Don't You Know Who I Am?

Piers
MORGAN

Don't You Know Who I Am?

EBURY
PRESS

1 3 5 7 9 10 8 6 4 2

Published in 2007 by Ebury Press, an imprint of Ebury Publishing

Ebury Publishing is a division of the Random House Group

Copyright © Piers Morgan 2007

Piers Morgan has asserted his right to be identified as the author of this Work in accordance with the Copyright, Designs and Patents Act 1988

The Random House Group Limited Reg. No. 954009

Addresses for companies within the Random House Group can be found at www.randomhouse.co.uk

A CIP catalogue record for this book is available from the British Library

The Random House Group Limited makes every effort to ensure that the papers used in our books are made from trees that have been legally sourced from well-managed and credibly certified forests. Our paper procurement policy can be found on www.randomhouse.co.uk

Printed and bound in Great Britain by Clays of St Ives PLC

ISBN 9780091913915 (hardback)
ISBN 9780091921521 (paperback)

First picture section: p1 top © Big Bictures; p1 bottom © Rex Features; p2 top © Craven Herald; p2 bottom © Charlie Gray; p3 top Soren Solkaer Starbird/*GQ* © Condé Nast Publications Ltd; p3 bottom © John Rogers; p5 top © Jez Smith www.theofficelondon.com; p6 middle and bottom, p8 © Getty Images; p7 top © Desmond O'Neill Features; p7 bottom © Rex Features.

Second picture section: p3 top and bottom, p5 top © Ellis Watson; p4, p5 middle and bottom, p6 top, middle and bottom, p7 top and middle, p8 top © NBC Universal, Inc.; p7 bottom © Getty Images; p8 bottom © Corbis.

All other images from the author's personal collection.

To Grande,
my incomparable grandmother

ACKNOWLEDGEMENTS

I'd like to thank Jake Lingwood, my brilliant editor at Ebury Publishing, for his patient, intelligent work on the text of this book. It's not easy transforming my smug, self-inflating prose into something loosely resembling occasional humility, but Jake somehow manages it.

Thanks also to my equally brilliant literary agent, Eugenie Furniss at the William Morris Agency, for helping me work out the concept for this book, reading it more times than any human being should decently have to, and being so entertaining over dinner.

Books like this take an awful lot of work by an awful lot of people, most of it not conducted by the author. So my heartfelt gratitude goes to Jake's splendid colleagues at Ebury, for their sterling support and help: Ken Barlow, Nicky Henderson, Fiona MacIntyre, Kym Wheatley, Rachel Rayner, Diana Riley, Rae Shirvington, Hannah Telfer, and, of course, his delightful boss Gail Rebuck.

Thanks, too, to the following people, who just make my existence easier:

My PA, Tracey Chapman, for all her hard work running my ridiculous life.

My parents for their continued unflinching love, support and encouragement – even in the face of overwhelming evidence that I have behaved like a chump.

My grandmother, for proving that age most definitely cannot wither you, nor custom stale your infinite variety.

My brothers, sister, and our huge and incredibly entertaining extended family for their stoical defence of my antics to horrified friends.

My three sons, Spencer, Stanley and Bertie, for being the best, and funniest, mates any dad could wish for.

Their mother, Marion, for encouraging them to be the above.

Simon Cowell, for 'creating Frankenstein's monster' and giving me the chance of a lifetime.

And to the serenely beautiful Celia Walden, for making me laugh, introducing me to the delights of gluten-free oatmeal, and extracting entries from my diaries that she said 'make you look an even bigger ass than normal'.

A NOTE FOR THE READER

There are hundreds of people mentioned in these diaries, often only by their first name. To help you keep track of who I am talking about, you may find it useful to refer to the Cast of Characters at the back of the book.

INTRODUCTION

For twenty years I worked in Fleet Street as a newspaper journalist. First as a showbiz reporter for the *Sun*, then as editor of the *News of the World* and *Daily Mirror.*

It was the only professional life I knew, and I loved every second of it. But then, on 14 May 2004, at 6.10p.m., I was sacked from the *Mirror* for publishing what the government said were hoax photos of British troops abusing Iraqi civilians – and everything changed.

Overnight, I lost my job, PA, expense account, driver and identity. I was thirty-nine, separated with three sons, and I remember waking up on 15 May, laughing to myself, and thinking: 'Right ... what the hell am I going to do for the rest of my life?'

I could make a reasonable living from writing books and articles, public speaking, giving interviews, and other commercial activities linked to my former job – though the obvious, more permanent, answer was to move into television full time. I'd presented a few series for the BBC and Channel 4 during my editing years, and had slowly improved my broadcasting skills.

But it would be a big leap to become a fully fledged 'TV personality'. To go down that route would mean automatically, and quite deliberately, trans-porting myself into the world of celebrity, with all the nonsense that entails.

I'll be honest now and say that I've always had a pretty healthy scorn for celebrities, particularly those with no discernible talent. The whole showbiz circus seems rife with shallowness, paranoia, arrogance and greed. On the other hand, it also spells – for the ones who crack it – big money, fast cars, flash houses, hot women, the best restaurant tables, and public adoration. All of which I suspected I could cope with quite easily!

So I went for it.

This book tells the story of what happened next, in all its tawdry, humil-iating, yet often utterly hilarious detail. What I experienced, I admit, challenged my whole view of celebrity: I learned more than I ever thought I would about the ever more frenzied 'star' culture we all now live in. And to my surprise, my trenchant views on that culture changed in a way I never thought possible.

But first, let me take you back to a magical day when a handsome young man came face to face to with his destiny …

PROLOGUE 1990

It's a blazing hot day on Malibu beach, and all I can see are beautiful blonde women in red bikinis running after a big guy in red shorts.

He has wavy brown hair, a finely honed physique and a permanently smug grin.

His name is David Hasselhoff.

I had flown to California to observe him on the set of his smash-hit TV series for the *Sun*, where I was showbusiness editor. At the time, *Baywatch* was the biggest show in the world, and he was its biggest star.

Never before had I witnessed such sheer unadulterated job satisfaction as David Hasselhoff seemed to derive from his work. He strutted, preened, marched and cavorted around the beach like he owned it. And who could blame him? Imagine being paid millions of dollars to chase Pamela Anderson around a beach all day?

I could feel pure envy sweating from my every pore. In that moment I wanted to be David Hasselhoff more than anything in the world.

Having said that, I was being paid £50,000 a year to jet first class around the world and stay in the best hotels to interview and party with celebrities.

I sat back on my sunlounger, sipped my ice-cold beer, nibbled on a freshly caught giant prawn and watched three *Baywatch* babes take a quick shower ten yards away. I laughed to myself. How could my life possibly get any better than this?

1

5 August 2004

ITV rang this morning to invite me to appear in the new series of *I'm a Celebrity, Get Me Out of Here!*

The fee is absurdly large, and for a moment a tiny part of me was tempted – it is, after all, one of the biggest shows on television – but how could I even think about doing it without losing all semblance of whatever credibility I have left? It would be simpler to walk up and down Oxford Street with a placard round my neck saying, 'WASHED-UP HAS-BEEN'.

The whole reality TV thing is out of control. As the number of digital channels explodes, so does the number of moronic 'celebrities' the reality genre spawns.

The editor of *Heat* magazine admitted recently that he'd rather have a Jade Goody interview than a chat with Tom Cruise, because Jade would say more and sell more copies. Which is probably true, but what does it say about us that we'd rather devour the latest gossip on an illiterate, talentless former dental nurse from South London who came third in *Big Brother* than hear the views of one of the biggest movie stars of all time?

Having said that, Cruise is a shocking control-freak bore and Jade's quite fun, so maybe I'm missing the point. Perhaps the Jades of this world have soared to celebrity high office precisely because they're not boring, speak their mind and live the dream every *Heat* reader aspires to: being a celebrity.

I used to aspire to that goal, too, if I'm honest.

When I was interviewing stars for the *Sun* as a cub reporter, I really wanted to be famous myself. It seemed such an exciting, glamorous life. I even regularly appeared in my own column, with my arm draped around celebrities, and rather enjoyed the subliminal fame-by-association it brought me.

As an editor I became more cynical about the 'star' business, having seen at first hand how fucked-up, egotistical, haughty and self-deluded so many of them are.

Watching them surrounded by sycophantic agents, lawyers, PRs, make-up artists and fans, I didn't envy them, I just thought how ridiculous and fake the whole circus seemed.

Money and power corrupt, that much has been obvious since the Romans stomped around the globe, but I reckon fame corrupts more, because it's so inherently shallow.

Why should you get a better table in a restaurant, or an upgrade on a plane just because you're famous? Why should you be automatically treated more reverentially just because you're on TV or in a movie?

And how, frankly, can you expect to stay normal and grounded if people treat you differently just because they know your name?

I can understand adulation when it's linked to awesome talent. If you're Tiger Woods or Anthony Hopkins, then you deserve to be treated differently, because you can do things very few others can do. But being a star these days no longer depends on talent. You can become one just by sleeping with a footballer, or appearing on some cretinous reality TV show, or just by going to the right nightclub and taking your clothes off.

My problem is that all the TV work I have ever done has been linked in some way to my 'talent' as a newspaper editor, whether it's *Question Time* or *GMTV*. I wasn't a celebrity, I was an editor who appeared on TV occasionally, but now that I'm no longer an editor, my televisual *raison d'etre* has changed, and if I am not careful I could end up being one of those awful people who are on TV just for the sake of it. That way madness and ridicule lie.

I won't deny I'm attracted to the limelight, and always have been, but I've been around enough famous people to know that it's a double-edged sword. Great in parts, hideous in others.

The most likely career path for me now is to become a television presenter. I've done a fair bit of it now, and I'm slowly getting better at what is a much trickier art form than it looks. But if I do pursue the TV route then I have to also accept that I will become, by default, a fully fledged 'celebrity'.

And so I guess the big question is: Do I actually want to be a 'celebrity'? And the honest answer is: Yes, I think I probably do, because the obvious benefits seem quite splendid.

But at what cost?

One thing I'm absolutely sure about is that it won't be in an Australian jungle eating repulsive bugs with Paul Burrell and Joe Pasquale. If that's what being a celebrity is, then get me out of here.

6 August

Michael Parkinson has invited me for lunch at The Ivy in a few weeks' time. I have more time to really enjoy fun encounters like these, where I can turn my phone off, drink too much fine wine over amusing conversation, and then enjoy a long, lazy siesta afterwards. I eagerly accepted.

Ironically, Parky and I now share the same TV agent, John Webber. I signed with John a few weeks after leaving the *Mirror* because another of his clients, Anne Robinson, rang and ordered me to. 'You need someone like John if you want a career in television,' she said, and she was right, I do. He's a tough, no-nonsense Jewish dealmaker, and his assistant, Tracey Chapman, is the nearest thing to Kerrie I have found since leaving the *Mirror*: highly organised, calm, hard-working and unafraid to tell me when I'm being an arrogant arse.

Popped into the Harbour Club next door to my riverside flat in Chelsea for a personal training session with Wendy.

I've skilfully avoided her for weeks on the pretext of finishing my book, but she was having none of my 'I'm tired' moaning, and threw me around various instruments of torture for an hour as I panted, wheezed and whined.

'You look bored,' she said.

'That's because I *am* bored,' I replied.

'What are you doing for the rest of the day?'

'That's the problem. Nothing.'

'What, nothing at all?'

I stopped rowing and looked at her bemused face.

'Well not exactly, no. I've got a bloke coming to fix my blinds, a BT engineer setting up my broadband, and I'll probably nip down to Sainsbury's to do my daily shop, then watch a crap matinee on TV and wait for the clock to strike six, so I can have a glass of wine without feeling too guilty.'

'Oh dear,' said Wendy.

Yes, oh dear indeed.

7 August

Down to Newick for a week of cricket, sunbathing and writing. I bought the other half of my parents' house there a few years ago, and converted my garage into a cottage for my grandmother soon afterwards. What with frequent visits from my two brothers – Jeremy, an army officer, and Rupert, a nightclub manager – and my sister Charlotte, who's married to an army colonel, and their large families, it has become not unlike *The Waltons*. But it represents a permanent oasis of calm away from frenzied London.

Took the boys to the nearby Chailey airshow, an entertaining day out with lots of old military planes zipping about the skies. Quite a few people came up to say hello, or offer their 'condolences' (always the most annoying thing anyone can do – makes you feel like you have literally died). Then one short, squat bloke in Union Jack shorts and covered in tattoos gawped at me by the ice-cream van and laughed to his mates, 'Hey! It's 'im, that prat who faked those photos.'

A delightful epitaph if ever there was one.

17 August

Tennis with Andy Coulson at the Harbour Club. We are usually pretty well matched but he beat me easily today. It's not a lack of fitness – I just felt sluggish and uncompetitive, two things I never felt at this time of the morning in my years as an editor.

We had breakfast afterwards and Andy was fired up about various stories in the papers that didn't really interest me now I no longer have to be professionally interested. His phone rang three times, each time from the *News of the World* office needing urgent answers to things. My phone didn't ring at all, and wouldn't for another few hours. Life outside a newspaper office is much calmer, quieter. Seeing Andy bouncing off the walls reminded me how sedentary my life has become. His day will be packed full of problems, breaking news, meetings, lunch with someone powerful. Mine will be spent writing, watching TV, and generally doing not very much.

I read the papers when I got back to the flat. I used to get all ten national newspapers every day when I was an editor, but I no longer have to worry about 'missing' anything that might lay me open to humiliation from my staff. Mainly because I don't have staff any more! So now it's just the *Daily Mail*, *Sun*, *Mirror*, *Telegraph* and *Guardian* – a mix that gives me a suitably balanced blend of bigotry and bias from all sides of the political spectrum.

Thought about listening to the *Today* programme, as I always used to, but opted instead for Magic FM. Who needs John Humphrys baying for some poor defenceless politician's blood when you can have Johnny Mathis soothing your ear lobes?

At 10a.m., I headed with my laptop for the balcony. I'm in the middle of writing my memoirs, a diary of my editing years called *The Insider*. It's been a hugely cathartic experience, and reminds me what fabulous fun it all was. But sitting outside now, with the sun streaming down across the river, I feel extraordinarily liberated. No boring meetings to endure, no rows with bean-counting managers or advertising executives, no business lunches with people I loathe, no twelve-hour days cooped in a tower block waiting for something to happen. There's a lot to be said for avoiding proper gainful employment if you can afford to.

Walked to Sainsbury's at lunchtime, and bought a chicken salad to eat while watching an Alan Partridge DVD. I probably went to a supermarket five times in the whole eleven years I edited papers. Now I go most days, and rather enjoy aimlessly floating down the aisles searching for that elusive can of Ambrosia cream rice that I'll never actually eat, but makes me feel better for having in my fridge. I get recognised occasionally, but people are always very friendly, if completely predictable. 'What are you doing now?' is all they ever ask. I understand why, but hate the question because I don't really have an answer. 'Oh, I'm writing a book and doing a bit of TV' doesn't have quite the same ring to it as, 'I edit one of the biggest papers in the world.' I can see them looking rather sorry for me, which is the last thing I want them to do because I don't feel remotely sorry for myself.

Kelvin MacKenzie called. 'How much are you putting in this book then?'

'Everything,' I replied.

'How can you remember it all?'

'Because I kept emails, tapes, letters, photos and memos, that's how.'

'Oh dear, oh dear,' he cackled. 'Well, just leave me out of it.'

'Kelvin, you're one of the stars.'

Fell asleep on the sofa, and woke after half an hour feeling refreshed and ready for action. Only there wasn't any action! So I called the boys, and asked if they fancied whacking a few golf balls. Spencer's eleven now, Stanley seven, and Bertie three. They've all got a great eye for a ball, any ball, and a ferocious competitive spirit. We spent an hour on the driving range in Wandsworth before it ended, as it usually does, with the three of them kicking seven bells out of each other. One of the best things about being jobless has been the amount of time I've been able to spend with them. I always tried to get to all their school stuff, even if it meant trekking across London during rush hour to do it, then dashing back to Canary Wharf in time for the first edition. Now I can be more spontaneous, and in less of a hurry. We went to Pizza Express for tea, and Stanley informed me that one of his schoolmates had called me an 'ex-predator' the other day.

I choked on my Sloppy Giuseppe.

'I think he meant to say ex-EDITOR, Dad,' he added, hastily.

'Are you sure?' said Spencer, smirking. God he's growing up fast.

'Dad,' said Bertie.

'Yes?'

'What do you do now?'

'That, Bertie, is a very good question.'

Dropped them back with Marion. She's great about the kids; I can see them whenever I like. And she is a terrific mother. We've been separated for four years now, and are embarking on the tortuous divorce process. But we've stayed good friends and talk every day.

Met a few friends for a drink in my local, the Lots Road Pub and Dining Room. On a bad night, Robbie Williams – who lives nearby – is in there, drinking orange juice and whining about fame. But on a good night like tonight, it's the nearest thing to a country pub I know – good comfort food, real ale, a fun atmosphere and staff who greet you warmly when you walk in.

None of the people with me were tabloid journalists, so the conversation wasn't dominated by tabloid chatter. It's only now I am removed from the game that I can see how boring it must be for non-journalists to listen to a bunch of hyped-up hacks boasting about how they snared some C-list celebrity for sleeping with someone they shouldn't have. Real people might be mildly interested in such things, but they don't CARE. Tabloid journalists work themselves into a fury of absurd indignant rage, oblivious to the sheer hypocrisy that goes with it. Most journalists I know lead the kind of lives that would fill the *News of the World* for a month if they ever became famous.

Got back to the flat, fuelled with four pints of bitter, turned on the TV and watched some imbecile from the *Daily Express* reviewing the first editions of the papers. I caught the front page of the *Mirror* and felt an instant pang of irritation: That headline should be a WOB (White on black type), not a BOT (Black on tone) ... then realised that nobody was listening any more, and went to bed.

I enjoyed the day, but I'm beginning to feel a creeping restlessness about my life. Writing the book has kept me occupied for three months now, but what the hell am I going to do when it is finished?

20 August

Spent most of the day looking forward to Ian Botham coming for dinner at my flat this evening with Kath and his daughter Sarah. I prepared a sumptuous gastronomic feast, which in Ian's case meant spending a lot of time choosing a lot of very fine wine.

'I need some really special stuff,' I told the Australian manager at my local Majestic warehouse.

'OK, who's coming to dinner, then, the King of Spain?'

'No, no, much bigger than that: Ian Botham.'

The manager whistled with excitement. 'Blimey, mate, you're right there. Beefy *is* bigger than the King of Spain. What does he like to drink?'

'Well, almost anything, but from what I can gather he is currently into really good Spanish reds and French burgundy. I want to impress him with something special because he's always been very hospitable to me.'

'Got it, mate, no worries.'

He returned with what he described as a 'magnificent Mersault' and a 'Rioja that will knock his stumps over'.

I paid the fairly vast bill for a case of each (you can never have enough supplies for a Botham visit) and headed back to the flat.

The Bothams arrived soon after 8p.m. Kath and Sarah completely sober, Ian slightly less so, after an inpromptu drinking session following the end of the day's play at the Oval.

'Right, what we drinking then?' he bellowed.

'I've got some really good…'

He cut me off in full boast.

'I don't want any of this French shit,' he declared, brandishing my 'magnificent Mersault' as if he'd just found a bottle of rotting soya milk. 'Where's the Chardonnay?'

I gulped. There wasn't any Chardonnay. I'd been specifically led to believe that Beefy was *off* the Chardonnay and *on* the 'French shit'.

'How about a red?' I suggested desperately.

'Oh all right then, what have you got?'

I led him to the 'Rioja that will knock his stumps over'. He stared at it for several long, agonising seconds.

'Good stuff that. Looks like you've been saved by the bell, Morgan.'

My sigh of relief was only matched by Kath and Sarah's disapproving tutting at Ian's behaviour.

It was a very entertaining evening, with Beefy getting more and more vociferous as the case of Rioja slipped away. 'We can't take him anywhere,' Kath sighed. But you can tell they both adore him, and he them. Whatever problems there may have been in the Botham family, and having a whirl-wind character like Beefy as a husband or father is self-evidently never going to be the easiest ride on the funfair, they are as tight as they come now.

At 2.30a.m., Beefy drained a fifth bottle of Rioja and announced, 'Right, I'm on air in six hours, so we'd better go home…'

Kath and Sarah grabbed an arm each and virtually carried him down-stairs to their taxi, still tutting and smiling.

21 August

Woke at 9a.m. feeling like a horde of rats had invaded my brain and were now scraping their filthy little nails over my cranium.

I fumbled for the TV remote, switched on Sky Sports and saw Ian Botham giving his live predictions for the day's play, looking and sounding like he'd spent the evening sipping cocoa before a good ten-hour sleep.

28 August

Saturday mornings were always sacrosanct for me when I was editing. It was the only time when I could have a lie-in and not be bombarded with millions of phone calls. Now Saturday is just another day, so I agreed to go on the new Eamonn Holmes sports show on Radio Five Live.

It was his first day and chaos reigned.

'Can you stay on a bit?' he mouthed when my ten-minute slot finished. 'I could do with some help here…'

I stayed on air for another hour and a half, watching Eamonn struggle with the perils of a live radio show. He's a pro, though, and by the end he began to relax and enjoy himself, as did I.

It was nice to get out of the flat and do some actual work, even though it was unpaid. I get endless offers at the moment to do soundbites for TV and radio stations when a story with even the vaguest 'tabloid' agenda breaks, but there are only so many times you can answer your phone at 7a.m. to someone from BBC Radio Birmingham asking what you think of Prince Harry's new girlfriend before your patience, and will to live, expires.

2 September

Dinner at The Ivy with Simon Kelner and Roger Alton, two of my favourite journalistic characters. Both were fascinated by LAE, or Life After Editing to give it its full name, and I regaled them with stories of long lunches with the phone turned off, leisurely days watching cricket and balmy nights drinking in country pubs without a care for the Blairs.

'Must be nice having all that free time,' said Roger wistfully.

'It sounds wonderful,' said Simon. 'Though I read recently that most people die out of sheer boredom within five years of retiring.'

I spluttered into my Chablis.

'*Retire? RETIRE?* I haven't bloody retired.'

But I am in danger of dying of boredom. That much is true.

5 September

Took Spencer and Stanley to Botham's box at Lords for the one-day international against India.

For most of the morning they were given a life tutorial by Lord Jeffrey Archer, spanning the full range of lessons he'd learned. They were completely enthralled – he is, after all, a master storyteller.

Other parents might have been less pleased at having Lord Archer as their children's moral guide, but I was unphased. Archer might not be everyone's cup of tea, but then neither am I, and I'd rather my sons led a life full of excitement, incident and drama than work as assistant managers in a high-street store selling cheap DVD players and oversized bras.

'Dad, he's sold one hundred and twenty million books,' said Spencer later.

'How do you know that?'

'He told us.'

6 September

Mentorn, the TV production company that makes *Question Time*, approached me in the summer to see if I'd be interested in presenting a new political interview show for Channel 4.

Today, John Webber rang to say they were looking at Amanda Platell as a possible co-presenter.

'Do you know her?'

I smiled. Amanda and I are old friends. Before she became William Hague's ill-fated spin doctor, she was, briefly, editor of the left-wing *Sunday Mirror* when I was at the *Daily Mirror*, proving that she's nearly as adaptable politically as I am.

'Yes, very well. I like her. The show sounds fun, what's the idea?'

'It's based on the American show *Crossfire*. You two grill a politician about the big issues of the week, but you also grill each other. You coming from the left, Amanda from the right.'

I liked the concept – a serious show made by serious people, with a dash of theatre – and it would get me back into the Westminster loop, which would be useful.

I'm still really not sure what I want to do with my professional life. I feel pretty sure that I'm done with newspapers, but is TV going to be enough to keep my juices flowing? There's always so much faffing around with TV work – waiting in green rooms, re-recording stuff, travelling to pointless 'new' locations. It lacks the immediacy of a newspaper newsroom.

7 September

Went to the GQ Man of the Year awards in London. Elton John improved my general mood of mild disenchantment by coming up and saying, 'Hey, Piers, looking for a job?'

'What kind of job, Elton?'

'Well, the thing is, I'm short of a gardener at my Windsor place.'

I laughed through clenched teeth. I'm trying very hard not to be bothered by the constant jokes about my employment status, but it's not that easy to be honest. Particularly when this evening I had to once again fend off dozens more people asking, 'So what are you doing now?'

For twelve years that question never arose. But now I'm an oddity: someone who used to have a big job, but doesn't any more. And nobody's quite sure how to behave towards me.

To compound my misery, Carol Vorderman and Des Kelly loomed into view, bounding over full of false bonhomie. They are the two people who displayed the most shocking disloyalty when I left the *Mirror*.

I've let them have it with both barrels in my diaries, but they are oblivious to this fact, and will remain so until *The Insider* is published next March.

I played along with the game, letting Carol sit on my knee and coo with shocking insincerity about how 'really, really upset' she'd been about my sacking. Not upset enough to call me at the time, though.

Des stuck his hand out in that horribly uncomfortable, half-cocked sideways manner that insecure people like him have. 'All right, mate?' he said.

I was tempted to stick a fist in his gurning face, but instead I hit him where I knew it would really hurt: 'Fine thanks, Des. I'm so sorry you didn't get my job. Mate.'

Jordan cheered me up later, in the way that only she can.

'I bet you're getting plenty more now you're not having to work all day,' she giggled.

'More what?'

'You know what!'

'Is that an offer, Ms Price?'

'Do me a favour!'

'That's exactly what I'm suggesting.'

We both giggled. Jordan takes a lot of flak, but she makes me laugh.

She's earned millions out of being herself – a gobby, pretty Brighton girl with huge breasts who behaves badly in clubs.

'Doesn't it get boring?' I asked her.

'Nah,' she laughed. 'I'm only Jordan one day a week, that's when I get drunk and stick me tits out at photographers. The rest of the time I'm just me, Katie Price, and that usually means being at home doing nothing.'

'Are you talented?' I said.

'Nah, not really. I can pose for the camera, though, which is a talent I s'pose.'

And she's right, it is. Nobody harangued Twiggy when she was a modelling superstar, so why should we have a go at Jordan for being a coarser version?

I got home at 2a.m. feeling drunk and restless. I used to laud it at parties like that, careering around, laughing at celebrities and playing the big-shot tabloid editor. It doesn't work in quite the same way now, obviously. An SAS marksman reduced to firing blanks.

27 September

Very tedious day, wasted away on the usual treadmill of gym, Sainsbury's and daytime TV. Thank God I've got lunch with Parky tomorrow, I'm really looking forward to it.

28 September

Bollocks! Parky cancelled lunch at the last minute – something to do with a 'diary clash'.

It's what I used to say at the *Mirror* when I checked the week-ahead diary on a Monday morning and realised I had to spend two hours with someone not important enough to warrant two hours of my valuable time. Now I have all the time in the world, but my importance to other people has reduced dramatically.

Cancelling lunch with a tabloid editor at the last minute would be professional suicide for a TV star. Cancelling lunch with an unemployed *ex*-tabloid editor is an altogether easier decision.

1 October

Filmed the pilot for *Crossfire* today. It seemed to go OK, though two people interviewing the same subject at the same time is not an easy dynamic. It was like a bear pit at times, with everyone shouting louder and louder in order to be heard.

Amanda Platell and I had a definite chemistry, though, and the Mentorn team seemed excited by what they'd seen.

I hope we get a chance to make the show, it could be just what I need to kickstart my TV career again.

7 October

A soldier was charged today over the Iraqi abuse 'hoax' photos that got me sacked. The news came out of the blue and I spent the day fielding calls from the world's media, including TV stations from America, the Middle East, Australia and Germany.

He's twenty-five, and although the exact charges haven't been revealed yet, they clearly think he's the guy who allegedly faked the pictures.

I don't know what to feel. On the one hand I'm angry at what appears to be confirmation that I was indeed a gullible fool, as I can't imagine they'd charge him without compelling evidence. But at the same time I feel relief that I might finally find out what *did* happen. It's always struck me as odd that I should lose my job over an alleged hoax without anyone knowing for sure who took the photos, where they took them, why they took them or what they depict. Now we might find out the answers, so at least I'll know.

I was never told the names of the two soldiers who brought the photos to us. Details like that are often deliberately kept from editors to save them facing legal problems at a later stage regarding their sources. But I did know they were both squaddies serving with the Queen's Lancashire Regiment in Basra in the summer of 2003, and that they were both with the Territorial Army. By a remarkable coincidence, the soldier who's been charged was a member of the Territorial Army, and served with the QLR in Basra in the summer of 2003.

14 October

Good news. John Webber rang to say that *Crossfire* has been commissioned by Channel 4, so my new life as a Jeremy Paxman wannabe will start soon. I'm pleased. It's a proper job, the money's great and they're saying it could run for years if we get the first series right.

18 October

John Webber called again.

'How do you fancy co-presenting *This Morning* with Fern Britton while Phillip Schofield is off for three days?'

'What do you think?' I asked.

'I think it would be great live experience, even if it's not the kind of thing you want to end up doing,' was John's sensible reply.

I'm intrigued by the idea, but slightly concerned at the prospect of plunging myself into cheesy daytime telly. Is it really what I should be doing when I've just landed *Crossfire*, an altogether more serious TV platform?

2

26 October

First day of *This Morning*. I was still apprehensive about it, but consoled myself with the thought that nothing can go wrong with a programme like this.

I was given Phillip Schofield's dressing room, which was full of his clothes and personal effects. I once wrote an unofficial biography of Phil when I was on the *Sun*, which had upset him, despite it being one of the most sycophantic tomes ever written. Now here I was stepping in for him – a bizarre turn of events.

I felt curiously nervous as I paced the room. Two hours of live TV is a lot to get through, and there seemed to be far more frantic activity than I'd expected.

Fern came in to say hello and couldn't have been nicer or more reassuring.

'Just be yourself,' she said, 'and remember that I'll always be next to you if anything goes wrong.' It was a genuinely comforting thought.

The first show went OK, though I got a little overexcited when Rachel Stevens – who I'd personally persuaded to come on as a guest – showed me her naked foot live on air. She has tiny size 2 feet and I grappled with it like a lifer in Wormwood Scrubs who's been let out for the day.

'Would you like some bromide with your tea?' asked Fern pointedly in the next commercial break.

I quite enjoyed the interview stuff, but the peripheral shopping, face-lift and cuddly-toy nonsense grated. I don't think I'm designed to sit in six multi-coloured chairs, testing them for the nation's housewives, and I'm sure my discomfort showed.

Any notion I'd had that live TV would be easy was dispelled pretty sharpish. It's fast, chaotic and you have the entire control room of producers and directors jabbering away in your ear the whole time. Fern handles it with extraordinary ease, barely flickering an eyelid as another script goes down or an interview subject suddenly disappears off line. She's smart, calm and warm – three essential ingredients for this kind of show. I'm still a hard-nosed cynical tabloid hack at heart, and find the cosy sofa style of presenting difficult to adjust to.

'You did very well,' said Fern as we debriefed with the production team afterwards. 'No mistakes, apart from leching over Rachel's foot, and you began to really relax by the end.'

I stifled a yawn, not out of boredom but sheer exhaustion.

'God, it's bloody knackering this live telly lark,' I said.

They all laughed knowingly.

'Toughest thing in television,' said one producer. 'Fern and Phillip just make it *look* easy.'

27 October

They say you can always remember where you were when pivotal moments happen, such as losing your virginity, your first child being born or Elvis dying.

Let me just add another to the list: the moment I sang a duet to the 'Macarena' with Timmy Mallett, wearing appropriately ridiculous oversized glasses, live to millions of people on *This Morning*.

We were taking part in a pop quiz, with Fern and I as captains, and one of my forfeits was to perform the 'Macarena' with the man who had memorably murdered it in the charts a few years earlier.

As I stood in my suit next to the multi-coloured human strobe light that is Timmy Mallett, I could feel every sinew in my body pleading with me not to do it. My mind raced to the *Daily Mirror* newsroom, where I could imagine my former colleagues watching their TV screens in abject horror as the man they'd once called Boss committed slow professional suicide.

'Hey, Macarena … Hey, Macarena,' the words hung in the air like a particularly pungent corked wine. Beads of sweat developed on my stiff upper lip and down the base of my spine. When the quiz finished, I slumped back in my chair as a beaming Mallett said, 'That was fun, wasn't it. Did you enjoy that?'

'Well, it's a long way from the Iraq War, isn't it?' I replied.

I got back to the flat where, out of curiosity, I read the *This Morning* website message boards to see how I'd gone down.

'Who is this repulsive man?' read one. 'Pierce someone,' replied another. 'Never heard of him, but he's rubbish, isn't he?'

'Did you see him groping Rachel Stevens yesterday, the dirty old man.'

Perhaps most damning of all was the one that said, 'Bring back Michael Ball as a stand-in, PLEASE.'

28 October

Just when I thought it couldn't possibly get any worse I had a day of abject humiliation, and it wasn't even my fault.

I arrived at *This Morning* determined to make a go of it and put the 'Macarena' horror of yesterday behind me. The production team were incredibly supportive, and Fern was brilliant again, telling me it was all going fine and that all I had to do was slow down a bit and relax. She laughed about the message boards: 'Oh God, never read those.'

A researcher elaborated: 'You should have seen what they said about Phillip when he started. He replaced John Leslie, and John's fans were so incredibly nasty about him it reduced him to tears. He won them round eventually, though, and now they love him.'

Something tells me I won't be back to turn them round.

I sat in the studio with Fern at around 10a.m., having a coffee and waiting to do a quick ten-second live promotion during *Trisha*, saying what's coming up on *This Morning*. It's a simple daily process: we get a twenty-second countdown from the studio in our ears, a red light comes on the camera in front of us and we read a brief script from the autocue before going back to our coffee. The first two days had been no problem at all, which lulled me into a false sense of security. Today, very few people were on the studio floor because they were recording an outside broadcast of the pop group Busted arriving at the show.

I was unconcerned as Fern and I chatted about life and the universe. We got round to the impending American elections at the weekend and the growing fears of another Al-Qaeda attack. As I was talking, I noticed the red light on the camera was on. I turned to Fern, who looked bemused and said, 'What's that light doing...' I turned back to the camera and instinctively began to read the autocue: 'Today on *This Morning*...' But the red light turned off almost as soon as I started speaking. Fern and I looked at each other again. 'Were we on air then?' I said, panic rising in my voice. She looked furious. 'I think we were, but I have no idea why. This has never happened to me on this show before.' A flustered production woman ran onto the floor, red faced and apologetic. 'I'm so sorry, with all the fuss over the Busted OB, we forgot to cue you in.' Fern was not amused. 'So what the hell did people hear us saying?' My heart sank. All I could remember were the words 'Al-Qaeda' and 'Possible attack this weekend'. We sat in silence for a minute or so.

'Are we in the shit, Fern?' I asked. 'Oh don't worry about it,' she replied, laughing nervously. We started the show fifteen minutes later, but I could feel a rising sense of unease among the team. Eventually the director came over and explained, 'Look, we're going to have to say something on air to the viewers. We've had hundreds of calls from worried housewives.'

'What about?' I asked, fearing I already knew the answer.

'Well, it's erm, it's about you telling Fern to stay in at the weekend because you reckon Al-Qaeda are going to blow something up to coincide with the American elections.'

I gulped and Fern looked queasy. 'OK,' I said, 'I'll say something to calm them down.' I suggested a few thoughts to Fern, she tweaked them a bit and we prepared to address the nation.

Fern went first, explaining, 'I want to put everyone's minds at rest. We had a little slip-up earlier when we didn't realise we were live on air. Don't panic, nothing is going to happen. Is it, Piers?'

I tried not to laugh: 'Erm, we were getting a little political and I was talking to Fern about a leaked CIA report that said they were worried about a terrorist attack in America before the election. Obviously I don't know anything, so if any of you are worried that I have some inside information on a terrorist attack, I don't. I hope that clears things up. I'm sure nothing will happen.'

Fern added, 'That's something you don't have to be a spy to under-stand, that possibly with an election something might happen.'

Now I did laugh. 'Trust me, nobody tells me anything any more.'

We cut to an ad break, and Fern and I giggled like schoolkids who'd been caught smoking on the bus.

Then a horrible thought dawned on me.

'What if there *is* a terrorist attack this weekend now? I'll be accused of being in on it with Bin Laden.'

Fern laughed: 'God, at least it wasn't yesterday when we were talking about Frank Bough...' The rest of the show went by in a blur as I imagined the next day's papers. Only I could terrify millions of women with an Al-Qaeda-related fuck-up on a morning TV show. Sure enough, as we came off air the press officer was waiting. 'We're getting a few calls, Piers, do you want to say anything?' All I wanted was to get mindlessly drunk, but I decided that may not be the most appropriate statement to make.

I drove to Oxford in the evening to take part in an Oxford Union debate on whether George Bush should be re-elected. I was on the 'Not in a million light years' side with Richard Dreyfuss and Will Hutton. And we were up against David Trimble, an ex-Bush advisor called Grover Norquist and some mad-eyed woman from an organisation I'd never heard of called Republicans Abroad.

I sat opposite Trimble over dinner, and was struck once again by how impressively dull he is, and how utterly, implacably intransigent his views are.

Dreyfuss, who I only really know from *Jaws*, was barmy but entertaining. He raged against Bush in a demonic manner that caused most of us to question his sanity, but it was reassuring to hear that at least some Americans realise Bush is not the greatest leader they've ever had.

The students all seemed really young, which can only mean one thing: I am getting old. Still, they loved me revealing how I'd cocked everything up on *This Morning*.

Perhaps I could carve out a lucrative new career simply telling audiences what a halfwit I am?

29 October

The papers are full of my disaster. MORGAN PUTS FOOT IN IT AGAIN WITH TV TERROR WARNING screamed the *Independent*.

I am a national laughing stock, the perfect start to my new career as a D-list TV presenter. Christ.

I sought solace in a pork pie from Sainsbury's, only to be met with various blue-rinse grannies pointing at me and laughing.

One came up and said, 'You dropped a bit of a clanger, didn't you, lad,' with pure unmitigated glee.

Is this what I am reduced to? Bumbling around daytime TV, then fending off the mocking Doris and Mabel brigade as I shop for my lunch?

30 October

A card arrived from Fern. 'I've really enjoyed these three days working with you. Hope we see you soon, and remember to tell all your cocky pals that daytime fluffy stuff is harder than they think.'

God, she can say that again.

2 November

Stayed up to watch the American elections, and it's pretty clear Bush is going to win again, which is completely baffling to any sensible observer. But then I suppose it's no more baffling than us re-electing Blair next year, which looks a racing certainty at the moment. Two gung-ho leaders take their countries into an illegal, unethical war and their electorates respond by saying, 'Well done, guys, have another four years.'

5 November

Crossfire started production today. Or *Morgan and Platell* as it's been renamed after legal issues involving the rights to the American show's name.

Morgan is first purely for alphabetical reasons, but as I said to Amanda this morning, 'In Hollywood terms, there's only one No 1 in the billing and that's the first name on the posters.'

She took the jibe well, kicking me firmly on the shin as the credits rolled, while beaming sweetly at me.

Our first guest was supposed to be Greg Dyke, who would have been a lively opener, but he pulled out and a desperate last-minute scramble left us with Tory frontbencher Michael Ancram, a charming fellow but a serious candidate for Dullest Politician in Britain.

The production team were all very enthused afterwards, thinking we'd got off to a good start, but I found it all rather uninspiring.

9 November

Had dinner at No 11 with the Browns and various political chums of theirs, including Harriet Harman, Margaret Hodge and Sue Nye.

Gordon is a strange Jekyll and Hyde character. Over dinners like this one, he's relaxed, chatty, gossipy and extremely charming. Then I watch him on TV and he turns into one of the Thunderbirds, speaking in a relentless high-speed monotone, performing one of the worst staged smirks I've ever seen when he thinks he should lighten up a bit and generally coming across as a dour, stiff Scots bloke who looks after our money. Which is a perfect image for being Chancellor, but hopeless if you want to make the move to Prime Minister.

His 'people' are all from the same mould. Ed Balls is quite fun away from a screen, and so is Alistair Darling. But put them on *Newsnight* and it's like an undertaker's taken over the airwaves to announce mass euthanasia programmes for anyone who laughs in public.

Sarah's got an astute PR brain, and I know she's working on 'relaxing' her husband when he's on public duty, but I can't help worrying that in their desperation to be seen as more serious than spin-flam Tony, they are going too far the other way.

11 November

Robert Kilroy-Silk was our second guest on *Morgan and Platell*, and he was much livelier. He'd been sacked from his BBC talk show earlier in the year after branding Arabs 'suicide bombers, limb-amputators, and women repressors' in a newspaper column. Since then he's been the high-profile frontman for the UK Independence Party, a new far-right political group.

We gave him a fairly rough ride, but he gave as good as he got, and I came off the set feeling far more pumped up than last week.

The production team, however, seemed less pleased.

'You've got to stop heckling the guests so much,' said Eamonn Matthews, the executive producer.

'I didn't. I just wasn't going to let him waffle.'

'I promise you that you did,' he replied. 'And it will alienate the audience.'

I went home feeling deflated and confused. What the hell do they want from me? I thought the whole point was a 'crossfire' not a bloody tea-party chat.

13 November

Boris Johnson was sacked by Michael Howard tonight after more stories of his alleged nocturnal activities hit the papers. Howard laughably said he made the decision to remove Boris from his front bench because it was an issue of 'personal morality'. Which, if that was genuinely the criteria for being a senior Conservative, would, I expect, wipe out almost their entire shadow cabinet.

At least there were loads of great Boris shagging jokes doing the rounds on email within minutes of the news breaking. My favourite was the suggestion that the final straw for Howard came when he confronted Boris and asked what his view of the Northern Ireland position was. 'Not sure, boss,' he replied, 'haven't got round to trying it yet.'

The whole Boris the Buffoon act makes me laugh. The guy is incredibly clever and knows exactly what he's doing. Boris worked out long ago that the public are suckers for that dithering, bumbling upper-class twit stuff, so he gives them exactly what they want, and they lap it up.

Underneath the phoney bluster is a keen political brain calculating a path to power. The problem is that Boris genuinely thinks he can be prime minister, which raises the alarming prospect of him having his finger on the nuclear trigger. At which point the joke doesn't seem quite so funny any more.

14 November

A.A. Gill has reviewed *Morgan and Platell* with his usual generosity in the *Sunday Times*: 'Piers Morgan and Amanda Platell's new show is huggably appalling. It's like watching her driving a van full of sugar and him driving a van full of weedkiller, and them crashing in slow motion, being trapped and catching fire. The emergency services turn up just so we can all stand and watch this brilliant pyrotechnic wreck.'

And then the bit that really made me laugh: 'It is the most awful political show in living memory... even more jaw-droppingly grim than Jeffrey Archer's chat show.'

His wasn't even the nastiest review. That award goes to Charlie Brooker, TV critic of the *Guardian*, who said, 'It's hard trying to work out which of the hosts you'd like to smack in the cakehole first. Morgan spends the entire time looking twice as smug as a man who's just learnt to fellate himself. Yet miraculously it's moon-faced putty-nose Platell who snatches first position in the punchability stakes, because there's something about her that suggests she thinks she's gorgeous and pouting. It's a bit like watching a drunken old spinster pinching the waiter's arse at a wedding reception. Still, there is one remarkable side effect to all this, it is the first political show where the politicians are far the most likable people in the studio.'

Trailing in a tired third was Rod Liddle's tribute, also in the *Sunday Times*, which contained just one good line: 'Morgan hops around all over the place like a demented kangaroo with Tourette's.'

I don't actually mind bad reviews. In fact, if they're going to be bad, then you need them to be horrifically, memorably awful, as then the reader thinks the critic has some personal issue with you. The worst bad reviews are the dismissive, non-abusive ones that make your show sound rather pointless.

If I hadn't seen *Morgan and Platell* yet, then these reviews would definitely make me want to tune in, which makes me pleased with the ferocity, although I know it will only serve to confirm the production team's view that I'm going over the top.

Spoke to Mum tonight and she was appalled by the reviews.

'Why do they have to be so horrible about you?' she asked, as any mother would.

'Because – and I know this might come as a shock, Mother – a lot of people *do* think I'm horrible.'

15 November

Eamonn Matthews emailed me some 'advice' after watching the Kilroy show again.

'There's great pace and vigour to the interview, but I think you need to ease up a bit and let the guest answer the questions. Don't allow me to pull in your wonderful ebullience and TV presence, that's what makes the show sing.

'But if you can't get the balance right then the format will fail, and the spin doctors will write us off as lightweight. It is a touch on the tiller, but it must happen or we're on the rocks. Watch Paxman, he's the best. He has edginess but he gets stuff from people. Remember, it's not a gladiatorial contest.'

So it's not a gladiatorial contest, but he wants me to be like Paxman, the ultimate TV gladiator.

I'm not only confused, I'm quite irritated by the patronising tone of this email. I'm not used to being criticised like this. When you're an editor, you're the king and nobody would dare say things like this to you. Of course I'm not the king any more, and I know there's a lot of truth in what he is saying. Eamonn is a highly experienced and talented TV producer. I am still a novice at this TV game, and I know I should stop being so sensitive and start listening for a change, but it really goes against the grain.

17 November

Had lunch with Simon Cowell at the Cipriani. I've known Simon since my days editing the Bizarre showbiz column on the *Sun*, and he hasn't changed a bit. He's now one of the biggest TV stars in the world, thanks to his cruel judge act on *Pop Idol* and the US version *American Idol*. He finds the whole thing hilarious.

'If someone had told me I'd be doing this one day, I'd have laughed them out of my office,' he said. 'But I am, and it's a lot of fun. You just have to take it all with a pinch of salt.'

We spoke about my various career options.

'You could have a good future in television,' he said. 'You just need to make the transition from tabloid editor to TV presenter in the public's minds. I'd like to work with you on something, let's think about what it could be and talk again.'

Simon insisted on paying the bill – he always does – and treated me in exactly the same way as he used to treat me when I was an editor. I like that. I'm amused by how differently people treat me now I'm no longer so 'important'.

22 November

I'm getting quite a few speaking offers at the moment, paying anything from £10,000 to £15,000. There are two types of gig: the after-dinner speech and hosting awards. The former are much easier, because the audiences tend to be smaller and more attentive. The latter can be rowdy, tricky affairs, with up to 1,000 people getting drunk and misbehaving.

Tonight, I hosted the British Society of Magazine Editors Awards at the Hilton, a lively crowd of some 800 magazine journalists. I thought they might give me a tough time, but they were fine, even laughing at my rather poor Sly Bailey jokes, which were just revised versions of clichéd blonde gags:

1) 'I should have seen the warning signs in Sly's first week I suppose, when she sent me a fax and put a stamp on it.'

2) 'But I forgive her for sacking me. Sly herself went through a harrowing dismissal from a workplace. As a teenager she used to work in an M&M's factory, and got fired for repeatedly throwing out the Ws.'

When I finished presenting the awards, the organiser ran up, thanked me and said, 'We'd love you to come and do it again next year.'

Sure. Easy money.

23 November

Janet Street-Porter accepted the 'media personality' slot on *I'm a Celebrity Get Me Out of Here!*, which I turned down, and is making a complete arse of herself.

For a bright woman with a sharp populist antennae, I think she's dropped a massive error by agreeing to cavort semi-naked in the jungle. At least her performance has convinced me that my decision was right.

There really isn't any amount of money in the world that could possibly compensate for the prospect of a randy Janet straddling my hammock at 2a.m. in a leopardskin bikini with lust in her eyes.

24 November

Veronica Wadley offered me a weekly column in the *Evening Standard* today, and I jumped at the chance. It doesn't have the biggest circulation in the country, but it is influential, and read by all the top journalists, politicians, etc.

'What do you want me to write?' I asked.

'Oh, just be yourself,' she replied. 'I'm sure you're not short of a few opinions…'

Some will see doing a column in the *Standard* as a bit of a comedown from editing a national paper, but I don't care. I've always enjoyed writing, but never got much of a chance to do any when I was an editor. And it's not like it's my new full-time day job, though having said that, what is?

Am I a TV presenter, a journalist, a columnist, an author, a public speaker or, as most of the public seem to believe, just the idiot who got hoaxed by those Iraqi photos?

Perhaps it doesn't matter, though. At least this way I can't be sacked again, because I can always claim that whatever I was sacked from wasn't my proper job anyway.

4 December

Took Rob McGibbon to watch Arsenal play Birmingham in the Premiership. On the way back the Mercedes I've kept from my editing years started making strange chugging noises, slowed down and then stopped bang in the middle of the frantically busy Holburn Viaduct.

We pushed it to one side and tried to work out what was wrong.

'Must be electrical,' I said.

'Or mechanical?' Rob suggested.

Neither of us had a clue.

I called Mercedes, but nobody was answering the phones at the various places I had in my contacts book, and as it was Saturday, most garages were shut, so eventually I gave up and called a breakdown service to help.

I turned on the car TV while we waited, and *Morgan and Platell* happened to be airing on Channel 4.

'Oh, God,' said Rob, 'to be in a car lumbered with *two* Piers Morgans is more than anyone should suffer.'

Bored with waiting, and with listening to myself bang on about Europe on TV, I tracked down a number for Mercedes headquarters in Germany and they put me through to an engineer.

By now we'd been sitting there for nearly an hour.

I explained what had happened, and he offered a number of possible reasons for the problem.

As he spoke, the breakdown man arrived and set to work.

My German friend then casually asked, 'I assume you have petrol?'

I laughed. 'Of course I do.'

Then I looked at the gauge, which showed I had no petrol at all.

'Erm, actually, I might be out of petrol.'

The breakdown man stared at me in disbelief.

I thanked the engineer and hung up, then asked the breakdown man if he could lend me some petrol. He sighed and poured in half a gallon. I turned the key in the ignition and the car started as normal.

Rob was curled up in a little ball by this time, convulsed with shame and joyous laughter.

10 December

Bertie had his nativity play today and the omens were not good. At the summer nursery school ballet performance back in July, he had been required to don a tutu, something that provoked considerable mirth in his two older brothers.

'You've got to wear a dress, you girl,' said Stanley, helpfully, as Bertie headed off to school that morning. Bertie's angry young eyes suggested this might not be a foregone conclusion, and sure enough, he was nowhere to be seen as the other kids pranced about on stage.

Eventually he was frogmarched out by two teachers, fuming in his combat trousers. Bertie wriggled free, ran to the front of the stage and shouted at the top of his voice, 'I don't do bloody ballet.' An announcement that caused equal measures of horror and hilarity among the audience. I regret to say that I belonged in the latter camp. I'm not sure I want my sons doing 'bloody ballet' either.

Today he was supposed to be a star in the nativity play, and he seemed even more furious. I watched from a few rows back as he was once again frogmarched out against his will, and not in costume, during a touching rendition of 'Away in a Manger' by his schoolfriends. Bertie, snarling menacingly, aimed a whack at Joseph before turning to the ensemble and shouting at the top of his voice, 'SHUT UP, YOU FREAKS!'

17 December

It was the fabled *GQ* Christmas lunch today, much enlivened this year by the performance of one Rod Liddle. We have certain things in common: he, too, got sacked – as editor of the *Today* radio show – and we both drink too much and have a penchant for attractive blondes. There, the similarity ends rather abruptly, at least in Liddle's eyes. He is one of those guys who exudes an air of intellectual arrogance and pomposity. And the few times I've met him, he's expelled that air right in my face, as if the concept of even talking to me is somehow beneath his intelligence and stature. Which makes me laugh, because to me he's just a fattening old whinger in his forties with terrible – and I mean *shocking* – teeth.

Anyway, his most recent clever contribution to intellectual debate has been to have an affair with a twenty-two-year-old girl who works at the *Spectator* called Alicia Monckton. His wife Rachel Royce kicked him out and the mutual slanging match has gone on all summer – poor old Liddle's rapidly become the laughing stock of London's chatteringly dull literary classes.

I was sat on his table at lunch, but he barely exchanged a word with me, preferring to throw as much alcohol down his neck as he could.

As lunch drifted into early evening drinks in one of those dark throbbing dens of iniquity that Dylan Jones specialises in, I found myself sitting on a sofa with Miss Monckton. Liddle, it seemed, had been dragged away by an urgent work-related matter.

To my surprise, Alicia was rather good fun.

'I've got to ask,what on earth is a girl like you doing with that revolting old goat Liddle?' I said, as another tray of mojitos arrived.

She giggled: 'Oh, I *love* him. He's the only man in the world for me.'

It was my turn to giggle. 'Alicia, I wouldn't be quite so hasty about that if I were you.'

'But Rod's so clever and funny,' she insisted.

'Yes, well so is Dawn French, but I manage to keep a lid on my burning sexual desire for her.'

Alicia's phone rang; it was Liddle. She refused to answer.

'He's always calling me when I'm at things like this, I think he gets jealous.'

The phone rang incessantly, but she just laughed and let it ring off.

'I think you should answer it and say you're having a nice drink with me and I'm looking after you really well,' I said.

She burst out laughing. 'Oh my god, he'd go completely crazy if I did that.'

'Exactly.'

Two more mojitos arrived and her phone kept ringing. This was a desperate man.

'Go on, answer it and wind him up a bit; it will be amusing if nothing else.'

Alicia giggled and answered.

'Hi darling.'

I could hear a man's voice ranting and raving in the background.

'Calm down, Rod, I'm just having a drink with a few of the *GQ* crowd...'

More ranting and raving, a bit louder this time.

'Oh, you know, Piers Morgan and—'

If Vesuvius had erupted at that moment it couldn't have made a bigger noise than the roar of fury that emanated from Alicia Monckton's mobile.

'Rod, don't be so ridiculous, we're just having a drink.'

As she'd predicted, he was going completely crazy.

'Tell him we're just going to have a dance,' I mouthed. Anything to increase his torment.

'We're just going to ... Rod, stop it ... Please, Rod, just calm down, you're being ridiculous.'

Eventually she hung up.

'He's not happy,' she said with a grin.

'Another mojito?' I replied.

Fifteen minutes later a huge commotion erupted near the club's entrance.

A large, sweaty man with wild hair was tussling with security men, trying to get in. Closer inspection revealed it was Liddle.

Seconds later he was charging through the startled guests like an elephant after too many Red Bulls, shouting, 'Where's Alicia?'

'Oh dear,' she said.

He looked demented. His eyes were out on stalks and he was foaming gently from the right side of his mouth; his hair was all over the place and his appalling teeth were bared ferociously. The wild man of Borneo reborn.

'What the FUCK do you think you're doing?' he shouted.

Alicia had the look of someone who had seen it all before, many times.

'Rod, don't make a spectacle of yourself, come and sit down.'

'No, I won't fucking sit down. What the fuck do you think you're doing?'

'I'm having a drink,' she said calmly.

He stared at me, death in his eyes. 'Why don't you just fuck off?'

I laughed. 'Now, Rod, why don't you calm down like Alicia suggested. It's all perfectly innocent...'

He turned back to Alicia, who suddenly looked about fourteen.

'I turn my back for one fucking minute and this is what you do?'

Liddle, unfortunately, looked and sounded about eighty-seven.

I made my excuses and left the grim domestic scene.

8 January

I've taken the boys to Portugal for a week, and tonight Spencer and I braved the Sheraton Hotel bar, where a German singer/guitarist was performing.

To say he was bad would be to insult the legions of really bad musicians out there. This guy was off-the-dial bad, an evil cocktail of karaoke and techno, with a dash of Joe Dolce.

We amused ourselves by asking him to play some of our favourite songs, then watching him absolutely murder them.

'He's really terrible, isn't he, Dad?' said Spencer after 'Moon River' had been annihilated.

'Son, this is historic stuff. I have never heard a worse singer in my life. Just sit back and enjoy it.'

And enjoy it we did. Me with a Montecristo No 2 and large glass of amaretto. Spencer with a Diet Coke and packet of crisps.

For many of the songs we didn't exchange a word – a mere raised eyebrow proving the catalyst for more uproarious laughter.

I don't know who the guy was, but he did more for father–son bonding than he will ever know.

12 January

The Insider is nearly ready for the printers, so I've decamped to Antigua for ten days to check over the proofs in peace. I think it's a good read, and I don't owe anybody any favours. But I have to confess to being rather surprised how far I've gone with some stories, and some people. This book will either be my rebirth into the London glitterati scene, or my burial.

Holidaying on your own is a strange experience, especially during the evenings, when cooing couples sit holding hands by the palm trees munching pieces of freshly sliced coconut together, as you scribble on a manuscript by the bar trying not to look too lonely and pathetic.

This morning I was lying on the beach reading yet more proofs when an English guy came up, clutching a faxed copy of that morning's *Times*. The front page was full of photos of British troops abusing Iraqi civilians. They had emerged from a court-martial case in Germany and been released with the full approval of the Army and MoD. The same Army and MoD who had condemned the *Mirror*'s photographs last May, even if they were genuine, because publication might inflame anger towards our boys on the ground in Basra.

The man on the beach said, 'You were right, then.'

I wasn't sure what to say. I guess the pictures do vindicate my claim that we'd exposed a wider truth and that this kind of abuse had been going on. But they don't mean the *Mirror* photos were genuine, and I'm not going to get my job back. The one inevitable consequence of these photos coming out was that my phone and Blackberry stayed in a permanently vibrating state as the world's media clamoured for my reaction.

I couldn't see any upside in saying anything. People can make their own minds up about what these photos mean and whether it changes their view of what the *Mirror* did. It nails the lie that there was no abuse, but I'd still love to know the truth about those 'hoax' pictures.

By the end of the afternoon, three more people had approached me on the beach to congratulate me and offer their sympathies. It felt rather satisfying.

23 January

I was waiting for my bags at Gatwick when a ruddy-faced man walked past, took a double take and came back to peer at me intently. I could see his mind whirring away, trying to work out how he knew me.

After what seemed like minutes, but can't have been more than a few seconds, the lights came on and the bells went off and he exclaimed triumphantly, 'I love your gardens!' before walking off again.

I stood there crushed. I don't do gardens. I have absolutely nothing to do with bloody gardens. Who the hell did he think I was? Alan Titchmarsh?

My recognition factor has definitely risen since I left the *Mirror*. Two weeks of being on the news during that 'will he, won't he resign' debate significantly increased my profile. But my level of 'fame' is a weird one. I can go for days with nobody batting an eyelid, then spend an hour walking down the King's Road where one in ten people react to me in some way.

Anyone who says they hate being recognised is lying. It's a buzz. But I can see how very famous people grow to dislike their lack of anonymity. Particularly with the explosion of mobile-phone cameras, which has turned everyone into amateur paparazzi.

25 January

The BBC have approached me about presenting a live daily entertainment show on BBC TWO. It sounds potentially brilliant, but they want me to work on a pilot for a month with their internal production team and see what we come up with. It would go out at 6.30p.m. and, if it gets commissioned, would be the biggest TV project I've been involved in. I feel ready for another proper job. *Morgan and Platell*, which is returning for a second series in a month's time, is fine, but it's just one day's work a week and I don't particularly enjoy grilling slippery, dull politicians. Very few of them are open and honest, so the interviews become a game of cat and mouse, with Amanda and I trying to prise some gaffe out of them and them trying not to let us. The viewer might be amused by the confrontation, but the voter is rarely given much of an insight into genuine policy or idealogy.

3 February

An amusing lunch with Alan Rusbridger at The Ivy today. Before he became editor of the *Guardian* he used to be the paper's diarist and loves a good gossip. He seemed obsessed with how much money I've made since I was fired, from the pay-off, book deal etc., so eventually I told him, in strict confidence. 'Fucking hell!' was his only comment. 'You won't repeat that, will you, Alan?' I responded, slightly alarmed by his wild excitement. 'It always sounds disgusting when people like me start banging on about how much money they earn.' He gave me his solemn word and I'd know if he did repeat it, because I gave him a figure that was ever so slightly different to the real one.

6 February

The media diary in today's *Observer*, sister paper to the *Guardian* and boasting one Alan Rusbridger as its executive editor, carried an intriguing item today, claiming I've been going around boasting about how much money I've made from my pay-off, book deal etc., and then detailing the exact amount I've earned. Or rather, the exact amount I told Alan Rusbridger.

Once a gossip columnist…

8 February

Bertie has been complaining of toothache for weeks now, but a trip to my dentist last week ended in failure when he refused point-blank to go anywhere near the chair.

The dentist suggested I take him to Guy's Hospital where he can have the teeth that need removing taken out under anaesthetic, so today we queued up for several hours to see if they could fit him in.

They could, and a thorough examination of his overcrowded mouth concluded that he had an emerging abscess and that he'd need to have six teeth removed.

'I won't have any left,' he exclaimed, with understandable concern.

'You will, mate, don't worry.'

A nurse arrived to lead him away and I felt a sudden shudder of fear race through me. I don't care how safe the procedure, how good the hospital, or how reassuring everyone is, any operation involving a four-year-old boy is something you want over and done with as soon as possible.

I paced the waiting room for what seemed like hours but was in fact no more than fifteen minutes before the nurse returned pushing an unconscious Bertie on a trolley.

'Hello, Mr Morgan, here's Bertie. Everything's fine, he'll just be a bit groggy when he wakes up and he may start thrashing around.'

No change there then, that's how he normally is in the mornings.

I sat next to his bed for another twenty minutes or so before he started stirring. And boy did he stir – kicking his feet in the air, punching wildly at anything he could hit and shouting at the top of his voice.

I tried holding him down but got several clumps on the head for my troubles. Then a load of blood gushed from his mouth onto my white shirt, not the cleverest item of clothing I've chosen all year, I must say.

'Bertie, it's Daddy, calm down, mate.'

'GO AWAY!' he screamed, more blood sploshing all over me as he smashed various tubes out of his eyeline. It was like a scene from *Mad Max*.

'Shh, Bertie, it's all going to be fine.'

'AAAGGGGHH!' He let rip with one last full-throttle wail before collapsing in my arms and murmuring gently.

I held him in my arms for the next half an hour as he recovered, rocking him gently and trying not to dwell on how I would leave the hospital with him, dressed in my bloodstained shirt, without looking like some crazed kidnapper.

When he finally woke up properly, he whimpered a bit and then opened his mouth wide so I could inspect his teeth, or rather the lack of them. It was quite shocking, he'd gone from Donny Osmond to Alf Garnett in an hour.

'Do I look OK, Dad?' he asked.

'You look great, Bertie, just great.'

They say parents should never lie to their kids, but in situations like this, of course you should.

9 February

I have invited George Michael to my book launch (everyone who appears in the book is being invited), and he replied today, saying he'd watched and enjoyed the recent *Morgan and Platell* interview with George Galloway.

'I fully understand your choice of Amanda Twat from Hell as your foil,' he wrote. 'She comes up with such utter shite that you are always going to look like the good guy in comparison.'

As for the book, he said: 'I'm sure it'll be a good read. I hope our Tony comes out of it looking as good as he should.'

He then added one of the funniest PS's I think I've ever received: 'PS you probably think it's a bit strange that I never bother to change my email address, but that's because I'm realistic enough to know that I've probably been under GCHQ surveillance since "Shoot the Dog", in which case firewalls and changing my address aren't going to make a blind bit of difference. You are in the same boat I should think. Anyway, I hope they like my taste in men...'

Good old George. I wonder how he will take my references to him in the book. He ought to laugh, as I've only been like him – indiscreet and gossipy. But these rock stars can be rather touchy when it comes to gossip about themselves. For instance, I would wager good money that his venom towards Amanda is prompted by something she once wrote about him rather than her performances on *Morgan and Platell* – where I think she comes over as smart, funny and confident.

Did a lengthy interview this afternoon with the *Daily Mail*, who have bought the serialisation rights to *The Insider*. When I saw who they had sent to interview me, my heart sank. Mary Riddell is a very good interviewer, but I once sacked her as a columnist from the *Mirror*.

She was very cheery, though, and when the interview finished she said, 'I must say that I've never seen you looking healthier or happier. Being sacked seems to have done you the power of good.'

It's true that I feel much fitter than when I was an editor, but I'm getting slightly twitchy about the book now the publication date is looming. I've had a great laugh writing it, but I suspect some people won't see the funny side quite as strongly as I have...

15 February

Simon Hattenstone, the *Guardian*'s top interviewer, came to grill me at the flat for a couple of hours. He's quite camp in a heterosexual way, but his interview technique was flawless – well-researched, detailed and forensic.

He and his photographer somehow persuaded me to pose for pictures holding a frying pan containing a hard-boiled egg, for reasons that were supposedly linked to my difficulties in adapting to normal life. The whole thing left me feeling slightly twitchy, that is until I found a sheet of paper on my kitchen floor after they'd left.

It contained a handwritten itinerary from Simon's partner for the next fortnight while he looks after their kids, including such gems as: 'Monday, put bins out, tape *Friends*, buy organic carrots', and so on.

I called him at his office and started reading out the list.

He burst out laughing. 'Oh *no*!'

'Oh *yes*!' I replied. 'I think this means you're going to be very nice to me, doesn't it, Simon – or the organic carrots go public.'

'I was going to be very nice to you anyway,' he replied. 'But you're right, the carrots need to remain our little secret.'

An old *News of the World* colleague, Bill Anslow, was retiring tonight, and on a whim I decided to make the trek to Wapping and see him off with a drink. He's a slightly mad but incredibly hard-working and talented guy.

It was weird being back in a room full of journalists again, and it's the first time I'd experienced it since leaving the *Mirror* nearly a year ago. The conversations were the same as I remembered, lots of moaning about management, budgets, expenses – and plenty of black cynical humour about life and the universe.

Journalists operate in a strange bubble, insulated from the real world by the alien nature of newsrooms, the sprawling hives of news and gossip that leave you immune to shock and often emotionally detached from the reper-cussions of what you publish.

16 February

Filmed the pilot for the BBC TWO entertainment show this afternoon, and it couldn't have gone much better. Dale Winton was our star guest, and said to me afterwards, 'I smell a hit here, Mr Morgan.'

The idea for the show came from Alison Sharman, head of BBC daytime programming and one of the rising stars of the corporation. And she was apparently very pleased with the pilot. All it needs now is Alison's final say-so, which should come in a few weeks.

I came home feeling excited and confident. This could be it, my new day job. Doing what I think I do best, live think-on-your-feet interviews, news and celebrity chat.

26 February

The *Daily Mail* interview appears and Mary Riddell has effectively branded me a gloomy drunk struggling to recover from the shock of being sacked.

So much for, 'I've never seen you looking so healthy and happy.'

27 February

Spent most of the day in negotiations with the *Mail* over the first day of my book serialisation. I know from my own experience as an editor how important it is not to let a single word, photo or headline appear without your prior knowledge. I also know that the *Mail* will want to make it all sound as scandalous and outrageous as they possibly can, which is perfectly fair given the money they're paying.

At 3p.m. a *Mail* executive rang to tell me they are running a huge front-page promo and six pages inside: the sort of coverage they would usually devote to a major news story.

I gulped.

'Erm, did you say *six* pages?'

'Yes, the editor likes it very much,' came the worrying reply.

Now, Paul Dacre is a brilliant editor, but hearing that he was suddenly excited enough to devote six pages of his paper to my book on day one alone left me feeling not a little uneasy.

'What's the headline on the first spread?'

'It's … er … well it's…' The executive's hesitation did nothing to allay my mounting anxiety. 'It's … STOP FUCKING LYING TO ME, TONY.'

I gulped again.

'But I never said that to Blair.'

'No, not exactly. But it's kind of generally what you said, isn't it?'

'No, it's not, because he didn't ever lie to me personally, not as far as I know anyway.'

'I see. Well, if you're unhappy about it, I'll talk to the editor.'

I gulped for the third time. Dacre was not going to react well to me rewriting his headlines. I didn't want to be difficult, and I definitely wanted the serialisation to be sensational, but it's me that needs to be able to defend the headlines and text when I hit the airwaves later this week, and I couldn't justify this one.

Half an hour later the executive called back.

'The editor says if you don't like it, then think of a better one yourself.'

I laughed. Dacre would be loving this, and I didn't blame him. There can be few things more satisfying than having an ex-rival editor, and one who'd given him a fair amount of stick over the years, squirming around.

'OK, well I'll try and do just that.'

'I'm caught in the middle here,' she said. 'It's not easy trying to please two editors at the same time.'

I laughed again.

'Well if I were you, I'd concentrate on pleasing the one who is currently your boss, rather the one who no longer edits a paper bag.'

She laughed nervously.

I phoned back with a suggested headline twenty minutes later.

'See if Paul will accept STOP THE FUCKING LIES, TONY. It's the same length, but doesn't imply that he has necessarily done the lying. Others in his camp lied to me all the time, so I think that works just as well and has the benefit of being accurate.'

Dacre liked it, and we have passed the first potential flashpoint between editor and ex-editor.

28 February

All the other papers got their JCBs out and lifted huge chunks of the *Mail* serialisation. It was a quiet news day, which helped, and everyone seemed to be talking about the diaries, which was the whole point of the serial after all. I can't deny that it feels great being back at the centre of things again.

There was a Variety Club tribute to Arsene Wenger tonight, and I decided to go and pay homage to the great man.

He smiled when I went over to say hello. 'I was reading your book in the paper today. It's pretty hot stuff, especially about the Blairs.'

'Yes, well I thought you'd appreciate me getting you out of the headlines for a few days, Arsene.'

We chatted for fifteen minutes, and I was struck once again by what a smart, cultured, charming guy he is.

'Why don't you buy Michael Owen?' I said. 'He and Thierry Henry would be fantastic together.'

'He wants to come, I know that, but he gets too many injuries. He won't play more than twenty games most seasons.'

1 March

Fiona Phillips emailed me from her *GMTV* office:

'Hello. I am addicted to the extracts from your book in the hideous *Daily Mail*. It's bloody brilliant. Can't wait to read the book. Slightly miffed that you clearly found Princess Diana slightly more intoxicating than me. Still, I'm gradually getting over it. What does your mum think? Has she read it yet? Anyway, I'm far too busy etc… Fiona X'

What does Mum think?

Well, she read the dedication to her and Dad and burst into tears. Then she read the book in three days and was so emotionally wrought up by the end that she didn't know what to say to me. 'I'll have to read it again,' she said.

Mothers never read these things like anyone else. Every tiny slight, slur, punch or criticism of her 'little boy' hurts.

The book's already attracting some splendidly bitchy comments. My favourite has to be from David Aaronovitch, the portly spleen-venter in the *Guardian* who wrote in his column this morning: 'Morgan shows himself to be an ill-mannered, thin-skinned, easily flattered, narcissistic ignoramus, given to stupid jokes, banal observations, casual rudeness and hypocritical pieties.'

Very hard to argue with any of that, to be honest.

3 March

A bizarre letter appeared on the internet today purporting to be something George Michael had sent to the *Daily Mail* that they declined to publish. I've no idea if it's genuine or not, but it certainly sounds like him:

'Dear *Daily Mail*

'As much as I am saddened to have to write this letter in full view of the general public, I feel I have no choice but to defend myself (and my partner Kenny, in a way) from some of the comments that Piers Morgan has made in his book due to be published.

'Piers Morgan knows very little about George Michael, and that's a fact. We have spoken rarely in the last ten years, and what would probably surprise people is that we have never discussed my private life. Well, apart from that once at dinner. Those really close to me, straight or gay, would tell you that I am not secretive at all, in fact the phrase "too much information" comes to mind occasionally, and with Piers it was sometimes like that. Like at the mentioned dinner. Sadly, as I like to be open about myself, I was always aware that Piers is the busiest rumour mill in town, and that respect for my privacy was not exactly guaranteed.

'I have travelled the world many times and, at forty-one, I think I have earned the right to a quiet life, with loads of paid-for sex with a countless number of men (most of which had no names; other than "hot stud", "londonqueer2478", "bighairygay69" and "wellhung231"), which I truly love, and maybe Piers just can't relate to that. I am a bit surprised that Piers seems to have forgotten me telling him I've slept with ... a story he very well could have published and given me credit for.

'Yours sincerely,

'George Michael'

If it is George, which I can't say for certain, then my fears about him having a sense-of-humour failure over the book appear to have come true.

4 March

Mike Graham, editor of the *Scottish Daily Mirror*, emailed me: 'Speaking to my oppo Bruce Waddell at the *Daily Record*, who saw Blair in Scotland last night. Cherie "not too thrilled" about your revelations. Blair said, "Piers is a bit of a naughty boy." Just thought you'd like to know...'

6 March

Stanley and Marion have appeared in a *Mail on Sunday* Mother's Day feature. The highlights included:

Q: What is the best thing about your mum?

A: She ate squirrel when she was cycling around Laos for charity. And she's very good at nit check at school.

Q: Does she ever embarrass you?

A: Yes, when she drops me off at school and winds down the window to shout, 'I love you Stan,' in front of all my friends. And when she cries at films that aren't even sad.

Q: Do you want to be like her when you grow up?

A: I'm not a girl.

Q: Do you think she is pretty?

A: No. But once when she was going out she came down the stairs and looked like a beautiful princess.

Meanwhile, further tributes pour in for *The Insider*. Someone called Richard Brooks, writing in *The Sunday Times*, says, 'I've never read such a monstrous ego trip in my life.' Which was particularly amusing given its placement next to A.A. Gill's column. Mr Brooks adds, 'Given the dire sales of books by other media types like Greg Dyke and Michael Buerk, how many copies will it sell? Random House paid Morgan £1.2 million so must sell 80,000 copies to get its money back. If it does I'll eat my proverbial hat.'

Now there's a challenge...

9 March

Had my book launch for *The Insider* at the One Aldwych hotel in Covent Garden.

I'd invited everyone who was in the book, knowing that most of them wouldn't attend in a million years unless I was going to be immolated at some point between the champagne and canapés.

If you can judge a man's character by the company he keeps, then I wonder what Sigmund Freud would have made of the 'company' who turned out for me, including Mohamed Al Fayed, Richard Branson, Ian Botham, Anne Robinson, Sir Trevor McDonald, Jon Snow, Leslie Phillips, Kevin Pietersen, Ross Kemp, Tara Palmer-Tomkinson, Fiona Phillips, Michael Winner, Andrew Marr, Andy McNab, Andrew Neil, and Kelvin MacKenzie.

Word came down that Graham Norton was outside trying to gatecrash.

'Let him sweat for another five minutes, then he can come in,' I said. May as well squeeze as much amusement out of the evening as possible.

Cilla Black bounded in at 11p.m., flanked by four very camp young male friends. ''Ello darling,' she cried, 'where's the champagne?'

Stan was the only one of the boys who came – Bertie was too tired and Spencer wasn't feeling well – but he was in his element, marching around introducing himself to celebrities and posing for photos before eventually crashing out on a sofa with a contented grin on his face.

I tried making a speech, but the acoustics in the room were terrible and everyone was far too pissed to care about anything I had to say anyway.

After two gags fell flat, I appealed for calm. 'Look, it's my party, the least you ungrateful bastards can do is listen to my speech.'

A hail of catcalls and whistles filled the air.

'Right, that's it, I'm giving up,' I shouted, assuming this would shock them into respectful silence.

'HURRAH!' came the jubilant response.

Despite this shocking lack of respect for the author, it was a great night, and an encouraging one. If I can get that kind of turn-out for my book launch then I'm not completely finished.

Yet.

10 March

Kerrie, my long suffering *Mirror* PA, emailed: 'I bought your book today – £9.97 in Tesco's (it's scandalous what you were charging last night!). I'm looking forward to reading it. I am, of course, considering bringing out my own diaries – something along the lines of 'Replied to J.J. Worgan's letter … Piers's mum called … went and got a cheese and pickle sandwich … News 24 called for an interview … read *OK!* magazine.'

I don't miss the job, but God I miss Kerrie running my life for me.

12 March

Filmed the live quiz *Test the Nation* for BBC ONE tonight.

I've appeared before, as an 'expert' commentator, but never as part of the 'celebrity' team.

I sat next to John Kettley the weatherman, *Coronation Street* stars Bradley Walsh and Tina Hobley, impressionist Jan Ravens, BBC news reporter John Pienaar, and cricketer Darren Gough.

It seems that no matter what I think about it, I am now officially a celebrity.

But what does that mean?

You get recognised, asked to sign autographs, can get a table at The Ivy and people suck up to you.

Other than that, what's the point of it all?

You lose your privacy, which can be very annoying sometimes. Mind you, there's nothing worse than a celebrity squealing about privacy given the voracious way almost all of them sell their own down the river to papers, magazines and TV networks.

And you can very easily lose your perspective on life too, or 'disappear up your own arse', to use the vernacular.

The other teams included dustmen, vets, bankers and surfers.

All of whom are comfortable, I expect, in knowing exactly what they do. My world is changing and there's very little, it seems, that I can do about it.

Afterwards I spoke to Anne Robinson, who hosts the show, and she told me how she dealt with the whole morphing-into-a-celebrity process.

'It's a very strange thing at first, but you just have to realise it's all a bit of a game. A serious game involving serious amounts of money, but still a game at the end of the day. Don't take it too seriously, but find something that suits you and make it work, like I have done with *Weakest Link*.'

Anne's a sharp, gutsy woman, who made the transition from newspaper journalist to TV star via a lengthy bout of alcoholism.

'Do you like being a celebrity?' I asked.

'Oh God yes, it's better than slogging your guts out in some office all day, isn't it?'

3

15 March

A strange day of hugely conflicting emotions. It was the British Press Awards tonight, an event I haven't missed in twenty years, but my Aunt Lorna died suddenly in Ireland at the weekend, so instead of attending the annual bun fight, I flew to Dublin with mum and Jeremy for the funeral tomorrow morning. Lorna was the only sister of my natural father Vincent, who died when I was just one, but she had kept in touch with us all over the years, and was a bright, opinionated, kind and amusing woman. Her death, which was completely unexpected, has hit her delightful family hard.

As I was driving in a taxi to Heathrow, my phone rang and it was my publisher Jake telling me that *The Insider* had gone straight into the non-fiction charts at No 1 after selling more than 10,000 hardback copies in a week.

WOW!

I felt a rush of adrenalin and excitement coursing through my tired, deflated body. And yes, a certain sense of 'fuck the lot of you' too, directed at all those who had so gleefully enjoyed my demise back in May. Normally I would have celebrated such a momentous event by getting wildly drunk and performing a naked conga on Chelsea Bridge at 4a.m., but instead I had a glass of warm red wine in the BA lounge at Heathrow with Mum and Jeremy.

After landing in Dublin, I turned on my mobile to be greeted by a torrent of text messages that made my phone vibrate so much it nearly jumped out of my hand.

All of them were from former colleagues in the national press at the Press Awards.

'All kicking off here – Jeremy Clarkson just called you an arsehole on stage!'

'Geldof's branded us all small dicks.'

'Carnage – everyone threatening to pull out next year.'

'Newsflash: Geldof fight with Dickie Wallace in loo.'

And so on.

By 3a.m., there were further unsubstantiated text claims of unethical fornication, illicit drug-taking, more brawls in nightclubs, allegations that the awards had been rigged and various drunken resignations.

There are not many times when I've missed Fleet Street and all its madness, but tonight was definitely one of them.

16 March

An email from Victor Lewis-Smith: 'Loved the book. What's astonishing is that we both hate the exact same people.'

And a note from Paul Dacre at the *Daily Mail*: 'I have done some terrible things as an editor, but making you a hero must be the worst! Seriously, though, a rip-roaring, tantalizing read. Dinner on me soon. PS please don't reproduce this letter in the next volume of your diaries.'

21 March

John Webber invited me to a glittering Board of Deputies dinner tonight, one of the biggest nights in the Jewish society calendar. Tony Blair was the guest speaker, so this would be the first time I had been in the same room as him since the book came out.

I arrived early and immediately bumped into Victor Blank, who was as charming as ever. Admittedly, he helped sack me when the heat got too close to his own chair, but I hold no grudge against him. It was Sly Bailey's idea, not his. He introduced me to Gerald Ronson, the business tycoon who has fought his way back from the Guinness Four disgrace. Before I could exchange pleasantries, Ronson started berating me for being too anti-Israeli on the *Mirror*. He was all red-faced and spluttering, as if he was my boss bollocking me for stealing paperclips. 'We always tried to be impartial, Mr Ronson,' I said firmly. But he was having none of it and carried on venting his spleen until I gave up defending myself and walked away. A quite extraordinary performance.

I found John, who said Cherie Blair was not likely to be coming because 'something had come up'. We agreed that it was probably her breakfast when she saw the guest list and realised my name was on it, but minutes later Tony arrived to a huge fanfare, with Cherie by his side. They were sitting just ten feet away on the top table, facing me. This was going to be a fun night...

Lord Levy appeared by my side during the first course, and couldn't have been friendlier.

'Hi, mate, how are things?' he said cheerily. Whatever people say about Levy, he didn't mind being seen talking to me in front of the PM, and that's not something that can be said of most senior Labour people right now.

'I'm fine thanks, Michael. How's it going your end? I see Milburn's beginning to make a few leadership noises…'

'Fuck Milburn,' said Levy, with a steely glint in his eye. 'If he makes any attempt to make a move on Tony then I will guarantee that none of the money in this room goes anywhere near him. Let's see how he gets on then, shall we.'

I laughed. You'd want Michael Levy on your side, definitely.

'How's Tony?' I asked.

'He's fine.'

Levy then bent down, pulled my ear to his hand-covered mouth conspiratorially, and whispered: 'He knows you're here. He's relaxed about it, but he probably can't speak to you: it's all a bit too close to the book coming out. You understand.'

I laughed again. I suspect Blair would rather stick a large fork in my skull than talk to me, but Levy was doing his best to smooth things over in that skilled way of his.

'Well, send him my love,' I said. 'I've always liked him, you know, it's just Cherie I can't stomach.'

Levy raised his eyebrows to the ceiling. No words were necessary.

As the plates for the first course were being removed, I spied a shadowy figure creeping through the room. It was Cherie, clad in full Sari and flashing that grin to all and sundry. As she reached our table, John sprang to his feet and said, 'Mrs Blair, I wonder if you've had the pleasure of meeting Piers Morgan?'

The table fell silent, as did several around us. Cherie's eyes fixed on mine, a mixture of loathing and curiosity on her overly made-up face.

'Yes, I know Piers Morgan.'

I laughed out loud: 'Hi Cherie, why don't you come over and sit with me in the Catholic corner, and forgive and forget?'

She smiled regally, in the same way the Queen did when I first met her – not a smile of warmth so much as a grimace of controlled revulsion.

Then she puffed her chest up, stretched her head as high as it would go and pronounced slowly and deliberately, 'Piers, even the world's greatest sinner is forgiven in the eyes of the Lord.' And with that, the First Lady turned on her heels and glided away to another table.

I was stunned. Cherie in sense-of-humour shocker.

30 March

My fortieth birthday. I should be feeling thoroughly depressed at this doom-filled landmark. But oddly, I rather like turning forty. If you've spent, as I have, your entire adult life being called 'The Boy Morgan' then it's rather comforting to be finally viewed as officially 'old'. I had a big dinner party at Floridita tonight, a lively Cuban restaurant in Soho, for forty friends and family – a party that ended with a water disco in a friend's indoor pool at 5.30a.m. It's safe to say that I saw off my thirties with a bang.

1 April

I was due to fly to Dublin today, to appear on the popular *Late Late Show* and promote the book, which is still, amazingly, No 1 in the charts.

But the Pope's health has been deteriorating fast in recent days, and it doesn't look like he'll survive the weekend, so a researcher called me this morning and said, 'I'm really sorry, Mr Morgan, but we're doing a whole programme on the Pope now, so we'll have to postpone your appearance.'

'I'm an Irish Catholic if that makes any difference?' I replied, only half joking.

'Are you? Well perhaps you could come on and talk about the Holy Father then? Did you ever meet him?'

I felt a sudden attack of self-distaste sweep through me.

'I think we'd better leave it. Don't worry.'

5 April

Alison Sharman has been promoted to the head of the BBC's children's programming, CBBC, which means she no longer makes decisions about BBC Daytime, which means my BBC TWO entertainment show pilot *First Edition* will now almost certainly be aborted. The worst thing about TV is that everything hangs on the whim of whoever happens to be running a channel at any given time.

I rang one of the production team.

'Are we fucked?'

'Not necessarily.'

'But it's not good news, is it?'

'Well, it means that the pilot will now revert to the BBC TWO Controller, Roly Keating, for a decision on commissioning, and obviously it wasn't his idea and he may have his own ideas for that slot. So no, it's not great news.'

'When will we know?'

'Soon, I hope.'

I hung up and cursed. Just my sodding luck that this should happen. I was sure that Alison would give us at least two months in the summer to try it out.

6 April

Had a long-arranged lunch with Kevin Lygo, the Channel 4 boss today, but spent last night puking my guts up in Sussex and had to cancel. No idea what's caused it, but have genuinely not been this sick in years.

It always sounds awful cancelling lunch on the day, nobody ever believes an 'I'm suddenly sick' excuse, and it's not a great career move to stand up one of the most powerful men in television, but if Lygo had seen me crouching on all fours in my garden, retching into a large yellow bucket as my concerned mother and grandmother stood over me suggesting dried toast or soup for tea, he might have been more convinced.

7 April

Still feel as rough as a badger's arse. The focus of my investigation is centring on a foul-tasting burger at Arsenal on Saturday, but food poisoning doesn't usually last this long.

Sophie Raworth called to see if I'd come in and help the BBC ONE Royal Wedding commentary team on Saturday for Charles and Camilla's nuptials. She is anchoring the coverage with Dermot Murnaghan.

'I'd love to, but I can't, I've been vomiting every hour for two days,' I said, lying flat on the sitting-room floor, clutching a Lucozade and feeling another wave of vicious nausea heading my way.

'Oh come on, Morgan, what are you made of?' she replied.

'Seriously, Sophie, there's no way. I can't even walk without chucking up at the moment.'

'Well I'll call tomorrow and see if you're any better.'

'I won't be.'

I crawled back to my bedroom, stuck an ice-cold towel on my fevered head, lifted the now empty bucket to its constant resting position by my pillow and tried to sleep as convulsions raged inside my tormented intestines.

If this *was* a burger, it was the world's worst-ever football ground burger, and that is truly saying something.

Spoke to the boys tonight on the phone.

'Dad, how many times have you been sick?' asked Stanley.

'About twenty times.'

'Wicked! Hey, guys, Dad's been sick twenty times!'

Spencer and Bertie were suitably impressed.

I've achieved a few accolades in my otherwise chequered life, but this was the first time I could hear genuine admiration in my sons' voices.

8 April

Sophie rang at midday.

'Better?'

'No,' I groaned. 'Had two hours' sleep and five more dashes to the loo. Nightmare.'

'Oh come on, it's just a bug, you'll be fine by tomorrow.'

'I won't. Why do want me anyway?'

'Because the powers-that-be think the tone of the whole thing needs to be slightly less reverential and serious than previous big royal events. The public mood seems to be for something a bit more jolly, and your name came up as someone who could provide some…'

'Some jolliness?'

'Exactly.'

'I don't feel very enthused with jolliness at the moment, Sophie.'

'I know, but you will tomorrow, especially when the adrenalin kicks in.'

I wanted to do it, to be part of the royal wedding coverage would be a great laugh, but I still felt diabolical.

'How long would you want me on for?'

'Oh, ten minutes, max.'

'OK, well let's say a tentative yes then, depending on a last-minute fitness check.'

'Brilliant, thanks.'

Sophie Raworth could persuade an eskimo to buy an ice bucket.

9 April

Woke up feeling slightly better. Still a bit sweaty, and not eating anything more substantial than a piece of dry toast, but definitely better. And I want to do this job, now.

At least ten million people will watch the BBC coverage, and if I make a good fist of it then perhaps I'll get more 'commentary' work. It suits my personality, because you need to be quick-witted, able to spot funny or interesting things as they happen, and stay cool amid all the live chaos – three things that every tabloid editor needs in abundance.

I rang the BBC to say I'd definitely make it, and two hours later I was on my way to Windsor Castle. I assumed the journey would be slowed to a crawl by hordes of people descending on the town, but it was conspicuously empty, which was a rather worrying sign for the royals, with just three hours until the wedding. I've always thought that the monarchy's biggest enemy is not the press, or even themselves, it's apathy. If the public no longer care, then the game's up.

I stared at the uncrowded streets and feared the end was nigh. If the future is Charles and Camilla, and nobody can be bothered to even attend their wedding, then the royal family is going to be finished in my lifetime.

The cab driver shared my view: 'Weird, isn't it?' he said, as we approached the castle. 'I thought there'd be tens of thousands here, but it's quieter than a normal Saturday morning.'

I found the BBC makeshift studio and said hello to Sophie and Dermot. A producer came over to inform me I'd be needed in twenty minutes or so for a ten- to fifteen-minute commentary.

'That will probably be it, I should think,' she said.

Loads of celebrities flittered in and out. Stephen Fry, Richard E. Grant, Trinny and Susannah. All we needed was an *OK!* magazine photographer and the occasion would be complete.

By 2p.m. there were thousands lining the streets – perhaps they'd all just done their shopping early.

When I got the call to go on air, I found myself sitting next to Penny Junor, one of the myriad royal watchers who make a living out of talking very, very, *very* seriously about the often ridiculous daily shenanigans of our monarchy.

I made a couple of less than reverential remarks – nothing too rude, just not the sort of thing you'd normally hear in a BBC royal wedding broadcast, and nobody seemed to mind very much. In fact, Sophie and Dermot seemed delighted to have someone to lighten the atmosphere a bit.

This was, after all, Charles and Camilla. A couple who have been laughed at and ridiculed more than any other in modern history, with the possible exception of Neil and Christine Hamilton.

I rather like them both. Charles has always been incredibly charming and polite whenever I've met him, and Camilla's just a good laugh, so obviously better suited to him than Diana ever was. The level of vitriol they attract seems absurd to me. Charles is probably the best-behaved Prince of Wales we've ever had.

I finished my slot and assumed that would be it, but the producers asked if I could stick around, and before I could finish my cup of tea I was wheeled back on for another round of jokey analysis of the Big Day.

I loved every minute of it, particularly the long arrivals part, where endless totally unrecognisable foreign royals clambered out of cars to bemused applause from the crowd and even more bemused looks from the commentators.

The production team kept prompting Sophie and Dermot with names via handwritten notes:

'And there's Crown Prince Alexander of Yugoslavia,' said Sophie with a straight face. I peered at the monitor to see a man I had never seen before in my life, and who I was damn sure Sophie hadn't either.

Commentating protocol dictates that you keep all the secrets to yourself and don't dob your fellow commentators in it, but this was too good to miss.

'You don't know who Crown Prince Alexander of Yugoslavia is, Sophie!' I exclaimed.

The producers started frantically shaking their heads and stage whispering, 'No, Piers, NO!'

Sophie froze, fixing me with a steely smile. 'Yes, I do.'

We could be heard but not seen by the viewers at that moment, and though I didn't pursue my line of questioning, I did fall about laughing during the five-minute break that followed.

'That wasn't funny,' said Sophie, giggling.

'It was,' I said.

'No it wasn't,' said the producer.

'Am I off, then?'

'No, you can stay, but only if you promise to behave yourself.'

'I promise.'

Twenty minutes later Harry and William took their seats in the chapel, and immediately started clowning around with their various cousins.

'And there's that naughty boy Harry up to mischief again,' I said.

The producer hastily scribbled a note and shoved it across the table at me.

'Tone. Please remember TONE.'

'Why, is Blair here then?' I mouthed back pathetically. She was not amused.

'Piers, please keep it serious when we are actually inside the chapel.'

'Righto, sorry.'

Then they wheeled in their big gun, the BBC's royal correspondent Nicholas Witchell, for a stint. Charles had recently been caught on camera saying, 'I can't bear that man,' while looking at Witchell, which had caused the royal pack a lot of entertainment given the extreme gravity with which Mr Witchell goes about his business.

He started droning on and on about the 'difficulties the couple will face' and saying things like, 'They will never escape entirely from the shadow of Diana, Princess of Wales, but it is their hope, and the hope of their friends and officials, that the public will accept this marriage and come to respect the new Duchess of Cornwall. Royal officials know that it won't be altogether easy. The very fact that she is to be known as Duchess of Cornwall, rather than Princess of Wales – and in due course, when he succeeds to the throne, as Princess Consort rather than Queen Consort – is a clear acknowledgement of public sensitivities over her role and status.'

The sort of guff that Pathe News presenters used to come out with in the Fifties. I found it all hilarious and interrupted him in full flow to offer my sympathies for the Charles snub, saying I was going to launch a campaign to clear his name. Mr Witchell was aghast at my impertinence. Just after 2p.m. the Blairs arrived, and I observed that Cherie looked 'radiant' with as straight a face as I could muster. Sophie suppressed a laugh. I was on air for most of the three hours in the end and thoroughly enjoyed myself. The adrenalin definitely helped with my illness, too, and I'm feeling a lot better.

The wedding seemed to go very smoothly – nobody tried to shoot Camilla and the general reaction was positive. 'Thanks, you were great,' said Sophie afterwards. 'Naughty but great.' She and Dermot had been too. It's fantastically difficult to anchor these big live broadcast days, but they did it with flair, professionalism and humour, without ever once damaging the BBC 'serious news' brand.

I felt pretty pleased with myself until I got home to find a stream of text messages asking why I hadn't mentioned the fact that Harry had been goose-stepping during the walk to the chapel. What? I sped through the tape I'd made of the programme, and sure enough there was the little tinker performing what appeared to be a perfect goose-step. I'd been so engrossed in trying to be funny that I'd missed the only proper story of the day. Oh the shame.

11 April

Tea with Mohamed Al Fayed at Harrods. 'Let's buy a newspaper,' he announced. 'You'd be the editor, and between us we'll get rid of these Labour bastards who are ruining the country!'

'But then we'd just get the Tory bastards back again,' I said.

'You're right. They're all bastards, aren't they?'

It would be genuinely funny running a paper with Mohamed. Maybe I should do it.

All papers should be owned by megalomaniac billionaires with axes to grind: they'd be so much more entertaining, not to mention fearless.

13 April

Drinks party at Matthew Freud and Liz Murdoch's Notting Hill mansion.

I bumped into a lady by the kitchen door who I thought I recognised.

'Hello. Piers Morgan,' I said.

'Hello,' she replied, smiling, 'I'm Helen Fielding.'

The name rang a few bells but I couldn't place her.

She was early forties, attractive and bright. We exchanged small talk for a few minutes as I tried to work out how I knew her.

Then the penny dropped.

'I know who you are, you're Bridget Jones, aren't you?'

She laughed wearily. 'Yes, I am.'

'How exciting,' I panted.

Pause.

'Have you... have you got a bloke yet?'

Even as I said it I felt stupid.

How many times must she put up with an imbecile like me saying something like that? It's the same as builders shouting, 'A-ha!' at Steve Coogan, or teenage girls asking *Little Britain*'s Matt Lucas, 'Are you the only gay in the village?'

'Yes, I've got a bloke. And a baby, too, thanks.'

I apologised for my imbecility.

14 April

William Hague was the guest today on *Morgan and Platell*, and was witty, charming, on-the-ball and intelligent. He's just a guy whose time came too early, a bit like John Howard in Australia first time round. And just as Howard did, I can imagine Hague making a stunning comeback as Tory leader one day. There's an element of trustworthiness about him that few politicians these days possess, and he's great fun, too. The only question is whether he can afford to return to front-line politics. He earns £20,000 a pop on the after-dinner speaking circuit, which, if he's doing as many as I'm told he's doing, is a lot of money to give up and be a frontbencher again.

The show itself is going OK. Amanda and I get on pretty well, despite the odd handbags-at-dawn flare-up. She's intelligent and knows her stuff, but we're very different in the way we like to prepare. I never had a meeting that lasted more than fifteen minutes at the *Mirror* because I have the attention span of a gnat, so I prefer to be sent all the background material and prepare on my own. But Amanda likes to have long detailed group meetings to discuss everything, and so do the production team.

So I have to sit through hours of tedious discussion about every single line of questioning. I understand why they feel the need to do it, but I feel the life draining out of me every time. I just want to get in there and fire away at whoever's sitting in the hot seat. In my experience, you get a lot more out of them if you treat the interview as a spiky conversation rather than a forensic examination.

My obvious boredom and disinclination to do the meetings is causing friction.

19 April
A terrible day. I've been knocked off No 1 in the book charts – by the Pope!

Yes, *Pope John Paul II: In My Own Words*, has gone straight in at the top – the second papal hammer blow to my literary career in a matter of days. Still, as a good Catholic boy I can hardly complain.

I appeared on the *Today* programme this morning with Greg Dyke, both of us competing to be the most anti-Blair. It was Dyke's first visit back to the BBC since his sacking and he was quite emotional about it. I walked through the labyrinth of corridors with him afterwards and he admitted, 'I loved my time here and I still get very pissed off when I think how media people like you and me lost our jobs over Iraq-related stuff, but nobody from this fucking government has yet. It's scandalous.'

He seemed angry and bitter, far more so than I am.

As we walked, many BBC employees greeted him warmly and he was genuinely touched. Then he stopped, looked right and left with a puzzled expression and laughed: 'Fuck me, I'm lost!'

What a farce – two guys who'd held massive jobs and lost them in dramatic circumstances are now reduced to ten-minute radio rants, then fumbling blindly around the bowels of the BBC trying to get home in time for *Neighbours*.

'Do you miss it?' I asked.

'Sure,' he said. 'I never wanted to go, the governors stitched me up. I was just beginning to make a difference here and then bang, I was out.'

We shared not-as-important-as-I-used-to-be tales of life on the outside and agreed that it wasn't much fun really. It's easy to take for granted the infrastructure that comes with a big job – the PAs, the driver, the teams of people hanging on your every word, the sheer feeling of power you get from being the boss. And the basic companionship of working in an office with a team of lively minds.

As we finally worked out where the hell we were and reached the safety of the reception area, we stood for a few minutes more, chatting about our new lives. It struck me that the reason we were still talking was that we literally had nothing better to do.

Later, I had a book signing at the Westminster Book Shop, which is now owned by a friend of mine from Newick, Peter Tummons.

It was like every other book signing I've ever done: fairly soul-destroying. Unless you're a pop star or a footballer then hardly anyone turns up for these things. I got a steady trickle of people, but that soon faded to nothing. The hour was only enlivened by the sudden appearance of a completely bonkers individual in a bright raincoat and scraggy beard, who ran inside, hurled abuse at me and ran off again.

I seem to inspire this reaction in a lot of people.

20 April

Dylan Jones rang: 'How do you fancy interviewing celebrities for us every month? Q&A style, emphasis on fun.'

GQ is a 'cool' magazine, and every 'cool' celebrity wants to be in it, so there should be rather a big difference between securing interviews for *GQ*, and getting ones for the *Sun* as I did in my early twenties.

GQ also hosts all the best parties.

'Can I start Monday?'

He laughed and we quickly concluded a very generous deal.

I am pleased, because apart from the guaranteed income it will bring – always important in the precarious 'freelance' world – it will also give me access to big stars in an intelligent arena. No bad thing as I try to ditch the 'tabloid editor' stigma, and very useful if I ever get to host a chat show, which is one of the things I think I really could enjoy in television.

21 April

The court martial of the soldier accused of hoaxing the *Mirror*, and me, over those Iraqi photos was discontinued today, on the grounds that there was no 'military jurisdiction'.

All very odd.

MoD sources are spinning the line that they can't prove he faked the pictures in MoD time, so he could now face criminal civilian charges. But I'm hearing from *Mirror* sources that they just can't pin anything on the guy and he's denying faking anything. Fascinating.

22 April

Took the boys to see the World Wrestling Experience SmackDown tonight at the Excel Arena in East London.

All of them are completely obsessed with these huge American wrestling frauds charging around pretending to knock seven bells out of each other. It's exactly the same con act as British wrestling stars like Mick McManus and Giant Haystacks, who were on our TV screens throughout the Seventies and Eighties. And it's just as popular, judging by the snaking queue of excited kids.

There was a pantomime feel to the evening – the good guys get big cheers and the bad guys get booed and hissed – and loads of action, bangs, lights, rock music, fireworks and fake blood.

But there was also a moment of true transatlantic comedy towards the end, when one of the really bad guys, a Stetson-clad brute called JBL, hurled what he assumed was abuse at the howling crowd: 'Your Prime Minister Tony Blair is just a poodle to our President Bush … and your next Queen Camilla looks like a horse!' He stood back to receive his customary torrent of boos, but to his visible shock and dismay everyone just cheered their agreement.

23 April

Jeremy flew off to start a six-month tour of Iraq today. He was looking forward to seeing some live action, and to see for himself what it's really like out there. He's been out briefly before, but this will be a proper tour. 'Let me know if you find any WMD out there,' I said.

'Yes, very amusing,' he replied. Much as I would normally enjoy proving my brother wrong about something, this whole Iraq business has really upset him. Like many army officers he believed his government when they said Saddam had WMD and was going to use them. That's why he believed it was a just war, an essential belief if you're a soldier risking your life. Now he believes he was misled at best, lied to at worst. And the real problem for Tony Blair is not clearing up the hideous mess he's caused in Iraq, it's what happens when he tries to do it again. Because I fear the next time our Prime Minister goes to the military and says he needs their help fighting one of George Bush's battles for him on a spurious WMD-related pretext, the answer may be of the two-fingered variety.

Trust is vital between a government and its military, and nobody I know in the military would now trust Blair as far as they could shoot him.

24 April

Matthew Freud rang. 'Fancy becoming a press baron?'

'Er, possibly. Why?'

'*Press Gazette*'s for sale and I thought we might have a bit of fun with it.'

How amusing. The only trade magazine for newspaper journalists has given me years of stick, and the occasional carrot. It probably has the most influential readership of any magazine in the country, given that every major Fleet Street player reads it.

'What will it cost?'

'Not much, it's been pared to the bone and survives on the profit it makes from the British Press Awards. If we don't buy it, it will probably close down.'

'Let's go for it then.'

28 April

Had lunch with James Murdoch at Riva, a great little Italian restaurant in Barnes. He's been running BSkyB for a while now, and is slowly making a name for himself as a businessman who doesn't just trade off the Murdoch name, helpful though that must be, obviously. We had an amusing conversation, though he was massively more guarded than he used to be. I guess he has to be now.

A moment of high comedy came at the end when he went to pay the bill

– lunch was his suggestion – and I spotted that familiar rustling of jacket pockets that usually indicates a wallet-related issue. He was slowly turning a mild shade of pink – a second obvious giveaway – and I was in no rush to put him out of his misery: he is a Murdoch after all.

Eventually, after a long, painful minute, he said, 'Erm … look, this is really embarrassing, but I must have left my wallet at the office and I don't have any money on me…'

I laughed. 'James, it will be my pleasure. Can't have you Murdochs thinking you can buy my friendship anyway.'

Dylan Jones threw a dinner party tonight, where fellow guests included Jamie Theakston and his girlfriend, the supermodel Erin O'Connor. Jamie has a house in a village just a few miles away from Newick, we both play cricket for our local sides and both happily subscribe to the wine, women and song philosophy of life. Erin seemed very nice, but she'll be facing an uphill struggle with Jamie, whose attention span with any one female form seems startlingly limited.

30 April

Mohamed Al Fayed promised he'd promote my book at Harrods with a big book signing, and boy did he deliver!

I turned up at 10a.m. on a busy Saturday, and was directed underneath the store, across Knightsbridge, into a delivery area where a beautiful green and gold horse-drawn carriage awaited. I blinked – surely not?

But it was surely yes.

I was assisted up into the back seat, flanked by a very attractive scantily clad young lady clutching a billboard announcing that I would be signing copies of *The Insider* in the books section. We trotted right down the centre of Knightsbridge, with cars stopping to see who the 'superstar' was, and tourists gawping at me blankly from the street.

'Who *is* he?' was a regular mouthed refrain as we cornered the store, and continued down to the back where a small scrum was gathering for my big arrival. Mum had brought the three boys along, as well as Charlotte and her tribe, and there in the middle of them all was Mohamed, dishing out lollipops with a huge grin and giving what appeared to be a continuous interview to a TV crew. A Scottish bagpiper serenaded me as I clambered down from the carriage, and there was a ripple of polite if sceptical applause from the crowd.

'Mohamed, this is hilarious – I can't thank you enough,' I said, as he clasped my shoulder.

'It's my pleasure,' he chuckled. 'We did it for Victoria Beckham, so why not you?'

There were lots of very sensible reasons 'why not for me', but this was not the time to explore them. I must admit I was loving every minute.

'Right, follow me,' cried Mohamed, and he set off with me, my family entourage, the TV crew and the piper in hot pursuit. We marched round the whole ground floor first, attracting general bemusement, laughter, and the very occasional flicker of recognition for 'that bloke who got fired from the *Mirror*.'

Then we charged up the escalators to the book floor, where a huge number of people had congregated. I was completely taken aback. 'Are they all for me?' I asked one of Mohamed's assistants.

'Yes, Mr Morgan, it's been on the store tannoy system all day.'

A few seconds later I heard exactly what they were putting out on the tannoy system, and suddenly understood why there was such a big crowd. Unless you listened very, very carefully, you could easily mistake the announcement for 'Pierce Brosnan will be signing copies of his new book…'

They thought I was James Bond.

The look of bitter disappointment was etched all over their star-struck faces.

As news spread that I was *not* the Hollywood actor, the large crowd began to filter away, leaving a reasonable but not hugely impressive queue behind. Most of the defectors were Americans by the look of them. Oh well, I enjoyed being a superstar for half an hour, anyway.

Mohamed hammed it up for the publicity pictures with me, and left with more lollipops for all the kids and a cheery shout of, 'You must all have lunch at any of the restaurants, OK. Good.'

There was nothing in this for him, other than amusement, which is why I've always liked the guy.

I have to say, though, that I absolutely loved all the attention. It's nerve-wracking being centre stage like that, but exhilarating too. You can see why celebrities get so addicted to it.

4 May

Popped into a leaving party for Lorraine Heggessey, outgoing boss of BBC ONE, and it was the kind of star-studded send-off you'd expect from some-one as popular as she has been.

I stood at the back of the room with Ian Wright and Gary Lineker, trying to avoid taking part in the rather cringe-making song that had been composed for the occasion.

Lineker read a text message on his phone and suddenly grabbed my arm.

'Heard about Thierry Henry?'

'No, what?'

'Barcelona.'

'*No?*'

'Yes. Deal done this afternoon, thirty million quid.'

I looked at Wright, who simply nodded gravely.

'It's true. Terrible isn't it?'

I couldn't believe it. Arsenal's greatest ever player was leaving, this was worse than John Lennon getting shot.

Then Lineker and Wright exchanged a quick glance and exploded into fits of uncontrollable, back-slapping giggles.

'Only kidding.'

Funny guys. Very, very funny.

Later I was introduced to Roly Keating, the controller of BBC TWO. He looked rather embarrassed.

'Oh hi, Piers, I've been meaning to get back to you about your pilot.'

'Yes, well it has been three months now, Roly. Just wouldn't mind knowing either way what you want to do.'

'Yes, of course. The trouble is that I haven't actually heard it yet. They sent me a copy, but there was no sound on it.'

'No sound on it?'

'No, no sound on it. So I need to get another one with the sound on.'

'Yes, I guess you do.'

At that point we were all called to silence for the speeches and Roly used the chance to slip away from my incredulous face.

5 May

General Election day, and I spent most of it convincing myself not to vote in protest at Blair's Iraq folly. In the end I did cast my name for Labour because of the persuasive 'Vote Tony, Get Gordon' argument. The Tories are still all over the place, Charles Kennedy and his Lib Dems just seem a vacuous bunch of mediocre clods, and Labour have undeniably done an OK job domestically. Not a great one, just an OK one. It's just a tragedy that Blair has let himself, and us, be sucked into the horrific position of being America's poodle.

I exacted some light relief during the afternoon by appearing on *Loose Women*, where they presented me on air with a framed mock-up front page saying, PIERS MORGAN COMES ON LOOSE WOMEN which was in extremely dubious taste, however you read it.

Then I spent two hours interviewing Gordon Ramsay for *GQ*.

He crashed into his restaurant at Claridges like a mini-tornado. 'Fuck, sorry I'm so fucking late, had a fucking nightmare day!'

He may make Tourette's sufferers seem pure-mouthed, but I like Gordon.

A genius in the kitchen, he shouts from the hip, means every word he says, doesn't care who he upsets, has commendable zero-tolerance of mediocrity and flits from searing confessional to razor-sharp hilarity in a micro-second. And like most geniuses, he has overcome a pretty rough upbringing to get where he is: his father was an abusive, violent drunk who terrorised his mother.

'Did he ever once tell you he was proud of you?' I asked.

'Never. Not once. He just didn't like me. I pissed him off. I remember him taking me and my brother camping and leaving us fishing while he went drinking and then brought girls back to the tent. I told my mum and was obviously never allowed to go fishing again; he was really angry with me for that. He also dropped my brother, Ronnie, like a sack of shit when he had a drug problem, just the same as he dropped me.'

Gordon's relationship with fellow masterchef Marco Pierre White is another hideously complex one. They haven't exchanged a single civil word for four years after falling out over some business deal.

I recently tried to broker a rapprochement after Gordon said he was prepared to kiss and make up, but Marco was having none of it. 'I will never speak to Gordon again,' he snorted furiously.

I asked Gordon what it was like when they worked together at Harveys in Wandsworth.

'Marco was brilliant but mad. He made me arm-wrestle him one night. What a dilemma ... I sat there rolling up my sleeve, thinking, Do I let him win or do I knock the shit out of him? He was seething, his eyes were bulging and his wild hair was all over the place. And I thought, What the fuck am I doing here? So I decided to let him win. It was just easier. But then we started wrestling and I suddenly remembered all the abuse he'd poured on me and I just went mad and put his hand through the fucking table. I didn't care if he beat me up, this was my moment. He went mad and ripped the table up, but I'd beaten him, that was all that mattered. He may be a better chef, but I'm stronger than him.'

Gordon was laughing, but I could see the ferocious competition between them laid bare then and there, and it's something that's under-pinned their relationship ever since.

He then told me an incredible story of how he'd taken his wife Tana to the Fat Duck in Bray, where master chef Heston Blumenthal performs his chemist-like magic in the kitchen, and Marco suddenly walked in.

'He went up to Heston and insisted he chuck me out, then walked out to sit in the garden until I was gone. I couldn't believe it. Poor Heston didn't know what to do, but eventually he decided he had to go with Marco, so he came up and politely asked me and Tana to leave. I was furious, I mean my wife was with me for God's sake. So I stormed out to confront him, and he was sitting in a chair like fucking Don Corleone. I shouted, 'Get up you coward,' but he refused. I had the choice of hitting him or walking away, and I walked away.'

Now he was nice and riled, I pressed some more nuclear buttons.

'Can we discuss some of your other rivals now, using the names you have used for them?'

'Sure...'

'Ready Steady Twat?'

'Ah yes, Ainsley Harriott. Yes. Quite proud of calling him that, it was a good one. People tell me he makes them laugh, he's a comedian because of the voice and the eyes and the pepper mill. It makes me laugh when people say I'm bad for the industry and I see members of the public being humiliated on *Ready Steady Twat* because they can't cut cucumbers properly. It's so wrong.'

'Can't Cook, Won't Wank?'

'I did call it that, but it wasn't me that first called Antony Worrall Thompson a squashed Bee Gee, it was bloody Marco. Don't blame me.'

'You described Nigella Lawson as a sexy bitch from the neck up.'

'I never said that, and I told her I hadn't said it when we met the other day. She's a sexy bitch, full stop. I honestly never said it – that would have been a terrible thing to say.'

'Anton Mosimann – more famous for his bow ties than his cooking?'

'Fuck me, you've done your homework. Well he is, isn't he? He wears a shirt and bow tie under his chef's jacket, for fuck's sake. I was disappointed when I met him, such an affected Swiss load of old nonsense.'

'Novelli and Rhodes? The new Ramsays?'

'Do me a favour. Christ. Just didn't work, did it. Too many cooks spoil-ing the broth. It was embarrassing, wasn't it? Pair of dicks, honestly.'

Gordon was on vintage form – ridiculing, bombastic, arrogant, hilarious. I was choking with laughter after this little exchange.

He is an unreconstructed man, the way they used to make them and the way most women used to want them.

I asked if he was romantic.

'Yes, but only if I can get completely away from work. It's no good at home if I'm constantly being bothered by chefs going through lunch menus. I'm not one for slushy flowers that die after a few days, or text messages – never sent one in my life and never want to. Nor emails. Don't want to know about any of that crap. The thing about Tana is that she knows me very well; she knows what an arsehole I can be. And she knows when to back off, or offer support when I need it. We're from different backgrounds – I'm from a council house and a broken home, and she's from a really immaculate home life with great parents. She never gets involved in the business. I don't want to scream at her for not delivering food to table three on time. She is a very strong, normal person. And the sex is fantastic. I couldn't be with her if it wasn't. She looks amazing and I still wake up every morning with a hard-on. What more could you want at thirty-eight?'

I concluded the interview by asking, 'If you could have sex with one woman before you die, with Tana's permission, who would it be?'

'To make love to, or to fuck?'

'Either.'

'Liz Hurley.'

'Which method?'

'Oh, fuck her, definitely.'

10 May

I wrote a piece in my *Standard* column today about Elton John, saying:

'Elton John's not everyone's cup of tea. Vain, outspoken, and often impossibly vulgar, he personifies to many people the most hideous excesses of rock superstardom. But the revelation that he gave £22.6 million to good causes in 2004, a twelfth of his entire fortune, is something that deserves genuine admiration.'

Gary Farrow, our long-time mutual friend, rang this afternoon. 'Why did you have a go at Elton?'

'I didn't.'

'You did, you said he was vain and vulgar.'

'Well he is, but that doesn't mean I don't like him. And I was actually being complimentary about him if you bothered to read the piece.'

'That's not what Elton thinks – he's quite upset about it.'

I've upset a lot of people with this column, which is the nature of the beast, I suppose. It's tricky squaring being a fearless, sabre-toothed columnist with trying to make it in the world of television, which would require working with a lot of the people I write so critically about.

In the evening I went with Martin Cruddace to the twenty-fifth-anniversary party of the Dover Street Wine Bar, owned by George who sits next to us at Arsenal.

I'm not saying I was blind drunk, but at midnight I found my arm raised to the ceiling as I bid £1,000 for a night out with The Cheeky Girls, those mad Russian singing sisters.

As Martin put it when I was outbid, 'Mate, if you want a night with a Russian, you can get one a lot cheaper than that up the road in Park Lane.'

12 May

Elton John's stage version of *Billy Elliott* opened tonight, and the moment he arrived he marched over to where I was standing and said, 'Why did you have a go at me?'

'I didn't, I was being nice about you.'

'No you weren't.'

'Yes, I was.'

This was turning into a panto sketch.

'Well it didn't read like it.'

'Look Elton, I'm sorry if I upset you, that was not the intention at all. I was actually praising you for giving so much to charity.'

He was having none of it, though, and stomped off in a huff.

13 May

The BBC informed me today that Roly Keating had watched the pilot of my entertainment show, with the sound working this time, and would not be developing it into a series at this stage.

'I think we've been a victim of terrible timing,' said Karen Smith, one of the producers of the pilot. 'If Alison hadn't moved to CBBC it would definitely have been commissioned.'

'Don't worry,' I replied. 'I'm just pleased that Roly finally got to hear it.'

My day got even better when I was invited to take part in a new reality TV show, called *Celebrity Shark Bait*.

'We'd like you to sit in a shark cage off the South African coast and get attacked by sharks,' said the producer.

'Why on earth would you want me to do that?'

'Because it would make great telly.'

'What if I die?'

'That would make even better telly.'

These people clearly think I'm so desperate for work I'll do literally anything, however humiliating. A fact that in itself is humiliating.

Why on earth would anyone take part in something called *Celebrity Shark Bait*? It defies all reason. Yet I bet there will be a lengthy queue of famous people willing to do it just to be on telly.

14 May

Jeremy emailed from Basra: 'You'll be interested to know that I'm briefing your mate John Reid tomorrow. The Army is much relieved to have him in place of Buff Hoon – apparently we nearly got that tree-hugger Patricia Hewitt.'

15 May

Another email from Jeremy: 'It's 48 degrees and the sand gets everywhere. But we're all suffering in equal measure, there is no respite, it's stifling now and it's only going to get worse and we are all thoroughly bored with the subject. Reid gave an amusing speech to the soldiers saying that whilst we (Army) have 88 per cent approval rating in the eyes of the British Public, politicians have 7 per cent. However, our combined rating was therefore a healthy 95 per cent (ho, ho). I sat opposite him for dinner in the main cookhouse, but he was surrounded by soldiers telling him about the lack of welfare facilities, telephones, internet terminals and air-conditioning. By the time that was over he had to move on. All in all, though, he came across as a thoroughly good egg and went down well with the boys. Great improvement on Buff Hoon.'

19 May

Stanley had a starring role in his school play today, as a court reporter in *Humpty Dumpty*. It wasn't supposed to be a starring role as he only had one line, but in true Stanley style that was quite enough to steal the show. Dressed in classic reporter get-up – raincoat and pork pie hat – and clutching a notebook and pen, he marched to the front of the stage at the end of the thrilling *Dumpty* denouement in court and loudly declared in the most outrageous cockney accent you've ever heard, 'Oi've never 'eard anyfin' loik it in me loif!'

The audience collapsed with laughter as Stanley beamed with delight.

And I reflected on the irony of my middle son being centre stage as a cheeky journalist while I struggle to find my new vocation in life. I'd love one of the boys to be a journalist. Despite all the slings and arrows that came my way, it has to be one of the most exciting, unpredictable and amusing of professions.

20 May

The *Daily Mail* rang at lunchtime and asked if I fancied writing a piece about the 'death of celebrity', in light of all the abuse being fired at a new reality TV show called *Celebrity Love Island*.

'I'd love to,' I said, seeing as this whole celebrity subject has been on my mind so much lately.

I'd watched *Celebrity Love Island* the other night and could barely believe how cretinous it was. At one stage Calum Best, famous purely for being George Best's son, was asked to spell the word 'celebrity' – and failed. It seemed to sum up the whole ridiculous farce of modern-day Z-list fame.

Everyone thinks they can be a star now, just by prancing about on shows like this. And the worst thing is that they're right, they can.

I fired off 2,000 furious words, begging for a return to the days when real stars filled the airwaves, people with genuine talent like Sinatra, Olivier, or Eric Morecambe.

23 May

Channel 4 picked up on my *Daily Mail* article on the death of celebrity and want me to do a one-hour programme on it. I could make a good living simply commentating on the absurdity of modern celebrity culture. In fact, I could be a celebrity purely on the back of talking about celebrities. How utterly ridiculous!

24 May

Great survey in the papers today about global sexual performance. British men apparently last an average 7.6 minutes at sex, which is officially 0.6 minutes longer than American males. You just know that this will really, really annoy them.

26 May

Had to drive to Stratford-upon-Avon today to interview Shane Warne for *GQ*, and was looking forward to it enormously. The man's not just the greatest spin bowler the game of cricket has ever seen, he's also one of its most controversial and fascinating characters.

Pinning him down has been a bit of nightmare, involving endless texts and late-night calls, several cancelled appointments and lengthy negotiations over just how many free clothes he can wangle out of the photo shoot. These celebrities, honestly!

As I approached Birmingham, my phone vibrated. It was another text from Warne.

'Hi mate, any chance we can postpone to another day? We're about to lose, fuck me!'

Hampshire were indeed about to lose, in a very unexpected two-day thrashing to Warwickshire.

But I wasn't just going to turn round and drive all the way home, so I said we had to do it because the deadline was too urgent to rearrange at this late stage.

He reluctantly agreed, and I quickly worked out why he was so keen not to do the interview now: with a sudden unexpected free day looming tomorrow, he could get wrecked in Southampton tonight. And the sooner he got down there, the more time he'd have to party.

'Meet me at the hotel bar at 6p.m.,' he said.

I got there at 5.50p.m. to find another text.

'Room 121, come up in half an hour.'

Not the first time he has sent texts like that, I suspect, though I'm not his usual type.

I went up to the room and knocked.

Warne answered, looking knackered and clutching a freshly lit cigarette.

'Hi mate, come on in.'

I'd expected the best suite in the hotel. Warne is, after all, the biggest star in world cricket and a multi-millionaire many times over.

Instead I found him occupying a tiny little room, with just a bed, TV and coffeemaker for company. It looked rather grubby, the walls were peeling in several areas and there was a dank musty smell to the place.

This was a grim hotel room for a man of his stature.

'Nice place you've got here, Shane.'

'Yeah, I know, mate. Quality, eh?' He laughed at the sheer absurdity of his meagre accommodation.

'Christ, mate, this is like Alan Partridge.'

'Who's he?'

'Oh, he's a comic TV character who lives in a travel lodge room not dissimilar to this.'

'Never heard of him, mate.'

Warne uses the word 'mate' almost as much as I do, it's a form of punctuation that serves the very useful purpose of never having to remember anyone's name.

He also has a tendency to get into as many scrapes as I do, spending the last two years fending off drug, sex and betting scandals. Finally it looks like he's beginning to sort himself out, though he admitted, 'The problem is there's still a big kid inside me who likes to have fun. I am passionate about my cricket and I love my family, but I'm also a kid, and maybe I need to grow up … and maybe I don't. Life isn't a rehearsal, it's about having fun.'

'Do you feel you owe Mrs Warne one?'

'Oh, more than one, mate. You don't often get as many chances as I've had, and I would have understood if she'd wanted to walk. But I hope we can be together forever now, I really do. Christ, I'm starting to sound like Dr Phil on *Oprah*! Shall I start calling you Dr Piers?'

He was uncomfortable talking about all this, but also clearly wanted to get it off his chest. It was a surprisingly emotional outpouring from someone who has always come over as a typical fair-dinkum misogynistic Aussie.

Warne is the kind of celebrity I can properly admire, though. He is famous not just because he's a naughty boy, but because he can bowl like nobody else has bowled in the history of cricket.

27 May

Matthew Freud rang at 10a.m.

'Congratulations, we are the proud new owners of *Press Gazette*.'

What a laugh.

When the news broke an hour later, we began attracting a mixture of warm congratulations and blind fury.

'Why have you bought it?' one journalist asked me.

'So I can ban Jeremy Clarkson from the Awards,' I replied, which was about the most tactless thing I could possibly have said given the ongoing controversy over the British Press Awards – some papers are threatening to boycott next year's event unless the format is radically changed – but also the most satisfying.

I still haven't forgiven Clarkson for punching me at the Awards last year, though before all that nonsense we used to get on rather well.

28 May

My phone rang at 4p.m. It was Shane Warne.

'Hi mate, I've got a problem and might need your help.'

'OK, what's up?'

'Ah, some girl's gone to the *Sunday Mirror* with a load of crap about me and they're going to run it all tomorrow.'

'Right, is it true?'

Pause.

'I don't know, mate, I was out of it. Just can't remember much really.'

I took that as a yes.

He sounded sad and agitated. 'Is there anything you can do? Have you still got any mates at the *Mirror*?'

I've loads of friends at the *Mirror*, of course I do. And Tina, the editor of the *Sunday Mirror*, is one of my closest friends in journalism. But I can't just call up and get a story like this pulled, I'm not the editor-in-chief any more; they'd laugh in my face.

'I can make a few calls and see what's going on, Shane, but I doubt it will stop the story coming out.'

He went silent for a moment. 'Mate, my marriage is fucked if this comes out. Over.'

I was listening to a desperate man, and it wasn't a comfortable conversation.

Before I had interviewed him for *GQ*, I would have thought, 'What an idiot, you deserve all you get.'

But having seen him stuck in that poky little hotel room, and heard the way he talked about Simone and his kids, I felt a bit more sympathetic to the lifestyle issues that led to his behaviour.

I defy almost anyone to lead the life of a professional cricketer and not succumb to the temptation that gets thrown your way.

Warne loves his wife and family, of that I have no doubt, but he spends months on end living on his own in £80-a-night rooms, feeling, I should imagine, rather lonely and stifled. On the pitch he's a firebrand of passion, flair, energy and aggression. What's he supposed to do when he comes off? Put his pipe and slippers on and have a cup of cocoa watching *EastEnders*? Marital infidelity is never right, but the pressures of that kind of life cannot be underestimated. Warne's a good-looking, famous, rich sporting genius who has women hurling themselves at him like lemmings off a cliff.

Right now, though, he was just another cheating husband who'd been caught, and he was going through hell.

'I'm really sorry, mate,' was all I could think to say. 'My only advice is to say nothing and hope it blows over quickly.'

'I'm not going to say a thing, mate, but Simone's going to hear about this and she's going to go mad.'

29 May

The *Sunday Mirror* appeared without a word on Shane Warne. I could just about hear the sigh of relief all the way from Southampton. This is the downside of fame at its harshest. Everybody would love the money, adulation and freebies that come with celebrity, but who, if they're honest, would like their personal peccadillos splashed all over the papers? I know I'd hate it.

30 May

I've been writing my *Evening Standard* column for the agreed six months now and the contract is up for renewal. Today I was informed that it would not be renewed because I'm 'too expensive', which is probably just a polite way of saying they're bored with my rantings.

On the plus side, the *Press Gazette* news means everyone assumes I've given up the *Standard* to do that instead, so I don't get any MORGAN SACKED AGAIN headlines.

4

6 June

There is a famous pub cricket team called Lashings, owned by a millionaire called David Folb and based in Kent, that fields the world's greatest players. I've watched them play for years, and it's pure fantasy cricket as legend after legend strut their stuff against amateur opposition.

Every time I've watched them play, I've taunted their captain – former West Indies captain Richie Richardson – that Newick could stuff them out of sight.

David Folb rang me today to call my bluff.

'Hi mate, we've had a cancellation for a match in three weeks' time, do you and your village team finally fancy putting your boasts to the test?'

'Of course,' I said, before putting the phone down and thinking, 'What the fuck have I just done.'

I called Sam Carter, our scholarly and obsessive opening batsman.

'Sam, how do you fancy playing against eleven of the world's best players in Newick?'

I'm not quite sure what happened on the other end of the phone, but I fear it was a moment not entirely unrelated to Meg Ryan's memorable restaurant scene in *When Harry Met Sally*.

'Oh. My. God,' he stammered. 'Yes, yes, YES!'

'Good, because we've got three weeks to organise it.'

9 June

Jeremy read about the *Press Gazette* purchase in Basra and had a suggestion: 'You should try and add *Trout and Salmon* magazine to your stable, then you could appoint me editor and I could start leading a normal life again. I can see the headline now: EX-*MIRROR* EDITOR'S BROTHER RAISES THE FAMILY STANDARD WITH *MAGGOT WEEKLY*. I'm not sure I would survive in your line of business. You're nothing but a "rapscallion", according to the *Independent*, whilst I have managed to maintain my personal honour (and little else, admitedly) in an Establishment-approved vocation. The weather here today is ghastly: 52 degrees, windy and very dusty – we have a "shamal" (dust storm) blowing over us at the moment and the dust gets everywhere. It's actually quite difficult to breathe outside. I can't imagine why any human being would want to live in this place, but why would I want to give up the wonderful lifestyle I currently enjoy for better pay, the chance to go fishing five days a week and see my children grow up?'

13 June

Kelvin MacKenzie has given a big interview to the *Independent* media section in which he names *me* as one of his pet hates. I read it, then re-read it, in disbelief. I can only assume it was a gag and that the interviewer, Ray Snoddy, didn't get it. Things are really getting bad if even Kelvin's turning on me.

15 June

An email from Kelvin: 'Hi Piers, I'm so sorry that you appeared on my alleged hate list in the *Indy*. As you know, nothing could be further from the truth. I have spoken to Snoddy who said he must have misunderstood me!!!!!!!!!!!!!!!!!!!!!!'

It's taken him fifteen years, but Kelvin MacKenzie has finally apologised for something.

17 June

Bertie had a 'Taking Dad to School' day at his nursery. He thoroughly enjoyed marching me along by the arm saying things like, 'Come on, Dad, or you'll be late for school,' and then dissolving into fits of giggles.

18 June

I nearly died tonight, and it was all Shane Warne's fault. Driving up to London for Rob McGibbon's fortieth birthday party, I took a phone call from Michael Cohen, Shane's UK agent, saying he had a 'little local difficulty' that he needed some advice on. It was the same local difficulty that Shane had called me about a couple of weeks ago.

'Erm, it appears that a girl has gone to the *Sunday Mirror* claiming to have had an affair with Shane, and I don't need to tell you, Piers, that if this story appears then Shane's marriage is going to be in very serious trouble.'

At that precise moment there was an enormous bang and my car went into spiralling freefall down the M23. I'd been hit by something very hard and very fast, and realised in that split second that the middle lane of a motorway on a busy Saturday night is not a great place for this to happen. It's strange how lucidly you can think in moments like this. My mind flashed back to the time I drove a *Sun*-sponsored old wreck at a celebrity stock-car race in Wimbledon years earlier. 'Don't turn the wheel against the spin' was the training mantra then. The natural inclination when your car is turning at high speed is to try and correct it, but the clever thing to do is to try and ride the spin – that way you're less likely to turn over altogether.

It was all over in a few seconds, and when I came to a halt I discovered I'd spun straight down the road and ended up on the hard shoulder, as dozens of other cars had screeched past at high speed.

Michael Cohen was still on the line. 'What happened?' he asked, panic in his voice. 'Are you OK, Piers?'

'Er, Michael I'm going to have go, mate, something's come up,' I replied with what I thought was commendable understatement.

The car that hit me had careered into another Mercedes before writing itself off, leaving an elderly lady passenger with nasty cuts to her head. The driver and his passenger disembarked and were clearly off their heads on booze and probably drugs. To my astonishment, they reached back into their mangled smoking vehicle, turned the radio up even louder and began doing a wild dance in the middle of the motorway, cackling to themselves like hyenas. It was a surreal and alarming development. These guys were out of control and anything could happen.

At that point a car with a speedboat attached on a trailer skidded to a halt and manoeuvred itself into a position where it blocked off the offending vehicle. Three burly Scots jumped out and began shouting abuse at the two men, then one of them came over and asked if I was OK. 'You should be dead,' he said seriously. 'Those guys hit you at more than 100mph. I know because that was the speed they passed us at a minute ago. They've come up from Brighton veering across all three lanes and narrowly missing loads of cars. We saw it hit yours and just assumed everyone would be killed.'

I stood there in my shorts and T-shirt, feeling absolutely fine, not even a suggestion of whiplash. Other cars began stopping, full of furious people. One West Indian woman ran over to the two culprits and screamed, 'You fucking idiots, you could have killed everyone.' But they were too far gone to understand anything that was going on.

Minutes later the police arrived and after a good look at the scene, and talking to the Scots, one of them told me, 'Mr Morgan, it's your lucky night. If you hadn't been in a car as strong as your Mercedes S500 then I think you'd be dead now.' I stood by the side of the road dwelling on the incident. The two idiots were still swigging vodka from a bottle as police arrested them.

After about twenty-five minutes the phone went and it was Andy at the *News of the World*. 'You all right, mate, someone has just called the news desk saying you've had a bad road accident?' Another illustration of my burgeoning D-grade celebrity status. It felt rather odd to think that someone saw me standing by a smashed-up car and thought, Let's make a few quid out of it. But then, that's exactly what I did as a tabloid editor for a decade.

I considered my options and decided I might as well go to the party. The police dropped me at Gatwick Airport and I hopped in a taxi to Chelsea. 'What kept you?' Rob asked as I finally shuffled in at midnight. 'Erm, well, I nearly died,' I replied. He laughed and handed me a beer. At 6a.m. we watched thousands of women walking over Chelsea Bridge in bras, including my great friend Sarah Moriarty, taking part in some cancer charity race. As I said, a surreal evening.

21 June

Interviewed Simon Cowell today for *GQ*, over lunch at the Belvedere in Holland Park. He was even more sickeningly fit, tanned and relaxed than he had been last time we'd met.

American Idol is getting bigger and bigger in the States, and Cowell is rapidly approaching movie-star status.

'How crazy is it for you out there now?' I asked.

'It's mad. It's got to the stage now where if I pop into a shopping mall to get a CD or something, within a few minutes I'm completely mobbed, with 1,000 people circling me. I realise in those moments that virtually the whole of America must be watching the show.'

I was rather envious. Just three years ago Simon was a relatively unknown – if highly successful – music executive. Now, thanks to one lucky break when he was asked to be a judge on *Pop Idol*, he's become one of the most famous people on the planet.

'What's the barmiest thing that's happened to you?' I asked.

'I remember one old guy coming up to me in The Ivy in Los Angeles while I was having dinner and asking for a private word. I agreed and he then asked if I did private performances. I said, "Not really, no, but what do you have in mind?" And he said, "What would you charge to review my wife and I in bed? We'd be prepared to pay you $150,000." I thought it was a wind-up and started laughing, then I realised he was deadly serious. Unbelievable.'

The great thing with Cowell is that he never seems to take anything seriously at all, and will always answer any question you ask him with brutal honesty.

Since he'd brought up sex, I asked him what his worst-ever sexual experience had been.

'Oh God, having sex for the first time as a seventeen-year-old teenager. I lied and said I'd already lost my virginity to try and sound big. She hadn't lost hers either but admitted it, and on the day we planned to have sex it was like going to the gallows – I hadn't got a clue what I was doing. We went to the pub beforehand for a drink and I was forcing beer down my neck. I couldn't get enough of it to numb what I thought would be the most humiliating moment of my life. We went back and had a bath and she jumped out and said, "Simon, I'm ready," and I remember lying there contemplating ending it all there and then. Somehow I got through it.'

'Without prying too much into your personal grief, how many seconds?'

'I think that seconds might be too long a unit. I just wanted to get her out as quickly as possible so I could tell all my mates I'd done it.'

'Was she pleased with your performance?'

'I didn't ask her, actually, but I doubt she looks back on it now as the greatest sexual experience of her life, that's for sure.'

'You said recently that having sex with porn stars was a good idea because they're regularly tested for disease...'

'Yes, well there is a logic in that argument.'

'Does Terri (his girlfriend of three years) share that logic?'

'No!'

It's amazing to think that just ten years ago Cowell was completely broke.

'I was working for a record company owned by a public company that went down, taking us with it. I had borrowed a load of money from the bank to buy shares in the company and overnight they were worthless – as was I. I was literally down to the £4 I had in my pocket, and by the time I paid the cab fare home I was penniless, completely skint.'

'How did that feel?'

'It was, erm, grounding. Actually, the thought of it was much worse than the reality. There was a weird sense of freedom at having absolutely zilch but still having the energy and desire to change my life for the better.

I got rid of my house and swapped my Porsche for a £7,000 car I'd paid cash for, but that didn't embarrass me. It was just the way it was. Luckily, my parents asked me to live with them so I didn't have to pay any rent or anything. And to be honest, I felt fine about it. It was a wake-up call. I had to sort myself out. It came on the back of a very artificial time in Britain where everyone was buying things they couldn't afford and it was always going to blow up in our faces. I vowed then never to borrow money again. If I could afford something, I would pay cash for it; if I couldn't, I would wait. In an odd way, it was a very good thing for me.'

'Were you happier skint or now that you're fabulously rich?'

'Erm … money brings you security and choice. You can make decisions in a different way if you have a lot of money. But when you have nothing, you have a naivety, and a more fearless attitude because you have nothing to lose. To get money you have to be successful, which means you have to work bloody hard, and I did. I paid myself £5,000 a year, paid off my debts and learned more from the whole thing than anything else. I wasn't ashamed, I just accepted it.'

I asked him what his recipe for success was.

'My own saying is: "Create the hype, but don't ever believe it." And I always remember my father telling me that you have to remember that every single person who works for you or with you in your company has an invisible sign on their forehead that says, "Make me feel important." So if you have a very successful day, it's vital to remember who helped you and make them feel just as good as you do.'

We wrapped up the interview and sat chatting over coffee for another half an hour.

'Have you ever thought of working in America, Piers?' he asked.

'Not really. I'm completely unknown over there and can't imagine what I'd do.'

'I was unknown, too, and I worried about that a lot when they suggested *American Idol* to me, but it was easier than I thought. You'd enjoy it out there, it's fun.'

And I could tell by his beaming Hollywood-style grin that he was having the time of his life. Lucky bastard.

26 June

The big day has arrived: Lashings' all-star cricketers against the might of Newick village. Dozens of club members did a Herculean job preparing the ground for the match, filling it with beer tents, spit-roasts, ice-cream vans, Pimms bars and marquees.

At the house, the boys were wildly excited.

'Dad, can I bowl at Chris Cairns?' asked Stanley.

'No, mate. He is the world's biggest ever test match six hitter and you are eight years old. Leave Mr Cairns to your father.'

'Dad,' said Spencer. 'If he can hit Shane Warne out of the ground, I don't think he's going to be too worried about you now, is he?'

'He hasn't seen my doosra, has he, you impertinent little scamp,' I retorted.

They raced off to the treehouse in the garden, where shortly afterwards I heard a loud scream. I ran out to find Stanley crumpled on the floor, sobbing his heart out.

'I've broken my arm,' he said.

'No, you haven't, Stan, let me have a look at it.'

He winced in agony as I gently held up his wrist.

His face was ashen white and he was trembling. This didn't look good.

I checked the time. It was 1p.m., just an hour before the start of the first of two 20-over games.

'I'm going to miss it, aren't I?' said Stanley, unleashing another torrent of tears. 'And all because of my stupid bloody broken arm.'

'Stanley, don't use language like that. It'll be fine, don't worry.'

Mum inspected the wrist and thought it was probably sprained rather than broken, but said she'd take him to the local hospital for an X-ray to double check.

A crowd of well over 1,200 people had already turned up to watch on a perfect sunny day. It was the biggest village gathering I could remember outside of the annual Bonfire Night.

There'd been a small issue about charging people to get in, because technically the ground is a public playing field. But Lashings were waiving their usual £5,000 fee, and all they wanted were the gate receipts of £3 for adults and £2 for kids, which seemed very reasonable given the superstar status of their line-up.

As their players arrived, our mouths began to drop. There were three former West Indies captains – Richie Richardson, of course, Jimmy Adams, and Alvin Kallicharran – South Africa's current superstar Herschelle Gibbs, Indian legend VVS Laxman, Pakistan spinning maestro Saqlain Mushtaq... and Chris Cairns, 6 foot 4 inches of pure unreconstructed Kiwi beef.

Suddenly I didn't feel quite so confident.

Just before the game started, I heard excited squeals from my nieces and nephews. 'Stanley's back!'

And so he was, in a plastercast.

'Hi Dad, I broke my wrist.'

He'd been right, though it was just a greenstick fracture that shouldn't take too long to heal.

'I'm going to get all the Lashings players to sign my cast.'

Good old Stanley, his glass is always half full.

The match began and we started well, then Chris Cairns marched to the crease. On 11, he skied one straight to Miles Caldwell at long-on. He has the safest pair of hands in the club, but he dropped it. Five balls later, Cairns skied another one to Miles, who dropped it again.

'I don't give three chances,' laughed Cairns ominously.

He hit the next three balls for 6, each one bigger than the last. And three more in the next over. This was carnage.

I brought myself on to bowl. Cairns shouldered arms to my first ball, a sizzling non-spinning off-break. The commentator was impressed. 'Cairns giving Morgan real respect there.'

My second ball went into the field, as did the third, fourth and fifth. The last one was a mishit and only went for 4. I'd been hit for 28 in one over, and he hadn't bothered with the first ball.

He was laughing, my colleagues were laughing, 1,200 members of the crowd were laughing, Richie was on the floor laughing. And I could see Spencer, Stanley and Bertie howling with laughter by the boundary rope.

This was about the most embarrassing thing I'd ever experienced.

I took myself off, and Cairns carried on smashing everyone else into the field, going from 11 to 100 in just 29 balls.

When I finally got out, I congratulated Miles.

'You useless twat,' I said.

'Morgan, it was worth it just to see him humiliate you,' he replied.

It had been a fabulous day, though, the stuff of dreams for village cricketers like us. And it was only marred by the spectacle of several members of the parish council wandering around the ground murmuring to anyone who would listen about us charging for entry. Some people, honestly...

30 June

Met Sharon Osbourne at the Groucho Club to interview her for *GQ*. She brought along her PR, Gary Farrow, to keep her tongue in check, and maybe mine as well after the Elton John incident.

I'd heard she'd had some good plastic surgery, but that was an understatement. She looks incredible.

'Blimey, it works then,' I said.

'Yessss, darling,' she purred, putting on one of those voices normally reserved for Russian Bond girls.

'Looks quite an expensive refurb to me?'

'It is, my surgeon's name is Dr Leslie Stevens and he works in Beverly Hills.'

'What's he done for you?'

'Everything, my whole face – but not my lips, I hate that. Whatever you do to them, they always look false.'

'Price it up for me.'

'My face cost about £100,000 '

'Teeth? They're amazing gnashers.'

'Yessss. They were £65,000.'

'What else?'

'My arms, my boobs, my stomach, my bum, my legs…'

'How much were the boobs?'

'Oh, cheap. He gave me a special rate of £12,000 because I'm such a good customer.'

'How much would the whole body makeover cost, then? To do a "Sharon" cosmetically?'

'£3 million, I reckon. By the time you include all the extra costs for anaesthetists and so on. But darling, it's so worth it.'

'Is Ozzy happy with your surgery?'

'He doesn't give a damn. He's happy if I'm happy. Mind you, he does like my new tits. A lot.'

Sharon fell about laughing, as did I.

'Congratulations. Who would you say is the most grotesque example of how a woman should not look after surgery?'

'Bloody hell! I think Melanie Griffith has destroyed herself. She was this lovely, fresh, blonde Californian girl, and now she's just grotesque, it's so sad. Mickey Rourke… God! He obviously hates himself, doesn't he? If you're constantly seeking approval and celebrity then it can do that to you, which is scary. If you want to lead a nice, quiet life as a celebrity then you can, or you can turn up to the latest hot club or restaurant and start punching photographers for taking your picture, and I always think, Fuck off, mate. What the hell are you doing in that club if you don't want to be photographed? It's such bullshit. They should just grow up and stay at home.'

'Anyone else?'

'Michael Douglas, that's another terrible face job. Christ. Poor old twat. Ha ha ha ha ha ha.'

Sharon is the female equivalent of Elton John, wind her up and off she'll go, slagging off everyone and everything in a most amusing manner.

'Who would be at your nightmare dinner party?'

'Oh God, there are so many candidates. Bryan Ferry definitely. For fuck's sake, give me a fucking break. Him and Jagger are always up some lord or lady's arsehole on a fucking Persian rug. They make me sick.'

Gary chuckled nervously. The interview was definitely beginning to drift off-message.

'I'm going to the loo,' he said. 'Try to restrain yourself while I'm gone.'

I waited until he'd left the room.

'Madonna?'

'Oh my God, what a *cunt*!' Sharon squealed with laughter. 'Honestly, I'd like to punch her. She is so full of shit. She's into Kabbalah one minute, she's a Catholic the next, she'll be a Hindu soon no doubt. Fuck off, you cunt.'

I hastily double-checked the tape to make sure it was still running.

'Who else? Oh yes, Bono. What a twat. He has to be there. And Diana Ross. Awful woman.'

Gary returned and Sharon promptly excused herself.

'What else has she said?'

'Oh nothing much. Just called Madonna a cunt, Bono a twat and Diana Ross an awful woman.'

Gary gulped. 'Can we commute "cunt" to "twat"?'

'Why?'

'Just doesn't sound quite so bad, does it?'

Sharon returned and we decided to order some food, but the waiter informed us that we couldn't have a sandwich in the restaurant because it wasn't open yet – it was 6.10p.m. – but we could have one in the bar next door.

Sharon did not take this news well. 'That's fucking ridiculous,' she said. And she was right, it was. 'I want to see the manager.'

A minute later the manageress of the Groucho restaurant arrived, and we politely explained the nonsense of not being able to eat a sandwich in the restaurant but being allowed to eat one in the bar.

She pondered the issue for several moments and then declared solemnly,

'If this is an absolute first and last, and I have an assurance that you will not tell other people about it, then I will allow a sandwich to be served here.' Sharon, Gary and I all gave equally solemn assurances.

But as soon as she'd gone, Sharon shrieked, 'For fuck's sake! For fuck's sake! A fucking sandwich.'

I noticed an absolutely enormous diamond on her finger.

'How much?'

'Guess. It's from Graff.'

'£100,000?'

'Oh don't be so ridiculous, Piers.'

'Sorry, was that too high?'

'No, dear, way too fucking low. I'm not cheap and never will be.'

'A million?'

'More, darling.'

'Christ, £1.5 million?'

'Keep going.'

'£2 million?'

'£1.7.'

'Sharon, that's obscene.'

'I don't care. My favourite one that Ozzy gave me was stolen last year, this one means fuck all.'

'It just made you feel better?'

'Yessss.'

The interview ended and Sharon raised her hands in mock horror. 'Oh dear, Gary, have I been a bit too naughty?'

Gary laughed. 'Sharon, you're always a bit too naughty.'

I said goodbye and walked off down Soho, still chuckling.

1 July

It's the River Café quiz on Sunday night, and I'm struggling to put a winning team together.

Last year I pulled in Judith Keppel, but she can't come this time because she's renovating a house in France.

I've already got Simon Kelner and Roger Alton, which given that they are broadsheet newspaper editors should cover a few bases like pop music and gardening. Conor's there to provide 'hard news' answers – that's what he says, anyway – along with Larry the *Mirror* librarian, who won *University Challenge* and knows everything about everything.

But we need a quiz superstar, someone to strike fear into the opposition.

A person who, when they walk into the room, sends a message that we mean business this time and haven't come for second place again.

'What about Shaun Wallace?' Conor suggested several weeks ago.

'Who's he?'

'He was the first-ever black winner of *Mastermind* two years ago. Very clever guy and still likes doing quizzes apparently.'

It was a brilliant idea, but finding him has proved impossible. Shaun is a criminal barrister from Wembley and very hard to track down.

I had to trawl the internet until I found an interview he'd given to a Hackney Council magazine, contact the journalist who did it and beg for Shaun's number. But every time I've tried to call, his number has just rung out.

Today, at 6.30p.m., he answered.

'Shaun, sorry to trouble you, it's Piers Morgan here.'

'The *Mirror* bloke?'

'Used to be, yes.'

'Blimey, what can I do for you?'

'Well look, it's ridiculously late notice I know, but I've got a team for the prestigious River Café quiz on Sunday night and we need a superstar to help us win.'

'I see.'

'There's no money in it, but the food's great, and you get the chance to make people like Nick Hornby and Stephen Fry look stupid.'

Silence. Then, 'It sounds like a laugh.'

I tried to contain my glee. 'Great, I'll send a car for you on Sunday and see you there.'

'OK.'

I rang Conor: 'The winner of *Mastermind* 2004 is joining us.'

He chuckled. This is going to be fun.

2 July

Got offered a late VIP ticket to Bob Geldof's LIVE 8 show, but just didn't fancy it, so went to Ian Botham's box at Lords instead, where I found myself sitting next to former Rolling Stones guitarist Bill Wyman.

'I didn't fancy that LIVE 8 thing, either; sounds bloody boring to me,' he said.

Which was slightly ironic given Wyman's own 'bloody boring' image.

How wrong can you be about someone, though?

For virtually the entire day he kept me splendidly entertained with hilarious Jagger stories, merrily bitched away about endless showbiz legends, and came across as a funny, fascinating guy.

He said he still sees the Stones occasionally, but that there's no great love lost because he made nothing like the money everyone thinks he did from his years with the world's biggest rock band.

He laughed. 'Everyone thinks I'm fucking loaded, but I'm not. I've got less than two million if truth be told. Mick and Keith got all the money because they wrote the songs.

'I'm not bitter about it, I've got enough to be comfortable. And I'm happier with my life now than I suspect Mick is with his. But it wouldn't have hurt them to dosh it out a bit more, would it?

'They never really respected anyone else in the band. They just did what they wanted to do, when they wanted to do it. If me, Charlie or Ronnie wanted to do something they'd usually just say no.'

We discussed the current celebrity explosion.

'It's ridiculous,' he said. 'All these kids are leaving school wanting to be celebrities, but they don't have any talent to back it up. In my day you got a trade, and if you chose music then you learned how to play an instrument properly. Now they just flash their tits at premieres and everyone treats them like Marilyn Monroe.'

'But you walked away from the Stones at the height of their fame. Don't you miss all that?'

'Nah. Mick and Keith always needed constant attention and lots of people telling them how great they are. I just don't need that in my life any more. I've done so many interesting things since I left the Stones – photography, opening a restaurant, archaeology, playing with and producing other bands. And I found a woman who I really wanted to spend the rest of my life with, and when that happens to you, then you find contentment.'

I could tell he meant it. Bill Wyman had worked out that the only thing inhibiting his enjoyment of life was fame, so he just gave it up.

There was only one question I really wanted answering, though, and as the third bottle of red got opened, I asked it: 'So come on Bill, talking of women, did you have more than Mick or not?'

A long, smug grin sprouted across his gnarled old rocker's face. There was a lengthy pause for maximum dramatic effect as most heads in the box turned to him for the seminal Stones confessional statement.

''Course I fuckin' did.'

A polite smattering of applause for Bill rippled around the box.

It had been a fascinating insight into the mind of a genuine global star.

I'm sure millions of people would have swapped their dreary lives for his sex, drugs and rock 'n' roll career as a Stone, but he swapped it all for a comparatively dreary life when he realised that being a celebrity is just a pain in the arse most of the time – and best left to the insecure, fame-hungry, vain and greedy likes of Mick Jagger. I don't know Jagger, but I would imagine from what I read that he is considerably less happy with his life than Bill Wyman.

3 July

I got to the River Café quiz at 6p.m. for champagne in the garden. All the great and good of London's literary intelligentsia were there, from Jeremy Paxman to John Mortimer, and they all eyed me with deep suspicion after my Judith Keppel sting.

'Which ringer are you bringing this year?' said Paxman dismissively.

'I don't bring ringers, Jeremy, I bring winners. Everyone here has ringers, the only difference is that mine are better.'

Word spread quickly – 'Morgan's got some trick up his sleeve again, watch him.'

But as we were called in to start the quiz, there was still no sign of Shaun and I began to panic.

Then I noticed a small commotion by the entrance as a large, fit black man with spiky hair and a colourful shirt made an ostentatious entrance.

It was Shaun Wallace, and he was what can loosely be described as 'up for it'.

'Hey, captain, what's happening?' he bellowed as he spotted me by the door.

'Shaun, thank God, I was getting worried.'

'No need to worry, captain, this is going to be easy.'

He was even cockier than me.

I could see dozens of pairs of eyes grilling me and Shaun. Nobody seemed to know who he was, but they all knew he was my surprise guest.

'Who is he?' asked Alan Rusbridger from the *Guardian* table.

'Never you mind,' I replied, 'but I wouldn't prepare a victory speech if I were you.'

I took Shaun to our table and introduced him to the rest of the team.

'Chaps, this is Shaun Wallace...' I paused for effect. 'The winner of *Mastermind* 2004.'

Shaun high-fived his new teammates. Then Paxman called for quiet as he explained the rules, and I noticed Shaun suddenly go into some sort of trance.

'You all right mate?' I asked.

'Yes, just focusing.'

He looked like Linford Christie at the start of a race. Terrifying.

The first round involved tapes of famous pieces of sports commentary. We had to say what it was and the year in which it happened.

Within two seconds, Shaun banged his fist on the table and whispered loudly, 'Virginia Wade, Wimbledon, 9 July 1978.'

We glanced at each other in shock. This wasn't just impressive, it was bordering on the disturbing.

He rattled off the other pieces of commentary in even faster time.

'Boat race, Oxford sank. 1925 ... 6 April ... think it was a Saturday, about 4p.m. Really bad weather.'

It was like watching Dustin Hoffman in *Rain Man*. Only scarier.

Simon and I started giggling.

'Shaun, is there anything you don't know?'

'Not a lot, no,' he replied with an understandably arrogant smirk. 'But dates and things are my strong point.'

As the rounds went on, he grew more intense and aggressive. If we got something hard right, he'd insist on high-fiving everyone again, which was very amusing but certainly not the usual refined behaviour this event was used to witnessing at the tables.

Whenever Shaun was wobbly about something, one of the others came to the party. Roger was very strong on music and the arts, Larry on history, Conor on news and current affairs, me on the really difficult high-brow stuff like 'Which musical did John Travolta star in with Olivia Newton-John?'

But then came the round none of us had been expecting – sudoku, that ridiculous Japanese quiz game that everyone's going crazy about.

I looked at Shaun: 'Never done it, sorry.'

'Conor?'

'No, boss.'

'Larry, you must have done?'

'I haven't actually, sorry.'

This was becoming a crisis.

'Roger?'

'Wouldn't know where to start, old bean,' he laughed.

I wouldn't either. All eyes fell on Kelner.

If he couldn't do sudoku we'd had it. Nobody wins this quiz with a zero-scoring round.

'Simon?'

He stared at us, a slow beautiful grin appearing across his bearded chops.

'Gentlemen, leave it to me. I'm a sudoku addict.'

We cheered and passed the puzzle to him. Four minutes later he'd finished it. We were still in the trophy hunt.

As the competition neared its completion, tension began to mount. The *Guardian*, and the Mortimer/Hornby tables were both in the lead, but they'd already played their joker – where you choose a subject before a round starts and get double points – while we hadn't.

If we played ours and did well, we were home and dry.

Alan Rusbridger was jumping up and down to inspect the leader board like a Ryder Cup captain as the singles' results came in.

I caught his eye and winked. He wasn't amused.

'Bloody ringers,' he moaned.

'Better ringers, Alan, just better ringers.'

We played our joker and stormed the round, Shaun high-fiving us after answering virtually every question in two seconds.

There were tuts coming from almost every table now, and they were delicious to hear. They all pretend it's not competitive, but of course it is. Everybody there wants to win.

As the final round scores were inputted, and flashed onto the leader board, we saw our team's name – I had called us Press Gazette – at the top and roared. We'd won.

'Unlucky, Alan,' I said to a smouldering Rusbridger.

'Bloody ringers,' was all he could say, over and over again.

I was invited up to receive the cup, a handsome silver trophy, and took the chance to rub salt into the literary wounds opening up all over the room.

A small smattering of boos filled the air as I raised the cup above my head in triumph.

'I stand here rather as Douglas Jardine stood in Australia at the start of the 1932/3 bodyline series. As the bouncers started, one member of the crowd shouted, "You won't win many friends playing like that, Jardine," to which the great man turned with a bemused look on his face and said haughtily, "My dear fellow, I haven't come here to win friends, I've come to win the Ashes."'

More boos, shaking heads and general revulsion, punctuated by Shaun Wallace shouting, 'YEAH!' at the top of his voice and demanding one last high five.

4 July

Sky One want me to present a documentary about hoodies, those ghastly yobs who wear hooded tops and attack everyone they meet.

'What's the idea?' I asked.

'I think the idea is that you confront loads of hoodies,' said Tracey.

'Right, and what if they don't take too kindly to that?'

'Well I suppose you get beaten up as the cameras roll,' she laughed.

I've always fancied myself as a Roger Cook-style fearless interrogator. It must be great fun, not to mention bloody exciting, knocking on the door of some drug baron and confronting him, and there's something very commendable about it, too. Cook's too old for that game now, so perhaps there's an opening for me to take on his mantle. I could do a lot worse, frankly.

'OK, I'll do it.'

5 July

Matthew Freud and Liz Murdoch had an Independence Day party at their house last night. All the tables were named after American states, but one table – New Jersey – remained completely, and oddly, empty all night.

I ended up deep in conversation with Tony Blair's pollster Philip Gould. We drank a lot, laughed a lot, swapped Gordon and Tony stories, and as midnight approached we both had a sudden thought: 'Let's make New Jersey happen.' We marched to the empty table, sat down with a bottle of wine, and waited to see who would join us. Within half an hour, we had lured Sting, Claudia Schiffer and the Duchess of York into our lair.

New Jersey had most definitely happened.

6 July

Borders bookshops want me to speak at their annual conference for sales executives. It's in Birmingham in September, and is a good opportunity to ingratiate myself with the people who've been selling *The Insider*, and will hopefully continue to do so. I checked the date and realised it coincides with the last day of the last test match against Australia, but the Ashes will be all over by then, one way or another, so I accepted.

I took the boys to tea. Bertie was very excited because he's off on a school trip to the Natural History Museum tomorrow. It's his first proper 'Big Boys' trip.

7 July

Woke at 8a.m., made myself some tea and toast and put Sky News on while I read the papers.

Just after 9a.m., they flashed up some breaking news about a large explosion being heard near King's Cross Station.

First reports suggested it might be a gas leak or something, so I didn't pay much attention. But then more reports began flooding in of further explosions heard near Liverpool Street and other parts of central London.

This didn't seem like a coincidence, or an accident.

I turned the volume up and controlled bedlam would be the best way of describing the next half an hour as news anchors tried to work out what the hell was going on.

Eyewitnesses started phoning in with claims of buses being blown up and tube stations being attacked. London was under siege, and it was obviously terrorist-related.

My phone rang. It was Marion, sounding panicky.

'What's going on?' she asked.

'Not sure, but it looks like some bombs have gone off on a few buses and trains.'

'But Bertie's up there somewhere – on a coach.'

I froze. In all the chaos I'd completely forgotten about his school trip.

'Which way were they going?'

'I don't know, but the museum is right in the middle of town where everything seems to be happening.'

I turned to the TV again and saw a newsflash about a bus bomb in Tavistock Square. Where the hell was that in relation to the Natural History Museum?

'I'll try and find out what's going on. Can you call the school?'

It may be a cliché, but there is literally nothing worse in the world than thinking your child might be in danger.

Nobody was sure what had happened, but the situation appeared to be 'live' and there were fears of more attacks. It seemed that suicide bombers may have struck, though this hadn't been confirmed yet.

Marion called back. 'The school can't get through to anyone.'

Christ, this was a nightmare.

Another twenty minutes passed before she rang again.

'He's safe. All the phone systems are down apparently, but they just got a text from a teacher on the coach saying they turned back quite soon after leaving because the traffic was so bad as a result of what had happened.'

I sat back and sighed with pure unmitigated relief.

One theory emerged later that police may have deliberately closed the mobile networks, fearing the bombers were using phones as possible timing devices.

I spoke to Bertie in the afternoon.

'Dad, why are people bombing us?'

The honest answer is probably because we've been bombing them, but that would be too hard to explain to a four-year-old.

'I don't know, Bertie, but don't worry, the police will catch them.'

Which was totally untrue, because they were suicide bombers and were now all dead.

Everybody on TV is being very careful not to link this to Iraq and Afghanistan, but I don't know why. It must be bloody obvious to any sane human being in Britain that Blair and Bush's foreign policy is now coming back to haunt us.

Tracey emailed me this evening, 'What a nightmare horrible day. It's very scary. I've just been told that the Press Ball is cancelled tonight, for obvious reasons, and I can't believe I'm doing this, but here is your itinerary for next Friday:

2p.m. – Paul Danan

3p.m. – Rebecca Loos

4p.m. – Jade Goody

6p.m. – Abi Titmuss

What a joke.

As all my journalist friends would be piling into the terror story for the next fortnight, I'd be piling into a bunch of twats from reality TV.

I felt a pang of frustration that stayed with me several hours.

12 July

Jeremy's birthday. I sent him a note wishing him as much fun as one can have in Basra in midsummer.

He replied, 'Thanks. I actually managed to celebrate in some style, devouring a Magnum ice cream and a can of Lucozade mid-afternoon in the pleasant surroundings of the soldiers NAAFI, which was filled to the brim with sweaty, confused and slightly deranged-looking Royal Irish Regiment soldiers who had literally just arrived to start their six months in 50-degree heat.'

I asked him if he still had the same conviction about the war on Iraq he'd had when it first started.

His reply surprised me with both its honesty and vehemence:

'I totally concede defeat on this one. What history will remember:

'That in 2003, Iraq had no WMD and posed no military threat to its neighbours or anyone else.

'That the regime in Iraq never had any connection to Al-Qaeda or any other "global" terrorist organisation.

'That invading Iraq was inevitably going to make the world a more dangerous place.

'That invading Iraq was both illegal and immoral.

'That the "War on Terrorism" is a complete farce.

'That the biggest threat to the security in mainland UK is the British Government and its allegiance to that stupid mad mullah George W. Bush.'

He then sent me a story from today's *Taipei Times*, which quoted Max Hastings as saying, 'We must acknowledge that, by supporting President Bush's extravagances in his ill-named War on Terror and ill-justified invasion of Iraq, Blair has ensured that we are in the front line beside the US whether we like it or not.'

It really bothers me that my brother, a proud, loyal and hard-working officer for nearly twenty years, is now so utterly disillusioned by what he's found on the ground in Iraq. If he's feeling that way, then most of them will be. I hope Blair gets the occasional pang of guilt about what he's done, not just to the poor civilian population of Iraq, but to the shattered morale and pride of our armed forces.

Jeremy ended his email by noting, 'Baghdad alone loses over fifty people in terrorist action *every* day – twenty-four children killed in one suicide car bomb yesterday while collecting sweets from an American patrol (also killed). It's a mad world.'

15 July

If ever a day put my new life into sharp focus, it's today.

While Jeremy continues to risk his life in Iraq, I spent the afternoon interviewing Z-listers Rebecca Loos and Paul Danan for my Channel 4 documentary, *The Death of Celebrity*, based on my premise that we're becoming a nation of talentless wannabes at the expense of real stars.

Both of them have starred in the recent series of *Celebrity Love Island* and now consider themselves to be enormous international stars.

The sheer scale of self-delusion is awe-inspiring.

'I want to star in a movie with De Niro,' said Danan with a straight face.

'*Robert* De Niro?' I replied, hoping he meant some other C-grade celebrity imbecile I'd never heard of.

'Yeah, Bobby De Niro. That would be cool. Danan and De Niro, sounds good, dunnit?'

The most amusing moment came when I asked him what his fellow *Love Island* 'stars' did for a living, and when he got to Lady Isabella Hervey even he gave up trying to explain her status.

'She's a ... she's a ... she's a LADY!' he said, collapsing in a heap of laughter on the floor.

Rebecca is my second cousin by marriage, a fact that neither of us boasts about. She's undeniably pretty, but beneath the fixed smile lies a ruthless commercial animal. Poor old Beckham never stood a chance once he'd hired her.

What I really wanted to ask her was, 'What's the difference between you and a prostitute?' but I bottled it, and instead had to sit through an hour of self-justifying nonsense about why she's the most misunderstood kiss-and-tell bimbo in Britain.

Eventually I cut to the quick: 'Rebecca, do you consider yourself to be a celebrity?'

She paused, taking in the full enormity of the question, and replied, 'Yes, I think I am.'

It's official then. Sleep with a footballer and you're a celebrity. It's pathetic. But then all I'm doing by making a TV show about this ludicrous state of affairs is giving these imbeciles even more exposure and publicity.

I am helping them be just a little bit more famous. And that's all they care about. I mean, why worry about getting a proper trade when you can be a reality TV 'star', making a small fortune out of behaving like a fool for the public's delectation.

18 July

From the ridiculous to the sublime. I was due to interview the great Sir Michael Gambon at the National Theatre today, to see what he had to say about celebrity.

I arrived early and was asked to sign myself in. I looked at the sheet and saw Michael Gambon's name. And next to it? He'd signed himself in as Piers Morgan.

I found him, one of the world's leading actors, in his tiny hovel of a dressing room.

'This is my luxury home,' he joked.

'Are you a celebrity?' I asked.

'Good God no. Please don't call me that. I'm an actor. People may know who I am, but I am most definitely not a celebrity.'

I name-checked a few Z-listers, much to his amusement.

'Jade who? Abi what? Jordan – yes, I think I may have heard of her.'

'Basically…' I explained, 'she goes out once a week and exposes her breasts to the paparazzi, and from this she lives in a mansion, drives a Bentley and is a multi-millionairess.'

He gasped. 'My God!'

Then we showed him some tapes of wannabes trying to act.

'These people aren't actors,' he said witheringly. 'They can't act. I mean, just look at them. It's ridiculous.'

Once he'd warmed up, he was hilarious, and absurdly modest at the same time.

'All I've ever wanted to do is act,' he said. 'I remember sitting in this very dressing room after I had my first hit here, and people outside applauding when they saw me at the window. And that was so exciting, that was what I wanted: recognition of my work. But all these modern celebrities want is a quick buck, with no talent or hard work required. It's awful.'

What would you call this type of person?' I asked him.

'I would call them a cretin.'

20 July

My Z-list celebrity interview tour continued today with Ms Abi Titmuss, the former lover of John Leslie, who has made a million since his court case by flashing her breasts in magazines and generally flaunting herself around, trading off her notoriety.

The depressing thing, in her case, is that she's no fool. Titmuss used to be a nurse and is well educated, but the lure of easy money knows no bounds for the modern female celebrity wannabe.

She'd agreed to be interviewed because she has a new book out. I flicked through it this morning and it's basically low-grade literary porn.

'You didn't write this, did you, Abi?' I asked.

'Yes, I did.'

'No, you didn't. There's someone else's name on it, too. She wrote it, didn't she?'

'No, I did most of it.'

'Most of it? Come on, Abi...'

She blushed. 'Well, I wrote the introduction.'

'What's the point of Abi Titmuss?' I asked.

'What's the point of Piers Morgan?' she retorted. Which is, admittedly, equally unanswerable.

When we'd finished the interview, she handed me a signed copy of her book. She'd written, 'To Piers, lose some weight and I'll think about it. Love Abi.'

She should be so lucky.

22 July

The day I'd been waiting for all year. Lords, for the second day of the first Ashes test match against Australia. I come every year on this day with my village cricket mates and we always have a wonderful time, regardless of what happens on the pitch. In fact some of our best days have been when it's rained all afternoon, forcing us to take refuge in a local restaurant.

Today was sunny, the cricket was great, the beer and wine flowed copiously and the anecdotes poured out.

At 5p.m. my mobile rang; it was a reporter from the *Mid Sussex Times* asking for my reaction to the news that Newick Parish Council were threatening legal action against the cricket club for charging entry to the Lashings match, and even suggesting they might remove permission for us to play cricket altogether if there were any further 'transgressions'.

I should have said 'no comment', but I heard rumours of this earlier in the week and have been simmering with rage ever since. The day had been a huge success, most of the village had turned out and loved every minute, and both the club and Lashings had made good money out of it.

'Right,' I said. 'Have you got a pen?'

For the next five minutes I unloaded on the parish council:

'This is one of the most pathetic, spineless and puerile things I have ever seen, even by parish council standards.

'Here we had a team of world-class cricket players, and 1,200 people turned out on one of the most enjoyable days the village has seen for years.

'Every young cricket fan for miles around was able to see some of the world's greatest players on a village playing field.

'I would imagine most parish councils would think that was a very good thing for a cricket club to do and 99.9 per cent of people who came were willing to pay.'

The reporter couldn't believe her luck.

I ploughed on: 'By the scale of council horror stories I heard when I was editing newspapers, I don't think I have come across one as ridiculous as this.

'Burning them at the stake on bonfire night would be too good for them – I don't think we will do that but I'd like to try.'

The reporter gave a slight gasp, I suspect of suppressed glee.

'I think a lot of cricket club members feel that if we don't acquiesce we will be prohibited from playing there, but I have never acquiesced to this sort of behaviour in my life.

'I waged a campaign against the British Government over the Iraq war, so I'm sure I can deal with the parish council.

'The council's contribution to the village is to install a hut in the middle of the playing field, where the local layabouts and louts go to take drugs and generally misbehave.

'If they spent as much energy on stopping that as harassing the village cricket club they might do some good.

'I suggest these are the wrong people to be running the village. They are terrorising the village and if they had any decency they would resign. I suggest we have an emergency meeting to remove them. I might even stand as chairman myself.'

The reporter gasped again.

'Is that all, Mr Morgan?'

'That's probably enough for now, yes.'

I hung up and went back to my wine bottle. Within half an hour, I'd forgotten I'd even had the conversation.

Then word suddenly spread around the stand we were sitting in that a suicide bomber had been shot dead by armed police at Stockwell tube station.

The general reaction seemed to be unconfined joy that we'd 'got one of the bastards', but all I could think was that while I was watching cricket, my former *Mirror* colleagues would be racing around the newsroom trying to cover this extraordinary breaking news story.

25 July

The supposed 'suicide bomber' shot by police at Stockwell was an innocent young Brazilian called Jean Charles de Menezes.

I have great sympathy for the police – there can't be anything more diffi- cult to deal with than suicide bombing – but this mistake is a disaster, and the efforts to cover it up when the truth emerged after a few hours are utterly scandalous.

I wish I was back editing today. I'd be having a field day with this story, and the whole War on Terror nonsense. Blair is already saying that the 7/7 bombings had nothing to do with Iraq, but that's such bullshit.

Of course it's got to do with Iraq. If you kill tens of thousands of inno- cent Muslims over there, then Muslims over here are going to want revenge. It's not a difficult concept to grasp.

In his heart Blair must know now that the unrelenting fiasco of the Iraq War is an appalling historical legacy, and it will only get worse.

27 July

The *Mid Sussex Times* was published today, carrying my comments about the parish council under the headline: CRICKET FAN PIERS LASHES OUT AT COUNCIL'S 'LITTLE HITLERS'. I only knew this because I started getting texts from all over Sussex from people either congratulating me or asking if I was on some form of medication.

I read my comments in the cold light of sobriety and realised they were grossly offensive, tactless and totally demeaning.

Excellent.

29 July

I've been invited to write a travel feature on Sardinia for the *Daily Mail*, so thought I'd use the chance to spend some time with the boys, and took Rupert along for company. He's the perfect uncle to the boys because he's almost as big a kid as they are when it comes to stuff like sport, games and Playstations.

We are staying at a beautiful five-star resort, and tonight we left the boys with their nanny Caroline and headed to the bars for a few drinks.

As we sat chatting to a few English people at a table, I noticed a young man taking photos of me with his camera.

'What are you doing, mate?'

'Taking your picture,' he sneered. 'Why, don't you like it being done to you?'

His table fell about laughing.

'That's so clever,' I said. 'Nobody's ever thought of doing that to me before.'

He took some more pictures, revelling in his big moment.

'Think I'll sell these to the *Sun*,' he squeaked in a very Hooray accent. He was the kind of twenty-two-year-old burly-but-dim rugby player you get in Fulham wine bars at the weekend.

'Why don't you grow up, you little twat?' I responded.

'You're the twat,' he retorted.

It was like being back in the school playground.

Rupert was enraged. 'Do you get this happening very often, bruv?'

'Unfortunately, yes. And they always look and sound like him.'

Another flashblub went off.

I got up, walked over and asked him to put his camera down.

'Oooohhh, doesn't like it when it happens to him, does he?' taunted my friend.

'If you don't, then I'll make you,' I said, my patience now running on empty. This was absurd, but I returned to my seat and tried to ignore him.

More flashbulbs, more hysterical giggles.

One of his mates got up and brushed rudely past Rupert, which wasn't his brightest move, given that Rupert is 6 foot 4, very strong and runs night-clubs where dealing with drunken louts is part of the job description.

Rupert grabbed him by the arm and walked him at high speed into a nearby hedge.

At that point security guards arrived and broke up the fracas.

'What is going on?' they demanded.

'Those idiots keep taking pictures of my brother,' said Rupert indignantly.

To which the main idiot shouted, 'Yeah, that's because he's an idiot!'

I felt the red mist descending, marched over to him and stuck my hand over his face, pushing him back into his chair.

'Get off me,' he squealed.

'Bruv, leave it,' said Rupert.

I withdrew my hand, apologised to the security men and walked off. It had been a ridiculous incident and I should have risen above it, but the general uncertainty in my life has left me feeling tense and edgy.

Getting abused by drunken morons is not the way I want to lead the rest of my life, but what can I do about it? It's another example of the curse of celebrity. And there's no point whining about it. If you can't stand the heat, get out of the kitchen.

16 August

Started filming on my Sky One documentary, *Piers Meets the Hoodies*. The concept is that I go to some of the nastiest streets in Britain and confront that particularly unpleasant brand of thug sporting a hooded top.

It had all seemed a good idea when I was first approached a few weeks ago – I was excited by the chance to do a proper TV investigation, not just another celebrity interview. Who knows? Perhaps this will turn out to be my true TV vocation? – but right now, I'm not so sure. Today's trip was to Margate, in Kent, where the only hoodies we could find were young harmless kids on the beach who wouldn't chuck a stone in the sea, let alone terrorise a town. *Piers Meets the Hooded Choirboys* isn't really what Sky are after.

I knew things were going awry when the producer asked me to cycle down the seafront wearing a red hoodie over my suit as an opening link to the show.

I did as I was told, with the camera crew driving along in a van in front of me, recording it all for posterity.

We began attracting considerable attention – of the ridicule kind.

'Hey, it's that tosser who got sacked from the *Mirror*!' shouted one middle-aged fisherman, waving his rods at me gleefully. His mates started jeering as I pedalled on, revelling in my total ignominy.

I reached the end of the seafront and revealed my shame to the team.

'Oh dear, because I'm afraid we're going to have to do it again,' said the producer.

I desperately try and avoid being a prima donna on TV shoots because the industry gossip machine works fast and you quickly get a name for being up your own backside, but some things test even my patience, and this was one.

I peered back to see the fishermen still pointing and chortling.

'You're not serious?'

She nodded.

I got back on the bike and returned to my starting place, crossing the road to avoid the fishermen.

Then I set off again, red hoodie flashing through the sea air, feeling about as stupid as it's possible to feel.

'Here 'e comes again!' cried the fisherman, even more gleefully than before.

They whistled and jeered as I rode past. Mortifying. What the hell am I doing here?

17 August

The hoodie roadshow moved to Manchester, or to the backstreets of various Salford no-go areas to be more precise.

It reminded me of when I first became a journalist on the *Streatham and Tooting News* and covered the Brixton Riots wearing a completely inappropriate pin-stripe suit.

Now here I was again, suited and booted, marching around some of the roughest, toughest estates in Britain, looking for the roughest, toughest inhabitants, with only a female producer and two male camera crew for protection. The potential for something to go awry seemed rather high.

We interviewed a middle-aged woman whose life has been made a misery since she'd reported a local yob to the police and he was handed an ASBO.

Every day since she's been subjected to abuse, bricks being thrown at her house, graffiti and threats of violence. She's had a heart attack but still refuses to leave her home.

As we walked outside, a small crowd of hoodies gathered to shout insults, then zipped around on their bikes, disappearing through the maze of streets and alleyways that make up these sprawling estates.

They were always around, and though our interviewee wasn't scared, I was. I suddenly felt horribly vulnerable.

'Why don't you fuck off, yer tosser,' said one skinheaded kid on a motorbike. It was the ASBO boy, who wasn't supposed to come within 500 yards of our woman. 'Before we do yer.'

A few of his friends made throat-cutting signs.

Then a large, heavily tattooed woman, smoking and clutching a bottle of beer, charged out of one of the houses and began screaming abuse at me, the crew and our interviewee.

She walked over and clouted the ASBO boy in the head. Hard. It was her son, and she was angry about something he'd done. She was a violent, horrible creature, and in that moment I felt genuinely sorry for the boy. What hope did he possibly have in life with a mother like that?

Soon after, we beat a hasty retreat to the sanctity of our posh hotel in the smart part of town. It had been an unnerving snapshot of hoodie-land.

There's a whole underworld that exists in this country, where young people with no hope prowl council estates terrorising people because there's nothing better to do. There are no youth clubs, just miles of nothingness. It was a sobering and dispiriting afternoon.

23 August

Simon Cowell rang.

'Hi, Piers, I'm filming a pilot for a new ITV talent show and wondered if you'd like to come along and be one of the judges?'

I laughed. 'What, the new Simon Cowell, you mean?'

He laughed, too. 'Yes, something like that.'

'When is it?'

'September second.'

I checked the diary. 'I can't, I'm on holiday with the kids in Cornwall.'

'Can't you come back for the day? I think you'd enjoy it.'

I quickly considered my options. It was only a pilot, so might never make it on air, but it was Simon Cowell's show, and everything he touches turns to gold at the moment. It could potentially be my big break.

'OK, you're on. I'll fly back for it.'

'Great, see you there.'

26 August

Kevin Pietersen sorted me and Martin out a couple of tickets to the fourth test match at Trent Bridge today, so we drove up last night, booking ourselves into a tiny twin room at the Holiday Inn in Nottingham.

When we got to the ground this morning we discovered that our tickets were right in the middle of the players' wives and families enclosure, and we exchanged jovial banter throughout the day with Michael Vaughan's dad and Freddie Flintoff's wife.

By the time England came out after tea to bowl again, I was fairly merry, to put it mildly.

'Oh, not that bloody pie-thrower,' I observed loudly as Matthew Hoggard came on to bowl.

'Ssh,' came a tetchy voice from behind that I ignored.

I carried on mumbling and moaning for half an hour, convinced that Hoggard was going to single-handedly lose us the test match and therefore any chance of winning the Ashes.

'Get. Him. OFF,' I shrieked, to further widespread shhing.

Then he took three wickets in quick succession, bowling beautifully.
The crowd went wild, chanting, 'HOGGIE, HOGGIE, HOGGIE!'
I went puce with embarrassment.
Rachel Flintoff lent over. 'Piers, I think you owe that lady an apology.'
'What lady?'
'*That* lady.'
Rachel was pointing to the seat directly behind me.
I turned very slowly to find an attractive young blonde sitting with a grimly set expression on her face.
A sudden appalling thought flashed through my beer-addled mind.
'You're not … I mean, you can't be…'
'Mrs Hoggard,' she said, savouring the moment. 'Yes, I am. And I've been listening to your crap for the last hour.'
'Ah yes, well the thing is, let me explain…'
Mrs Hoggard raised her arm to silence me.
'There's no need to say a word, is there? My husband's made you look a right tit.'

1 September

I filmed the pilot for Simon Cowell's new talent show today and it was great fun. He stepped in as a judge as well at the last minute, and Fern Britton made up the panel, so I was with two people I knew well and got on with.

Paul O'Grady was the host, and did a superb job of keeping everything flowing. He's a natural presenter: smart, funny and incredibly professional.

Cowell and I took the piss out of each other throughout the recording, which the audience loved.

The concept of the show is simple. Anyone can come on stage and do any talent they like. They get two minutes to impress the judges, but we each have a buzzer and can buzz them whenever we want. Three buzzes and they have to stop. Then we give our verdicts and the winner is decided by a public phone vote.

My favourite act was a huge slob of a man called Big John, who said his talent was putting big things on his head.

I took one look at him coming onto the stage with a cement mixer on his head and hit the buzzer.

'John, no disrespect, mate, but you don't need a talent show, you need urgent psychiatric help,' I said afterwards. He was not amused, but Cowell was.

'You're a natural,' he said. 'Only Pete Waterman has got it so quickly before.'

'Do you think ITV will go for it, then?'

'Definitely. All their top people were down here watching and they all loved it.'

I suddenly feel rather excited by the whole thing. *Morgan and Platell*'s about to come back for a third series, and the ratings have held pretty steady, but it bores me to tears most of the time.

Today was the biggest buzz I've felt doing anything since I left the *Mirror*.

12 September

Death of Celebrity went out on Channel 4 last night and got a very respectable 1.8 million viewers. It also attracted some pretty favourable reviews, and they want to make a few more programmes on the back of it. I much prefer that idea to doing years more on *Morgan and Platell*.

It was the last day of the last Ashes test in the most thrilling series anyone can remember – it couldn't have been a more unpredictable, exciting plot if John Grisham had written the script.

I'd been there the previous two days and was offered two tickets to a hospitality box today by Freddie Flintoff's benefit manager Paul Beck, a very entertaining northern tycoon.

I rang Rupert: 'Fancy coming to the test today?'

'Oh my GOD. I'd love to, bruv, but I've got to work.'

'Rupert, we're about to win the Ashes.'

Pause.

'You're right, I'll come.'

I texted Pietersen en route to the Oval.

'This is your moment, mate. Good luck.'

'Thanks, China,' he replied.

The atmosphere inside was unbelievable. England started well, but then a rush of wickets, including Freddie for just 8, left us lurching on 122–4 at lunch. But Pietersen was 34 not out, and had survived three chances and some ferocious bowling from Brett Lee.

My phone rang and it was Sky News asking if I could do a quick live interview as they'd seen me in the box on their cameras.

'Sure,' I said, and went to meet them outside the main gate.

'So what's your prediction, Mr Morgan?' the reporter asked.

'I reckon Kevin Pietersen will score a hundred and we will win the Ashes,' I found myself replying.

Midway through the afternoon session, Pietersen went to his hundred with a fantastic cover drive. He'd come out after lunch like a man possessed, smashing Brett Lee out of the attack, swatting Warne for huge sixes, and slowly but surely wrestling the Ashes away from the Aussies.

The crowd, which had been eerily silent for most of the morning, began to celebrate, and by tea there was a deafening crescendo of noise around the ground.

Pietersen kept on smashing it until he was out for 158. It had been one of the greatest innings of all time, and in the context of this game, perhaps *the* greatest. There was a touching moment when Warne jogged over to put his arm round him and congratulate him, then KP looked up at our box with a massive grin on his face and we all roared our approval.

The England dressing room was right below us, and for the last hour Freddie kept up regular visual contact with the box. When England were finally declared Ashes winners, pandemonium erupted around the ground. It was like the Golden Jubilee, with a sea of Union Jacks and the sound of 'Rule Britannia' booming everywhere.

Freddie looked up to the box: 'It's gonna be a big one tonight, boys!' he shouted, and pretended to sink a very large pint.

'You coming partying?' Paul Beck asked me.

'Yes, mate,' I cried jubilantly as champagne sprayed everywhere.

And then, in the middle of my wildly celebratory conga, I suddenly remembered: the Borders store conference was in Birmingham tonight.

'Oh, no. I can't,' I said mournfully.

'Why not?'

'I've got to go to a book conference in Birmingham.'

Paul burst out laughing. 'That's a joke, right? Hilarious.'

'No, unfortunately not. It's true.'

'Can't you cancel it, mate, it's not every year we win the flaming Ashes?'

'I can't, I said I'd do it.'

Rupert interrupted my grieving process.

'I can come partying…'

'Great,' said Paul. 'Should be one of the best nights ever.'

'Unlucky, bruv,' said Rupert with a huge grin. 'I'll drink yours.'

I left to get my taxi to Birmingham, feeling deflated and miserable.

How could I possibly be doing this? How could I be turning down the chance to celebrate winning the Ashes with the team? With Freddie and the boys? None of it made sense, except that when I say I'm going to do something, I do it.

I got to the conference in time for dinner, after a tortuous two-and-a-half-hour journey, and told the organisers about the sacrifice I'd made.

'Oh you should have just called,' they said. 'We wouldn't have minded at all.'

His words tore into my heart.

'You wouldn't have minded?' I said slowly.

'Not at all, I mean, it's the Ashes, isn't it?'

I picked at my meal, wanting to die a slow, horrible death.

A text from Rupert arrived: 'Bruv, it's amazing here. On the lash with Freddie and the boys. You'd have loved it.'

Another nail.

I made my brief, five-minute speech – I was one of six authors they'd lined up for the evening – and nobody seemed too bothered about me being there at all, let alone speaking to them.

I sat down to muted applause, made my excuses soon afterwards and retired to my poky Jurys Inn room.

One word sprang to mind: Why?

13 September

I woke at 7a.m. to find a series of voicemails from Rupert. The last one said: 'Bruv, I'm completely smashed. Been with Freddie all night, and a load of the other boys. Best party ever! They can't believe you went to Birmingham instead?'

Nor can I, trust me. My taxi took me back to London, where I bought a copy of the *Standard*. There, splattered all over the front page, was a photo of Freddie Flintoff, drunk as a skunk in the bar of the England team hotel.

And there, right next to him, was the unmistakable blue shirt of my brother Rupert. His head had been cut off, but it was him all right, and IT SHOULD HAVE BEEN ME.

The hoodie documentary is coming together, but still lacks any real action on film. The stuff with the ASBO boy almost certainly can't be used because he's only fifteen, so tonight we headed for what the producer described as a 'target-rich hoodie environment': an estate in Tower Hamlets, East London, that was recently named the most dangerous estate in the city. A multi-cultural community rife with gangs, drugs and violence.

We had bodyguards today, in case things got out of hand.

I was wired up with a microphone and sent down into the bowels of one particularly notorious estate. It was quiet and eerie. I felt uneasy. The bodyguards were there, several hundred yards away, but walking around here in a suit suddenly didn't seem very clever.

For an hour, we didn't see anything, then a small group of hoodies emerged on a street corner and engaged me in conversation. They were young, no more than fifteen or sixteen, all Asian, and although quite animated they seemed friendly enough. One of them recognised me and we had a chat about why I'd been sacked.

As I started to walk away, one of them pointed at me and started swearing.

I walked a little faster, my heart starting to race, and hooded kids began appearing all over the place, some a lot older than the ones I'd just met.

By the time I reached the end of the street, there must have been thirty of them surrounding me – some on bikes, most on foot. The atmosphere had become extremely nasty very quickly.

'You think you're fucking clever, do yer?' snarled one pinch-faced individual.

I tried to engage him in dialogue: 'Not massively, no. I'm just trying to find out what life's like for you guys in places like this.'

'You don't care about us, you fucking wanker. You just want to come down here and make us look stupid.'

He was thick-set and stood just a few feet away from me, looking angry and potentially violent. The noise level had ratcheted up a few notches, and yet more youths began pouring out of various alleys to see what was 'going down'.

The answer, I was beginning to fear, was probably me.

A few of the bolder ones started circling me on their bikes, brushing me as they did so. It was potentially great telly, but I felt nervous and scared. There was a time, when I was editor of the *News of the World*, that I would have died for Rupert Murdoch, but dying for his station Sky One didn't have quite the same ring to it.

Cars began roaring down the road behind me, screeching to a halt a few yards away. Some of the occupants brandished baseball bats. This was all getting out of hand and I didn't like it.

Weird things go through your mind at moments like this, like having to explain to your children that the reason you're eating food out of a tube in hospital is because you went down to the roughest estate in London to find violent thugs and got beaten senseless.

A large guy in a white hoodie suddenly appeared on the scene, and the others filtered away when they saw him. He didn't say a word, he just stared at me. He was obviously some local big shot. Then he exchanged quick words in a language I didn't understand with the kid who'd asked me if I thought I was clever.

At that point my bodyguards shouted down the earpiece, 'Piers, get out of there. NOW.' I could see one of them running up the road towards me, and decided not to probe further into why they wanted me to exit stage right.

I just legged it as fast as I could down the road to the meeting place. The youths shouted and swore, but none of them ran after me.

I stood, catching my breath, as the bodyguards explained what had happened.

'They were Bengali,' said one of them, 'and I speak Bengali. The reason we pulled you out is because the big guy in the white hoodie told the other one to stick a knife in you.'

I felt a pinch of terror around my spinal chord.

'I see. Just as well I'm a coward then.'

The evening had worked from a televisual viewpoint and the footage would be great for topping and tailing the documentary. Live shots of me nearly getting stabbed by a gang of hoodies – perfect.

But as I drove home later that evening, I realised it had also served a secondary purpose: never again would I do something as bloody stupid as this.

Interviewing Posh Spice or going on *Question Time* is fine. Trying to get myself killed is not. I think I can safely rule out 'Investigative TV Reporter' from my list of potential careers.

5

16 September

An email from Jeremy: 'Life out here has changed a little. Temperature has gone down to mid-forties, insurgent activity has gone up significantly as we run up to the elections in mid-Oct. I should add that I am safely confined to our operational HQ in this miserable base with little chance of having to face any danger myself – I just send others out to face the prospect of a violent and pointless death. A chap I worked with in Cyprus was killed by a road-side bomb on Sunday, which was a bit of a shock. Thankfully only forty-nine days left. I heard Rupert had a good night with Flintoff & Co. I can't believe you managed to see all last three days of the last test of the greatest series ever – what an experience!'

I spoke to him later on the phone and he said that his regiment are now routinely patrolling Basra, and it's been pretty hairy some nights.

But we don't hear any of this stuff, the British public is just constantly told that Basra's safe and quiet and all the action is in Baghdad.

20 September

All the papers have been full of an SAS raid in Iraq, and today I discovered that Jeremy's men were right in the thick of it.

He emailed:

'Rather a lot of fun and games over the last few days. It started when the SAS arrested the bastard who has been masterminding the recent bombing campaign against British forces in Basra in the early hours on Saturday and brought him and a couple of his cronies into our camp for tactical questioning.

'Meanwhile his militia supporters started to get rather frisky and claimed revenge. Coincidentally, two British soldiers were lifted yesterday afternoon after a gunfight with Iraqi police (infiltrated with militia and often not on our side). The 'Police' refused to hand them over, and when we tried to get them back, riots kicked off across the city. So 1 RRW was ordered to send in our

C Company with their Warriors to get them back. C Company went in with over forty SAS troopers in the back of the Warriors, knocked down the perimeter, entered the compound, completely trashed it with the Warriors whilst delivering the SAS to the side of the building, where they blew holes in the wall to gain entry. After a quick search and a lot of gunfire, they brought out six soldiers who had gone in to negotiate the release of the two captives (headed by a chap I know well), but the captives had been moved and were missing.

'By good fortune, a surveillance that had been circling overhead reported that they had seen two people being hustled away to another building in another part of the city, so our boys loaded up the SAS in the Warriors and drove them there, where the SAS launched another assault and extracted their two blokes in one piece.

'It was an amazing night and kept us all rather enthralled. By the way, it was the Staffords Battlegroup that had their Warriors and soldiers on fire, not us, so no casualties and a job well done. Needless to say, this has broken the mindless monotony of our lives out here, leaving us all feeling rather buoyant and happy with life, but the legacy we leave here will probably be civil war, and the majority of the Iraqi civilians don't deserve that as a price for their "liberation".

'Whoever thought it was a good idea to come out here?'

25 September

The *Morgan and Platell* production team wanted Amanda and I to go to the *New Statesman* party at the Labour Party Conference in Brighton to show off a bit and try and sign up some guests. We're getting all the Tories and most of the Lib Dems, but the Labour big beasts won't go near us, mainly because they hate me almost as much as they hate Amanda from her days as Hague's spin doctor.

I trudged down to Brighton with a heavy heart. I vowed last year never to attend the party conferences again. They're such a waste of time, just loads of MPs, political hacks, lobbyists and very annoying researchers running around getting drunk and bitching about each other.

It was with these grim memories in mind that I entered the *Statesman* party, to be confronted by the usual air-conditioning failure, warm wine and heaving mass of sweaty, ranting torsos. Not an edifying spectacle.

I talked to a couple of 'delegates', who decided this was as good a time as any to give me their views on my career, and personality for that matter, something guaranteed to irritate me even more than I already was.

Then I spotted David O'Keefe, *Morgan and Platell*'s series editor and a lovely man, engaged in conversation with Charles Clarke, Home Secretary and one of the planet's most pompous people.

It was obvious from their respective demeanours that David was pleading with Clarke to come on the show and getting nowhere.

I was bored, so I decided to join in the debate.

'Ah, Home Secretary, how are you?'

'Ah, Morgan,' he replied, 'I was just telling your producer why I won't be doing your shitty little TV show.'

He appeared to have been drinking, as is normal with Mr Clarke, and his face was putrid and angry.

I considered how to respond for a moment or two. I'd been given strict instructions to behave myself, but Clarke was being deliberately provocative and I wasn't just going to stand there and take it.

'Tell you what, mate, why don't you just stick it up your big fat arse?'

David O'Keefe looked like he was going to have a seizure and began apologising on my behalf, giving it the full 'Oh, Piers is only joking, Home Secretary' act.

Clarke looked at me, a bit stunned.

I turned round and walked away, passing Jonathan Isaby, the ebullient deputy editor of the *Telegraph*'s Spy diary column.

'What happened there?' he asked.

'Oh, I just told the Home Secretary to stick it up his big fat arse.'

'Oh right, blimey,' replied Jonathan. 'Can I write that?'

'Sure, why not.'

I don't care any more. I'm bored with these ridiculous politicians and their equally ridiculous hangers-on. Almost all of them are conspiratorial, intellectually lightweight, humourless back-stabbers who would sell their children to get a job in the Cabinet.

I left my producer trying to appease Clarke, who was playing the wounded and distressed card for all he could, and jumped in a taxi to travel the eight miles back to Newick.

That is definitely the last time I'm ever going to a party conference.

26 September

The hoodies documentary was screened last night and attracted 160,000 viewers. About average for Sky One at 10p.m., apparently, but certainly not a big enough audience to justify nearly killing myself.

27 September

There are some invitations that land on your desk that you should automatically reject: lunch with John Redwood, Coldplay album launches and pretty much anything with the words 'carriages at 10.30p.m.' But there are others that sit there, luring you like an evil temptress.

Today, I had one of those from Anne Robinson – to appear on *Celebrity Weakest Link*.

I've always refused to do any reality shows with the word 'celebrity' in the title, or any quiz shows, because the potential for humiliation is too large. *Test the Nation* doesn't count, because your individual total doesn't get revealed (thank goodness).

So in the last year alone I've rejected offers to appear on *Celebrity Big Brother, Celebrity Love Island, I'm a Celebrity Get Me Out of Here! Celebrity Hard Spell, Celebrity University Challenge* and *Celebrity Who Wants to Be a Millionaire*.

But I like Annie, and it's not like it's *Mastermind* or *University Challenge*, is it? Or even *Have I Got News For You*, where my performance was later described by Angus Deayton as the third worst ever after Paula Yates and the tub of lard they used to replace Roy Hattersley when he pulled out at the last minute.

On the rare occasions I've watched it, *Weakest Link* questions don't seem that hard, and the other contestants tend to be quite dim. Plus the publicity might help flog a few more books for Christmas, so I've said yes.

But it raises the question again of whether I am a celebrity and, more to the point, whether I really want to be.

There is a massive difference between being a star with genuine talent – a great singer, actor or sportsman – and someone who the public know but consider vaguely ridiculous, like Jordan, Christopher Biggins or just about any soap star.

What kind of celebrity am I?

What *is* my talent if I no longer edit newspapers?

And if I don't have a great talent, then am I not in danger of becoming the very thing I despise most: a talentless Z-list wannabe celebrity, whoring myself around the TV airwaves just for the sake of being famous.

It's both a concern and a dilemma, and I don't know what the answer is.

28 September

The annual Press Ball, rearranged from 7/7, was enlivened by the auction, where one of the lots was a coach trip for twenty people to be personally escorted round Althorp, Diana's ancestral home, by Charles Spencer.

Kelvin looked at me and winked. Ten minutes of fierce bidding, and £5,000, later, Kelvin MacKenzie – scourge of the Spencers for most of his career – was the proud captain of a bus heading for Althorp.

2 October

A letter arrived via my publishers this morning from a young lady called Lucy, who wrote, 'I've been meaning to write to you for some time, since you mentioned your array of stalkers in a column for the *Evening Standard*. I was incredibly touched by the affectionate language that infused your description of these women. Indeed, you seemed fonder of them than any one of the men I've been out with over the last couple of years has been of me. So it struck me that I should abandon dating and offer myself as yet another of your stalkers. I appreciate the length of time it's taken me to write this letter might undermine my credibility in this respect, but I would urge you to overlook this slight aberration. I promise I am harmless, and I couldn't envisage ever stalking physically. Would the occasional postcard count? Or is it expected that I should send items of underwear? I have included a recent photograph of myself. Should you be happy to add me to your stable of stalkers, please let me know how to contact you in future.'

The photo was of a rather attractive young girl in naval uniform.

I toyed with replying – I am effectively a single man after all and she sounds quite amusing – but I resisted the temptation. I once received a letter when I worked on the *Sun* from a very pretty girl who enclosed topless glamour photos of herself and was asking for 'a drink, dinner, or whatever' in an effort to tap my 'brilliant journalistic brain'. I was engaged to Marion at the time, so sent back a po-faced reply saying the girl would get nowhere in journalism if she behaved in this kind of unseemly manner.

Which was just as well, because it was Marion and one of her mates who had written it...

4 October

Paul Routledge, the *Mirror* political commentator, has sent me a copy of a Yorkshire newspaper called the *Craven Herald & Pioneer*, which contains a large photograph inside of a fully grown sheep sitting in someone's house, watching a TV screen with me on it, presenting *The Wright Stuff* on Channel 5.

The caption reads: 'EWE'VE BEEN FRAMED. Interesting chap that Piers Morgan, or so this sheep seems to think. Photographer Stephen Garnett had to be quick off the mark when he saw this sheep watching television at a farm near Cononley. It seemed quite happy, but eventually wearied of the programme (we know the feeling), jumped down and wandered off again.'

6 October

George Osborne was the star guest on *Morgan and Platell* this week, which was good timing given the current furore over David Cameron's refusal to answer the 'have you taken drugs?' question.

Osborne, like Cameron, is a wealthy public schoolboy, so the answer is almost certainly in the affirmative, hence their joint disinclination to discuss it.

We had a lively production meeting in the morning about how to attack him over this point, and eventually I had a brainwave, but one that contained considerable personal risk.

'Erm, purely hypothetically of course, but if a Channel 4 presenter was to admit taking recreational drugs, would he or she get sacked?'

Everyone stared at me like I'd gone slightly mad.

'I would think you'd probably get promoted at Channel 4!' quipped one executive. 'Why do you ask?'

'Well, Osborne is a clever guy who, if we ask him the question, might well turn round and ask *us* if we've ever taken drugs. And it might be rather amusing if we answered him.'

Amanda spluttered into her coffee.

'Well I haven't taken drugs, that's for sure,' she said.

'No, I'm sure. But I have...'

Silence.

'But I'm not going to admit it if it means I get the sack.'

The executives said they'd 'have a word upstairs, purely on a hypothetical basis'.

Half an hour later, word came back that Channel 4 would be 'very relaxed' if that sort of admission was made, so long as it was an historic and not current situation.

'It's historic,' I said. 'Right, this is the plan. We ask him if he's ever taken drugs, and if he dodges it, we push him on whether public figures should admit to it in principle. Then he'll probably ask me if I have, I will admit it, and he will be cornered like a rat in the headlights.'

The team laughed, albeit nervously.

I went back to my dressing room and thought a little harder about what I was about to do. Is it really that clever to admit having taken drugs on TV?

The doubts raged in my head, but the upside of making a name for myself by cornering Osborne on a hot issue banished them to one side.

Once the interview had begun, we warmed him up with some fairly standard fare, which he dealt with competently and easily.

Then, ten minutes into the interview, I put the question to him.

'Have you ever taken recreational drugs?'

'I don't think public figures should have to answer that question.'

'Don't you? Isn't breaking the law a public matter?'

He paused, and stared at me. 'Well let me put it to you, then, have you ever taken recreational drugs, Piers?'

I paused.

'Hold it, hold it,' came the order from an excited team upstairs in the gallery.

I held it for several long, tantalising seconds.

'Yes, I have actually. Now, let me ask you again, Mr Osborne, have you ever taken drugs?'

He looked stunned, and trapped. I'd been honest, I'd answered the question, and now he had to do the same or he'd look slippery and evasive, having put me on the spot. I could see his keen political brain whirring, desperately looking for a way out.

'I'm not going to answer that question … for simple political reasons … and I think it's much better for our party if we don't directly answer that question as individuals.'

Game over.

'That was great,' said the gallery in ecstatic unison.

It's always great when a well-thought-out plan works like that. We leaked the exchange to the media, who picked it up like a Rottweiler with a nice big juicy bone.

I left the studio feeling re-energised about the show. We're halfway through the third series now, ratings are steady and we're getting good guests on saying good stuff at last.

10 October

Met the new BBC ONE boss, Peter Fincham today, a man who could be very important to my future career, whatever that may be.

He was smart, friendly and encouraging. And he's just given me the green light to present a six-part series called *You Can't Fire Me, I'm Famous*, which will involve me interviewing six celebrities who've been sacked at some stage in their lives.

I'm supposed to bring some personal empathy to the encounters, drawing on my own experience of getting the bullet.

It sounds fun, and BBC ONE is always a good place to be.

'I see you as my potential 10.35p.m. man, Piers,' Peter said as I left.

Better than his 1.35a.m. man, I guess.

11 October

I emailed Boris Johnson, asking him to be a subject on *You Can't Fire Me, I'm Famous*. He emailed back today: 'Dear Piers, I can't tell you how touched I am by your kind offer to allow me to revisit my moment at the epicentre of national derision … but on the whole I think I will wait until I am engulfed by the next disaster. A real biggie. Best, Boris.'

Jeremy emailed from Basra: 'We had a visit yesterday from Chris Hughes and Chris Grieve from the *Mirror*. Unfortunately I was too busy to see them, but apparently Chris Hughes told one of our captains that the last time he saw me I was standing on my head drinking a pint of beer and subsequently being sick.'

12 October

I'm half dead as I write this.

Stanley had his school run today, and parents were 'encouraged' to jog with their children. It was about two miles – twice around a field.

I've been keeping pretty fit by my standards, so I agreed to run – and regretted it by the end of the first lap.

'Come on, Dad,' cried my eight-year-old son, pounding along like an Olympic 5,000-metre runner.

'I'm trying, Stan, just don't go so fast…'

He scoffed.

Back at the flat, I emailed Peter Mandelson for the first time since *The Insider* came out, saying, 'Dear Prince, must be nearly time for you to talk to me again. How about coming on my TV show *Morgan and Platell* and being brilliant? Love Piers.'

Heyda! This is me giving a speech in Sweden, where the media-orientated audience seemed to find my stories massively more amusing than their British counterparts.

Easy tiger ... I plead with David Blunkett to show mercy at our 'turn-the-tables' encounter. But I needn't have worried – he had the probing interview technique of a robotic cuddly toy.

Well, I am an Aries ... This sheep was captured watching me on TV, but, like most of my viewers, it soon tired of what it saw and ran off. Baaahhh.

Hoodies? This lot in Margate looked about as menacing as a bunch of neutered choirboys. Hardly what Sky had in mind when they asked me to confront this evil social menace.

Take that, you Aussie bastards! Rupert and I celebrate in Freddie Flintoff's manager's private box, seconds after we won the Ashes at The Oval.

left: One for the road, Mr Flintoff? My brother Rupert took this photo of the great man at 5a.m. on the night/morning we won the Ashes. I was, inexplicably, addressing a load of book trade managers in Birmingham at the time.

below: 'Tell you what, Beefy, this bloody interviewer's a twat, isn't he?' Freddie and Ian Botham scoff at my pathetic attempts to interrogate them.

'I hope you know what the **** you're doing...' Sir Alan Sugar and I have a frank exchange of views as he prepares to fly me over the skies of Essex in his plane.

No escape. My brother Jeremy escorts Camilla Parker Bowles on the parade ground, strenuously denying all knowledge of me – obviously.

Celia poses for *GQ*. I can't think why on earth I even noticed her to be honest…

Celia and I get caught by the paparazzi at 2a.m. heading for Tramp nightclub in a dusty rickshaw. I don't appear to be too perturbed by this appalling intrusion into my privacy.

above: 'Thanks for the horse and carriage Mohamed, but where's my hamper?' My flamboyant mate Al Fayed greets me at Harrods for a book signing.

left: My tipsy sister Charlotte gets rather cosy with Graham Norton at my book launch. I may need to explain a few things to her...

below: Gordon Ramsay, Dylan Jones and I laughing at a party. I can only assume that we'd just heard something awful had happened to Jeremy Clarkson.

'Here's another glass of bubbly, Boris. Now just stay well away from my lady friend please.'

Smile Gordon, it's for the children ... The Chancellor helps me launch *First News* at Downing Street.

Man in the mask: this is the face that drove Kate Moss bonkers.

He replied, 'Don't torture me with the thought!! Px.'

I wonder if he's going through the same 'what am I doing now?' mental anguish that I am. We both used to be right at the centre of power. Now he's been shipped off to Brussels, and I'm reduced to begging MPs to come on a TV show that hardly anyone watches.

13 October

Michael Vaughan had his big benefit dinner tonight at the Hilton in Park Lane, and I was the host. It was a massive do, with well over 1,200 people, all paying a small fortune to honour the England captain. My main task of the evening was to interview Michael, and then get six more of the Ashes heroes up on stage for a further grilling.

Most of these Q&As tend to be rather boring, with the same old questions coming up time after time, so I decided to be a little different.

'Michael, it's been a great summer, but there's one question everyone in this room really wants to know…'

He craned his neck forward, the audience waited silently, I let the tension build for a second or two.

'… and that's this: Who pissed in Tony Blair's garden?'

Vaughan burst out laughing, as did the audience.

'Well let's just say it was a big man who's not here.'

'Called Fred?'

'He's not here, whoever he is.'

I was off and running, and by the time the other England boys got on stage my irreverence knew no bounds.

'So, Marcus Trescothick, why do the lads really call you "Banger"? It's got nothing to do with sausages, or has it?'

'Simon Jones, the last time I saw you was in a Barbados bar and you were heading off hand in hand with Jodie Kidd. What happened next?'

And so on.

It all went down very well. I think I'm getting the hang of this speaking lark, which is just as well since it's one of my biggest sources of income at the moment, though tonight's gig was unpaid.

I ended up in Annabel's with the cricketers, where they were showered with free champagne and mobbed by sexy posh blonde girls, as if they were pop stars.

It's been interesting watching the celebrification of cricket since we won the Ashes.

17 October

Down to the Savoy hotel today for a charity event called Turn the Tables, where politicians get to grill their media tormentors in front of a big audience.

I was to be David Blunkett's victim, which was perfect timing given that he has spent most of the last year immersed in a furious battle with the media over his affair with Kimberly Quinn.

Hilariously, I discovered that our encounter came up in the morning press briefing at Downing Street.

The No 10 website stated, 'Asked what David Blunkett's interview with Piers Morgan would contribute to the debate on welfare reform and pensions, the Prime Minister's Official Spokesman (PMOS) said that was a matter for the DWP.

'Asked if it was wise for David Blunkett to be doing such an interview, the PMOS said it was a matter he would leave to David Blunkett and his department, it was not a matter that would detain Downing Street for long. Put to him that perhaps it would be a matter for Downing Street when we heard what came out of it, the PMOS said that not only did that come under the heading of a hypothetical question but also, perhaps, wishful thinking on the part of the journalist.'

I was already at the Savoy when Blunkett arrived with his guide dog and various aides. He seemed considerably thinner than the last time I'd seen him, and nowhere near as confident or bombastic.

The audience were virtually baying for blood by the time we got up on stage, but Blunkett was strangely disengaged as we were introduced.

'No tricksy stuff or I'll go nuclear,' I joked.

'Don't worry, I don't want any more trouble,' he replied meekly.

His first few questions were more Parky than Paxman, and it only livened up when he made some dig about the press intruding on politicians' private lives and I replied, 'Well, we don't need to dig very far, you politicians seem quite capable of being caught with your trousers down without any help from the press.' Everyone laughed, except Blunkett, who just looked nervous and keen to move the conversation on.

He asked another very boring question, and I could feel palpable disappointment from the crowd, so I ignored it and said, 'I asked a few of my mates in the local pub for the best Blunkett joke they'd heard, and they came up with an absolute corker. But I will only reveal it if somebody bids at least £1,000 for charity by the end of lunch.'

Our ten-minute 'confrontation' had been a damp squib; we even suffered the humiliation of being out-laughed by the second sparring duo, Malcolm Rifkind and Jon Snow.

Lunch was an even drearier affair. In the good old days, pre the pair of us being mired in scandal and sacking, we'd have swapped insults throughout the meal and had a great time, but Blunkett just sat there, not eating or saying much, and looking thoroughly miserable.

He seems broken to me, a pitiful shadow of the man he used to be.

And that's a crying shame, because David Blunkett was always one of the more impressive politicians. Charismatic, clever, cunning and ambitious. A man who loved the rough and tumble of politics. Now he seems half-dead and desperate for a quiet life. Perhaps most telling of all, nobody was allowed to bid for my joke after the organisers of the event decided it would not be wise to further embarrass Blunkett.

The trial of the two former *Daily Mirror* City Slickers columnists started today, something I've been dreading for months.

Though I was personally cleared of any wrongdoing in the infamous share-tipping scandal in 2000, both by an internal Trinity Mirror investigation and the subsequent official DTI probe, I knew that this trial would inevitably rake everything up all over again, and my reputation would get further tarnished in the process.

Anil Bhoyrul has pleaded guilty to charges of illicit dealing, but his sidekick James Hipwell is pleading innocence. I'm surprised because Anil was less blameworthy in my opinion. Certainly he profited significantly less from their scam of buying shares before they tipped them when the share price rose on the back of their tip.

Hipwell's changed his story countless times, but the one thing he has been consistent about is bringing my name into absolutely everything in a pathetic attempt to get himself off.

I've not been called as a witness in the case, which surprised me. The only contact I've had with anyone, in fact, came from a lawyer for the third defendant, someone I've never even heard of, called Terry Shepherd, asking if I would help his client. I politely declined on the basis that I can hardly help a man I have never met.

The case is due to last six weeks, and I'm sure that by the end of it Hipwell will be found guilty, but I'm also sure that I will be so disgustingly smeared by then that everyone will think I was the real villain of the piece who just 'got away with it'.

It's infuriating and unfair, but there's nothing I can do about it because that is the story the media wants, and the media – as I know very well – usually gets what it wants.

18 October

Spent the afternoon interviewing Steve Coogan at Century, a private members club in Soho.

The last time I saw Coogan he was sitting on a luxurious, large red sofa, being fawned over by a group of very beautiful women.

Nothing odd there given his new status as Hollywood movie star. Except that he was in Stringfellows strip club, it was 4a.m., he was blind drunk and the four admiring ladies were all naked lap dancers who he was showering with endless bundles of cash. Nothing again, you might think, massively wrong with that. Except, perhaps, that he had been ditched by his new wife only months before after confessing to a sex and drugs romp with two other lap dancers in a London hotel. A cataclysmic event that might cause even the most louche of men to rethink their behaviour.

But then, Coogan has never been an ordinary bloke. A brilliant comedian, arguably one of the best in the country, he's also clever – very, very clever – and I have always found him both professionally and personally hilarious. Like many smart, funny performers, he has a massive problem leaving a cheering hysterical audience and heading home for a cup of cocoa and an early night with the wife.

The menu arrived, with a choice of two starters and two main courses. Coogan was delighted: 'See, that's the way a menu should be: hardly any choice. Makes life so much easier, and I bet the food is excellent as a result. We just get bombarded with choice these days, there seems to be this absolute belief that everyone wants millions of things to choose from. It's the same with hospitals and TV stations. We don't want to choose which one we go to or watch, we just want a bloody good one, don't we? I preferred TV when there were just four channels but it was all good stuff. (He was warming up into quite a head of steam now.) I mean, look at bloody mobile phones. Where can I get one that actually just lets me make a phone call? Is that too much to ask? You get these annoying little nerds who design all these useless functions that nobody apart from them can ever understand or use. I use my computer for emails and surfing the net and that's is it. What else do you need one for?

The waiter came back to take our order from the simple menu.

'Crabcakes and salmon please,' said Coogan.

I ordered the pigeon salad and the salmon.

His eyebrows pricked up. 'Actually, that salad sounds quite interesting, can I change my starter to that, please?'

I laughed: 'Getting a bit complicated suddenly, isn't it, that lack of choice.'

We talked about comedy. He had a theory about the importance of geography in the art of making people laugh.

'In places where there is a strong sense of identity, like Birmingham, Manchester, Newcastle and Glasgow, they're always up for it. They wear their hearts on their sleeves and let you know exactly how they're feeling, and that's great. You know where you are. But Southend and Watford are awful. They laugh, but not in the same way. There's a general lack of enthusiasm in those places, and it's probably because you never hear someone say they are proud to come from Southend or Watford, whereas you do with those other places.

'London audiences are tricky, too. They don't laugh as much as the northern audiences because, and I hate to say this, they are a bit cleverer normally and they pick up on all the little details and listen more carefully. They are more sophisticated. It's all about the commas and full stops down south...'

His publicist had made it very clear that Coogan would not wish to discuss his recent fling with Courtney Love. So I asked him anyway.

'You and Courtney were described as the most gruesome couple since Eddie Murphy and Mariah Carey. Thoughts?'

'Erm. I think enough has now been written about all that to satisfy the public.'

'No it hasn't. Come on, there are lots of unanswered questions, Coogan – time to fess up, mate.'

'All right. All right. I ... know ... her ... quite well.'

At which point he started gasping for breath.

'You're choking on your pigeon...'

'That brings back a few memories,' he cackled. 'I'm not saying any more about it.'

'Were you a Nirvana fan, or not?'

'You can't shake it off, can you? How long have you been out of that *Mirror* job?'

'You never lose it. Come on...'

'Well, yeah, I was as it happens. A big Nirvana fan.'

'Was that all part of the … erm … appeal?'

'*No*,' he groaned. 'No.'

'Come on, you're supposed to be a comic, you must be able to see the funny side of all this, surely?'

'Of course I can. And how clever was it to serve Fleet Street this little morsel in the middle of the silly season? Jesus Christ... Look, just trawl through all the old cuttings and cobble some shit together like you always used to...'

'It's not my fault you slept with Courtney Love, nor that this means you will be asked about her until you die...'

'I could have shagged someone more famous...'

'She was apparently quite upset to discover she had had sex with Alan Partridge.'

'All parties involved were fully aware of all issues before anything happened.'

'So she knew about your Nirvana collection and the fact that you are Alan Partridge?'

'She knew who I was, I knew who she was. Let's leave it at that. I'm just a good Catholic boy – I do naughty things and feel guilty about them.'

'Did you get her pregnant, then? You can confess and repent at the same time, if you like.'

'No, I didn't. I know that for a fact.'

'How?'

'I'm not telling you, but it's a fact. And since the source for that story was Miss Courtney Love, can I politely suggest the papers find more reliable sources in future?'

'Is she a fantasist then?'

'Let's just say she has certain issues … as have I.'

'Do you regret it? It's a bit unfortunate that it all came out when you have a movie launching called *A Cock and Bull Story*.'

'Actually, I thought the two things dovetailed quite well.'

At the height of his Alan Partridge fame, there'd been a rumour that Coogan had rejected a huge offer from McDonald's to do an advert because he was so right-on that it offended his senses.

'It's true,' he told me. 'A million quid.'

Pause.

'I wish I'd bloody done it now! It's a lot of money, isn't it? My decision wasn't entirely philanthropic or magnanimous. I mean, I made sure I leaked it so everyone knew and I got lots of good publicity out of it. I just thought it would leave a bad taste in the mouths of my real fans, who like the kind of comedy I do and probably don't like McDonald's.'

I asked him who is the best stand-up comic he's ever worked with.

'Oh, Frank Skinner. He's just brilliant. I made the huge mistake of touring with him when he was relatively unknown and I was supposedly the big name. He blew me off stage every night. It was a very un-PC act but bloody funny. He used to tell these shockingly coarse gags, then instantly apologise. Great trick, and he got away with it.'

'As do you.'

'Indeed.'

Coogan is one of those rare characters who seems to actively adore being a celebrity. He pretends he doesn't, but he lives the life of a rock star and takes full advantage of his fame whenever he can. If you can shrug off the adverse headlines that come with that kind of wild behaviour, then being a celebrity must be absolutely wonderful.

21 October

I set off to Pinewood Studios for *The Weakest Link*, with a ringing vote of confidence from my sons.

'I bet you come last, Dad,' said Spencer.

'Don't be ridiculous, son, I'm not that stupid.'

I arrived brimming with confidence, nay insufferable cockiness, and my sense of inevitable triumph wasn't entirely alleviated by noting that my rivals included Myleene Klass, Gail Porter and several other 'prime-time presenters' I'd never heard of. Though *Loose Women* hostess Kaye Adams was there, and she's a smart cookie.

One of the unknown 'celebrities' was a noisy long-haired bearded comic from the West Country called Justin Lee Collins. I introduced myself and he said, 'Oh you're bound to win, you were an editor, they're all really clever.' Others nodded their agreement.

Matthew Wright, an old friend, was a contestant, too, and we had a laugh in the green room about our rivals.

'Christ, mate, if we don't reach the final today we may as well top ourselves,' I said, suppressing a snigger.

He was more cautious.

'Have you seen the show, though?'

'Once or twice.'

'So you know all about the tactical voting that goes on?'

'Erm, what tactical voting?'

Before he could answer, the producer arrived to herd us off to the studio.

Suddenly I wasn't quite so sure of myself. What was all this tactical voting stuff about?

We took our places and I was right bang in the middle, straight in Anne's line of vision. I suspected she'd done that deliberately, so we could exchange regular banter as I progressed through the rounds.

The first round came, and everyone got their simple questions right. The same thing happened with the second round, but this time one of us had to be kicked off, something I thought only occurred when you gave a wrong answer. I should have watched the bloody show more often.

We were all asked to nominate someone to be the weakest link. I looked round to see a lot of faces looking at *me*.

'Tactical voting.'

The words reverberated around my head. As did the memory of Justin whatshisname saying I was bound to win because I was so clever.

My heart stopped. They wouldn't … would they?

Three of us got two votes each – me, Kaye Adams (who had also been identified as 'clever' in the green room), and Justin.

Because he'd been quickest with his answers, he was allowed to choose one of us as the weakest link.

This had just become my ultimate nightmare. I was facing first-off humiliation.

I pleaded for my life, begging Justin to spare me in a pitiful display.

He smirked. 'Sorry, mate, you're too clever.' And voted for me to go.

Anne could barely contain her glee.

'Fired again, Piers,' she chortled, as the audience roared their approval.

I trudged off, scarcely able to believe what was happening to me.

The director stopped me as I reached the steps.

'Sorry, we had a technical fault, can you do that again?'

I had to return to my position and let Anne fire me all over again. The audience loved it even more the second time.

There was another technical hitch, and then another, so I ended up filming my exit five times, each to a bigger ovation from the audience.

I had tried to keep my sense of humour, but this was ridiculous.

'I'm not doing it again,' I said and walked off to record my interview backstage, where a sad-looking woman said gently, 'I'm so sorry, Piers, are you all right?'

I was fine, I just wanted to kill someone.

Having made a statement about 'always being sacked by mediocre people' I returned to the green room to find a load of famous cricketers waiting to film another show, including Darren Gough.

'Did you win, mate?' said Darren.

'Not exactly, no,' I replied.

'Where did you come then?'

'Last.'

The room exploded with laughter.

I found my taxi ten minutes later and called the boys.

'I was the weakest weakest link,' I announced.

'Told you,' said a delighted Spencer.

'So you're now officially the most stupid celebrity in Britain, aren't you?'

'Yes, son, I suppose I am.'

The boys fell about laughing.

22 October

Anne Robinson emailed me this morning: 'Jealousy always follows talent, earning potential and good looks.'

Which was very nice of her, but makes absolutely no difference to my misery whatsoever. Can there be anything more embarrassing than coming last in a panel of D-list celebrity nobodies?

24 October

I did a speech in Wales to the prestigious Cardiff Business Club, and during the Q&A afterwards I was asked what I thought of Ian Blair, the Met Police chief, with regard to the enveloping scandal over the innocent Brazilian shot dead at Stockwell tube by cops who thought he was a suicide bomber.

'I think the guy at the top should always take the rap for these things, and if it's proven that he tried to cover up anything, then he should go immediately.'

Warming to my theme, I added, 'Ian Blair likes the sound of his own voice too much, he should shut up and get on with his job.'

I saw a bearded man in the front row eyeing me rather strangely. He came up to me afterwards.

'Hi, I'm Ian Blair's brother.'

SHIT.

'Oh God, I'm so sorry. I wouldn't have been quite so strong if –'

'Oh don't worry, I agreed with a lot of what you said. But what can you do with brothers, eh?'

26 October

A new book on Cherie Blair has just come out by a journalist called Paul Scott, who I have worked with in the past. It includes an anecdote where Cherie goes up to Michael Parkinson and starts laying into me, informing him that I told her and Tony I wanted his chat-show job. According to Scott, Parky concurs wholeheartedly with her uncomplimentary views and says I'll get the show over his 'dead body'.

I was furious when I read it because the only person who has ever mentioned the idea of me one day taking over from Parkinson was Tony Blair, when he had me round for dinner after I was fired from the *Mirror*. It was a typical piece of duplicity from Cherie, designed to turn Parky against me – a guy who I've always had huge respect for, and who I had always assumed quite liked me, too.

This is obviously the real reason why he cancelled our lunch date earlier this year.

I sat down and fired off a hurt and wounded missive, saying Cherie's claims were all bollocks and that I sincerely hoped he didn't really think I'd behave in such a manner.

27 October

Naynesh Desai, Ian Botham's amusing, generous and razor-smart lawyer, invited me to the Asian Achiever Awards in London, and I assumed I'd just be on his table getting slowly drunk with his other guests, who included Freddie Flintoff.

When I arrived, Naynesh took me to one side and whispered, 'Erm, you're the sort of guest of honour, is that OK?'

'*What*? How can I be, I'm not Asian and I haven't achieved anything this year other than getting the sack.'

'It's fine, the sponsors are a big Asian newspaper and they admired your editorship. You just need to make a little speech thanking them.'

Minutes later, Freddie arrived and seemed equally bemused. 'Naynesh told me it would be dinner for eight people. There are five hundred here...'

We were both led out in a procession before peeling off to our seats – Freddie on Naynesh's table, me on the top table.

'What the fuck are you doing up there?' he mouthed, incredulous.

'Chief Guest of Honour, mate,' I mouthed back.

He rocked his head back in complete hysterics, which were compounded seconds afterwards when I was formally announced and asked to come to the stage, where two very glamorous women put huge floral garlands on me to rapturous applause.

I caught Freddie's eye and winked.

After the meal, the awards were due to be presented, and I sidled over to tell Freddie some more good news.

'Seen the plaques they're giving out – they have a very special engraving on them.'

'What is it?'

'I can't say, Fred, but I think you'll like it.'

He eyed me suspiciously.

'And the Asian Achiever Sportsman of the Year is Mr Freddie Flintoff.'

The big man made his way to the stage, accepted his award with a brief, very genuine speech of thanks.

I saw his eyes drop to the plaque as he walked off stage, a quizzical raised eyebrow, then a look of horror and revulsion.

He came back and tossed the plaque towards Naynesh.

'Fucking hell, Naynesh, look what this says.'

Naynesh peered at the plaque a little closer, to see the words, 'Presented to Mr Freddie Flintoff in the presence of Mr Piers Morgan.'

28 October

I've been asked to host the Hair and Beauty Journalism Awards next month, to an audience of just seventy hair and beauty writers from magazines like *Vogue*, which has to be a candidate for 'Easiest Gig of the Year'.

2 November

News breaks in the City Slickers trial that I hadn't bought just £20,000 worth of shares in Viglen Technology, as everyone thought, but had in fact bought a total of £67,000, because I'd bought some in several PEPs as well.

I'd admitted all this to Trinity Mirror on the morning the story first came out, back in January 2000, and they had in turn informed all the investigating authorities, so it had never been a secret to anyone who needed to know.

But it was decided to keep the PEP purchase quiet from the media, unless directly asked, because I had bought those shares a few hours earlier than the ones on the open market, for the simple reason that I couldn't get my broker before lunch.

The significance of the timing was that the two Slicker boys had constructed their whole story around me wandering over to their desk in the middle of the afternoon, reading their column for the next day tipping Viglen, and then racing off to buy shares in Viglen myself. In fact, I first bought shares in Viglen hours earlier, long before they'd written their piece.

Nobody wants to believe all this, though, in the same way as nobody wants to remember other salient facts about this 'scandal'.

Namely 1) They'd tipped Viglen twice before in the previous fortnight and the share price had risen by over 30 per cent as a result. 2) My broker and my cousin already held shares in the company, and my uncle had recommended them to me the week before. 3) The Slickers story was based on an internet division advertising campaign that Viglen had been running in the national press for a month, in other words it was old news. 4) I didn't try to sell the shares when the price doubled overnight. 5) By the time the story came out the share price was almost back where it started.

Perhaps most pertinently, I had never once bought shares before any of their other tips, and they had made more than 2,000 tips in two years.

But no, as far as Fleet Street is concerned, I am the new Nick Leeson and must be treated as such. And there is nothing I can do about it other than wait to die, when I confidently predict that my obituaries will be headlined, DODGY SHARE-TIPPER DIES, AGED 86.

8 November

'Ulrika wants you to go to the house.'

The text message from Ms Jonsson's agent made me feel suddenly a little uneasy. This wasn't just any old house. This was the house where she romped with that moronic *Gladiators* star Hunter; the house she famously fled to when Stan Collymore beat her up; the house she hid in when the John Leslie furore erupted, and, most pertinently of all, the house she used as a kinky sex den for her secret fling with Sven Goran Eriksson.

I crept timidly up to the front door and banged twice. Within two seconds it was flung open and Ulrika was kissing me. OK, OK, on both cheeks. In a very, very platonic way. But that must have been how it started with Sven.

'I've come to talk about your ridiculous life for *GQ*,' I explained.

Ulrika cackled, 'Blimey, are you staying the night then?'

She sat me down in her sitting room while she made me a coffee.

And there, right in front of me, was an enormous oil painting of Ulrika – naked.

'Very nice,' I said when she returned.

'Thanks. The breasts are particularly good, aren't they?'

'Erm, yes, quite magnificent.'

'So they should be, I painted them myself.'

It turned out this was a self-portait Ulrika had done as part of her recent appearance on *Art School*.

'It gave me a great chance to rectify what God got wrong with my body.'

I laughed. 'I don't think he got it that wrong, to be honest…'

'No, but nothing an uplift, an implant, a repositioning and a bit of turning wouldn't improve – as you can see in the painting, where they are now perfect!'

I looked round the room and realised it was full of paintings of naked women.

'Ulrika, about all these pictures, I have to ask…'

'*Noooo*! I'm not a lesbian!'

I've known Ulrika since she was a *TV-am* weathergirl. She's what I would call a professional celebrity, someone who is just famous for being famous, doesn't mind admitting it and makes the most of what that brings her.

Every new tabloid headline means pound signs to her, the only enemy is public and media apathy.

It seems a soulless, rather absurd existence, but she seems happy enough.

It was the *Mirror* that broke the Sven and Ulrika scandal to the world.

'Do you regret it now?' I asked.

'No, not at all, I had a fun time with him.'

'But how can a man who shows so little passion on a football field fire himself up so passionately in bed, because you wouldn't have been with him if he couldn't, would you?'

She giggled. 'It's controlled passion.'

'You must have known it would hit the headlines and cause mayhem?'

'I kept saying to him that it was bound to get out and with the World

Cup only a few months away we were taking a huge risk, and he kept laughing and saying, "Some risks are worth taking, it's OK."'

'Sven was utterly spineless with you, wasn't he?'

'Oh fucking hell, yes, but at least I was able to work that out pretty quickly, realise what he was like and get out of it.'

'Which was down to me really, wasn't it?'

'You want me to thank you, don't you, Piers?'

'Thank me, spank me, whatever.'

'I'm not getting down on my knees to you.'

'That makes a change.'

'Oh ha ha. It would have ended a few months later anyway because I don't think he will ever have the balls to leave Nancy. I thought he would because he kept saying he would.'

'Was he sitting on this sofa when he said it?'

'Yes, he was actually.'

'Just sitting?'

'Yes.'

'What do you think now of your love rival?'

'Nancy bloody Dell'a-bloody-lollio or whatever her stupid name is? She should be thanking me. Have you seen how much make-up she wears?'

'She won, didn't she?'

'What did she win? A spineless little man, congratulations.'

'She's been quite bitchy about you.'

'Yes, but then look at her. She is deluded with a capital D. (Puts on hilarious mad Italian female voice) "Oh yes, I think this week we may adopt a baby. And next week we get married. And the week after I will become a geisha girl." Christ. She's off her trolley. It's quite endearing really, she's like a pantomime horse. I read somewhere recently that there is a country that has a law allowing you to marry someone even when they have died and I thought that would be her only hope with Sven. I can see her now, taking the dead hand of his corpse.'

At one stage of the scandal, Ulrika had started bleating about wanting her privacy respected. This from a woman who has happily invaded her own privacy for years.

'Do you think you have any right to criticise newspapers for intrusion when you relentlessly target famous men?' I asked her.

'RELENTLESSLY TARGET FAMOUS MEN! Is that a bloody joke! I have never targeted a man in my life, they target *me*.'

'Come off it, you've been out with just one anonymous bloke in twenty years, haven't you, your first husband?'

'That's just of the men you know about.'

'I see. Well how many men have you had sex with that I don't know about?'

'A few.'

'How many?'

'Er … umm … a couple. Neither of them was remotely famous and you never knew about them. So there.'

'Who is the best lover you've ever had?'

'The best lover?'

'Yes, if you could have sex with one of them again, who would it be?'

'I honestly don't think I have had the best sex of my life yet. Funnily enough as I head towards my fortieth birthday I find I'm getting more and more confident sexually. I don't feel like an insecure nineteen-year-old any more when it comes to men. I'm bang up for it these days.'

'Do you think you're good in bed?'

'Yes. Very. But you are only really as good as the person you're having sex with.'

'Have you been told you're good.'

'No.'

'You just know you are.'

'I just think if the other person is good to me then I can be very good, yes. Men always say you've got the most gorgeous arse or you're the best kisser don't they? I've heard it so many times.'

'Are those the two biggest lies?'

'Yes, along with "I won't come in your mouth, I promise."' To which Ulrika performed a repulsed gagging motion.

'Women lie, too,' I countered.

'Oh yes. I remember one guy asking me if it was the best sex I'd ever had and trying to be diplomatic because it most emphatically had not been, and I said, "Well, it's different because I love you." Which was a polite way of saying he was crap, I suppose.'

'Come on then, what is the best sex you've had to date?'

'I can't tell you that. It would embarrass the person.'

'Hardly!'

'All right, but it would embarrass all the others.'

'Can I guess?'

'Oh yes, I'd love you to guess.'

'OK, but how do you like your sex? That will narrow down the list.'

'I can't believe I'm listening to this.'

'I can't believe you're telling me. I would imagine that Hunter was all pecs and no action?'

'Well, men have different approaches, don't they? Some women want to be dominated and some prefer to be domineering. I like it when a man takes charge. I am very comfortable in that situation.'

'I guess that rules him out then.'

Raises her eyebrows in a confirmatory manner: 'Hmm. Next.'

'Your first husband, John Turnbull?'

Shakes head. 'No.'

'Collymore?'

Shakes head.

'He was too busy dogging, I suppose. Did he ever take you to car parks?'

Giggles. 'No. I didn't know what dogging was. Mind you, there were a few car-park visits, now you mention it.'

'Prince Edward?'

'No. We never had sex.'

'How far did you go with him?'

'No sex. Move on.'

'Who have I forgotten?'

'I had sex with my middle child Bo's father…'

'Ah yes, Marcus Kempen. The German. You're not going to tell me the best sex you've ever had was with a German, surely? The most efficient maybe, but not the best?'

'I will neither deny nor confirm.'

'That's a yes, then. Fascinating.'

'Hang on, I am being very unfair here. The best sex I've ever had was with my husband, my last husband, sorry my current husband.'

'That's a lie.'

'You say that if you want, Piers.'

'Are you a five-times-a-night girl?'

'No, no, no. It's quality not quantity. I read a survey in the *Sun* this week that said 65 per cent of people had their best sex in the back of the car, but when I did, it was the most uncomfortable sex I've ever bloody had.'

'When have you been most in love?'

'I think with Lance.'

'That's rather sad then, isn't it?'

'Yes, very sad. The biggest sadness of my life.'

'You don't seem that sad.'

'That's because I've taken happy tablets. No, I have to keep myself buoyant for the kids. I have moments, shit moments, really awful moments when I have to go and cry in the shower. I wear my heart on my sleeve and I don't postpone my pain in these situations. Men do, but I don't. If there was no reason to see each other again it would be easier because you could move on, but we are going to be linked forever because of our child and it will bring back good and bad memories. I'm hiding it quite well. I have to.'

'Is your heart broken?'

'Yes, a bit.'

'Has your heart been broken before?'

'James [Hunter] did initially, I guess. Stan just tried to break my neck, not my heart.'

'Sven?'

'God, no. We were never really in love with each other. I didn't cry over Sven, I can honestly say that.'

'I forgot to ask what Sven was like in bed? A tornado?'

'More of a rowing boat. With one oar. Going round and round and round.'

'A big oar?'

'Size isn't everything.'

'Is that just as well in Sven's case?'

'Yeah.' Laughs out loud. 'You're a terrible man.'

'Can you imagine marrying again?'

'No, if I ever say I'm marrying again will you please shoot me. If I ever come to you and say, "Piers, I have fallen in love and I'm going to get married and have more children," then you have my full permission to gun me down on the spot.'

'Are you worried about turning forty?'

'No, not really. I am aware that I don't look as young as I did, but I haven't succumbed to surgery yet. Nothing. No injections or anything like that. I have always thought the women who age the most beautifully are the ones who age naturally. There is a raw beauty about them you don't get with the botox and silicone brigade. But I don't know if men feel that way. I mean, my tits should not be down there, should they? And these lines on my forehead are getting worse.'

Ulrika was dropped like a sack of old spuds after the John Leslie scandal and is still bitter about it.

'It came on the back of Barrymore, Matthew Kelly and Angus Deayton. Presenters were dropping like flies, whether they were guilty or not, and being replaced by a new young crowd of pretty useless presenters who are rubbish at what they do.'

'Like who?'

'Oh, I don't know. Tess Daly is a good example. I mean, what does she bring to the party exactly? I'm sure she's a very nice person, but it's blanc-mange, it's nothing. Kate Thornton is another one. The show is so much bigger than the presenter that she doesn't need to be there. But she is, and you get all this unstructured shrieky shouting. The impression everyone gets is that TV is really easy to do – you just walk in, have your make-up done nicely, wear a gorgeous dress and shout a bit.'

We finished the interview and Ulrika giggled again. 'I've been rather naughty, haven't I?'

'Yes, *very* naughty,' I replied.

9 November

A handwritten note from Michael Parkinson arrived: 'Dear Piers, If Scott's account of you and Cherie is bollocks why would you want to believe a "source" quoted by the same author? You are not getting sensitive in your old age, are you? A cancelled lunch might have – and certainly did have – a perfectly logical explanation and have nothing to do with "general frosti-ness" as you put it. I am beginning to worry for you, my friend. You need to buy me a large lunch and I will bring you a meaty shoulder to cry on. I will settle for a good bottle of Puligny-Montrachet and a signed copy of your disreputable tome. Shall we set a place for Cherie? Much love, Mike.'

I read it twice and laughed out loud, both at the realisation of my shudderingly embarrassing overreaction and pitiful whining, and Parky's masterfully witty and perfectly pitched response.

I am in danger of disappearing up my own backside if I'm not care-ful. I'm more prickly than I used to be about perceived slights. A sign, perhaps, of my uncertain career path and lack of stability in my working life (and domestic life for that matter). I need to calm down and be more focused.

11 November

When you write a best-selling book, you get some amazing freebies thrown your way to turn up at parties or make speeches.

Today I flew first class to Dubai, where I'm being put up in a five-star hotel for a week, all expenses paid, and my only obligation is to turn up to a media networking group's party, and give an interview to the Middle Eastern edition of *Hello!* magazine.

It epitomises my life at the moment: fun, glamorous, but essentially vacuous, too. It's like I'm in some form of semi-retirement, doing one last lecture tour before I die. But I'm only forty, for God's sake.

13 November

The party was a very swanky affair, full of wealthy local businessmen, media people and glamorous women dolled up to the nines.

Halfway through I heard a familiar voice.

'Hello, mate.'

I turned to see the grinning face of Anil Bhoyrul in front of me – one half of the City Slickers.

'What are you doing now?' he asked.

I was momentarily lost for words.

'I'm, er, well, I'm doing lots of things,' I stuttered. 'How about you?'

Turns out he now works on a business magazine in Dubai and is having a great time. I was pleased, Anil was a bright, funny, mischievous guy who wrote a great column for me and didn't deserve to be sacked for his alleged crimes, which mainly benefitted his sidekick anyway.

The Slickers trial is, of course, already underway.

'I pleaded guilty and have been advised that I will probably get a community service order,' he said. 'But James has stupidly pleaded not guilty, so he'll probably go down if he's convicted.'

We agreed to meet up for a proper drink tomorrow. It was nice seeing him again.

14 November

Drinks with Anil and his girlfriend, a TV news presenter out here. He ordered about thirty lethal cocktails from the menu. Shots, shorts and stuff I didn't even recognise.

'Let's get smashed,' he said.

So we did. Absolutely, cartwheelingly, disgracefully smashed. And had a quite brilliant night careering around hotel bars and nightclubs.

15 November

Met Anil and his girlfriend again on the beach by the famous sail-shaped Burj Al Arab hotel.

As he poured me a cup of tea, my phone went and it was a reporter on the *Independent*'s diary.

'Mr Morgan, sorry to bother you, but I understand you may have bumped into Anil Bhoyrul in Dubai, which is obviously quite embarrassing for you given that the Slickers trial is still going on.'

'It's not that embarrassing, mate. He's pouring me tea on the beach, as I speak.'

Pause.

'I'm sorry? I don't think I heard that right.'

'No, you did. Anil is pouring me tea on the beach right now, and not doing a very good job of it I might add. He was always a useless teaboy.'

'God, I see. What else are you planning to do together out there?'

'Buy a few shares probably. Goodbye.'

Beneath the bravado lay a real sadness that the shares scandal had ever happened. We both agreed that it had been bloody stupid to ever trade in shares at all given our respective positions on the paper.

16 November

The people who flew me out here invited me to a party tonight in Abu Dhabi, at the new seven-star Emirates Palace hotel, which is supposed to be the most expensive and luxurious in the world.

'Who's going to be there?' I asked.

'Oh, Bill Clinton, people like that,' came the reply.

The drive was an hour and a half, but Abu Dhabi felt like a different world to Dubai. The latter has all the glitz, glamour and tourists. The former has all the oil, and therefore all the real money, but it's a much more conservative, traditional place.

We arrived at the 'party' to discover three things: 1) There were only 100 guests. 2) There was no alcohol. 3) Bill's plane was delayed so he wouldn't make it.

I ordered an orange juice and sat nibbling nuts, thinking it was a bloody long way to come and not have a drink.

'That's Benazir Bhutto,' said one of the people I'd come with.

'What, the former Prime Minister of Pakistan?'

'The very same.'

I walked over.

'Hello, I'm Piers –'

'Morgan, yes I know who you are. I'm reading your book. Most entertaining, especially about the Blairs.'

It's not often I'm lost for words, but this was one of those moments.

'Really? How amazing.'

I was genuinely shocked that someone as important as her was reading *The Insider*. And rather proud, it has to be said. She was immaculate, smart and funny, and we swapped small talk for a bit until I spotted a familiar head; in fact, one of the most famous heads in the world: Richard Branson.

I would be literally the last person on earth he would expect to see in a room full of Arabs at a business seminar in Abu Dhabi, so I tapped him on the shoulder.

'CHRIST! What the hell are you doing here?' He laughed.

'I was in the area. I've just met Benazir Bhutto and she said she's reading my book, can you believe that?'

Branson laughed even louder. 'That's what she just said to me.'

'What? That she was reading my book?'

'No, that she was reading mine!'

He was slowly getting mobbed, but said he was going to Dubai and we should catch up for a drink there.

As we drove back to Dubai for an hour and a half through the desert, I reflected on my trip. It's quite a laugh getting flown first class to glamorous parties and being told how marvellous you are by people you've never met before and will probably never meet again. But like anything, too much of it is boring.

17 November

Branson left a message on my phone: 'Piers, hi it's Richard. Look I'm really sorry but I can't meet for a drink because … well I've had a better offer: to have dinner with Bill Clinton!' Then all I could hear was more laughter.

At least he's honest.

18 November

Another airport, this time Gatwick, and another middle-aged man comes up to me and says, 'Excuse me, but I just want to say I follow everything you say about plants.'

I am *not* Alan bloody Titchmarsh. I don't even look like him. What is wrong with these people?

19 November

I am due to interview Sir Alan Sugar for *GQ*, and he is proving to be the nice, easy interviewee we all expected him to be. He sent his PR, James Herring, an email this morning politely outlining his thoughts on how the day should go: 'I am telling you now that I am *not*, repeat *not*, giving more than twenty minutes to the photographer. Do not bullshit him and say it will be OK for a day's shoot with Sir Alan, cos he will be very disappointed when he gets there. Tell him he has twenty minutes and I am off. I want you to tell him this so he knows upfront and is not disappointed. If he drives me mad I'll kick him in an area where he'll need to change his name to "Bathe it Daily".'

Vintage Sugar. But it was his next email that snapped my eyelids back.

'I have my small plane, which is really a boys toy (Brad Pitt just bought one and is learning how to fly it). If the weather's good I can take Mr Morgan up in it, put it in a spin and tell him to get out of that, son!'

I gulped. Oh my God, Sugar wants to take me out flying.

21 November

An appalling, embarrassing, hideously unforgettable night. For the second year running I hosted the British Society of Magazine Editors' Awards at the Hilton in Park Lane. It was a crowd I knew well, a venue I had spoken at many times. I'd gone down pretty well the previous year, hence my second invitation, and *GQ*'s Dylan Jones was the host. What could possibly go wrong? Answer: almost everything.

I suspected trouble when Dylan launched into a lengthy and extremely flattering introduction to me, only for it to be met by a mixture of silence, apathy and a few snide chuckles. However, nothing could quite prepare me for what happened next. Things started OK, but then I told one of my usual 'banker' stories from the book about Hugh Grant and Rupert Murdoch, waited for the punchline to provoke the usual uproarious laughter and ... nothing. Just an uninterested murmuring. I panicked, looking out at 1,000 people staring at me, demanding to be better entertained than this, and in that split second I realised why all stand-up comics are manic-depressive drunks and drug addicts. I could feel my cheeks go crimson, my breath shorten, my mouth parch. This was not supposed to happen. Everyone loves this story. And this is a media audience, they should love it more than anybody.

I ploughed on with a couple of Diana tales, to an increasingly deafening silence. Then a Cherie anecdote that never, ever fails to spark anything but huge guffaws. Except this time. I'd lost the audience now and there was no way back. Sweating profusely, I gulped down a glass of water and announced, 'Now for my penultimate piece of advice...' I was drowned out by a table in the far right-hand corner, which began cheering dementedly. It caught on, and most of the room began to join in. I was finally getting an ovation, but purely because I'd nearly finished.

I remember the wise words of a veteran after-dinner speaker: 'If you haven't struck oil after twenty minutes, stop boring and shut up.' I could at least see a glimmer of humour in the situation. 'Do I take it that you've had enough of me, then?'

'YES!' came the heartfelt reply.

My shame was complete and I abandoned the speech then and there – the first time I've ever had to do that.

Then came renewed horror as I realised I would have to stay up on stage and present dozens of awards to these people for the next hour or so. Dylan joined me, and never have I been more relieved to see any man in my life.

'Sorry, mate, this has never happened before...' I said.

'Don't worry about it,' he said, 'they're just a bunch of drunken wankers.'

He was grim-faced, though. No host likes to see their star turn go down like a divorce lawyer at a wedding. I stumbled through the awards, still burning with ignominy but trying to stay professional, and an hour later I crawled back to my table, wanting the world to be struck by a meteor.

Several people extended insincere sympathies, but most looked the other way. Only one laughed heartily. It was Celia Walden, the 6-foot blonde diarist from the *Daily Telegraph*. 'That was hilarious,' she said, 'one of the funniest things I've seen in ages.'

I forced a smile. 'Yes, unless you're the one up on stage dying on your arse.'

'Oh, who cares? They're just media people, they're always like that. I wouldn't give it another moment's thought.'

And she was right. I'd bumped into Celia a few times at parties, but never really spoken to her much. Yet her cheery hilarity at my downfall, and complete derision of the mocking crowd, had an oddly comforting effect on me.

We chatted for a while, and I found myself quickly forgetting the nightmare that had happened and focusing rather more intently on the amusing, bright and rather beautiful creature in front of me. 'I owe you lunch,' I said eventually.

'Love to,' she replied.

Andy Coulson came over to commiserate.

'Well persevered, mate, that must have been hideous. It's Peter Stringfellow's birthday party tonight if you fancy some light relief. Loads of hacks are going down apparently.'

Filling the next few hours with Jack Daniel's and Stringy's 'Cabaret of Angels' seemed a much better way to end the evening than going home on my own and moping. 'See you there,' I answered.

22 November

I woke at 6a.m., my head burning with hangover. I really caned it at Stringfellows, and the full horror of my speech had become a memory. But now every long, lingering, appalling second flooded back to me as I lay in bed. Why the hell had it all gone so wrong? I've done loads of speeches and never have I had such a terrible reaction. Perhaps they were just cynical magazine journalists who wanted to make a point about a newspaper guy. Or maybe they'd all read the book and had therefore heard most of the stories already, a theory floated by a few of the guests afterwards. Or perhaps, and this was the most worrying notion, perhaps I just wasn't very funny. I remember Dennis Pennis, that crazed TV stitch-up merchant, thrusting a microphone in front of Steve Martin once and saying, 'Hey, Steve, I'm from the BBC and I have a question for you.' Martin smiled graciously and went to speak to the man from the BBC.

'Steve, why aren't you funny any more?' came the question he least expected. The man, one of the funniest of his generation, looked completely devastated, and he was rumoured to have had therapy specifically to get over the shock of that encounter afterwards.

I know how he felt. There can be few things worse than being funny and then suddenly not being funny, of being able to work a crowd and then seeing 1,000 people staring at you in complete disappointment.

It's not just the shame of it all, either, I'm also worried about the possible economic fallout from this catastrophe. Word quickly spreads if you die on stage as an after-dinner speaker. I've had people on the phone within hours before, chortling away: 'God, did you hear about XXX at the Photojournalism Awards? Booed off stage, total car crash apparently.' By the end of the following day, the whole media world is reverberating from the seismic effects of that speaker's demise, and the one thing they are all agreed on is that he or she must never be booked to speak, ever again. One big high-profile flop on the after-dinner circuit can literally constitute financial suicide, never mind the emotional angst it causes the poor victim.

Mum rang to ask how it had gone.

'God, awful. Just awful. I fell flat on my face.'

'Oh, no … I'm sure it wasn't that bad…'

'Mum, there were 1,000 people jeering me by the end, it was horrible.'

There was nothing even she could say to make things any better.

I emailed Dylan to apologise. 'One day you're the cock of the walk, the next you're a feather duster. Sorry for being such a fucking duster last night, mate.

'At least I read the awards out properly and didn't hit anyone.'

He replied instantly: 'You were great, and they were a bunch of churlish cunts, but then, they are journalists after all.'

Just as I was recovering, I remembered it was the *Press Gazette*'s inaugural Hall of Fame party tonight, Matthew's clever idea to get all the great and good of Fleet Street under one roof for a few drinks, and honour the Top 40 of our lifetime.

After last night's disaster I spent most of the day dreading it. The media world would be chortling over my performance.

But it wasn't as bad as I thought.

The turn-out was impressive – virtually every editor, a sprinkling of proprietors, and most of the leading reporters, photographers, subs, columnists and commentators. As well as every diarist, including Miss Celia Walden, wearing the most magnificent boots I think I've ever seen.

We had a chat, and I introduced her to Roger Alton, the editor of the *Observer*.

'Ah, Roger, this is Celia Walden. I'm going to marry her one day.'

A quite bizarre thing to say given that I am still married and know almost nothing about her.

'What on earth did you say that for?' She laughed.

'I've no idea. You just tick all the right boxes, I guess.'

She grimaced. 'If you ever use the phrase "tick the right boxes" with me again, then the phrase "hasta la vista" will come into play, my friend. Now get me another glass of champagne and we'll pretend you never said it.'

She was right, it was a truly awful phrase, albeit perfectly apt in this particular case.

6

23 November

Celia Walden emailed to thank me for the party and express her sincere hope that I'd now recovered from my ridiculous marriage outburst, pointing out that there was 'less than zero' chance of this ever happening.

'Overconfident predictions are always a little tricky,' I replied. 'General Custer's last words from the brow of a hill during the Battle of Little Bighorn were, "Don't worry, chaps, they'll never hit us from … BANG."'

She then reminded me that she is due to pose next week for a series of scantily clad photographs for *GQ*, due to be published in two months' time, and I am penning some words to go with them.

I suggested dinner at The Ivy to conduct the interview.

'Fine, leave it to me,' she said confidently.

24 November

The very last thing I want to be doing today is the Hair Journalism Awards. It had seemed a cakewalk when I accepted the booking last month, now it represents possibly the most terrifying hour of my life. Seasoned speakers will all tell you that everyone dies some of the time, it's an occupational hazard, but my confidence is shattered and the pressure to perform is suddenly immense. I spent the whole morning honing my speech and changing gags that had always gone down well until Monday night. Then I sat through the one-hour lunch barely eating, trying to concentrate on how to ensure I was funny. The audience was 95 per cent female, and they all seemed to be in a nice relaxed mood, in direct contrast to the seething cesspit that the BSME became by 10 o'clock at night.

I was introduced at about 2p.m., cracked a quick gag, everyone laughed and I felt a massive rush of relief race through me. There were only a dozen or so awards, interspersed with the odd quip here and there from me as requested. It all went perfectly and they said they'd like to invite me back next year. And suddenly I don't feel quite as bereft about this speaking lark as I did yesterday. I floated out of the Berkeley Hotel on the kind of high you get after a particularly good massage.

25 November

Sat next to Geoff Miller at a cricket dinner in Birmingham tonight. He's a former England player and is now the leading after-dinner speaker on the cricket circuit. I regaled him with my BSME tale of woe and he laughed.

'Don't worry about that, mate. It's an occupational hazard. It's happened to me loads of times, usually when you least expect it. I spoke to the Barbados Tourist Board once and it was a total disaster. Absolutely terrible, and for no apparent reason. It comes out of the blue, and it happens to everyone. You just have to dust yourself down and forget about it, because if you try and rationalise it you'll go mad.'

I asked how he had honed his act over the years to try and avoid DOYA (Dying On Your Arse) syndrome.

He chuckled: 'The trick is to take the piss out of yourself. People love it if you call yourself useless, and it stops them doing it to you as well because they feel sorry for you!'

I watched 'Dusty' Miller – who does 250 lucrative gigs a year up and down the country – speak later that evening and he was brilliantly self-deprecating. His whole act revolved around stories that made him look, well, useless. And the audience lapped it up. I made a mental note to adapt my own act accordingly. Shouldn't be too hard…

27 November

I was hoping I'd got away with the BSME fiasco in terms of media coverage, but someone called Emma Duncan, who is apparently the deputy editor of the *Economist*, wrote a touching tribute to my performance in the *Sunday Telegraph* today: 'Some speakers are virtuous but dull; some are entertaining but nasty. Piers Morgan was unusual, in that he combined dullness with nastiness. I say this without malice, but with the express purpose of reducing his market value to the point where he gives up and nobody again has to sit through what we did.' The words 'without malice' made me laugh out loud, as did the sheer absurdity of being lectured on being entertaining by anyone from the *Economist*.

The *Independent*'s John Walsh did an amusing piece on the Hall of Fame party, in which he wrote, 'The *Telegraph*'s ridiculously beautiful diarist, Celia

Walden, confronted veteran scallywag Richard Compton-Miller, who had written scathingly of her talents, and left him expiring with *l'amour*.'

28 November

Lunch with Michael Parkinson today, and he didn't cancel.

I emailed Celia from the taxi to congratulate her on the 'ridiculously beautiful' compliment, and to enquire how she was getting on with booking our dinner.

'My "ridiculous beauty" doesn't seem to hold much sway with The Ivy receptionist, I'm afraid,' she replied. 'They've said they'll try and get us in, but they're fully booked at the moment.'

'Relax,' I said. 'I'm having lunch there with Parky today, as you do if you're a media luvvie arse, and will not leave until I have secured us the best table commensurate with your status as the most ridiculously beautiful woman in Fleet Street.'

I met Parky at 1p.m. and immediately ordered a very expensive bottle of Montrachet, as requested, then apologised for being such a sensitive little goon. Parky laughed it off. 'Honestly, you of all people shouldn't believe what you read, Piers...'

He's a splendid lunch companion – witty, indiscreet, highly opinionated and surprisingly profane. 'That man,' he said, referring to a well-known sports journalist, 'is a fucking idiot.'

We laughed about Meg Ryan and her diabolical performance on his show recently, where she clearly didn't want to be there and had zero sense of humour.

'I don't understand these people. If they don't want to do the show, then don't do it, but if you're going to come on, then the least you can do is fucking speak!'

'When did you realise it was going wrong?'

'Oh, when she started being defensive and you could sense the audience getting embarrassed. I could taste it! And then you get quite excited, because you know that although it's toe-curling, it's also great television. I was desperately trying to think of a way out of it, so eventually I reminded her that she had wanted to be a journalist before she became an actress, and she muttered, "Yeah." So I asked what she would have done if she was doing this particular interview right now and she said, "I'd wrap it up." You have to laugh, honestly...'

Parky asked me about the *Mirror* sacking, and I told him that Sly Bailey had lost her bottle, which was one of the perils of working for a weak PLC boss and not a billionaire proprietor.

At that precise moment I saw a mane of blonde hair and large breasts bouncing towards us. Of course it was Sly.

I stood up and kissed her on both cheeks, and she blushed slightly as she saw who I was dining with. Sly's always been embarrassingly star-struck. I remember her meeting Gordon Brown at the *Mirror* centenary party and almost having an orgasm as she stood there shaking his hand, then sending me a text message minutes later saying, 'I'm LOVING meeting Gordon!!!'

Not quite the way Rupert Murdoch behaves with senior politicians.

'Michael, this is Sly; Sly, this is Michael.'

Parky stood up and shook her hand graciously.

'I was just telling Michael how you stabbed me in the back,' I said.

She blushed even more furiously.

'Oh I didn't do that...'

We exchanged pleasantries for a couple of minutes before she tottered off to her lunch date. Parky loved the whole encounter.

As I settled the bill, I remembered my interview dinner date with Ms Walden and summonsed Mitchell Everard, The Ivy's brilliant general manager.

'Mitch, what are the chances of getting a table for dinner on Thursday night?'

'How important is it?'

'It's vital. I've promised a ridiculously beautiful woman called Celia Walden, who does the *Telegraph*'s Spy column, that I can get the best table after she was told you were full up. It's ostensibly for a magazine interview, but I think I'd quite like to marry her, too.'

'Right, well this sounds like an emergency, leave it to me.'

He returned two minutes later.

'OK, you're on for 8p.m., and it will be a good table, don't worry.'

'You star. If it all works out, you can be an usher, Michael will have to be best man obviously.'

Parky, who himself regularly writes for the *Telegraph* and said he enjoyed reading Spy, chuckled.

'Good work. If that doesn't do the trick, nothing will.'

I got back to my flat and emailed Ms Walden: 'Right, The Ivy is on for 8p.m. Parky sends his love.'

29 November

This could be my last day on earth, because I am due to fly with Sir Alan Sugar over the county of Essex in his little plane. And if he flies like he lives, then I'm in for a bumpy old ride to say the least.

I got to the Brentwood airfield at 11a.m. and it was absolutely freezing cold.

I found the *GQ* team shivering by some small planes outside.

'How's Sir Alan?' I enquired.

'Not happy,' came the reply.

'Oh, leave him to me,' I laughed. 'He hasn't been happy since the day he was born, and even then he was miserable apparently.'

Then the cold, quiet air was infected with a sudden verbal assault: 'Oi, Morgan, you ready to die, then?'

There he was, striding towards me like Stormin' Norman Schwarzkopf in a big brown Biggles jacket and black shades.

'Ah, Sir Alan, a delight as ever. Now this idea about you flying me around, I'm really not sure we need to do that...'

'Bollocks, we're flying,' he growled.

'In what?' I asked.

'In that,' he growled again.

I turned to see a tiny plane.

'That?' I asked, panic rising in my voice.

'*That.*' He nodded. 'A Cirrus SR22-GTS. Now follow me.'

A minute later Sir Alan was clamping me down with an extra tight seatbelt after physically shoving the photographer into the back.

'You've made a will, right?' he cackled.

I was feeling suddenly rather tense. I'm sure he's a very good pilot, but the plane was no bigger than my car.

'It's the ultimate boy's toy,' he said proudly. 'Small but quick. A bit like me.'

He strapped himself in and turned the engine on.

'Right, some safety stuff. If I have a heart attack, you pull this cord, right, then yank it back twice, then it will blow you up out of here, and in the unlikely event you survive you will probably parachute down into a big tree and die anyway.'

I tried to laugh, but no sound was coming from my mouth. I had a sudden craving for tarmac, the tarmac we were about to leave.

'You scared, Morgan?'

He was loving every second of my obvious discomfort, but his cowardice taunts helped me snap out of my doom-laden mood.

'Don't be ridiculous. Come on then, Maverick, let's see if you can manage not to make me the Goose figure in this farce.'

We taxied down the runway with Sir Alan jabbering away to air traffic control like a pro. He'd obviously done this many times before, and knew what he was doing, but still the nagging doubts lurked.

'You know the worst thing about this, don't you?' I shouted as we prepared to take off.

'What's that?'

'If we go down the headline will be ALAN SUGAR DIES IN PLANE CRASH, and I will get a tiny mention on page nine saying, "Also on the plane was disgraced former *Mirror* editor Piers Morgan."'

Sir Alan laughed loudly. 'Quite fucking right, too.'

Once airborne, my fears evaporated quite quickly. Sir Alan's a very good pilot and seemed to take it very, very seriously, which is no bad thing when you have other people's lives literally in your hands.

We sailed high above the Essex countryside, down to the coast at Clacton; it was a clear day and the views were incredible.

'I love it up here,' he said, looking more at ease then I'd ever seen him before.

'Nobody can bother you, there are no phones or faxes or bloody emails. And you can go anywhere you like, there's complete freedom.'

I had to agree, it was an extraordinarily peaceful and enjoyable sensation.

Until we turned round to come back and he announced, 'Right, your turn.'

I laughed hesitantly.

'What do you mean, *my* turn?'

'I mean *your* turn. Start flying.'

I grabbed the stick and began desperately moving it to what I thought was the right place.

'Pull it up – not that much, you twat, down again. Too far, you bloody halfwit.'

And so on. Suffice to say that Sir Alan would not make a great driving instructor.

Eventually I got the hang of it and flew us in a slightly wobbly line back to Brentwood.

With ten minutes to go, he regained control, only to promptly lose sight of a plane that our radar showed us was either right above or below us. I looked at Sir Alan and his lips were pursed in concentration.

'You know where that plane is, right?' I said.

'Course I fucking do.' His lips locked even tighter.

'You don't, do you...?'

'Yes. I. Fucking. Do. Just shut up, Morgan ... now where the fuck is it?'

I craned my neck out of the window but could see nothing. There were a couple of other small planes a mile or so away, but nothing where the radar said there was one.

Sir Alan craned his neck, too, but couldn't see anything either.

'Where is the fucking thing?' he growled.

My early apprehension returned with a vengeance.

Was this it? Was I actually going to die in a plane flown by Sir Alan Sugar?

The incident passed, with no plane appearing anywhere and both of us realising that there hadn't been one after all.

It had been an extremely disconcerting few seconds.

We landed a few minutes later and he looked disconsolate.

'What's the matter?' I asked.

'I've failed,' he said, shaking his head.

'What do you mean?'

'You're still alive, that's what.'

1 December

Dinner with Celia Walden at The Ivy.

A very entertaining evening was enlivened by the usual weird ragbag mix of people you get in there some nights. Louis Walsh and Kate Thornton from *X Factor* were at different tables, with Margaret Thatcher stuck in the middle of them with her former chief of staff, Charles Powell. And Salman Rushdie in the corner. Now you don't see that little group in the same room every day of the week.

As the wine slid down, my vocal cords flexed up. And by the time Lady T made her exit, I was ready for a chat.

She'd been my political heroine as a young man, the only Tory I have ever voted for. I still have a signed photo of her congratulating me on winning a nuclear disarmament debate at Lewes Priory Sixth Form College. I was arguing the anti-CND 'we must have a deterrent' side. I'd met her once, at a Rupert Murdoch drinks party in 1994 when I was editor of the *News of the World*, and she'd been just how I hoped she'd be: opinionated, argumentative, finger-wagging and commendably inebriated on vast tumblers of Scotch.

Recent rumours suggested she was a shadow of her former self, suffering various debilitating ailments, including ongoing torment from her teeth and slightly losing her marbles since her husband Denis had died.

She looked fine to me, though, and as she walked past, I stood up and offered my hand.

'Lady Thatcher, Piers Morgan, how nice to see you again.'

'Ah yes, hello.'

'We last met at Rupert Murdoch's flat when I was editor of the *News of the World*.'

'Yes, I know who you are.'

I had no way of knowing if she really knew who I was, but she pretended she did, which was good enough for me. Especially as most of the restaurant was now watching the encounter, many of them, I suspect, hoping that she'd completely blank me.

I introduced Celia.

'She writes the *Telegraph* diary, and I think you know her father, George Walden.'

'Yes, of course.'

Celia and Lady T had a friendly chat before she moved on.

It had been a surreal end to a thoroughly pleasant evening. The only problem was that in all the excitement I completely forgot to ask Celia any questions for *GQ*.

3 December

Morgan and Platell has been canned after three series. I'm not entirely surprised, or that upset. It had a good run – twenty-seven shows – and produced some lively interviews amidst a lot of dross, but in the end we were beaten by the schedule. Going out at 6.30p.m. on a Saturday with a political programme, at the same time as smash hits *X Factor* and *Strictly Come Dancing*, was always going to be an uphill struggle. The ratings for the last show dipped under 400,000, and that's just not good enough.

I can see the headlines now: MORGAN SACKED AGAIN.

4 December

As predicted, news of my latest sacking is met with chortling grave-dancing by the media. Lots of POOR PIERS AXED AGAIN gloating all over the internet. It's slightly dispiriting to see such obvious glee at my departure from the political airwaves, but my only real concern is that it's the Christmas party season and I'm now going to have to spend the next bloody fortnight answering that familiar old question: 'So, what are you doing now?'

5 December

Off to the Hilton in Park Lane, yet again, to speak at the Lord's Taverners' Christmas lunch. The Taverners are a bunch of wealthy, famous and eclectic cricket fans who raise small fortunes for charity, and I'd agreed to do the speech for nothing after a personal plea from *Daily Mail* sportswriter Ian Wooldridge, my boyhood journalistic hero.

This annual festive extravaganza usually breaks all known records for alcohol consumption, and after the BSME debacle I was more than a little apprehensive about addressing 1,200 pissed blokes in suits, especially as there were two more speakers coming after me who had been captioned 'comedian' on the menus.

I sat next to David Frost and Chris Tarrant, the latter responding to a gentle enquiry of 'How are you?' by replying rather oddly, 'Fine, apart from the bloody wife causing me grief.'

Richard Stilgoe, the songwriter and former *That's Life* star, must have picked up on my rather too obvious anxiety, because he scribbled a note and passed it round the table to me.

'Fear not,' it read, 'you are among friends.'

Then it added, 'You are also an anagram of Morag R Penis, A Sperm Groin, Minor Gasper, and Porn's Mirage.'

I looked over and he was gurning away in a slightly uncomfortable manner. A strange fellow.

The speech, though, went well. Mainly because I abandoned my usual script and told a stream of cricket sledging stories, which this kind of audience has heard a thousand times but still finds hilarious.

My personal favourite is the one from tubby Zimbabwe opening batsman Eddo Brandes to Glenn McGrath, after the Australian bowler asked him, 'Hey, Brandes, why are you so fucking fat?'

The answer: 'Because, Glenn, every time I fuck your wife she gives me another biscuit.'

6 December

I accepted an absurdly large fee ages ago to give a speech in Stockholm to celebrate the 175th anniversary of the big Swedish tabloid *Aftonbladet*. It seemed easy money at the time, but since the BSME experience, every speaking engagement seems fraught with danger and possible humiliation. In this case, massive ruddy alarm bells were sounding all round my head.

If my magical anecdotes had bombed in front of a British media audience, what was the chance of them working in front of a Scandinavian one?

I'd been assured that they all spoke good English and loved hearing about Diana, the Blairs and celebrities, but then I'd been pretty confident that British journalists would like them, too, and been proven hideously wrong.

I hit Google for inspiration, and found it in the name of Lars Johan Hierta, pioneer of the free press in Sweden and founder editor-in-chief of *Aftonbladet* from 1830 to 1851. He was a fearless, buccaneering editor who dared to take on the then King, Johan XIV, who he claimed ruled with a 'bedchamber government', and fought for free trade and freedom of expression, lower taxes, mass public education and a properly democratically elected parliament. He was prosecuted five times, the ruling classes loathed him, but he was loved by the working class populus.

When I reached the venue for my speech, I sat in my seat, looked up at the stage and saw huge photographs of Lars Johan Hierta everywhere. Whenever I mentioned his name, the audience erupted into applause, and by the time I'd finished my eulogy to Lars, they would happily have given me the freedom of Stockholm.

After that, the Diana, Blair and Sven-Goran Eriksson stories went down brilliantly.

The whole thing reinforced some cardinal rules about public speaking: know your audience, flatter them, show you've done some research into their event and don't ever assume you will automatically be funny – because you won't be.

After me, a Russian journalist called Anna Politkovskaya got up to speak. She was small, quietly spoken and seemed rather dull until she started telling us about her life investigating Putin's government and reporting from the front line in Chechnya. Then she became completely compelling.

'I've had many death threats,' she said. 'But they will never shut me up. The Russian people, and the world, need to hear the truth.'

I chatted to her afterwards and discovered that, despite a life spent dodging bullets and bombs in the name of journalism, she is also the mother of two young children. She was an extraordinary woman, who left me profoundly moved by the job she does and the astonishing determination and courage she displays while doing it.

7 December

Bertie had his first nativity play at his big school today, and I got there just in time.

Expectation levels after his last few theatrical performances were not high, but he came out all in white, with a halo on his head, and sang with great gusto while clasping his hands firmly together in a permanent state of prayer.

Bertie has become, against all expectations, a little angel.

8 December

Spoke to Celia today to try and rearrange our interview. 'It's my birthday,' she said. 'And I'm going to Le Caprice to celebrate.'

'Sounds good. Who with?' I don't know why I asked that.

'Ed Victor, my literary agent.'

Impressive. Ed, to many in the publishing business, is *the* literary agent.

'What are you doing with him?'

'A novel.'

'What about?'

'Oh, a beautiful bitch from Paris who ruins everyone's lives.'

'Autobiographical then?'

'Of course.'

I was just leaving the flat to get the train to Bristol for *Question Time* when I noticed it was 1.15p.m.

I called Le Caprice.

'Hi, it's Piers Morgan here, I understand Celia Walden is dining with you today?'

'Yes, Mr Morgan, she is.'

'Splendid. Now what's the best bottle of champagne you have on your menu?'

'We have a very good Krug, sir?'

'Sounds good. Can you take a bottle over to Ms Walden with the message, "*Bon Anniversaire, avec mes felicitations*, Piers."'

The reception manager chuckled.

'Of course.'

Took the train down to Bristol to appear on *Question Time*. They'd stuck all the guests in a block of seats together, which was slightly awkward given that I wanted to spend the journey preparing notes on how to savage them all.

Jenny Willott from the Liberal Democrats looked slightly terrified, which was hardly surprising since it was was her first *QT*.

George Osborne, the shadow chancellor, was late onto the train and groaned when he saw me waiting in the next seat.

'Oh God, as if my day wasn't bad enough,' he laughed. He'd been leading the news after Labour rebel Dennis Skinner got thrown out of the House of Commons for observing about the Tory handling of the economy in the Eighties: 'The only thing that was growing then was the lines of coke in front of Boy George and the rest of the Tories.'

I picked up the late edition of the *Standard* and showed him the front page, which screamed the story.

'Bloody Skinner,' he said, still laughing. If that had been a Labour minister, there would definitely have been no laughter. The impressive thing about these Tories is the way they take this kind of thing in their stride. How you handle a crisis is perhaps the most important thing any politician can learn.

'I hope you don't get too overexcited tonight, Piers,' Osborne said as we ordered coffee.

'Oh don't worry, George, I'm just going to very calmly carve you up like a kipper.' He seemed notably unaffected by my threat.

Two hours later we were sitting next to each other in front of millions of viewers as we waited for the first question.

The EU rebate. Fuck. It was the one subject I'd hoped wouldn't come up, so naturally it did. I stumbled through a lengthy, rambling and not very intelligent answer, then Osborne responded by having a go at Blair for surrendering part of the rebate, and I got a little carried away, saying it was pretty rich for him to criticise Blair given that Thatcher had opposed it to start with.

He looked at me in bemusement.

'What do you mean? Lady Thatcher was the one who got the rebate in the first place.'

I froze. He was right, she had. I'd got it completely, utterly, 100 per cent wrong. I could feel myself blushing furiously. What the hell could I do to get out of this? I just sat there in silence, preferring to say nothing than try to wriggle my way out of it.

It was excruciatingly embarrassing. The only possible escape clause being that very few people at home would probably have any idea what we were talking about, so my stupidity would only be revealed to the political types.

Osborne smirked; he knew he'd got me and he knew he'd got me in the first round. I was on the back foot and praying for Iraq to come up. That was always my banker question because every *Question Time* audience gets very heated about it and always agrees with me.

Fortunately it did, and I was able to launch into my usual soundbite-heavy rant about the mayhem we've caused with the fatuous War on Terror. The audience howled their agreement and the EU rebate clanger seemed forgotten.

The last question was a funny about whether we agreed with those people who splatter their houses in absurdly over-the-top Christmas lights.

'No,' I said. 'They should all get ASBOs.' The audience fell about, the show ended and I could relax.

We had the usual dinner with David Dimbleby afterwards and not a single person mentioned the EU rebate mistake. Nor did I get any texts or emails about it. It was as if it had never happened. Quite bizarre.

Dinner was fun, mainly because we spent most of the time taunting Osborne about the pictures in the *News of the World* of him with a black hooker and suspicious-looking white powder all over the table.

'It wasn't what it seemed,' protested George to general laughter.

'No,' I said. 'I suspect it was a lot worse.'

To his credit, George giggled loudly.

9 December

Woke up to the news that the CPS will not be prosecuting the soldier charged with faking the *Mirror* photos that got me sacked.

They said there was 'insufficient evidence for a realistic prospect of conviction', so he's an innocent, free man, and nobody has been successfully convicted of hoaxing us.

I got a few calls throughout the day from various papers and radio stations, but nobody seems too bothered by this extraordinary twist in the ongoing 'hoax' saga.

I feel a little irritated by the apathy. If this guy didn't take them, who did?

Even more curiously, I later learn that he is likely to be a chief prosecution witness in the trial of a number of soldiers facing court cases in connection with the death of an Iraqi civilian, Baha Mousa – all of them from the Queen's Lancashire Regiment, the same regiment the *Mirror* accused of abusing Iraqi civilians.

Interviewed Faria Alam this afternoon for *You Can't Fire Me, I'm Famous*. She was the secretary who got stiffed by the Football Association after stiffing Sven.

I expected to loathe her, but she was quite fun when she stopped feeling sorry for herself. And quite sexy too. I could see why Sven got so over-excited.

10 December

Last summer I painted my flat balcony a rather fetching Moroccan red to go with a table and chairs I bought in Marrakesh. Everyone who has seen it thinks it's great, and creates a suitably Kasbah-ish feel to an otherwise extremely anodyne white-walled area. Technically, you're supposed to keep the balconies white so we all look exactly the same, but nobody's complained and frankly, who the hell wants to look exactly the same as all their neighbours anyway?

Nobody in my block can see my balcony, you'd have to be virtually in the river to do that. But, there's always one, isn't there?

An anonymous typed letter was stuck through my flat door today saying, 'Mr Morgan, during a recent television programme, you said that people who install Christmas lights and decorations that annoy their neighbours should be given ASBOs. What about people who deface buildings in contravention of the terms of their lease? Please paint your balcony white, as it should be. I have recorded the TV programme in question and will happily send it to the press, together with a photograph of your ghastly red balcony.'

I read it twice and laughed out loud. What a pathetic, cowardly, petty little piece of neighbourly nonsense.

I could see the headlines now: SHAMED MORGAN IN NEW RED BALCONY OUTRAGE.

13 December

I appeared on the *Today* programme on Radio 4 with Amanda Platell and Greg Dyke, the subject being, 'Who runs Britain'.

Iraq came up in discussion and I said, 'It's an absolute farce that the only people who have lost their jobs over Iraq are me, Andrew Gilligan, Gavyn Davies and Greg Dyke. If it's MI5 that's behind it they should all get promotions and pay rises. They can't find weapons of mass destruction, but by God, they can get media people out of their jobs.'

Just as I was getting on my high horse, James Naughtie jumped me with a question about the City Slickers trial.

I'd been expecting it, and launched an equally impassioned defence on that, too, pointing out once again that I hadn't been prosecuted, was not facing trial and could therefore reasonably expect to be considered innocent of any crime.

This evening I was jumped again, this time by Melvyn Bragg during a Q&A session after a speech I gave to a high-powered media society called the 30 Club.

He harangued me about the fake photos, so I harangued him back, going over the whole story in detail. How we'd given the MoD the photos at midday, how they'd never made a murmur about authenticity, how nobody has yet been found guilty of 'faking' the photos and how compelling evidence has emerged of much worse abuse by rogue British soldiers against Iraqi civilians.

Melvyn, who I see at Arsenal occasionally, came up to me afterwards and said, 'That was a very powerful defence, congratulations.' So was his hand-shake, quite the biggest bonecrusher I've had in a long time.

Nevertheless, on days like this I feel under permanent attack. I have got to find something that changes the agenda, that stops people banging on about the past and allows me to move on from being an ex-tabloid editor.

14 December

Simon Cowell rang. 'Hi, Piers, good news. ITV want to do the Paul O'Grady talent show, and they want you as a judge. We're going to announce it tomorrow.'

'That's great, Simon.'

And it is. I'm thrilled. This will be my first prime-time TV break in Britain, and it'll be one in the eye for all the critics who've written off my TV career since *Morgan and Platell* was canned. It's also right up my street – judging talent, battling my wits with a live audience and being centre stage again.

Met Celia again for a second attempt at interviewing her for *GQ*.

We dined at Marco Pierre White's new place Luciano, and spent another two hours laughing but forgetting to actually do the interview.

'Do you want to come to a party?' she said as we got the bill.

'Yes, OK. Whose is it?'

'The *Telegraph* features department.'

'You're joking, aren't you? That's like Hannibal Lecter turning up at Sandringham for afternoon tea.'

'It'll be hilarious. Come on.' And I was whisked off down the road to a Soho bar.

As we walked in I could feel an icy chill blast through the room. Heads turning, then frowning. Urgent, muttered whispers. The general gist seemed to be as I'd predicted: 'What on earth is *he* doing here?'

But Celia found it all terribly amusing and led me round, introducing me to various subs and writers.

Just when I was beginning to settle in, we were off again, this time to the *OK!* magazine Christmas party. We got there in a fairly inebriated state to find what can only be described as an 'interesting' assortment of characters.

'There are supposed to be loads of big stars here,' Celia said.

I spotted Vanessa Feltz.

We had a glass of champagne and decided to move on quickly.

'Let's go to Tramp,' I suggested. I've been a member there for years but only go once every six months or so.

There were no taxis outside, but there was a man in a rickshaw.

It was freezing, but it was better than walking and Tramp wasn't far away. As we sped off, several photographers gave chase, 'papping' us in the back of the rickshaw. It was turning into an amusing night.

We drank more champagne in Tramp, then called it a day.

'We forgot the interview,' I said.

'Oops,' she replied.

15 December

News of the talent show broke this morning. PIERS MORGAN TO JUDGE ITV TALENT SHOW was the *MediaGuardian* headline. Within minutes I started getting congratulatory texts and emails. This could be massive, I can feel it in my bones.

Being a judge on a show like this is one of the hottest gigs in TV at the moment. Everyone knows what it did for Simon Cowell, and I can't pretend that I wouldn't absolutely love it to do the same for me.

I spent the afternoon Christmas shopping in the King's Road, or more accurately, wandering aimlessly around trying to find something, *anything*, to buy people. I loathe shopping with a passion. It's such a senseless, dull, tiring and ultimately expensive thing to do. I can't wait for all shopping to be done on the internet, so I never have to walk around real shops again.

I walked into Waterstones to check out the Christmas books, and as I did so, one of the managers came rushing up to me.

'Hello, sir, how wonderful to have you in the store.'

'Oh, thanks very much.'

'Would you mind signing some copies of your book while you're here, sir?'

My chest puffed with pride.

'No, not at all.'

This happens quite a lot – eagle-eyed book-store managers spot authors (usually checking to see where their own tomes are placed) and ask them to sign a load of books they can then sell as 'signed by the author'.

I followed the manager downstairs, but rather than take me to the biography department, we headed into the gardening section.

'Now then...' he said, hesitating slightly. 'It's ... um ... I'm so sorry, what was the title again?'

I laughed. 'Well it's not in the gardening section, mate, I can tell you that for sure.'

He blushed. 'Oh, right...'

'Who do you think I am, if you don't mind me asking?'

'You're Diarmuid Gavin, aren't you?'

Christ, so *that's* who they all think I am. Not Alan Titchmarsh.

'No, I'm not.'

'Oh. Well who are you then?'

'I'm Piers Morgan.'

Pause.

'Oh God, I'm so sorry.'

Another pause as he collected his thoughts.

'Well, since you're down here, would you mind signing some copies of your book, Mr Morgan?'

I got home to find an email from Conor at the *Mirror*:

'Mate, I'm just looking at a series of pictures of you on our browser. You're in a rickshaw. In Wardour Street. With a "mystery blonde" in red boots. Explain, please.'

16 December

Christmas drinks at Matthew Freud and Liz Murdoch's sumptuous Notting Hill pad. You know what you're going to get with those two – amusing, influential guests, magnificent wine and at least three or four 'incidents' that will have the London media scene reverberating with shockwaves for at least a week. Tonight was a lively party, even by their standards. I took Celia as my guest, a decision I regretted almost immediately as Jamie Theakston reeled drunkenly into view the moment we arrived, announced he had been for a nine-hour lunch with Simon Kelner and placed his hand on Celia's right buttock in a commendably shameless declaration of lustful intent.

I like Jamie, but his seduction technique is like his batting – aggressive and with a careless disregard for his own (and anybody else's) wicket.

A steaming drunk Jamie Theakston is not the man you want to see seconds after arriving at a glamorous party with a woman you might quietly be trying to impress.

Sure enough, he spent the next thirty minutes pursuing Celia around the party like a hyena on heat, lunging indiscriminately towards her body at frequent intervals and trying to drag her into various side rooms. It was, to put it mildly, an unedifying spectacle.

Celia, to her credit, fended him off as best she could, but although we were there together in a purely platonic capacity, I could feel the red mist rapidly descending, and concluded that I should quietly leave before doing something I might regret.

I passed Matthew on the way out and explained, 'Sorry, mate, but unless you want Theakston's blood all over your nice carpets, I'm out of here.'

My last sight as I walked out was Theakston physically pulling a startled Celia towards him and whispering not so sweet leerings in her ear.

Once outside I marched off down Ladbroke Terrace feeling decidedly pissed off. There is something very beguiling about Celia, and it has this weird effect on the male species that renders most of them instant dribbling letches.

As I turned the corner, I heard the sound of running feet and turned to find Celia looking bemused and upset.

'Where are you going?' she asked.

'Oh, sorry, you must have mistaken me for a guy who likes watching his guest be groped and fondled all night by a slavering twat like Jamie Theakston.'

'It's not my fault,' she said quite reasonably.

'No, I know. It's just embarrassing, so I would rather not have to stand there watching, to be honest.'

It was bloody freezing and we were both shivering.

'Will you come back in with me?'

'What's the point?'

'I'd like you to. Jamie's just drunk, ignore him.'

He was and I should.

'OK, but any more of that nonsense and I'm definitely out of here.'

We walked back in to a low-level murmuring. Word had quickly spread about some sort of incident, but nobody was quite sure what it was, other than the fact that raised voices had been heard in the street.

I headed to the bar, where I bumped into Gordon Ramsay.

'I hear Theakston's been trying to pull Celia,' he said.

'Hmm. Trying is the word.'

'Are you two an item then?'

'No, no. Just friends.'

'Oh yeah,' cackled Ramsay.

At that moment Theakston reappeared from the garden and saw Celia next to me at the bar; his predatory eyes lit up and he pounced again.

As his hand headed towards her, I grabbed it in full flight.

'I don't think so.'

Theakston stared at me, barely able to focus. 'What's it got to do with you?' he slurred.

'She's my guest, that's what. And if you touch her one more time I'm going to touch you, and not in a way that you'll enjoy. *Comprende, amigo*?'

Ramsay appeared at my shoulder, laughing loudly. 'Go on, hit him,' he goaded. 'I'll be here if you need any help.'

Theakston weighed up his options.

'Jamie, I mean it. Just leave her alone or you'll regret it.'

I was behaving like a jealous boyfriend when I barely knew the girl.

'*Hit* him,' cried Ramsay, loving every second.

Theakston stumbled, then grinned maniacally, blew Celia a spittal-fuelled kiss and headed back to the garden.

The crisis was averted. I didn't really want to hit him, because I knew by the morning he'd be sober and mortified and we'd always got on well.

'Thank you,' said Celia. 'You're my knight in shining armour.'

Ramsay was devastated. 'Fuck it! I was looking forward to a big fight there, what a shame.'

In one of those surreal evolutions you only experience at parties like this, I turned away to find myself face-to-face with David Cameron and George Osborne, the two likely lads of the rejuvenated Tory party.

'Ah, gentlemen, what a nice surprise.'

Cameron was instantly charming, and not in that laboured Blairite I-want-to-be-your-best-friend-for-a-while way. He just seemed nice and normal and smart.

'When are you going to come back to the Conservatives then?' he asked.

'When you guys sort your act out,' I replied. 'Which to be fair may not be very long the way things are going.'

'You could be our attack dog against New Labour,' said Osborne, mischievously. 'You must dislike them almost as much as we do now.'

I laughed. 'I rather like that idea. You could stick me in a cage, feed me raw meat and unleash me on some cabinet minister in the afternoon.'

Cameron and Osborne exchanged a quick glance.

'Erm, seriously, you should think about publicly renouncing Labour and coming back to us.'

They're quick thinkers, I'll give them that. They didn't really want me working for them, that would be madness on both sides, but an ex-*Mirror* editor defecting to their side right now would be a useful piece of propaganda.

'Well, let's see if you've got any policies first, shall we?'

They laughed, easily and confidently. 'Oh we will, don't worry.'

I liked them. They have a freshness and candour about them that's impressive, especially in contrast to Labour's paranoid wrecks.

'Blair saying he won't fight the next election was a massive own goal,' I said. 'It means you can effectively campaign for the next three years, while whoever takes over from him has just a few months. Momentum is everything in politics, you could win if you play it right and keep your noses clean.'

Osborne groaned. He knew what I was getting at.

18 December

A fascinating email arrived this afternoon from Sarah Botham:

'Year 1981

'1. Prince Charles got married

'2. Liverpool crowned soccer Champions of Europe

'3. Australia lost the Ashes

'4. Pope Died

'Year 2005

'1. Prince Charles got married

'2. Liverpool crowned soccer Champions of Europe

'3. Australia lost the Ashes

'4. Pope Died

'PS In the future, if Prince Charles decides to remarry, please warn the Pope.'

20 December

GQ's annual Christmas lunch at Vogue House is always the most riotous party of the season.

Simon Kelner made a funny speech ridiculing Dylan for his relentless in-magazine plugs for his favourite fashion designers, the outrageous suggestion being that Mr Jones ends up with a permanently free wardrobe from his grateful benefactors. Dylan cheerfully admitted it, and why not? The best advert these guys could ever have is the editor of *GQ* wearing their clothes, and Dylan's far too fashion conscious to wear anything but the very best.

As the afternoon wore on, a splinter group sidled off to Dylan's office, where he had a huge revolving chair in the corner.

Tracey Emin was there, off her head as usual.

I sensed a commercial opportunity.

'Any chance of doing me a few quick doodles?' I asked.

'Why?' she said, immediately and rightly suspicious of my motives.

'I collect art,' I replied unconvincingly.

'Do you fuck,' she scoffed. 'You just want to sell 'em on eBay, don't you?'

She'd got me in one.

'Well, I'm hardly going to hang your filth on my wall now am I, Trace?'

'You little sponging git. Fuck off.'

21 December

Lunch at Cecconi's with *Mirror* boys Richard Wallace and Conor. Around 4p.m., a waiter came over and said he'd like to offer us a glass each of 1957 Calvados on behalf of the restaurant's new owner, Nick 'Soho House' Jones.

We beamed with delight and tucked in greedily.

'Would you like another?' he then asked. It was at that point that a slight misunderstanding crept into the conversation.

'We'd love to, thanks.'

Fifteen more 1957 Calvados £30-a-shot glasses later, things were getting a little blurry all round.

But not blurry enough for the bill to be illegible to our drunken eyes.

Food – £175

Drink – £475

'Erm, we thought the Calvados was on the house?' Conor slurred.

'Yesh,' Richard and I agreed.

The waiter looked bemused.

'No, no, just the first one.'

We toyed with calling Nick Jones to see if he would bail us out with his legendary largesse, but decided we weren't sober enough to make any sense on the phone, so paid up and staggered into the night.

23 December

Sometimes I love my life.

My 'work' today involved going to a large suite at the Dorchester and interviewing the supermodel Rachel Hunter for two hours for *You Can't Fire Me, I'm Famous*.

She was smarter, funnier and a lot sexier than I thought she'd be, and we had a great laugh romping through her life with Rod Stewart, Robbie Williams, and the rest.

Rachel hit me three times with a pillow during the grilling, but as I told her: 'You're just playing hard to get.'

It was a fun, revelatory, entertaining chat, perfect for the 10.35p.m. slot. I think Mr Fincham will like it.

28 December

The *Daily Mail* have sent me on another travel feature, this time to Bahrain. I took the boys, Rupert and his girlfriend Chloe. We flew over in BA's new business class seats, which now face each other. This, as I soon discovered, can be a little disconcerting when watching a slightly risqué film like *The 40-Year-Old Virgin* with your twelve-year-old son. Catching Spencer's eye after 'gags' like, 'You know how I know you're gay? You have a rainbow bumper sticker on your car that says, "I like it when balls are in my face,"' is not the most comfortable experience I've ever had as a father.

The villa we were staying in was so massive I thought for a moment that we'd uncovered a new United Arab Emirate. And it came with a charming Indonesian man called Samsul, our 24-hour 'lifestyle' butler, which appears to be a modern euphemism for 'slave'.

The trouble with little children, however, is that they watch too much TV, and just as Samsul and the three other members of staff who had just arrived waited for us to express our joy, Bertie performed his favourite *Little Britain* impression: 'Don't like it.'

There was an uncomfortable silence. 'Bertie, sssshhh,' I stammered. 'Of course you like it.'

He grinned, shook his head and repeated very slowly: 'Don't. Like. It.'

Poor Samsul looked on the verge of tears, so I escorted Bertie, by his ear, to bed.

29 December

We woke at 9a.m. to find a sumptuous breakfast awaiting us. Plates of fruit, fry-ups, pancakes, freshly ground coffee, juices.

Bertie took one look at it and said, 'Don't like it.'

By now Samsul was in on the joke, so no further damage was done.

We watched the Arsenal game on TV tonight, and a commentator absurdly said that my least favourite Arsenal player of all time – the stupefyingly untalented, bald French imbecile Pascal Cygan – was 'at the centre of things'.

Stanley observed firmly and hilariously, 'Dad, Cygan should never, and I emphasise the word "never", be the centre of *anything*.'

30 December

Nothing, it appears, is going to be too much trouble for Samsul. I woke at 8a.m. today to hear the following conversation: 'Hi, Samsul, it's Stanley. Please could we have a football, the *Wedding Crashers* DVD and some Coke. Thanks.'

Rupert later rather exceeded the spirit of the relationship, I thought, when he rang to request nailclippers, but Samsul reacted as if this was the least humiliating thing he had ever had to provide.

The only spanner in the works of this earthly paradise came when Spencer discovered there was a German family staying next door and immediately hid our football, explaining, 'You can't be too careful with the Germans, Dad.' Later in the day he declined an offer to play a match against them, saying, 'England beat them 5:1 recently, for God's sake – it's an insult to me that any German could contemplate playing football with me after that.'

Where do they get this stuff from? As their father was the man who wrote the notorious headline ACHTUNG SURRENDER, I may not have far to look.

31 December

I took the boys to dinner in the main hotel tonight, and as it was a trek of at least, oh, 1,000 yards, Samsul insisted on driving us there in a golf buggy. It was nearly dark, and as we approached a back door leading up to the restaurant I didn't notice that another buggy was right behind us, containing another family.

Stanley suddenly dropped his voice to an urgent stage whisper.

'*Dad* … it's Carol Vorderman.'

I laughed at his obvious wind-up and walked on.

'*Dad* … it really *is* Carol Vorderman.'

Stanley never repeats the same wind-up twice in quick succession, he hasn't got the patience.

I turned my head very slowly and saw Carol sitting on the other buggy, dressed like the Queen of Sheba in her later years. Next to her was Des Kelly, my oh-so-loyal former deputy at the *Mirror*, and they were accompanied by Carol's children.

I hadn't seen either of them since *The Insider* came out, though I'd heard that Des threw a tantrum on finding a copy of the book in the *Daily Mail* newsroom, where he now writes a sports column again, and had tossed it out of a window.

My description of them as the 'Harry Redknapp and Tina Turner' of journalism had not gone down well, apparently, so anything could happen now.

It was just my buggy and their buggy, their butler and my butler, Carol's kids and my kids.

Spencer was all for having a fight right there in the foyer. He holds quite deep grudges against all those he has concluded were disloyal to me over the *Mirror* sacking, and Des Kelly would be just below Sly Bailey on his hit list.

I didn't know what to do. It was such a totally bizarre coincidence.

Kelly bounded off his buggy like a hyperactive puppy and held out a hand, and for some inexplicable reason I shook it, to Spencer's visible disgust.

Carol ignored me completely, marching ahead with her nose in the air, playing the indignant hard-done-by victim. It was a hilariously pompous performance, even by her standards.

They walked on as Spencer and Stanley dissolved in fits of laughter.

'That was *so* funny, Dad,' Stan spluttered.

And he was right, it had been. What made it even funnier was that they'd always been so pathetically paranoid about anyone knowing where they were going on holiday. Even I, his editor, wasn't allowed to be told. For fear, I suspect, that the paparazzi might catch Carol without make-up and airbrushing, and put a slight dampener on any more of her cabbage and seaweed diet books.

Spencer's mind was firing away with potential revenge attacks.

'Why don't we take photos of her on the beach and sell them, Dad?'

It was sorely tempting to be that juvenile, but after considering the plan I concluded it would ultimately be self-defeating.

Instead, I chuckled at the knowledge that our encounter will have sent their paranoia levels so high that it will have absolutely ruined their holiday.

3 January 2006

Word of my Vorderman encounter spread quickly, mainly because I told everyone I could think of. Celia's deputy at the *Telegraph*, Jonathan Isaby, called me about it and ran the following quotes from me in today's Spy column:

'Short of finding Jeremy Clarkson and Ian Hislop snorkling in my pool, I can't think of two people I would less want to bump into on holiday.

'Judging by Ms Vorderman's stony little face, she wasn't massively thrilled either. My sons are now prowling the shores with their cameras trying to get paparazzi photos of the "real Carol" on the beach.

'And Spy will, of course, get first glance should they be successful.'

Later in the afternoon my phone rang.

'Hi, is that Des?'

'Sorry?'

'Is that Des Kelly?'

I laughed to myself. 'Erm, who's that?'

'I'm ringing from the *Daily Mail* diary, returning his call.'

'No, this isn't Des. This is Piers.'

Long silence.

'Oh, I see. Gosh, how embarrassing, sorry.'

'It's not embarrassing at all. Thanks for calling.'

Had to queue for an hour at Bahrain airport, behind an appallingly loud and vulgar family from Texas and an even more irritating group of golfers from Berlin.

Rupert, standing beside me, sent me a text: 'Americans and Germans, it's tough to know who to dislike more.'

4 January

The splendid Richard Kay diary in the *Mail* quoted Des Kelly today as saying: 'Morgan's been desperately hoping someone in Bahrain will recognise him. Unsurprisingly they haven't, so he's been reduced to ringing newspapers back home to try and find someone who'll take notice. He told one paper he plans to send his children out to take paparazzi photographs of Carol. Why bother? If the children are anything like their father, they'll just fake them anyway.'

Ooooh, get him...

My amusement was short-lived, though.

The following item appeared in today's *Independent* diary, Pandora: 'Piers Morgan has always been careful to prevent details of his occasionally colourful love life entering the public domain. Until now, that is. For in this week's *Easy Living*, the former red-top editor contributes to an article on that old chestnut: "Does size matter?"'

'Asked about a straw poll of female readers, which suggests that it jolly well does, Morgan comments, "Slightly above average, and with a skilled and energetic technique, will keep any woman happy. Small dicks and huge dicks bring frustration and surgery. That's why I'm so in demand."'

'Hmm. Does anyone out there have reason to disagree?'

I read it and froze in the kind of horror Hugh Grant must have felt when that LAPD officer shone his torch in the car when he was asking Divine Brown for directions to Sunset Boulevard. What the hell was this all about? Then it slowly came back to me ... a few weeks ago I'd taken a call from Rachel Johnson, the equally mischievous sister of Boris, grilling me about this issue for a new magazine column she was doing.

I'd assumed it was all off the record, but sought instant emergency email clarification: 'Erm, Rachel, you didn't actually quote me *direct*, right?'

Half an hour later my humiliating fate was sealed: 'Yes, I did. I thought it was harmless and you knew I was quoting you. Are you angry? Please don't be. I was just showing off that I talk to you.'

I replied: 'Rachel, as you well know I have spent the last eleven years refusing even to admit I have a private life, let alone discuss it in public. Now, thanks to you, the world knows how big my dick is and how massively in demand this supposedly makes me.'

She responded: 'Piers, I am sorry. I was wrong to quote you without checking first. You're right on every count. *Mea culpa*. Thanks for being so, um, big about it.'

I am trying to see the funny side of this, but can only see a potential can of worms of epically embarrassing proportions opening. For years I've advised celebrities never to discuss their private life if they want to have their privacy respected. Now I may as well have taken out an advert in the *Times* inviting every woman I have ever slept with to offer their detailed thoughts on the precise size and performance of my genitalia.

And God knows what Celia will think about it. Boasting about my supposed sexual prowess is hardly the best way to woo a woman, is it? And woo her is what I seem to be subconsciously doing.

My fears have not been allayed by a constant bombardment of texts from amused friends gleefully seeking further 'dick' revelations.

5 January

I was awoken at 7a.m. by the thud of newspapers outside my door. I raced to the *Independent* like a condemned man galloping to the gallows.

My sweaty hands flicked to the Pandora column, where my eyes flashed like lasers until they rested on the words 'Piers' and 'Morgan'.

I read on: 'I noted Piers Morgan's brassy claim – in an interview for *Easy Living* magazine – to be "above average" in the trouser department, with a "skilled and energetic" bedroom technique. Readers with reason to disagree were asked to get in touch, and one of you, who we shall call "Sally", had the good sense to do just that.

'"Due to an unfortunate incident I try to forget, in a hotel room a few years back, I can tell you that Piers is some way off the mark," she writes.

'"For a person of over 6 foot, he was normal, maybe even disappointing, but his real problem was an embarrassing tendency to let himself down at key moments. Piers apologised a lot, but even with help, 'Mister Floppy' was certainly not 'skilled and energetic'."

'Over to you, Mr Floppy!'

I sat on my tiled floor, head in hands, feeling vaguely nauseous.

This is a bloody nightmare. 'Mr Floppy' – Christ almighty, there's no way back from this. I remember Jamie Theakston once being branded 'small' by a kiss-and-tell merchant and never being able to shake off the tag, but at least she never called him 'Floppy'.

I have no recollection of anyone called Sally, or anything like the incident to which she referred, but that's hardly the point. 'Ex-tabloid editor squeals about inaccuracy and invasion of privacy' is not the most winnable public campaign I could mount right now.

I emailed the offending item to Ms Johnson under the subject heading, 'It gets worse...'

She replied quickly: 'I am beside myself with embarrassment and contrition.'

That's not going to help stem the tide of yet more horrific revelations.

I resorted to perhaps the only weapon left to me, humour.

'Dear Pandora, I don't recall the incident to which you allude in today's column. However, it would be fair to say that Arsenal can't always raise their game against Hartlepool United in quite the same way as they can against Real Madrid. Love "Mr Floppy".'

The column's editor Guy Adams emailed back a little later, 'Fear not, I've just received further testimony from one very satisfied customer, so we'll put it down to a blip in form.'

Never have the words 'further testimony' appeared more ghastly to the naked eye.

6 January

I woke at 6a.m. and spent one hour and eleven minutes pacing my flat, waiting for the 'further testimony'.

Pandora duly recorded: 'It pains me to say this, but Piers Morgan may be a more competent swordsman than we originally thought. Yesterday, readers heard from "Sally", who had dubbed the former *Daily Mirror* editor "Mr Floppy", following an unsatisfactory encounter in a hotel bedroom.

'Today, I give you testimony from "Jessica", who writes to tell me, "I can't agree with a single word that Sally spat out. Piers was a tower of strength in the trouser department. In fact, for a lazy bed-mistress such as myself, it was like sexual boot camp with a naked, 6-foot marine. He made me laugh almost as many times as he made me..."'

I had no recollection of 'Jessica', nor to be perfectly honest do I have any memory of this alleged incident either, but it's funny how much less distressed I suddenly feel about this ongoing 'nightmare'.

It reminds me of a conversation I once had with George Graham, the football manager who'd been exposed a few times by women he'd slept with.

'So long as they say I went at it like a steam train six times a night, then kiss-and-tells are fine. It's when they say you were hung like a hamster and went at it like a tortoise that it can cause untold damage!'

7 January

Tracey rang to say that Johnnie Walker want me to be the face of their new Blue Label whisky campaign, and are prepared to pay a rather large sum of money for the privilege.

Since I drink the stuff anyway, this strikes me as a quite splendid piece of business.

8 January

Finally got round to writing up my *GQ* interview with Celia today.

I have made it jokily gushing, over-the-top and journalistically disgraceful, suggesting that I've been sucked into Ms Walden's web and abandoned all pretence at a detached critique the moment I saw the eight pages of photographs the magazine was carrying of her in various states of Agent Provocateur undress.

Which is not entirely inaccurate.

The article reads as follows:

'The phrases "ridiculously beautiful" and "Fleet Street hack" are rare bedfellows. There is, frankly, a shocking lack of aesthetic excellence among the ranks of our Fourth Estate.

'But in the case of Celia Walden, editor of the *Daily Telegraph*'s diary Spy, the description was recently deployed by no less a man than John Walsh, literary bon viveur of the *Independent* and someone whose opinion on the female form should be trusted implicitly.

'Celia is twenty-nine, at least 6 foot in her heels, blonde, bright (Cambridge), amusing, trilingual in French, Russian and Italian, and writes a splendidly mischievous gossip column.

'Her picture byline is, by *Telegraph* standards, 'racy' and has spawned a lengthy debate from her crusty old Tory readers about the suitability of her sporting what appears to be a slinky négligée at the foot of the letters page.

'But in the words of Brigitte Bardot, Celia's iconic heroine, as this *GQ* photo session reveals, "Men are beasts and even beasts don't behave as they do."

'Born in Paris, she is the daughter of George Walden, former Conservative MP, diplomat and author of a hilarious memoir detailing, among other things, his frequent amorous encounters around the globe.

'She loves France because "they take pleasure seriously there: good food and wine, looking as good as you can".

'And like Bardot, our Celia loved getting her kit off.

'"At first I felt slightly shy, but then the music and the photographer put you in the mood – with a little help from Agent Provocateur. In fact, towards the end I was enjoying myself a bit too much. I kept having visions of waking up the next morning, thinking, Oh God, what did I do?"

'The answer is simple. Like Bardot, she has brought a lot of basic pleasure to a lot of basic lusty men.

'And talking of men, Celia has such refreshing views.

'"I like someone who doesn't pander to my whims, refuses point-blank to placate me and eats like a man. Oh, and blokes who wear short-sleeved T-shirts over long-sleeved ones do something weird to me."

'She dated the exotic French chef Jean-Christophe Novelli and they remain close. "He thinks his best asset is his looks, but in fact it's JC's kindness that's the most remarkable thing about him. What I also found attractive was the fact that he loved women so much. He used to look at other women a lot and I liked it. Hell, I'd even point them out most of the time."

'Celia's a very sharp journalist beneath the glorious exterior. She breaks stories, stirs up trouble and inspires equal doses of admiration, lust and fear.

'She loves champagne, wants to meet John Updike – "the greatest living author" – and would rather have lunch with John Prescott, because "With Prezza I reckon you'd end up on a two-day bender: he'd be giving you a headline a minute and flirting in a brilliantly basic way," than Tom Cruise, because "it's all PR nonsense with big fat US stars like him".

'She is starting to do television, and unashamedly loves the camera almost as much as it loves her.

'And she is writing a novel, "a twisted love story based in Paris ... some is autobiographical, but not the main character, thank God – she's a complete bitch".

'So there we have her.

'Celia Walden is indeed "ridiculously beautiful", likes her men to treat her mean and to love other women, can make you laugh out loud over a bottle of Krug, and is, as I write, resolutely single.

'When God created woman, he blessed Hollywood with Bardot and Fleet Street with Walden.

'Form an orderly queue now, gentlemen.'

Now if that doesn't get me another dinner date, nothing will.

9 January

Had breakfast with Celia at the Lanesborough Hotel to show her the copy. She feigned embarrassment, but I could tell she loved every word.

'Need a lift to work?' I said.

'That's very kind,' she replied.

We were driving along the Embankment at 4mph when I gently nudged into the back of a white van.

The owner, a strapping young white man with dreadlocks, sprang out like a raging hyena and raced to my window shouting and swearing. I wound it down slowly.

He stared at my face and exploded, 'Oh, fucking hell … I might have fucking guessed it was you, you PRICK!'

I kept my temper in check. 'Sorry, mate, I wasn't concentrating. Let's swap numbers and I'll sort this out later if there's any damage.'

He raced angrily back to his van to get a pen and paper, we exchanged details and I apologised again.

'Oh, don't worry, mate. I just overreacted. You're all right really.'

Celia watched the whole thing in stunned amusement.

'Does that kind of thing happen to you a lot?'

'I'm afraid so, yes.'

10 January

Disaster. Paul O'Grady has quit ITV for Channel 4, which means he will almost certainly be banned from presenting the talent show, and without him, there will probably not be a show at all. Just my bloody luck. Every time I get close to landing a new day job, something like this seems to happen. It's incredibly frustrating.

7

12 January

Lunch with Channel 4 boss Kevin Lygo at The Ivy. He was cock-a-hoop over O'Grady's defection, and laughed even more when I told him it had almost certainly buggered up my own prime-time break.

We discussed the astonishing comeback of Noel Edmonds, who hosts the hot new game show *Deal or No Deal*.

Kevin said, 'He didn't want to do it. I rang him several times and tried to persuade him, but Noel was adamant it would be the wrong vehicle for him.

'He thought daytime TV was a step backwards for someone who had spent virtually all his career in prime time, but I just knew he'd be perfect for it, Noel is a brilliant live presenter.

'In the end he agreed, and now he can see it was probably the best decision he's ever made.'

I understand Noel's reluctance, though. Television these days is so flaky that it might easily have bombed, and then he'd have received a tubload of vile abuse about being a washed-up old has-been. As it is, he's basking in the glory of being in a hit show again.

Had dinner tonight at the Cambio de Tercio with Ian Botham, Freddie Flintoff, various other Bothams, and a few of their mates who'd helped with his last leukaemia walk.

Beefy has raised nearly £10 million with his charity walks now, a staggering sum of money. It remains an enduring and shameful mystery why he's never been knighted for this alone, never mind being one of the greatest and most inspiring sportsmen we've ever produced.

By 2a.m. I was incapable of speech, stability or sense.

Another huge jug of sangria arrived.

'Come on you lightweight,' taunted Freddie, who had guzzled enough alcohol to sink a cruise ship but seemed completely sober.

He's very similar to Beefy: physically massive and strong as an ox, true to his friends, hard playing and hard drinking, smarter than people think, and already almost as iconic.

Since the Ashes, Freddie has become as famous as Beckham in Britain, but just finds it all rather funny.

'I come out of me 'ouse in the morning looking rough sometimes and there's all these photographers taking me picture. And I have to laugh. I mean, who wants a photograph of me looking rough?'

I laughed: 'Everyone. Welcome to the world of celebrity, Fred.'

'I'm not a fucking celebrity,' he scoffed.

'Oh yes you are,' I replied. 'So get used to it.'

As I got up to leave, Beefy stood up and declared, 'Right, you've avoided doing any of my walks in the whole time I've known you, so this year, you're doing it. No excuses.'

He looked deadly serious, as did Freddie, who added: 'Yeah, right,' in the way Grant Mitchell does when his brother Phil threatens someone in *EastEnders*.

'OK, OK. I'll do it.'

I'm banking on them all being too drunk to remember.

15 January
Spoke to Simon Cowell.

'What's going to happen to the talent show now O'Grady's gone?'

'Well he can still host it if he wants to,' said Simon, 'but it's not massively helpful, obviously.'

I could tell by Simon's voice that he's very disappointed. O'Grady was perfect for the show, and there are very few others who could adequately replace him.

16 January
Celia emailed: 'In case you haven't heard, there could be another, major obstacle to your marriage plans. The Hoff is getting a divorce … and will soon be back on the market.'

I snorted with derision.

'David Hasselhoff? Do me a favour. If he's my love rival, then this is going to be easier than I thought.'

Celia hates flowers, probably because she gets bombarded with the contents of Kew Gardens every week from admiring suitors. But boring roses are one thing … I had an altogether more sinister idea in mind. I called my brilliant local florists Molly Blooms and asked them to track me down a Venus flytrap.

Donna, the manageress, came back with a better idea: 'It's not really the season for flytraps, but there is something available called a nepenthes pitcher plant, which looks rather good.'

I checked it out on the internet. It was a revolting-looking, highly carnivorous little number that traps insects in its pitcher, sucks them down to its floral bowels and drowns them in water and enzyme fluid. Some grow so big they can kill frogs and rats. And to add to the fun, they spew out their liquid every now and again, like an angry spitting cobra.

I attached a message: 'Careful, Celia, it traps things then kills them.'

She rang in the afternoon, slight hysteria in her voice.

'You disgusting man. That ugly plant you sent me has just shot some vile substance all over my desk, causing mass newsroom panic.'

'You liked it, then?'

'I loved it.'

Later she emailed me: 'There has been another casualty from your earlier spurting missive: my priceless suede stilettos, which have now been reduced to a cheap, leathery texture more akin to Jodie Marsh's skin than anything else.'

18 January

Interviewed Vinnie Jones for my BBC ONE series. It was classic Vinnie – tough, uncompromising, surprisingly emotional, confrontational and amusing. I like the guy.

Halfway through I checked my phone for messages and found one from Martine McCutcheon asking me to ring her urgently. I did, and discovered she was holed up in a Barbados hotel room, surrounded by paparazzi and thoroughly fed up about her holiday being ruined.

'It's a bloody nightmare,' she said. 'They're everywhere, in the bushes, on the beach, on boats. I can't go out and it's wrecking everything. I thought you might be able to give me some advice on what to do?'

'Well, what are you doing out there?'

'I'm doing a piece for a magazine.'

'And they're paying for it?'

'Yes.'

'That doesn't massively help your invasion-of-privacy argument now, does it, Martine?'

At least she had the good grace to giggle. 'No, I know that. But it still shouldn't mean they can stalk me all day, should it?'

'No, but they'd argue that you're flaunting your wares for cash and publicity, so why shouldn't they get a piece of the action. I think you have several options. You can go to a quieter island, which isn't swimming in quite so many photographers, or you can simply go up to these guys, ask what they want and give them some photos. It's sometimes easier to do that and maintain some form of control over what they take. They will usually be up for a deal like that.'

'I'm not doing that, why should I? I'm on holiday.'

'Well, prepare for pictures you have no control over to appear in the papers, then.'

'That's what I'm worried about – my big arse all over the front of the *Sun*.'

'I'm sure your arse would look lovely, Martine, but if you take my advice you'll be in a position to choose which photo of your arse they use.'

'Well, I'll think about it.'

19 January

I spent the afternoon posing for photos to promote Johnnie Walker whisky today, wearing a dinner jacket and lovingly holding up a glass of Blue Label.

I felt like Bill Murray in *Lost in Translation*. Just without, unfortunately, any Scarlett Johansson to share it with.

The tabloids are full of Martine McCutcheon's arse clambering onto a boat in Barbados. They were very flattering and looked like she knew she was being photographed. I sent her a text: 'Did you take my advice, then?'

She replied: 'It was too late, the buggers already got me.'

'Well never mind, your arse looks great.'

'Thanks, I think that's the nicest thing you have ever said or written about me! See you when I get home.'

It must be awful being a female celebrity when it comes to holidays. It's fine if you look like Gisele. Not so fine if you've put on a few pounds, forgotten to shave your legs, or developed a rash of pustulating zits on your face.

That's why so many of them do secret deals with the paparazzi where they get 'accidentally' papped on the beach at a pre-arranged time when they look their best, then get to approve the photos and even split the money when they're sold on to newspapers and magazines.

It's a cosy relationship where everyone wins, apart from people like me, who prefer to see snaps of celebrities looking terrible.

20 January

Anil Bhoyrul was sentenced to 180 hours' community service today for his part in the City Slickers fiasco, but the judge warned James Hipwell that he faces a custodial sentence. This is the right result all round.

Had lunch at The Ivy with my literary agent Eugenie, enlivened by the appearance of one Dale Winton, who ran over to say hello and declared, 'If I get one more friend repeating what you said about me in your book I shall DIE, darling.'

The relevant entry in my previous diaries read, 'Dale Winton called me today to say he loved me and thinks I'm incredibly talented and very handsome. I feel a little unnerved.'

I couldn't think of what on earth to say as he towered over my table, so I just spluttered, 'Well just don't start bloody kissing me in here, for Christ's sake, Dale…'

With that, Mr Winton bent down, grabbed me forcibly by the shoulders and began to 'snog' me in full view of almost every other diner.

The room fell almost completely silent, bar some embarrassed titters from a table of Essex girls nearby.

'We're just good friends,' I cried lamely as Dale cackled like a hyena who'd just tucked into a large, juicy, defenceless antelope.

I could see what everyone else was thinking: 'Yeah, right, Piers. And there's still a heterosexual Lib Dem left in parliament.'

Still reeling from my Dale encounter, I popped down to the 606 jazz club near my flat tonight with Conor and his girlfriend Rosa, the *Mirror*'s political journalist. It's an underground dungeon run by genuine jazz enthusiasts, where you can eat, drink and listen to some of the best musicians in the world.

I bumped into Celia, who was there with some friends.

'What are you doing here?' we asked simultaneously.

She smiled: 'My brother Fran is a professional saxophone player and he and his band are on tonight.'

We joined tables later in the evening, much wine was consumed and by midnight we were dancing a slow waltz to her brother's stunningly good sax playing. I don't think either of us quite knows what's going on here, if anything, but as we danced, I spotted Guy Adams, the *Independent*'s diarist, staring at us with a mischievous grin on his face. It's never a good sign when a gossip columnist smirks at you.

23 January

Interviewed Richard Madeley for *GQ* in his office. It was busy, with lots of researchers and production crew running around.

'You must miss all this?' he asked.

'I miss the people and the buzz,' I replied, 'but not the job itself. It was all-consuming.'

'I can understand that,' he said. 'Judy wants us to wind down a bit, she thinks we work far too hard and she's probably right. But it's not easy, is it?'

'Well, it is if someone fires you!' I replied.

I've always rather admired Richard for the way he brings a proper journalistic rigour to his daytime TV job. It's not easy, and he takes a lot of flak for it from supposedly 'serious' TV journalists. But he's a good interviewer, asks the questions that need asking and always seems well researched about his subject.

I asked him what his worst professional moment had been, and he spat out an extraordinary story that reveals a lot about where he sees himself as a presenter.

'We landed a world-exclusive interview with O.J. Simpson, and it was all going well until ITV ordered us not to do the whole show with him as we wanted to.

'They wanted us to do three interviews, so we would actually cut O.J. off after twelve minutes and go to Neil fucking Diamond. I mean, it was madness. And we were worried because we knew that wouldn't be enough time to really grill him, and the press were already working themselves up about us giving him an easy ride. In fact, I remember you calling our PR a few minutes before we did the interview, asking him to tell us not to go easy on O.J., and to really work him over or we'd get hammered.

'We were very grateful, but we already knew that, and now we knew we didn't have enough time. When we met O.J. backstage it got worse, because he was fucking loquacious and obsessed with the tiny details of his trial – we could see a real potential for him to just drone away so we could hardly get a word in.

'It was a nightmare. We were arguing right up to the start of the show, but in the end we had to do it the way our bosses told us to, and it was awful because we actually did a good interview – we were just getting to him a bit and his top lip was beginning to sweat when, bang, the twelve minutes came, we had to go to the break, our bosses were shouting down the line to move on, and Judy had to say we would be ending it there and coming back with Neil fucking Diamond. The audience gasped and O.J. looked totally bemused; it was humiliating beyond belief.

'I was fucking furious, and in the break all hell broke loose. We pleaded with them to let us stay with O.J., but they refused, so he was led away and that was the end of that. The papers absolutely crucified us.

'And because I do think I'm a pretty good journalist and interviewer, it was just bloody terrible. The worst thing in my career. They all said we fucked it up, asked shit questions and let him off the hook. Awful. And not our fault. It was the injustice of it that really annoyed me.

'It made me sick to the pit of my stomach actually and ruined the rest of my week.'

I changed the subject: 'Do people still shout "shoplifter" at you in supermarkets?' [Richard was arrested in 1994 and charged with stealing champagne from a Tesco store. He was later acquitted.]

'No … not any more, thankfully. I remember at the height of it all, when I was facing trial, being in Marks & Spencer and this spotty little squirt walked up to me and said in this whining, high-pitched nasal voice, "I think you're a bloody disgrace coming in here. You can't nick any more champagne from Tesco so you've come here to shoplift, have you?"

'He went on and on, and I started trying to explain how I had been charged with something but was innocent, when Judy marched up and said, "Why don't you fuck off?"

'He looked totally stunned and replied, "I have the right to free speech, madam," or something ridiculous. And Judy responded, "No you don't, you have the right to jerk off, you little wanker." A crowd of people had gathered by now, and they started applauding and saying, "Good on you, Judy." It was great. She was great.'

I laughed.

'Do you like getting pissed?'

'Yes, but I don't do it very often. The last spectacular time was one Christmas Eve a few years back when I got completely hammered. At 2a.m., Judy and I went to bed, and the next thing I knew it was 4.30a.m. and I was stark naked on my hands and knees in a downstairs cupboard with the light on, and in my hand was a can of fake snow.

'I thought, What the fuck is going on? Then I remembered that my son

Jack and I had wanted to cover the Christmas tree in fake snow, and Judy said it was totally naff and wasn't going to let us. I walked from the cupboard to the tree and saw I'd turned it completely white in my drunken stupor. I turned everything off and went back to bed, then expressed complete surprise in the morning. I didn't get away with it. I never do with Judy.'

'Are you aware that an anagram of your full name, Richard Holt Madeley, is "the old daily charmer"?'

'Yes, but I don't think I am remotely charming. I'm a bit spiky, a bit hyper, but not a charmer. Actually, I do occasionally find myself irritating. I watch myself sometimes and think, Stop being such a fucking irritating twat, Richard.'

Afterwards I went to The Ivy to meet a couple of women who claimed they were about to launch a national newspaper and wanted me to front it. This seemed highly unlikely given that they could only get a lunch table for 2.30p.m., but I went anyway.

The women were Sarah Jane Thomson, who runs a huge media data company called Thomson Intermedia with her husband Steve, and Nicky Cox, who I remembered as Nicky Smith when she used to edit teenage pop magazines. Nicky had gone on to set up the BBC children's magazine department, launching thirty-six magazines.

They had money and credentials – I was a little more intrigued.

'So come on then, what's this nonsense about launching a national newspaper.'

They smiled and showed me a dummy front page.

'*First News* – the national newspaper for children.'

It was my turn to smile.

'That's a great idea.'

And it is. There's never been a proper kids' paper. Various adult ones have carried supplements for children, but nobody has tried a stand-alone tabloid-format paper before, and I think there's a real market for it.

By the end of lunch I agreed to come on board as editorial director, and I feel rather excited about it.

24 January

One of the hazards of editing a tabloid newspaper is that almost every party you attend becomes a potential war zone, so it's been a blessed relief since I was fired from the *Mirror* not to have to fend off endless bile-spewing celebrities and raging public figures over the canapés and champagne any more.

There's still the odd occasion when I get confronted by some foaming relic from my red-top past, though. At a Channel 4 party tonight, I was approached by Virginia Bottomley, former Tory minister, and to many the absolute person-ification of old-style haughty Conservative arrogance and pomposity.

She looked slightly demented, and immediately started hectoring me loudly about some story the *Daily Mirror* had done on her daughter being disciplined at school for underage boozing back in the mid-Nineties.

All I could remember about the original incident was that she was the only politician ever to call the chairman (then Sir Robert Clark) at home and ask him to pull a story. Something he commendably refused to do.

Anyway, as she huffed and puffed and hissed and spat, I suddenly realised that I didn't have to put up with this kind of nonsense any more, and particularly not from tragic Westminster has-beens like Ms Bottomley.

'Virginia,' I said, as graciously as I could, given her ridiculous behaviour. 'I'm terribly sorry, but rather like the nation, I really couldn't give a monkey's cuss what you have to say about anything any more.' She looked momentarily bemused and then completely crushed as I ambled off to talk to the much more interesting Jon Snow.

If there's anything more pathetic than an ex-Cabinet minister behaving like he or she still runs the country, then it's probably an ex-tabloid editor doing it. But at least I know that.

28 January

The *Mail on Sunday* rang at 1p.m.

It's never a good thing when a Sunday paper rings you on a Saturday afternoon. In fact the last time the *MoS* had rung me on a Saturday, it was to tell me the MoD were 'raising doubts' about the photos the *Mirror* had published the day before of British soldiers abusing Iraqis.

'Mr Morgan, I have to put something to you.'

Oh God, what was it? Drugs, lap dancers, my former friendship with Gary Glitter?

'It's about your relationship with Celia Walden.'

Phew.

'What relationship? We're just good friends. I'm a huge admirer of her work.'

'Well, you were seen smooching in the 606 jazz club last week.'

'Smooching?'

'Smooching.'

'I see.' Guy Adams has clearly been doing what comes naturally – gossiping.

'And we have got your *GQ* article on her, which, to put it mildly, is very complimentary.'

'Ah yes, well that was just a bit of fun and shouldn't be taken too...'

'So are you an item?'

I laughed. I'd spent years harassing celebrities about their private lives like this, and now it was happening to me.

I tried to remember my own advice: keep calm, be polite, give an ambiguous answer that cannot later be exposed as a lie.

'I think the key phrase is "in my dreams".'

I phoned Celia.

'Oh God, what did you tell them?'

'I said we weren't having a relationship.'

'Good, because we're not.'

'No, I know. That's why I said that.'

'Good.'

29 January

I assumed that my 'non-relationship' with Celia would be a few paragraphs in the *Mail on Sunday* gossip column, but when I bought the paper I discovered it was the whole of page 11, a proper 'news' page.

The article was illustrated with some very sexy photos of Celia from the *GQ* shoot, and one of the two of us together, which must have been lurking in the files before we ever really knew each other and used to meet at the odd showbiz party.

The headline was less than ambiguous: I DO ADMIRE HER WORK, SAYS SMITTEN PIERS.

I read on: 'As an ex-newspaper editor, Piers Morgan has given many a young journalist the benefit of his professional expertise. Now the latest writer to catch his eye is Celia Walden, the Amazonian daughter of former Tory MP George Walden.

'After she posed for this series of provocative shots for a men's magazine, the former *Mirror* editor and bestselling author provided a breathlessly complimentary article to accompany them.

'In the interview, Morgan describes Ms Walden, a journalist for the *Daily Telegraph*, as "ridiculously beautiful" and compares her to the French actress Brigitte Bardot, gushing that "like Bardot, she has brought a lot of basic pleasure to a lot of basic, lusty men".

'The ardent tone of the article in *GQ* magazine will add to rumours about Ms Walden, 29, and 40-year-old Morgan. Last weekend, Morgan, who has separated from his wife Marion, was spotted slow dancing with Ms Walden into the early hours at London's 606 Jazz Club, near his Chelsea bachelor flat.'

It ended by saying, 'Last night, Ms Walden said her slow dance with Morgan had been "entirely innocent" and denied they were romantically involved. "We are not an item," she said. "He is just a good contact."

'Morgan, who lost his job in 2004 when the *Mirror* published hoax pictures of British troops abusing Iraqi prisoners, said, "We are just very good friends. I am a huge admirer of her work. The key phrase is 'in my dreams'."'

So now everyone's going to think I'm dating someone who I'm not properly dating yet. How weird.

I rang Celia.

'You seen it?'

'Yes.'

'Thoughts?'

'I can't believe these journalists just make this stuff up…'

There was then a prolonged self-reflective pause as we both digested the sheer hypocrisy of this statement.

3 February

Met the *First News* team for a catch-up lunch at The Ivy today. Jamie Theakston was at the next table and hung his head in shame when he saw me.

'Congratulations, mate, you were quite disgusting at that Freud party,' I said.

'Oh, don't. I'm still trying to live it down,' he replied, looking genuinely mortified. 'How bad was I?'

'Well, let's just say that I nearly hit you for groping Celia, Rebekah slapped you for trying to grope her, and apparently you even tried it on with Liz Murdoch as you were led away by security.'

He went bright red.

'Fucking hell, that's bad.'

'Actually, it seems quite funny now. I wouldn't make a habit of it, though.'

'No, quite. It's Simon Kelner's fault. I'm never going to lunch with him again.'

ITV want me to appear in a celebrity charity edition of *Who Wants to Be a Millionaire*. After the *Weakest Link* debacle the last thing I want to do is another TV quiz where I confirm my status as the dumbest celebrity in Britain, but another part of me wants to prove I am *not* the dumbest celebrity in Britain, so in yet another moment of vain weakness, I agreed.

'Who am I on with?' I asked.

'Ann Widdecombe,' came the reply.

Now *that* is funny.

8 February

Tracey rang me in a state of high excitement.

'*Cosmo* magazine want you to strip naked and be a centrefold for a special charity issue,' she said.

I put down my toast.

'WHAT?'

She read me the email:

'We are pleased to tell you that Piers Morgan has been selected by the Cosmopolitan 2006 Nomination Committee to be invited to join the Centrefolds Hall of Fame. Piers has been deemed so desirable by our 2 million readers that we would be honoured to photograph him to appear in the Centrefolds VIP section of *Cosmopolitan*. Since the first Centrefold appeared in 1972, *Cosmopolitan*'s iconic images of gorgeous male celebrities have become a firm favourite with our British readers.'

Tracey made some further enquiries and established that I will apparently be pictured in an illustrious line-up including Radio 1 DJs, a Brit actor who's been in *Human Traffic*, the England rugby team, a celebrity chef who's everywhere at the moment and one of Keira Knightley's exes...'

I emailed Celia to see what she thought.

'Do it. If you never wish to see me again in your entire life.'

9 February

To Lord's cricket ground for the official launch of Freddie Flintoff's benefit year. I've been asked to host a Q&A with Freddie and Ian Botham, the kind of assignment I would pay for the privilege of doing.

It was a tough night, though.

The 1,000-strong audience was full of City boys all wanting to drink themselves into oblivion and meet some celebs, and the room was a strange long, thin oblong shape, stretching miles down either side, which made the acoustics a nightmare. Chris Tarrant was hosting the event, and when I saw he was struggling to control the crowd I knew we were in for a difficult evening.

'That was murder,' he said as he rejoined our top table, sweating slightly in the nervous way you do when crowds behave like this.

Max Boyce did a good job reeling them back in with his old Welsh rugby routines. I'd heard them all before, but he delivers the stories with such extraordinary gusto and passion that it still makes you roar with laughter.

Then it was my turn to grill Freddie and Beefy. It went OK, but I could tell that half the people at the back couldn't hear a thing, and when you're paying £500 for a ticket, the least you expect is to be able to hear the speakers.

Freddie and Beefy were entertaining, as usual, but they were both itching to get off stage, away from the baying, restless crowd and back to the wine.

I was sitting next to Freddie, and within seconds of us returning to our seats he started to be bothered by autograph and photo hunters. Hordes and hordes of drunken City traders wanted to slap him on the back, make some inane joke about Shane Warne's nocturnal habits and get a souvenir. He dealt with them all with remarkable patience, but it was hot and increasingly uncomfortable as the scrum around him grew.

It's hard to tell people to piss off at your own benefit do, but some of the behaviour was appalling – people pushing and shoving others to get to Fred. Most of them didn't even appear to be proper cricket fans, just big suited-and-booted blokes from Essex with lots of wonga who'd probably won the tickets in an auction.

A couple of Freddie's benefit team eventually appeared to persuade the throng to return to their tables.

Freddie was bright red and sweating profusely.

'That was fookin' 'arder than bowling at the Aussies,' he laughed.

Then he gripped my shoulder, harder than I would have wished, lent forward and growled in my ear, 'I need a drink Morgan, and I need a drinking partner.'

I gulped. There are many quick ways to commit suicide, and being Freddie Flintoff's drinking partner appeared to be one of the more reliable ones, but this was no time to be a lightweight.

'You couldn't keep up with me, Flintoff,' I scoffed, not entirely convincingly.

He cackled, very convincingly.

'Do fook off, you cheeky twat!'

'White or red, you northern lightweight?' I demanded.

'Red.'

I took one of the open bottles on the table and poured us both large glasses.

Freddie took his and drank it in one mouthful. It was like watching a gorilla drink a bottle of milk. Fast, furious and unnerving.

He eyed me suspiciously. 'Come on then, hotshot.'

I took my glass and drank it straight down. Not quite so fast, but not slowly either. It's at times like this that you need Jeremy, who can drink a pint of beer standing on his head in four seconds. Though he once tried it with a warm flagon of lager in a Wandsworth wine bar and projectile vomited all over the tables, chairs, walls and other diners.

'Fill 'em up!' came the order. So I did. And Freddie gulped his straight down again, faster than the first one.

'That's better,' he laughed.

I swigged mine down, too, slower than before, and with a slight convulsion near the end.

'Oh dear, having trouble already, are we?' he taunted as he grabbed the bottle, filled his glass again and threw a third straight down his vast throat.

I was in serious danger here, and we both knew it.

I began drinking the third one, but stopped halfway through, pretending my phone had rung.

'Sorry, mate, must be the office.'

I don't, of course, have an office.

By the time I'd taken my 'call', Freddie had finished the bottle and was laughing and joking with some other mates. I'd escaped before a stomach pump was necessary.

20 February

Did my Johnnie Walker gig tonight – they wanted me to interview the bald Italian football referee Pierluigi Collina, so I was effectively getting paid a lot of money to interview a bloke I admire about a sport I love, in the name of a whisky I drink anyway.

Collina was striking in the flesh – tall, slim, athletic and with those ferocious eyes.

I asked him if he'd been having a nice time in London.

'Yes, though I got attacked by a *Big Issue* seller today.'

'What?'

'Yes, I needed some new shoes, so I went to Selfridges and this guy was there trying to talk to me. Eventually I got in my car and he started chucking rubbish at the vehicle. It was quite frightening, though I can laugh now.'

'What was his problem?'

'I don't know – either he was annoyed that I didn't buy a copy of the *Big Issue*, or he remembers some penalty I gave years ago that he disagreed with!'

21 February

I've been nominated for Book of the Year in the British Book Awards, and to add to the delicious sense of anticipation, so has Jeremy Clarkson.

I was asked for a comment, so I said, 'I am absolutely desperate to win, purely to see Jeremy Clarkson's face as I do a little celebratory conga on stage.'

I should really stop this feud with Clarkson. It must be getting very tedious for everyone else to keep reading about it. But whenever I see the scar on my forehead where his ring-encrusted fist sliced into my flesh, all thoughts of 'forgive and forget' are instantly banished from my mind.

The other competition for the book prize isn't up to much: Jamie 'two million books' Oliver, Sharon 'heading for a million' Osbourne and some woman called J.K. Rowling.

22 February

Went to watch Spencer play football in conditions so freezing cold I could feel my flesh hardening, my eyeballs frosting and my will to live receding by the second.

The match was a closely fought, if uneventful clash, but by the middle of the second half it was so icy that I seriously contemplated calling that explorer lunatic David Hempleman-Adams and asking for tips on how to survive Arctic conditions.

Only a handful of other parents had braved the weather, and we stood in a close huddle in the middle of a wide-open set of playing fields as the wind howled bitterly into our bowels, comparing notes on who was suffering the most.

It's at times like this that you pray for a miracle, something to end the pain. And I got one.

Spencer, loping around in midfield as usual, received a pass from one of his mates while still a good 15 yards outside the penalty area, and just smacked it instinctively straight into the top corner of the goal. It was the sort of thing you'd expect from Ronaldinho at the Nou Camp, not your twelve-year-old son on a rough old pitch better suited to a cow field. I don't know who was more stunned, me or Spencer.

Suddenly the cold was replaced by heat, my shivers by trembles of excitement, the agony by ecstasy.

It was, and there's simply no other phrase for it, a wonder goal.

The final whistle went soon after, meaning it was a match-winning wonder goal, too.

I ran onto the pitch to embrace the hero.

'Spencer, that was unbelievable.'

'Dad, stop being so embarrassing.'

But I could tell he was chuffed to bits.

Andy Coulson, Neil Reading and I took Peter Stringfellow to The Ivy in the evening to belatedly celebrate his sixty-fifth birthday.

'What are you drinking, Pete?'

'Just water for me, boys.'

Andy and I looked at each other in bemusement.

'Very funny, Pete. Come on, champagne or vodka?'

He laughed. 'I'm on the wagon, have been for six months. And I've never felt better.'

He looked terrible.

'What do you do in the club without a drink?' said Andy.

'I drink soft drinks, it's great...'

This was unbelievable.

'Presumably you console yourself with a few lap dances,' I suggested.

'No, no, Bella doesn't like me having dances, so I've stopped that as well.'

'You'll be trying to tell us you've been completely faithful to her next,' I said.

'I am, mate, completely, and I love it.'

Andy and I exchanged further incredulous looks.

'Pete,' I said, 'let me get this absolutely straight. You are now teetotal, faithful and banned from having lap dances in the club where you spend every night of your life?'

'That's right, yes.'

'And you expect us to believe you've never been happier.'

'I haven't.'

At which point all four of us burst out laughing.

23 September

Woke up to discover that Paul O'Grady is refusing to host Simon Cowell's talent show. In fact, he's refusing to work for ITV ever again, saying, 'I'd rather sweep the streets after the way they've treated me. I've told them I won't do the Soap Awards or Simon's show.' So that's that then. Great. I land a prime-time TV show, and the host buggers off before we even start. I can't think who else they could get who would be anywhere near as good as Paul, and if the show was going to be called *Paul O'Grady's Talent Show*, then I'd wager that without Paul O'Grady, it's dead in the water.

I caught a cab to the One Aldwych at lunchtime to interview Billie Piper for *GQ*, which should alleviate some of my irritation.

We've never met before, though I spoke to her on the phone when she was still with Chris Evans.

She was already sitting at the table when I arrived. Prettier than I'd expected, and very friendly.

Every interview I've read with her smacked of squeaky-clean, and the first half of our chat was uneventful.

Then I tested the water by asking, 'What are your best assets?'

'Erm, I like my arse. I often admire it in shop windows. It's big and I like big butts; I find them really sexy. I love looking at other women's arses as well.'

She looked at me, smirking. This had just got interesting.

'Do you fancy women, then?'

'Yeah, big time. I check women out more than I check men out.'

'Have you ever slept with a woman?'

'No.'

'Do you want to?'

'Maybe.'

'If Beyoncé begged you to sleep with her, would you?'

'No, because although I like the look of her, I don't think she's that dirty.'

'And that's what you're after, is it?'

'Sure, if you're going to do that you may as well do it properly. I have a few female friends who I've often talked to about this, and if we were going to have a threesome, then I'd do it with one of them.'

'You know which ones?'

'Yes. We'd have to have a few bottles first.'

'Is your boyfriend Amadu aware of this?'

'No, I couldn't do this with him, I'd have to be single.'

'Are you auditioning for the third partner in this project?'

She gave a long filthy cackle: 'Why, are you my man, Piers?'

'Let's keep it professional, shall we?'

'My friends are so hot, too. You'd be in for a real treat. If I was single again and leading a crazy hedonistic lifestyle, that's what I'd be doing, definitely. But I'm not at the moment.'

'Are you good in bed?'

'I like to think I'm great.' She roared with laughter. 'But then, every woman does, don't they? I like to think I've got a few special tricks.'

'Do you like porn?'

'Yes, but not gay porn. I just don't find that sexual. I like dirty straight porn. It's my favourite kind; it's the only kind.' Squeals with laughter.

'If you're like this after a Diet Coke and two glasses of water, then what on earth are you like after one of your benders?'

'You don't want to know!'

'Oh I do, I do…'

'You definitely don't.'

'I definitely do…'

'Trust me, it's lethal.'

'Do you have a high sex drive?'

'I go through phases. Sometimes I like being on my own and don't want sex at all, I just want to do my thing quietly. Other times my sex drive goes through the roof.'

'Are you a morning or evening girl?'

'Morning! It sets you up for the day.'

'Coffee first?'

'No. Straight in. Followed by a latte. There you go, Piers.'

'I wonder if this was the kind of interview your agent, Michael Foster, had in mind when he suggested you do it.'

'Michael Foster is going to fucking kill me.' She laughs hysterically.

'HARDCORE FILTH FOLLOWED BY A LATTE – BILLIE TELLS ALL. Dear oh dear.'

'Such a laugh.'

'This could already be one of the most shocking celebrity interviews of all time, given your squeaky-clean image. How do you feel about that?'

'Very excited. I do think this is the most frank interview I've ever done.'

'It has been reported that Amadu is an expert at tantric sex, is that true?'

'He likes to think so, but it's not true. We call him Mr T, and he loves people thinking that, but frankly, who wants to bang on for hours anyway? Nobody does. Who wants to have sex for three days without having an orgasm? Answer: fucking nobody, unless you're insane. You just want a quick in-and-out most times, do you know what I mean?'

'Are you always honest?'

'I like to be, yes. I don't think you can go far wrong if you're honest, though we'll soon see when this interview comes out, won't we! God, I'm suddenly feeling so hot.'

'Indeed. Billie, you were hilarious.'

'Oh God, I'm in such trouble. I'm going to have to go home, have a cold shower and lie down. What have I done?'

This interview was now totally out of control.

'I need to go to the ladies' room,' she said.

'Yes, well have some bromide while you're there,' I suggested.

Billie blushed. 'I am feeling rather overexcited actually.'

'Where are you going now?' I asked.

'I'm going to go home, have a cold shower and watch a filthy porn movie.' She sighed. 'I don't know what I've just done, but I fucking enjoyed it. What about you?'

'I'm going to call the editor of *GQ* and tell him to clear a few extra pages.'

'Am I in trouble?' she said, looking like she very much hoped the answer was affirmative.

'Yes, Billie, *big* trouble. But in a nice way.'

She kissed me goodbye. 'That was fun. We must do it again some time.'

I rang Dylan Jones: 'Erm, I just had the nearest thing to sex with Billie Piper I'm ever going to have.'

A car was waiting to take me straight to the *Who Wants to Be a Millionaire* studios at Elstree, where Ann Widdecombe was waiting with various instructions.

'Now don't be flippant, Piers. I want to take this seriously and raise a lot of money for charity.'

'Who is your charity?' I asked.

'It's a donkey sanctuary.'

I stifled a laugh. The irony of making a complete ass of ourselves was too delicious.

We went through the system without an audience, and without the real questions obviously. Chris Tarrant was there throughout, hopping around like a hyperactive bee. His enthusiasm is infectious, though, and pretty amazing given the length of time he's done the show.

'I never get bored with it,' he said. 'It always throws up something new.'

I laughed. 'You're right. I'm going to sneeze my way to a million quid.'

We sat in the green room watching the first celebrity couple, Russell Grant and Sheila Ferguson.

They did well, getting up to £125,000 before making a mistake and falling back to £32,000.

Ann, watching on the monitor in our room, answered almost all of their questions before they did in a clipped matronly manner. She is obviously very well read and very clever, so with my populist background we should do well.

I kept making jokes, but she was having none of it.

'This is serious, Piers. I don't want any guessing, or any jokes. Just tell me if you know the answer, OK?'

I laughed and she grimaced.

When our bit started, she was off like a firecracker, answering all the easy questions before all four options had been displayed. I just kept quiet and let her get on with it. You can't stop a tornado in full flow.

Eventually we got a cricket question and she turned to me in blind panic saying, 'I have no idea, do you?'

'Relax,' I said. 'Matthew Hoggard.'

I answered a question about a Bond girl next, and we sailed through to £4,000 without using a lifeline.

But then we hit trouble.

Ann knew the answers to the next two questions but wasn't absolutely certain, so we used up all three valuable lifelines confirming her view.

I'd lined up Judith Keppel as one of our phone-a-friends, but when the time came it was a history question and I opted instead for Larry Lawrence, the *Mirror* librarian, who knows everything historical and gave us the right answer.

We'd reached £16,000 but had no lifelines, and then got asked which book a certain phrase had been the first line of.

Neither of us had a clue.

I was prepared to gamble, but she was having none of it.

'This is a lot of money for donkeys,' she said. And half would be going to a fireman's charity I had nominated, which concentrates the mind a lot harder than if the cash is coming your way.

It just seemed such a disappointing result. One more question and we could start gambling in the knowledge we'd get at least £32,000.

'We're taking the money,' said Ann firmly.

I nodded.

'She'd promised to kiss me if we got to a million, so I'm quite relieved in a way,' I joked. She didn't laugh.

We got back to the green room and people were very nice to us, but looked disappointed. Every charity must dream of getting £1 million, and we'd had high expectations of doing well. So £8,000 each was a dud whichever way you looked at it.

I went home, ringing the boys on the way.

'How did you do, Dad?' asked Spencer, hoping the answer was £100.

'Not very well. Just sixteen thousand pounds.'

'Oh Dad, that's terrible. But Jonathan Ross only got a thousand.'

'Did he?'

'Yes, and so did Alastair Campbell.'

That cheered me up enormously.

24 February

Billie Piper's agent, Michael Foster, called me.

'Piers, we have a major problem with your interview.'

'Do we, Michael?'

'Yes, Piers, we do. You can't put anything in about sex or drugs.'

I laughed. 'Erm, well that's going to be rather difficult because that removes pretty much the whole interview.'

'Yes, well, Billie is a very young girl who has said things she now regrets.'

'Michael, Billie is twenty-three and didn't sound to me like she regretted anything, other than the prospect of telling you what she'd done.'

'Piers, I am telling you not to put this stuff in. It's a small town, you know.'

I laughed even louder. This was hilarious, he was trying to put the arm on me like some mafia don. Only Michael Foster is about 5 foot 2 and as menacing as a legless armadillo.

'Michael, when I was an editor I got threatened by the IRA, Combat 18, football hooligans and the American government. Do you honestly think I am going to pull stuff from my interview with Billie Piper because you might seek some terrible retribution?'

'I didn't threaten you … I just … erm … I just asked you to consider her age.'

'Bollocks, you threatened me and I don't respond very well to that kind of thing. As for her age, your client married another of your clients, Mr Evans, and spent two years flying around the world having the time of her life. She isn't exactly a shrinking violet, now, is she?'

'How bad is this going to be, Piers?'

'Not bad at all. She comes over as a feisty, funny, bright young woman who tried a few drugs and likes sex. Big. Deal.'

'Well, I hope you think very carefully about what you're doing here. That's all.'

'Oh, I am thinking very carefully, Michael, don't you worry.'

I put the phone down, laughed to myself and called Dylan to relay my conversation with Mr Foster.

'What do you want to do?' asked Dylan.

'Put it all in, including his pathetic little threats.'

Dylan cackled. He loves a bit of mischief.

25 February

Jeremy Clarkson writes in his *Sun* column today: 'A simple bird flu information film on TV should do the trick. Just the facts: how it travels, how it spreads, and how we can direct it straight through Piers Morgan's letterbox.'

Jeremy … LET. IT. GO.

26 February

Found myself in the unlikely setting of the Laurence Olivier Awards tonight, where, to my astonishment, I'd been asked to present an award for Best Supporting Performance in a Musical.

I waited in line backstage with Kathleen Turner and Maureen Lipman.

It was curiously nerve-wracking. Do you say anything, and if you do then do you try and be funny or keep it serious? I kept changing my mind.

Much as I would love them to view me as a TV presenter and author now, the reality is that I will be seen by most of the audience as a revolting tabloid editor.

I walked out with Catherine Tate, my co-presenter, who seemed even more nervous than I was, and she is one of the top comedians in the country.

My head was racing: Speak, don't speak; crack a joke, don't crack a joke.

I walked to the microphone to what can best be described as a very mild round of applause.

'Ladies and gentlemen, forgive me if I'm a little nervous, but the last time I was at such a distinguished awards ceremony Jeremy Clarkson got very upset at not winning Motoring Writer of the Year and punched me in the head three times. All I can say is that if it helps, I'll be sitting on Table Thirty later if you lose and want to take it out on someone.'

They laughed and I quietly thanked Jeremy Clarkson.

27 February

Simon Cowell called today from his Hollywood home.

'I'm still hopeful about the talent show,' he said. 'But we've got to talk it through with ITV properly now that Paul's out of the picture. Funnily enough, I've sold it to NBC over here. They saw the British pilot and loved it.'

'Well let me know if you need a judge,' I said, joking.

'They want an all-American panel, so I doubt your talents will be needed, Piers,' he responded unsurprisingly. The Americans have never heard of me, and one mean Brit taking the mickey out of them is probably quite enough for their liking.

8

4 March

I was a crossword clue in the *Daily Mail*'s *Weekend* magazine today, something that ought to have brought a slither of pleasure. Only the photo of me they used had three chins and a bright red face, and the caption said simply, 'Media pundit Piers'.

I stared at those three words for a few seconds, contemplating my life.

Is that what I am now? A 'media pundit'. A poor man's version of Professor Roy Greenslade or that miserable old toad Stephen Glover?

I have always refused to write a media column on the grounds that nothing in the world could be more depressing than penning one of those 'it ain't as good as it was in my day, guv' pieces.

But here I was being described as a 'media pundit' anyway. Just another rent-a-quote talking head for the country's papers and airwaves.

It's a sobering thought that this is now perceived as my day job. And I don't like it.

11 March

Alan Sugar, gracious as ever, emailed me first thing this morning: 'You lot have as much chance of winning the Champions League as I have of becoming Pope in my lifetime and yours.'

I replied, 'In that case, I'd buy yourself a cassock pretty sharpish.'

'Yeah,' he wrote, 'and I would change the Lord's Prayer to "Give us this day our daily Amstrad".'

A nice letter arrived this afternoon from Dorothy Byrne, head of news and current affairs at Channel 4.

'Dear Piers, it's been so much fun working with you, and genuinely an honour. The programme was great – real quality political debate as good as anything on television and often more original. You gave the whole project and team so much support, but in the end the schedule always wins.

'I hope we can work together again, not least because half the department is in love with you. I could not possibly say which half I am in!'

I couldn't help thinking that if the show was that good, and they all love me so much, then why the hell are they canning it?

But to be honest, I've had enough of it anyway. I wasn't cut out to be a Paxman, Humphrys, or even a Jon Snow. You've got to really love politics to be one of them, and I just don't. I find most of it crashingly dull – boring people spouting boring claptrap about usually very boring things. Most of them would sell their proverbial granny to get up the Westminster ladder, or stab their colleagues in the back if they had to, and I view their tired, cliché-ridden antics and refusal to answer perfectly fair questions with increasing cynicism. Give me an Alan Clark over a Patricia Hewitt any day.

13 March

Had lunch with James Nesbitt for *GQ*.

I've bumped into him at numerous showbiz events over the years, when we've both normally been under the influence of vast quantities of alcohol, and invariably he's made me laugh.

He's kind, too. When I was sacked from the *Mirror*, he sent me a very long and clearly heartfelt text message about a month later, and it was genuinely one of the most touching things anyone said or wrote to me throughout the whole sorry episode.

His long-suffering wife Sonya is a splendid woman. The last time I saw her was in a hotel bar at 2a.m. a couple of years ago, and she laid into me and other tabloid hacks about our disgustingly intrusive practices in an animated and highly entertaining manner. What shone through most vividly was that this was a woman who really loved her husband, and was damned if she was going to let some trashy newspaper exposés, or the tramps who sold them, ruin their relationship.

Her ferocious defence of her man was somewhat surprising given that only a few months before he'd been caught snorting cocaine and having sex with a twenty-two-year-old legal secretary. But as I watched Jimmy and Sonya Nesbitt kissing and cuddling their way into the 3a.m. moonlight, I realised that their marriage was made of stronger stuff than most.

As I sat down at Cecconi's restaurant in Mayfair for the interview, Jimmy made it clear he wasn't massively keen on baring his soul about 'all that stuff a few years ago', and who could blame him. Yet we ended up talking about hardly anything else, and I saw a new, much more serious and thoughtful side to him.

What followed turned out to be not so much an interview as a therapy session, with me playing the unwitting role of the therapist.

My favourite exchange was this:

'I was checking your early career CV this morning and it was quite revealing. Your first starring acting role was as the Artful Dodger, you then appeared in Pinocchio, and your heroes are George Best and Alex Higgins. There does seem to be a bit of a character-shaping process going on here, Jimmy...'

He laughed loudly: 'I see what you're doing, Piers...'

'A devious, lying, booze-sodden sex maniac?'

'Fairly damning, isn't it...' He started to chortle. 'To be fair, the Dodger was a very charismatic guy ... and so were George and Alex.'

'Do you see anything of yourself in that particular brand of "charisma" though?'

'Yes ... er, I mean no.'

15 March

I found out today that Marion's been seeing Rav Singh, the *News of the World* gossip columnist. So we're both now seeing gossip columnists, which must mean something sinister, but I can't work out what. Anyway, everyone expects me to be really distressed by the news, but I'm not. Rav's a good bloke, and I've always got on well with him. If he makes Marion happy and is nice to the boys, then that's all I can ask for.

20 March

The first British Press Awards since I became co-owner of *Press Gazette* – and therefore the awards too – took place tonight.

Matthew rang: 'Let's skip them and go gambling instead.'

'Why?'

'Because everyone will expect us to go down there and lord it around, so let's do the complete opposite and not go at all. That way you can at least guarantee nobody will punch you.'

I rang Celia: 'Fancy going gambling at Aspinalls?'

We met Matthew at 9p.m. and watched him play the tables like an old pro, slamming £5,000 chips all over the roulette wheel with barely a second glance.

Determined not to be outdone, I went next door to the blackjack tables, cashed in £500 and lost it in nine minutes.

Regular texts from the awards suggested everything was going very smoothly, even as one put it: 'Boringly smoothly'.

22 March

A text message arrived at 9.31p.m. tonight saying, 'Hi Piers, are you working 2night?' I have absolutely no idea who this is, so ask them to identify themselves. 'Laura' comes the reply. I only know one Laura, my cousin, and she has never shown the remotest interest in my working schedule. 'Why do you want to know?' I ask. 'Because I might need a lift later.' Now I am completely bemused. What the hell makes my cousin, lovely though she is, think I am going to give her a lift to her home in Dorking later tonight? I call the number.

'Laura, it's Piers, have you been drinking?'

'Yes,' comes a slurred reply that doesn't sound like my cousin at all.

'Erm, which Laura is this?'

'Laura Bruno, you fool. Are you free later?'

Laura Bruno? Frank Bruno's ex-wife?

'Laura, this is Piers Morgan, what the hell are you talking about?'

Silence for several long seconds, followed by squeals of drunken laughter. 'Oh my God, I'm so sorry! I've got a local cab driver called Piers who takes me home occasionally if I've had a drink. His number must be next to yours on my mobile.'

I wish Laura goodnight, pour another glass of wine and ponder the thought that however grim things get, at least I'll definitely never be Laura Bruno's late-night cab driver.

26 March

Mother's Day, and the *Independent* asked me to write a piece about what my own mother has taught me. I wrote the following:

'1. Humility – Oh, OK, that was just my little joke. (Although my mother is the polar opposite to me when it comes to lauding her own achievements.)

'2. Tenacity – My mother has spent her entire adult life fighting for her children's rights against what her own mother would call the 'po-faced little pocket Hitlers of officialdom', whether it be getting us into schools, village cricket teams or Brighton Pier on a busy Saturday afternoon. All her four children have inherited that determined dog-with-a-bone streak, which can be slightly awkward when we all decide we want the last piece of lamb at Sunday lunch.

'3. A 'glass half full' mentality – My mother is the kind of person who if I told her I had just committed ten murders would instantly seek some sort of positive from the news, along the lines of, "Well, at least it wasn't eleven, darling."

'4. Worrying – My mother ought to have been a Jewish momma in the Maureen Lipman Beattie mode, so relentless – and often, it must be said, completely needless – is her worrying about her four children and ten grandchildren. Only yesterday, in the space of a five-minute conversation, she diagnosed sinusitis, bird flu, asthma, bronchitis, possible tuberculosis, and couldn't rule out testing for meningitis and pneumonia – all just from hearing my groggy voice. The disappointing reality is that I've got a bad cold. Unfortunately I now do the same with my children, to their constant irritation.

'5. A hard work ethic – My mother has worked far too hard all her life. For a decade she and my father ran a popular country pub in Sussex, slaving away seven days a week with hardly any holidays, often catering for up to 300 people in a single day, while simultaneously manning the two bars and caring for four young children. And I have no memory of feeling even remotely neglected, which is a great shame because there is loads of money in those "my childhood hell" misery books. I was brought up to believe you should work hard and then play hard. And I still do both with equal enthusiasm.

'6. Generosity – My mother would give you her last penny, and sometimes I suspect she has done just that to help out a friend or family member. Money for her is just something to pay the bills with and spend on the family, and I have inherited much of that sentiment. I like earning it, don't get me wrong, but I like squandering it just as quickly, too, on friends, family, sport and splendid wine. And my mother, of course.

'7. Humour – My mother laughs a lot, even when things are inutterably depressing. This is a great trait, which I hope I've inherited.

'8. Enthusiasm – I can't stand inherently cynical people and nor can my mother, who is one of life's great enthusiasts, and never fails to get wildly excited about even my most low-level antics. I am the same with my three sons, even when it mortifies them.

'9. Impatience – My mother likes to get on with things and get the job done. And so do I. Neither of us have time for ditherers or lazy bastards.

'10. Creativity – My mother gained a BA Hons degree in Fine Art at the age of fifty-nine, two years ago, and has always inspired her large family to be creative and artistic. Which is why none of us are bankers, accountants or tax officials, and why we all love our lives.'

27 March

Have flown out to Los Angeles to interview Ozzy Osbourne for my BBC ONE series *You Can't Fire Me, I'm Famous*. As a showbiz hack on the *Sun*, I used to nip to the States all the time to interview big stars, but apart from the last Concorde flight, I haven't spent more than a day there in a decade.

People often ask me if I could work in America, and I've always said no. They just don't seem to understand me over there, least of all the predominantly Mexican cab drivers.

I got a taxi to drop me at my hotel, the Beverly Hilton – repeating the correct name slowly three times – and instead he dropped me at the Beverly Hills. By the time I realised, he was gone, and I had to wait a further twenty minutes for another cab to turn up.

During that time I watched a procession of super-rich surgically masticated and chronically smug, rude and irritating Hollywood society types lumbering in and out of their Bentleys and Ferraris.

They all seemed so false, so insincere and so gripped with paranoia about their appearance. LA is a nice place, but I wouldn't want to live here.

28 March

Arsenal were playing Juventus today in the Champions League, so my producer Gary and I headed down to the Cock and Bull pub in Santa Monica to watch it with about a hundred other noisy fans.

Some bloke behind me kept up a constant stream of foul-mouthed commentary. It wasn't funny, just irritating.

Eventually half-time came, the lights went up, and I turned to see who had been ruining it for everyone.

It was Johnny Rotten.

Standing there with orange spiky hair, a pint in one hand, a fag in the other, still trying to be a Sex Pistol but old enough to be a grandfather.

Part of me had to admire his refusal to face up to the ravages of age. But another part of me wanted to put a large sock in his big Tourette's-ridden mouth.

Someone else in the pub told us that Rotten got beaten up a couple of weeks ago by a bunch of Scousers while behaving in a similar way during a Liverpool match.

The Ozzy interview went brilliantly. Once he warmed up he was charming, funny, surprisingly lucid and brimming with great anecdotes.

I felt like I knew every part of his house already, because it starred, of course, in the MTV programme, *The Osbournes*, but Ozzy gave me a proud little tour, including a visit to his personal gym.

'I do an hour and a half in here every day,' he said, turning on the step machine.

'That's incredible,' I said, genuinely impressed.

'Yep, every day,' he insisted.

Two minutes later he had to stop walking because he was breathing so heavily. I don't know what he does in that gym for an hour and a half, but it's not vigorous exercise – I can say that without fear of contradiction.

29 March

Got back to London very jet-lagged, and went straight to the National Book Awards. Saw Gordon Ramsay by the entrance.

'Just seen Jeremy Clarkson – he wants to chin you again,' he chortled.

There's nothing, as I know from the Theakston incident, that Mr Ramsay likes more than a good fight, particularly if I'm the one getting hit, but I could really do without physical violence tonight.

'Where is he?' I asked.

Ramsay burst out laughing. 'Only kidding, mate. He's not coming.'

When it came to the Book of the Year category, a camera crew suddenly appeared at our table and zoomed their lens at me. A sign that good news might be on its way?

I straightened my tie, sat up straight and started hastily preparing a graceful acceptance speech.

'And the winner is...'

My chest began to swell.

'J.K. Rowling.'

Cue the biggest spontaneous chest deflation since Jordan's implants burst.

The camera stayed on me, so I decided to ham it up a bit, hanging my head in my hands and mouthing, 'NO ... NO ... what has she done for the book industry?'

Jamie Oliver caught my eye and laughed. 'We were robbed,' he said.

I went over and asked if he fancied writing a column for *First News*.

'Sure,' he said. 'Come and see me tomorrow.'

30 March

My forty-first birthday. Met Jamie Oliver for a coffee at his restaurant, Fifteen.

'Happy birthday,' he said, presenting me with a bottle of his own olive oil and a signed copy of his latest cookbook.

I don't know how he knew, but it was a rather nice touch.

We had a long chat about a possible column, and I became rapidly enthused with his passion and crusading zeal when it comes to getting our kids healthy again.

I'd make him Health Secretary tomorrow – it's what this country desperately needs: real people in government, speaking their mind and having big ideas that really work.

Every night I see our supposedly top politicians on programmes like *Newsnight* and *Question Time*, and marvel at their complete inability to give straight answers or commit to any plans about anything.

The BBC had a big party in the evening and I saw poor old Davina McCall, whose chat show has been a ratings disaster. She had that haunted look of someone who knows she's in a turkey but has to finish the series.

'I'll come and boost your ratings,' I said.

'Will you? That's *so* kind of you, Piers,' she replied, sarcastically, before sticking her tongue out.

Davina's experience has shown me once again how brutal the television world can be. One false move, one wrong show, and you get buried.

31 March

Down to Brighton to do a speech for a Sussex cricketer called James Kirtley, who is launching his benefit year for the county at the Grand Hotel on the seafront.

I spent years with Jeremy, watching Sussex at their Hove ground back in the late Seventies, bowling to greats like Imran Khan and Tony Greig in the nets and generally making a nuisance of myself. It was where my love of cricket was cemented, and it's nice to be able to give a little back to the county side now by doing the odd speech here and there at various functions.

This one, however, turned out to be a complete bloody nightmare.

As I stood up to speak to warm applause, a fat, bald bloke at a table a few feet from me shouted, 'WANKER' at the top of his voice.

I was completely taken aback. This was a fundraising event, for Christ's sake. I wasn't getting a penny for it and I was getting heckled before I even started.

I ploughed on, hoping it was a momentary lapse in manners, but the bloke was drunk out of his thick-set tattooed skull and utterly determined to hound me off the stage.

'Yawn, yawn, yawn,' he declared, adding a huge elaborate theatrical yawn for good measure.

Other guests tried to shush him, but he was having none of it.

'You're *boring* me, Piers,' he slurred.

It was all hugely disconcerting, but there's nothing you can do except carry on, which is what I did.

Every punchline was met with a 'Boring' or 'Not fucking funny' or 'Heard it before', and it descended into near farce as more and more people tried to shut him up, and he responded by becoming louder and more belligerent.

I stopped speaking at one stage and turned to him as he spat out another insult. 'Look mate, everyone else seems to be enjoying it, so if you really hate it that much why don't you just leave?' People loudly applauded, but it made no difference to the big oaf.

'Why don't *you* just fucking leave?' was his considered response.

Eventually two large guys went over to remove him, which was easier said then done. He writhed around like a giant harpooned lizard, still clutching his pint glass and cursing away.

After an angry two-minute struggle he finally left, and I got the biggest round of applause of my whole speech.

I finished up soon afterwards, and sat down feeling slightly shell-shocked.

Bob 'The Cat' Bevan, one of the best speakers in the country and the compère for the day, lent over. 'He was an idiot, and you dealt with him very well. I've had loads of them.'

It was mildly comforting to know it wasn't just me that inspired this sort of behaviour. But the fact remained that I was down in Brighton at a benefit lunch for a county cricketer, and had just been hammered by a drunken heckler for no apparent reason.

It hurt, I can't pretend otherwise. It sort of crystallised my current situation. Drifting aimlessly from speaking engagements to TV studios, penning travel features and shopping in Sainsbury's. Nothing means very much.

I called Celia.

'I've just been heckled at a bloody freebie benefit speech,' I wailed down the phone as I walked off down Brighton's promenade in persistent drizzle towards the station.

'How *hilarious*!' she giggled.

I stopped in the middle of the pavement and laughed out loud. It was hilarious, there's no better word for it.

These things are only as bad as you let them be, and the reality was that while one imbecile had heckled me, the rest of the audience seemed to really enjoy the speech. It was a classic 'glass half full' versus 'glass half empty' moment, and in my self-indulgent misery I had failed to realise that it was actually all rather amusing.

As I turned the corner, I saw my verbal assailant puking into a rubbish bin, then pulling out a used McDonald's box and licking the remains. In that moment I understood the absurdity of taking his onslaught remotely seriously.

Later in the afternoon I did an interview with Jan Moir for the *Daily Telegraph*. Given that Celia works for the *Telegraph*, it seemed inconceivable that one of her colleagues would stitch me up, so I was in a relaxed mood.

Jan was a big cuddly lady who quickly informed me that she 'absolutely loved' my book, thought I'd been treated 'very shabbily' by the *Mirror* bosses and generally praised me professionally and personally in a manner so profuse that alarm bells should have rung all over my inflated head.

But after the battering I'd had earlier in the day, I was just happy to hear anyone say something nice about me.

We chatted for an hour and a half, had a glass of wine towards the end, at her instigation, and got on very well, I thought. Jan laughed in all the right places and kept saying how much she was enjoying the interview. A fact that should have made the alarm bells ring louder. I've read her stuff for years, and she either loves you or stitches you up, there's rarely any middle ground. She's a good, entertaining writer, and I had been looking forward to the challenge.

By the time she left, I was convinced it couldn't have gone any better.

I rang Celia. 'Went really well, think she liked me a lot.'

'Great, my parents read the *Telegraph*, so this could be perfect timing.'

'For what?'

'For admitting that I even know you.'

I ran a bath and luxuriated in my own genius. This media game is so easy sometimes.

1 April

Had a very long, very boisterous forty-first birthday party at Cambio de Tercio tonight. As I stumbled into the night at 2a.m., the waiters all queued up in a line and formally presented me with a genuine matador hat, which I wore for the next ten minutes as I tried unsuccessfully to hail a taxi.

'It might be easier to get one to stop if you don't pretend to be El Morganese,' suggested Celia.

I took the hat off and a cab stopped immediately.

2 April

Lunch at Andrew Neil's house, along with Michael Portillo and his charming wife, and the usual exotic assortment of guests that Andrew likes to have around him.

We drank fine wine, ate superb food, argued ferociously about everything from the Euro to Victoria Beckham's dress sense, and ended up dancing to Barry Manilow at 10p.m. A splendid way to spend a Sunday.

6 April

Took Sarah Brown to The Ivy for lunch. We had a great laugh, gossiping about the Blairs – it's safe to say that things with Cherie are still hell-freezeth-over-before-we-talk-again cold – various newspaper editors, the delights of children and so on.

She was very interested in *First News*, the children's paper I'm involved with.

'Where is the launch party?' she said.

'We're still trying to find somewhere,' I replied.

'How about No 11?' she suggested.

I was gobsmacked.

'Well that would be fantastic, but are you sure that's not a massive imposition?'

'Not at all, we do things like that all the time if it's for a good cause, and you're going to be giving money from the cover price to charity each week, so that sounds a very good cause to me.'

10 April

The *Telegraph* interview appeared today with a huge strapline across the top of the masthead saying, I'M NOT SUCH AN AWFUL HUMAN BEING, SAYS PIERS.

'There you are,' I gloated to Celia as we enjoyed a lavish breakfast at the Wolseley. 'Told you she liked me.'

I turned to the interview inside and speed-read it.

'Oh dear, Piers, where shall we begin,' wrote Ms Moir. 'Perhaps with the words you inscribed on my copy of your autobiography, *The Insider*. "Please be gentle with me," you wrote, in your curiously girlish handwriting, before putting one sweet little kiss at the end.'

I began to sweat.

'Gentle with you? You big sap. Why should I? Why should anyone be gentle with Piers Morgan, the former editor of the *Daily Mirror* who was famously sacked in 2004 after publishing hoax photographs of British soldiers abusing Iraqi prisoners?

'Well, according to Morgan, he deserves clemency because his national caricature as a galloping clot, a blithering drunk, a dodgy share-tipper and the chump's chump is not just getting a bit out of hand, it was undeserved and exaggerated in the first place.'

It got worse: 'In his stylish London riverside apartment, with its Italian limestone floors and walls painted an interesting shade of yellow that he describes as "hay", Morgan opens a bottle of wine and settles down on his plush, cream sofa.

'In the background, soft music plays and scented candles add a romantic touch as we gaze out at the setting sun glinting on the Thames. Like a fool, I'm happily enjoying this tranquil and rather glamorous moment before it becomes obvious what Morgan's intentions really are.

'Within minutes, he makes it clear that what he most wants to do is show me his … oh my God! Put that away, it's disgusting! You revolting boy. Don't put me through this, please, I beg. Yet Piers Morgan insists. Nothing can stop him now. He wants to show me his sensitive side.

'"Very little offends me," he says quietly, "but I am aware that people who don't know me could read some of the things written about me and think, 'Really, he is an awful human being.' I don't particularly enjoy my caricature, even if I do get a lot more attention because of this assumed mythology about what I'm like."

'That's so sad. One might have imagined that his eleven rumbustious years as a tabloid newspaper editor, playing hardscrabble with the lives of the rich, the famous and the downright unfortunate would have inured him to the brickbats and wicked ways of Fleet Street, but tragically this seems not to be the case.'

I felt my chest tightening.

'Are you all right?' said Celia.

'She's stitched me up like a kipper,' I said.

'Oh no, how?'

'Well, like this for instance: "Morgan is so thin-skinned that there are moments when you can practically see his heart constrict. So sensitive!"'

I skipped to the last paragraph:

"'One day he just might, like a white grub turning into a June beetle, metamorphose from overgrown schoolboy into elder statesman, but don't hold your breath.'"

Celia and I looked at each other for a few long, thoughtful seconds.

I would normally laugh at something like this, but I just felt rather embarrassed, and awkward.

I'm forty-one now, and reading once again that I'm some sort of overgrown schoolboy suddenly doesn't seem quite as funny as it used to.

It's also a bit worrying that every time I do an interview now, I get turned over. It wouldn't bother me if I was still editing the *Mirror*, but a lot of TV executives will read this *Telegraph* interview and wonder if it's worth investing airspace in a man whose public image is increasingly that of a hyperactive chimp.

12 April

Recorded the *Davina* chat show last night with Jade Goody – words I never thought I'd say, but it's my job now. If you're a celebrity, then this is the kind of thing you have to do to keep your name in the public eye.

I tried to liven things up by taking the mickey out of Jade and telling a few juicy stories, but Davina seemed totally distracted by all the flak she's been getting, and there was a general stench of death around the studio.

There is nothing worse than a TV series that everyone knows is terrible and has no chance of being recommissioned.

'Just forget about it,' I said. 'You're a great talent, it's just not been the right show for you.'

She smiled, without an ounce of happiness. 'It's been very hard, but I won't give up, and things definitely have improved.'

I was due to interview George Galloway for *GQ* today, and spent a longer time than usual preparing for the duel.

I met him at his Westminster office, laden with photos of Che Guevara, Fidel Castro and even Saddam's old right-hand man Tariq Aziz.

He was deeply tanned, smoking a cigar and chuckling.

But I had a cunning plan to wipe the grin off his face because, having read all George's recent interviews, it was clear that he would be in tricky territory if I pursued his Iraq arguments.

More specifically, it would be very hard for him not to say that it was morally justifiable for Tony Blair to be assassinated as revenge for the war. And if I could get him to say that, then we would have a big news story on our hands.

My plan worked perfectly. This was the exchange:

Q: 'Since many people view the invasion of Iraq now as an illegal, unethical war, are retaliatory strikes against the perpetrators morally justified even if innocent civilians die?'

A: 'No, it's never morally justified to kill innocent civilians.'

Q: 'But how do you defeat an evil force like Hitler without also killing innocent civilians?'

A: 'Innocent people may be killed during the bombing of legitimate targets, I accept that is justified. But the carpet bombing of innocent people in Dresden, for instance, was morally unacceptable, not to mention a total failure.'

Q: 'Were the atomic bombs of Hiroshima and Nagasaki acceptable?'

A: 'No. The evidence now suggests strongly that the Japanese were on the verge of surrendering anyway. And even if you sought to justify the first bomb as a way to end the war, there can be no justification for the second one whatsoever. It was purely designed to be an example to the Soviet Union of the enormous power of the American military.'

Q: 'If the suicide bombers in London on 7/7 had targeted Tony Blair and senior military leaders instead of innocent civilians, would you say that was justified?'

A: 'Well it certainly ... that's a difficult question, isn't it? The people who prosecuted an illegal murderous war on Iraq could hardly complain if someone sought to strike back at them. My problem would be that it's very likely that innocent civilians would die if such an attack was mounted. I would much prefer to see those who prosecuted [?] the war brought to court at the Hague and charged with war crimes.'

Q: 'Being a great politician, George, you've avoided the question. Would a simple assassination of, say, Tony Blair by a suicide bomber, if there were no other casualties, be justified as revenge for the war on Iraq?'

A: 'It would be morally justified, yes. I am not calling for it, but if it happened I believe it would be of a wholly different moral order to the events of 7/7. It would be entirely logical and explicable, and morally equivalent to ordering the deaths of thousands of innocent people in Iraq, as Blair did.'

Bingo. I had my news line. But perhaps he could be pushed even further.

Q: 'If you knew it was going to happen, that Blair was going to be assassinated by Iraqis, would you alert the authorities?'

A: 'My goodness this is a moral maze, Piers. Erm … yes, I would. Because such an operation would be bound to be counterproductive because it would just generate a new wave of anti-Muslim, anti-Arab sentiment, whipped up by the popular press. It would lead to new draconian anti-terror laws, and would probably strengthen the resolve of the British and American services in Iraq rather than weaken it. So yes, I would inform the authorities if I knew it was coming.'

Damn. Wrong answer.

He then revealed an extraordinary confrontation with Blair just before the war started:

'The Prime Minister keeps saying he was surprised by the ferocity of the Iraqi resistance. And I have to laugh, because I told him man-to-man, face-to-face, outside the gentlemen's lavatory in the library corridor inside the Commons, just me and him. I told him the Iraqis would fight him with their teeth if necessary, for as long as it took. There will be endless resistance. This was early 2003, just a couple of weeks before the war. I even went through exactly the kind of resistance it would be. I said there would be endless suicide bombs, roadside bombs, assassinations – it will spill all over the world.

'I looked him in the eye and said, "Please listen to me, Prime Minister, it will be a complete disaster." And frankly it was like talking to Rory Bremner. He went into his usual hands-out, Princess Diana dead moment, choke in the voice, and restated the standard line he's trotted out.

'I hope that in his quieter moments in the last three years he has had time to reflect on the fact that everything I and the anti-war movement have said about Iraq has happened and everything he said turned out to be wrong.'

You'd expect someone like Galloway to be a hard-drinking, storytelling, possible drug-abusing bon viveur when he's not terrorising MPs, but he shocked me by saying, 'I've never had a drop of alcohol. Nor did my father before me and nor has my daughter after me. My father brought me up strongly against drinking; he thought it was the curse of the working classes. He used to point to children who had their arses hanging out of their trousers while their father was staggering drunk from the pub and say, "That what's happens with drink." I feel the same as he did. I hate seeing drunks.'

'Have you ever taken drugs, then?'

'No, in fact I must be the only man my age who has never even seen a drug. I don't know what cocaine looks like, or hashish. Nothing. Spending most of my life in Muslim countries means I have never felt I'm missing out on drink or drugs.'

'So by a process of elimination your only vices are sex and cigars?'

'Yes, I suppose so. Cigars are problematic, because the best ones only come from Cuba, and when the US embargo is lifted the American market will buy them all long before they get to us, so I'll have to give up cigars.'

'So that just leaves you with one option George…'

'Yes, but as I grow older that too will become less and less prevalent.'

I'd enjoyed the interview enormously. It was good to get my teeth into something serious again, to debate things that matter with someone who knows his stuff.

And George seemed to enjoy it too, but that's because I don't think he realised quite what he'd said.

I rang Dylan. 'Galloway says it's morally justified to murder Blair.'

Dylan whistled. 'Fuck me.'

13 April

Charlotte rang to talk about her extraordinary day yesterday at Sandhurst, where Patrick is a top colonel. Prince Harry was commissioned as an officer in the famous 'passing-out parade' – and my little sister had to formally accompany the Royals throughout the day.

This meant that all the TV footage and newspaper photos had endless images of Charles, Camilla and the Queen enjoying Harry's big moment – next to Charlotte and Patrick.

'I was absolutely terrified!' she admitted. 'But thrilled too, of course.'

After the parade, Gabby, Phoebe and Georgina all got to present the Queen and Camilla with posies, sealing a memorable day.

18 April

Had dinner at the Groucho tonight with Ellis Watson.

As we went to leave, a French man came running up to me and exclaimed, ''Allo! I am a big fan of your work.'

I thanked him, curious as to what a Frenchman would know about my work.

'I think you have some great ideas and you come over really well.'

I thanked him again, but the curiosity remained.

'Yes, and although nobody thinks you 'av a chance at the election, I think you do.'

I laughed.

'I'm sorry, who do you think I am?'

'You are David Cameron,' he said proudly.

'No, I'm not.'

Pause.

'Oh I understand, you don't want people saying you were drinking in a nightclub. Don't worry, I won't tell anyone.'

And with that he was gone.

23 April

I was bored out of my brains at home this morning, wondering how to fill the yawning day ahead, when a text arrived from Simon Cowell:

'Hi Piers, I may be getting NBC to accept a Brit judge for the talent show. If so, would love you on it. Filming is end of May for three weeks and then six weeks from mid-June. I wanted to check your dates before I push NBC and see if you are up for it. Simon.'

I stared at my mobile screen for several seconds before the reality of what I'd read sank in properly. Appearing in a talent show on NBC in America is big time. Very, very, very big time. I waited … oh at least ten seconds before replying: 'Definitely. Sounds brilliant. Piers.'

Blimey. What have I let myself in for?

25 April

Cowell rang: 'OK, I've spoken to the NBC guys again; they've seen the pilot we did for the UK version and they like you. But they're nervous about having another Brit judge, people saying we're just copying *American Idol* and so on. So they want to meet you to discuss all the issues and see if you're right for the job.'

'OK, where and when?'

'Thursday morning, my place in Beverly Hills. We are less than a month away from starting filming, so we need to get on with it.'

'Righto. So I need to fly out…'

'Tomorrow. You're booked on the BA flight.'

Bloody hell, he doesn't muck about, Mr Cowell.

'Great, see you then.'

This was moving at a mad pace.

Arsenal played Villarreal tonight in the second leg of the Champions League semi-final. With just one goal in it, anything could happen, and it was comfortably the most important match in the history of the club.

So where was I at kick-off?

At the Marriott Hotel in London, hosting an awards event for legal clerks, that's where. I'd accepted the booking months ago, and failed to realise the significance of the date. From the moment I *did* realise what might happen tonight, I've been in living hell.

My club, my boys, playing in the greatest game of their lives, and I'm poncing about on stage doing my Jimmy Tarbuck routine. Oh the shame.

Fortunately my dilemma was explained as I was introduced, so I got an unexpectedly warm round of applause just for turning up – which made a nice change.

And throughout the awards I was given constant updates by fellow Gooners in the audience. The news was all good, nobody looked like scoring and our 1–0 home win would be enough to see us through.

Towards the end, someone shouted, 'Penalty!' and I stopped speaking in mid-flow.

Villarreal had a chance, in the very last minute, to level the scores and perhaps go on to win.

I asked the crowd to be silent while we awaited the result of the penalty. A hush descended, then a huge roar. I just couldn't work out if that was gleeful Arsenal fans celebrating a save, or Chelsea fans celebrating a Villarreal goal.

'HE SAVED IT!' came the cry from table eleven.

Jens Lehmann, our mad German goalkeeper, had made a brilliant save and Arsenal were through to the European Cup final for the first time ever.

I made an emotional address to the room: 'I never thought the day would come when I'd thank God for a German, but tonight it has.'

I phoned Martin the moment the awards were over and we instantly started planning our trip to the final in Paris on 17 May. What a night that will be, the night I've dreamed of for thirty-seven years.

26 April

John Prescott was revealed by the *Mirror* today as having had an affair with one of his parliamentary team, a lively young lady with the splendid name of Tracey Temple. There were hilarious photos of a dishevelled Prezza winching her around the dance floor at a Christmas party. Rather like that video footage of him punching a yob who threw an egg at him, I suspect this will all play rather well for the old bruiser. When you're a laughing stock to start with, it's very hard to be damaged by anything, as I've discovered myself over the years.

I boarded the BA flight to Los Angeles feeling excited. This could be a really big moment in my life, the chance to go to America and be a proper 'star', with all the wonderful nonsense that entails. I watched *The Player* on my laptop to get 'in the mood' for Hollywood and thought about Simon's last words to me yesterday: 'Piers, I won't mislead you. It's fifty-fifty that NBC will accept you as a judge – probably a little worse actually. This is a big show for them, and having an unknown Brit on the judging panel is a massive risk. I am pushing hard, but in the end it will be down to how you perform in front of them on Thursday. Just go for it.'

I landed at LAX at 4p.m. for the second time in a month – after thirteen years away from the place.

Simon had arranged for me to see the live *American Idol* results show, and I arrived just in time, feeling tired but exhilarated. I sat in the front row, just a few yards from the judges' desk. They came out to cheers (Randy Jackson and Paula Abdul) and jeers (Simon).

He spotted me and grinned cheerfully, before bringing the others over to say hello. 'Welcome to my mad world,' he laughed.

And he was right, it was crazy. Over 1,000 people going bonkers in the audience, and 35 million Americans watching at home.

The show was over quickly. It was slick, perfect, emotional and dramatic.

Cowell said only about two sentences, because there's no judging on the results shows. He leaned over as the credits rolled and said, 'That's one way to earn $400,000.' Then roared with laughter, as did I.

'Come to my dressing room,' he said, before a phalanx of burly armed bodyguards led him away.

I found him ten minutes later, lounging on a sofa, cuddling Paula Abdul's minuscule dog. He hates kids but loves animals.

With him was a woman with the fabulously exotic name of Cécile Frot-Coutaz, who runs Cowell's co-production company, Fremantle, in Hollywood. She is French, and smart in every sense.

We got down to business.

'Tomorrow's meeting is very important, Piers. It will literally decide whether you do this show or not.

'They will want you to justify yourself, to explain why you are qualified to be a judge on this show. And the answer, I think, is to say how, as a newspaper editor, your job every day was to identify talent and write about it, to promote real stars when you found them. Stress how you helped break some of the big bands, like Take That and so on, how you've met most of the world's biggest stars. And try and sound like you know what you're talking about!'

I was starting to feel a little nervous.

Simon drove me back to my hotel in his brand-new Bentley.

He had no bodyguards now.

'They're just for show, really,' he said. 'Though we've had a few hairy moments when acts I've criticised have been waiting out the back with baseball bats, so you have to be careful. But that's more of a problem in places like New York and Chicago than here.'

'Do you enjoy it out here?' I asked.

'Oh God, yes. It's very different to the UK, but I like that. They are very enthusiastic here, and if you have a hit show they love you. You don't get any of that mean spiritedness you get sometimes in Britain, where people resent your success.'

We arrived at the hotel, where Simon was greeted like a visiting president.

He gave me one last rally cry: 'Right, look Piers, this gig is yours for the taking. And if you get it, then it could change your life.

'It has the potential to be as big as *Idol* one day, I really believe that. And that means you will get obscenely rich and absurdly famous very fast and thank me for ever. See you in the morning.'

I am back in my room now, it's 9p.m. and I'm sipping a glass of beer, contemplating tomorrow's meeting.

I feel rather like I did back in 1993 waiting to see Rupert Murdoch for breakfast in Miami. Nervous; very, very nervous. But excited, too, and realising that I might be on the verge of a stunning career move again.

On that occasion I was made editor of *News of the World*. Now I might land a starring role in a huge American TV show.

The enormity of all this is quite hard to grasp. If I get this job and the show is a hit, then perhaps I will finally have found something to fill the void of being a newspaper editor.

27 April

Woke at 6a.m. and paced around nervously for a couple of hours until the gym opened and I could sweat off the jet lag.

The meeting was at 11a.m., and I got to Simon's house half an hour early.

It's a big, rambling Hollywood mansion, with huge imposing gates.

His assistant met me at the door, and took me inside for a cup of tea while Simon finished off another meeting.

I could hear lots of animated debate going on outside by the pool, but it was clear that Simon was the one making the decisions.

When it ended, I bumped into the departing guest and discovered it was Louis Walsh, Simon's *X Factor* co-judge.

He looked severely harassed.

'Good luck,' he said. 'Simon's just rejected everything I offered him!'

Simon was pumping by the time I got outside, full of creative energy and enthusiasm.

'Feeling OK?'

'Absolutely. I've never auditioned for anything before, so this will be an experience if nothing else.'

The NBC executives arrived, Craig Plestis and Meredith Ahr.

We shook hands and got down to business.

Simon explained why we were there, and then invited me to introduce myself.

'You're probably thinking: Who the hell is this guy, and why the hell should we put him in our show?'

They nodded.

At least I'd got something right.

'Well, I did a bit of statistical research last night and found out that Regis Philbin has 800,000 hits on Google to his name.'

Simon had told me that Regis – generally considered to be one of America's biggest TV stars – was being touted as a possible host for the show.

They nodded again: 'That's because he's a major star.'

'Yes, I know. Which is why you may be surprised to learn that I Googled myself as well, and I've got 901,000 hits.'

The NBC duo looked stunned by this revelation.

I paused for effect before delivering the killer punch: 'And that's before I've even come to the States...'

They seemed impressed. All I knew for sure about American TV network executives is that they love ratings and adore statistics.

And I'd given them clear, undeniable statistical evidence that I was not an unknown after all.

For the next half an hour I unloaded the full range of my spurious claims to fame and infamy. I let them have it all, from my mates Diana and Tony, to my old boss Rupert Murdoch, to what a great editor I'd been and how successful I was on British TV.

By the end of my humility-free virtual monologue, I was beginning to convince even myself what a well-connected genius I was.

'So in conclusion, I can't think of anyone better qualified to judge this show than me.'

Simon laughed. 'Right, well you certainly can't accuse Piers of lacking the confidence to do this, anyway!'

Craig Plestis stood up and shook my hand, saying as he did so, 'It was nice meeting you, Piers, shame we won't be seeing you again.'

I could tell he was joking, so I held his hand in mine in a vicelike grip and said, 'Craig, with all due respect I'll let *you* know if I want the job. OK?'

There was an uncomfortable silence, and for a split second I thought I'd overdone the soufflé and blown it big time. But then Craig and Meredith both laughed, Simon sighed with relief and we said our goodbyes.

'That went very well, Piers,' he said after seeing the NBC duo out. 'I reckon it's in the bag, but we won't know for a few days. I'll call you as soon as I hear.'

'Who else are you thinking of having on the judging panel?'

'Oh, it's not confirmed yet. But Brandy might be one. And I'm thinking of David Hasselhoff for the other chair.'

'David Hasselhoff? Is that wise?'

'Why?'

'Because he's the only bloke I know with a bigger ego than mine, and he's supposed to be barking. We'd clash like mad.'

An evil grin appeared on Cowell's face.

'Precisely!'

I left his house and got my limo back to the airport. The stark reality of what I might be taking on is only just beginning to hit me. If I get this job I will have to spend most of the summer out here. That means no cricket, no seeing the boys and not much seeing Celia for that matter.

And all for what? To be a judge on a talent show that nobody I know will ever watch.

Do I really want to live here? What if it flops spectacularly and I have to come home in shame to more ridicule? Most of the shows that launch in the States get canned pretty quickly, it's ruthless beyond belief.

This could be the biggest gamble of my life. But then, if I think about it harder, what have I really got to lose?

3 May

I was nominated for Interviewer of the Year at the PPA awards tonight, one of the two big magazine awards nights, for my *GQ* stuff. My biggest rival was Alex Bilmes, who also happens to be the Features executive at *GQ* who sets up most of my chats. We've exchanged increasingly ill-tempered banter for the last few days, deliberately spurred on by Dylan Jones.

When I got there I discovered that the host for the evening was Ian Hislop, who holds the unique distinction of being the only man I loathe more than Jeremy Clarkson. And the feeling is perfectly mutual.

The prospect of him having to present me with an award was too wonderful for words, and for the next hour I carefully planned what I'd do if I got up on stage. I settled on starting a speech, then running across and pretending to hit him, but stopping mid-punch and saying, 'Only joking, mate.'

Knowing him as I do, I would confidently predict that the shock might cause an embarrassing 'trouser incident'. He's like all school bullies: not so keen on it coming back at him.

The nominations were announced, and he theatrically groaned and made some quip about praying it wasn't me, before saying the words I'd feared most, 'Alex Bilmes'.

4 May

A weird, surreal day. The launch party for *First News* started at No 11 Downing Street at 3.30p.m., and at 3.45p.m. I was standing by the window of Gordon Brown's study peering out at the No 10 garden with Spencer when Tony Blair suddenly darted down the steps and began strolling around with his right-hand woman Sally Morgan. I quickly realised that if we stayed exactly where we were then Blair would come straight into our eye-line when he went back inside.

Fifteen minutes later I spotted an aide scurrying out with a message, and sure enough Blair trotted back up the steps and looked straight at us. 'Wave, Spencer,' I laughed. 'It's the Prime Minister.' Blair saw two hands waving at him and cheerily waved back in that 'Hi, guys, wanna be my new best mate' kind of way that he does so well. Spencer and I waved slightly more furiously and I added a loud 'coo-ee' for good measure. Blair blinked through his glasses, peered a little closer and then recognised me. It was like he'd suddenly been injected with leprosy. His hands withered downwards, his smile evaporated, his head bowed, his shoulders stooped and he almost ran inside.

'Doesn't he like you any more, Dad?' said Spencer.

'Hmm, obviously not son,' I replied. Then we both giggled.

Gordon made a very nice speech, saying how pleased he was to 'welcome Piers back to Downing Street'. Not a sentiment that I would imagine was shared next door at that precise moment.

Later he told me an amusing story about Tony Benn's son Hilary, who is making quite a name for himself in the Cabinet at the moment.

'He's just come back from South Africa, where he met Nelson Mandela,' he said. 'Mandela asked him how Tony was, so Hilary said, "Oh, he's fine thank you, considering he's now eighty-one." Mandela looked shocked apparently and said, "Tony's eighty-one? I had no idea he was so old." Only then did Hilary realise that Mandela was asking about the Prime Minister, not his dad.'

I introduced Celia to Sarah Brown, who promptly grabbed Gordon and said, 'This is Celia, Piers's girlfriend.'

Celia raised an eyebrow. 'Am I?' she whispered.

'Yes, I think you probably are now,' I replied.

So Celia and I formally shook hands on it, as the Prime Minister was probably formally shaking hands with some head of state right below us.

I got back to the flat at 8p.m. Still no news from Cowell, so I texted him to see what was happening.

He responded quickly: 'Your fate is being determined in the next two hours. Going now to NBC.' I felt tiny beads of sweat starting to glide their way across my upper lip. I poured a glass of Montrachet and waited.

At 10p.m. I had a shower to try and cool down.

While I was splattering myself with cold water, Cowell called and left a message. 'Piers, it's Simon, give me a call.'

His voice was deadpan, non-committal. I played it back again to try and deduce any fragment of a clue as to the answer. There was nothing. The man is the world's greatest non-giver-away-of-clues. It's what he does best.

I called back but now he was on voicemail, so I left a message requesting another call, mumbling about being in the shower and trying desperately not to sound too … desperate.

At 10.17p.m. he called back. 'Piers, it's Simon.' He sounded utterly miserable and my heart sank like a stone. 'Look, I'm really sorry, it's not good news.' Make that two stones.

'Oh well, never mind, it was fun thinking about it anyway,' I said cheerily, belying my abject disappointment.

Silence.

'Yes,' said Cowell, 'I tried everything I could, but NBC had made their decision and that was that.'

'Well, thanks for trying, Simon, I really appreciate–'

'So I'm afraid … you're going to have to come to Hollywood and star in my new talent show.'

WHAAAAAATTTT?

The little smirking, devious, cruel, contemptible … wonderful human being! I'd been Cowell-ed, suckered into thinking I'd failed like one of his poor victims on *X Factor*, only to discover I was through to the next round after all.

'You BASTARD!' I shrieked, to his audible pleasure. He would have made a great Roman emperor, sparing and executing gladiators with the same hugely satisfied smirk on his face. 'Piers, it was unanimous. The NBC guys liked you and you're in. We're going to have a lot of fun.'

I rang the boys to break the good news. Spencer chuckled with sheer incredulity.

'Really?'

I laughed. 'Yep, really.'

'That's cool,' he replied. The first time I think he has *ever* said that word in relation to his father.

Then I called Celia.

'What would you say if I said I was going to work in Hollywood this summer?'

'I'd say it's been fun knowing you.'

Pause.

'I'm joking. Of *course* you must go – it's going to be brilliant.'

There are certain pivotal moments in any relationship, and this was one.

5 May

I was booked on BBC Breakfast News to do a quick chat about *First News*, but it was the day after the local elections, and when I got there everyone was buzzing around like blue-arsed flies. I'd been told I was going on at 8a.m. – a prime slot when you get the biggest audience – but that quickly became 8.20a.m. after Menzies Campbell turned up to explain why the Lib Dems had performed with stunning mediocrity, then a flustered young BBC researcher came up to me and said, 'I'm awfully sorry, Mr Morgan, but I'm afraid David Cameron has turned up, so we'll pop you back to eight forty-five.'

The poor kid couldn't have been more than twenty-two, was sweating profusely from all the running around he'd been doing and didn't even know what I was there for. I felt sorry for him; he's probably being paid peanuts for this, too. But as the clock slipped on, I realised all the mums I'd hoped to target with the paper would be on the school run, so this was rapidly becoming a complete waste of time. I passed Cameron in the corridor. 'I've been bounced down the order for you ... oh the indignity.'

He laughed and apologised in that wonderful Blair-like way that indicates he couldn't be less sorry. 'Let's have lunch or something soon,' he said as his aide frogmarched him off to yet another studio. 'Sure,' I said, knowing he was just being polite. There's not much I can do for David Cameron now, other than advise him to never, ever read the papers.

Later in the afternoon, I was due to appear – by phone – on Chris Evans' Radio 2 show. I had been assured it would be a good ten-minute chat about the paper. It wasn't.

When I finally got through to them, a young woman explained I'd be taking part in a ten-second quiz instead. 'But you can plug your paper if you get the questions right.'

'I thought I was doing an interview?' I replied. 'Hang on, let me talk to Chris.' I heard some frenzied muttering.

'Chris says take it or leave it.'

'I see. Well in that case I'll leave it. Thanks very much.'

All rather irritating.

A while later, Spencer and his amusingly mischievous schoolfriend Theo, who is spending the weekend with us, started giggling uncontrollably. I saw my mobile phone in their hands and froze. 'What are you laughing at?' Neither was able to speak properly, but Spencer eventually mumbled something about someone being on the phone for me. I grabbed it with mounting terror.

'Hello?'

'Mate, it's Kevin Pietersen, what the fuck is going on? I've just had your kids on the phone wanting to talk about the next test match.'

I had to laugh. 'Sorry, mate, they nicked my phone. Look on the bright side, they didn't call Freddie, did they...'

He laughed: 'Bloody kids, ha, ha.'

Then a darker thought entered my head. I hung up on KP and turned to Spencer. 'Did you call anyone else before that?'

He and Theo shifted uneasily on their devious little feet. 'Erm, well just one person...'

I checked the dialled calls and saw one word: 'FAYED'

'You did what? Christ almighty, you stupid boys. Don't ever do this again, OK.'

They were still giggling. It reminded me of the early teenage years I spent locked in phone boxes with a few mates and a load of 2p coins, randomly calling our teachers and shouting abuse at them. Very, very silly, but it seemed hilariously funny at the time.

I called Fayed's office. 'Hi, it's Piers Morgan here. Have you just had my children on the line?'

The PA laughed loudly: 'Yes, Mr Morgan, they were demanding to be put through to the chairman.'

'Oh no, look I'm terribly sorry.'

'Oh please, don't worry about it, it was most amusing.'

Newsnight had a panel of critics to assess *First News*, and all of them gave it a thumbs-down. But since the panel consisted of Paul Morley, Johann Hari, Michael Gove and Julie Myerson, I feel quite encouraged.

6 May

Woke up to discover that Charles Clarke's been sacked as Home Secretary, Jack Straw's been demoted to leader of the Commons and Geoff Hoon's been pensioned off to Europe. The three government ministers who chortled loudest when I got sacked are all being carved up at once. What a delightful start to the day.

8 May

Simon Cowell rang. 'We start filming on 19 May,' he said. 'I suggest you get out there a few days before because the jet lag can be pretty bad and you're going to have a long day.'

'OK, no problem. Have you confirmed the other judges yet?'

'Yes, it's definitely going to be Brandy ... and David Hasselhoff.'

'You are the devil in disguise, Simon.'

He chuckled.

I put the phone down and checked my diary – 19 May was a Friday. I'd have to fly out on 17 May at the latest to have a day to acclimatise ... which was the day of the Champions League final in Paris.

I stared at the diary, willing it to change. I couldn't miss the game, I just couldn't. Martin had booked the Eurostar, we had great seats in the ground and various five-star restaurants and bars were being targeted for the mother of all celebrations.

But there was no way I could go to the game and get to Los Angeles in time for the filming. It was logistically impossible, unless I flew from Paris the morning after the match, arriving in LA late Thursday evening. But I'd be knackered, and any delays would mean I'd be late, which would be professional suicide.

I rang Martin.

'I can't go, mate. I've got to be in America.'

He was almost as upset as I was. We'd followed Arsenal together for a decade and now, in our most glorious moment, we would be thousands of miles apart. And I would be stuck in a country where their idea of football involves a rugby ball, helmets and pads.

I poured a Jack Daniels and let out a small yelp of pain. This was the ultimate cruelty. For a brief moment I even considered telling Simon to forget the show, to explain that some things were just more important than some silly prime-time American TV show. But then I looked in the mirror and said, 'Piers, don't be a twat. This is your chance at the big time.'

A bottle of champagne arrived at 6p.m., from Conor.

'Congratulations, boss, absolutely sensational! I *told* you we should have published those Iraqi pictures.'

9 May

Saw Anne Robinson for a cup of tea. She stormed America with *Weakest Link* a few years ago, then it all ended as fast as it began when the show fell victim to overscheduling and 9/11, an event that turned Americans off a lot of light entertainment shows for quite a while. 'It's a shark pool,' she said. 'But fun while it lasts. What's your deal?'

Ah yes, 'the Deal' – all anyone in American entertainment cares about.

'Erm … well, we're still negotiating. Their first offer wasn't exactly great.'

'Don't tell me, $5,000 a show?'

I laughed: 'That's exactly what they offered me. How did you know that?'

'Oh, that's what they offer everyone first, and presumably some people are stupid enough to accept it. I wasn't, and nor are you.'

Anne talked me through how she negotiated a huge suite at the Beverly Hills Hotel, first class flights for her and her husband Penrose, a driver and a six-year deal to present the show.

'Doesn't that lock you in a bit too much?' I asked.

'It means nothing,' she said. 'The moment the ratings dip, they cancel the show and you get sent back home in economy!'

Anne's a tough cookie and her advice was sound and kind:

'Go there, be yourself, have fun,' she said. 'It's a fabulous opportunity, but don't get sucked into all the nonsense out there or you'll forget who you are.'

10 May

Cowell has put me onto his agent, Alan Berger at CAA, one of the most feared and respected agents at one of the most feared and respected agencies, who has just successfully renegotiated Cowell's megabucks *American Idol* deal for four more years – for a rumoured $100 million.

I emailed him to explain that I knew roughly what salary and perks Anne Robinson got in Hollywood, and I was expecting the same.

He replied: 'The difference is that Annie was a proven host of the show in England and they really couldn't do the show without her. She was also the only host. In this case there are two other judges and you are still unknown, in the US. And *Weakest Link* didn't really work over here.

'Money will come to you in good time. Do the first one, be a big hit and we will deal with subsequent seasons. This is not about getting rich quick, this is about establishing you over here and expanding your businesses and personality on this side of the pond.'

Hollywood's not about getting rich quick? I see.

I spent the afternoon watching Spencer play cricket. It would be the last time I would do this for quite a while, a realisation that hit me hard as I lay in the freshly cut grass by the boundary and watched him bowl a tight line and length for four excellent overs. There are going to be many sacrifices I'll have to make chasing my Hollywood dream; it's not going to be easy.

11 May

Appeared on *Question Time* today with, among others, Michael Heseltine. There was an excruciating moment near the start when he tried to remember the names of Blair's big reshuffle victims and had a complete blank. As he sat there dithering, I wanted to help but had no idea what to do. If I said the names for him, it could have looked really patronising, but by saying nothing we all let the great man suffer palpable embarrassment.

Eventually David Dimbleby helped him out, but by then the damage was done and the audience at home would have been left with the feeling that Hezza's brain was going, when the truth, as I discovered by chatting to him in the green room, is that he's just as sharp as ever.

Hezza ended the question red-faced and flustered. He knew how it must have looked and it hurt his pride, but it seemed to galvanise him at the same time, and he roared through the rest of the show like the mane-flowing lion we all remembered. It was like watching Muhammad Ali come off the ropes in his third comeback fight and floor his opponent with some surprisingly nifty uppercuts.

Afterwards he admitted, 'I just couldn't remember their bloody names.'

'I wouldn't worry,' I replied. 'They're very forgettable people.'

Had a quick drink with Dimbleby in the green room.

'What are you doing now?' he asked.

'I'm going to Hollywood to star in a big TV show for NBC,' I replied.

'No, seriously,' he chuckled.

'I am serious,' I said. 'I fly out next week.'

I have rarely seen a look of greater bemusement than the one that crept across David Dimbleby's face in that moment.

12 May

Text from Ellis Watson: 'On a plane with Preston from *Big Brother* who, on commenting to his PR on the choice of her reading material, just asserted that the author was a "bit of a prat". And the book? Yours...'

14 May

Spent the afternoon ringing friends and family to say goodbye.

'I'm off to Hollywood,' was my glorious mantra.

'See you when it flops,' was the almost universal response.

9

15 May

My Hollywood adventure begins. It's 9p.m. in Los Angeles and I'm sitting in a palatial suite at the Regent Beverly Wilshire, where the movie *Pretty Woman* was filmed. I feel tired, jet-lagged and a little disorientated. The truth is that, amidst all the bravado, I don't really know what the hell I've let myself in for. I'm out here, on my own, entering a world I know little about, but which is described by those who've experienced it as the nastiest, most brutal tentacle of the entertainment industry in the world. Prime-time American TV, who would have thought it...?

16 May

I woke at 4a.m., watched a surprisingly powerful movie called *Jarhead* about the US Marines, had a ridiculously large breakfast involving endless plates of fruit, croissants, Mexican omelettes and tortillas, then went for a walk. The hotel is at the foot of Rodeo Drive, the most expensive shopping street in America and the very epicentre of Beverly Hills. The surrounding area is surprisingly pretty – tree-lined streets, nice wide roads, not many cars, smart houses. It's the one thing I didn't really expect from LA: tasteful. I had another breakfast, then a Starbucks coffee (they are, literally, on every street corner over here) and found a nearby newsstand selling faxed copies of same-day UK newspapers. Everyone is very friendly, and not in quite the vacuous 'have a nice day' way I had feared; the locals just seem chilled out and genuinely pleasant. But there is something wrong: the weather.

It's cloudy and a bit chilly. This is springtime in California, for goodness sake, I thought it was always hot here?

17 May

Found an emailed invitation to a Hugh Hefner Playboy party this morning.

Fantastic! I've been here two days and I'm going to be skinny-dipping in the infamous Heff Grottos already.

Then I read on and realised the party's in London, not at the Playboy Mansion ten blocks away. Dejected isn't the word.

19 May

First day of filming. I drove to the Paramount Studios lot in Hollywood, scene of some of the greatest movies ever made, entering by the famous Melrose Gate. Then I walked through a series of makeshift studios until I found Studio 7, the permanent home of *America's Got Talent* for the next few months.

A short, very friendly guy came up to me and introduced himself with the immortal words, 'Hi, Mr Morgan, I'm Bobby, welcome to Paramount Studios, let's go to your trailer.'

'Sorry, Bobby, what did you say?'

'Your trailer, Mr Morgan. Over here…'

I looked to where he was heading and saw this large mobile home sitting there with the letters 'PM' on the door. He wasn't joking, I was genuinely getting my own trailer. I stifled a laugh, walked inside and found a large sofa and sitting room, bathroom with shower, a fully stocked fridge, microwave, DVD and CD player, wardrobe, writing desk and a box full of sweets and chewing gum.

'Let me know if there's anything I can do for you, and I mean *anything*, sir.'

'Well, a cup of tea would be nice,' I replied.

'You got it.'

Four minutes later a piping-hot cup of English breakfast tea arrived. This was better service than the Beverly Wilshire.

I heard the unmistakable roar of a Ferrari outside, followed by a knock on the door, and another unmistakable noise:

'Well, I never thought I'd see the fucking day when I saw Piers Morgan sitting in his trailer on the Paramount movie lot,' cried Simon Cowell, shaking his head slowly.

'Would you like a cup of tea?' I said.

'Love one, thanks.'

Bobby nodded. 'You got it.' And raced off again.

I'd only known Bobby five minutes, but I already knew I was going to miss him terribly.

Simon shut the door. 'Right, Piers, I don't want to teach you how to suck eggs, but a few words of advice. Just be yourself, enjoy it and be honest.

People don't mind you being rude out here, so long as they think you mean it and aren't just being gratuitously offensive. And it helps if they agree with you ninety per cent of the time.'

'Can I swear?'

'Nooooooo. Well, you might get away with a bloody or two, but that's it. This is a family show and the networks are incredibly sensitive about things like swearing and nudity. Remember all that fuss when Janet Jackson's boob popped out at the Superbowl? It's crazy, but that's the way it is.'

Simon sat back on the sofa and for the next half an hour told me the whole amazing story of *American Idol*. How the show was rejected by every network until Liz Murdoch phoned her dad Rupert and told him how brilliant *Pop Idol* was and how Fox had to buy it.

'Everything changed that minute,' he said. 'Fox literally bought it that day. Rupert told them he didn't want a thing changed from the British version of the show, but I wasn't sure I wanted to do it; it seemed a big risk when everything was going so well in England.

'I had to be persuaded by trusted friends that it could be the biggest thing I ever do, and thank God they did, because it has been.'

'What was your first deal like?'

'Oh, very average. Nobody new gets much to start with here if you're an unknown. But if the show's a hit, it's a very different story.'

The first series of *Idol* did well, but not brilliantly. It was the second series that really took off, and average ratings for the latest, sixth season have been nearly 30 million, a huge number.

'Is it true your new deal is a hundred million dollars?'

He smirked. 'It's so vulgar talking about money, Piers.'

'I'll take that as a yes.'

He smirked again. 'Let's just say that was a very good day at the office.'

'Do you enjoy living here, though?'

'Yes, very much. It's a nice lifestyle, and I always go home for a few months when the show finishes, so it's perfect. I get the best of both worlds.'

Bobby knocked on the door.

'Wardrobe is ready when you are, sir.'

I was bemused. 'Er, I'm wearing my wardrobe.'

Bobby raised a quizzical eyebrow. '*Right*. OK. No problem. How about make-up?'

'No, I'm not wearing my own make-up.'

'OK, well let's get you over there.'

Bobby led me down to a golf cart. We set off and stopped after 12 yards.

'Everything all right, Bobby?' I asked.

'Yes, Mr Morgan, we're here, sir.'

I looked up to see the make-up trailer. I had just been driven from one side of the narrow street to the other.

'Bobby...'

'Yes sir?'

'I can probably walk next time.'

'You got it.'

At that moment I heard a loud noise and turned to see David Hasselhoff clambering into the make-up chair next to me, jabbering loudly at what looked like his extended entourage.

He was taller than I expected, pretty fit for his age, extremely animated and gesticulating dramatically.

I waited for a moment of calm and introduced myself, 'Hi David, I'm Piers.'

He stared me up and down intently.

'Oh hi, man, nice to meet you.'

'We've met before actually. I interviewed you on Malibu beach years ago when you were in *Baywatch*.'

'You did? Who for?'

'The *Sun* in London.'

He looked like I'd just told him he had two weeks to live.

'The tabloid *Sun*? I know them all right, bunch of lying wankers. You guys were always sticking it to the Hoff!'

The Hoff. How amusing. When big stars talk about themselves in the third person it's normally a sign of quite advanced and incurable egotitis, but there's something endearing about calling yourself by your nickname.

We sat in two chairs a metre apart, and two delightfully friendly make-up artists, Mezghan and Amy, went to work.

'Hey, can you guys stick some peroxide in my hair?' asked the Hoff.

'Sure, David, but why?' said Russell, our hairstylist.

'I just thought I could sit in the sun for a bit and my hair might go lighter and make me look younger.'

I started laughing, assuming this was a joke, but it quickly became clear that he was deadly serious.

Russell pondered his answer carefully. I got the distinct feeling that it is *never* a good idea to question a big star when he or she wants something on set.

'It's probably not a good idea to do it so close to filming,' he said diplomatically.

At which point the Hoff sat up with a start and said, 'Oh God, I've already put some on actually. Is that going to be OK?'

'It should be fine, David,' said Russell, with alarm in his eyes, 'but maybe stay out of the sun.'

What else could he say: 'Well, Hoff mate, I reckon you'll be bald as a coot by teatime,' which must be at least one possible side effect of dosing an ageing mane with buckets of peroxide.

The Hoff was so pumped up it was slightly unnerving. He took his appearance incredibly seriously, examining every mark on his face, every blade of hair, every inch of his clothes. He knew *exactly* how he wanted to look.

It was fascinating to watch, and understandable, too. He has a lot riding on this series. The Hoff was the biggest TV star in the world in the *Baywatch/Knight Rider* days, but his career has been on the wane since then, he's fifty-three and in desperate need of a hit if he's not going to end up on the celebrity scrapheap.

He kept up a near relentless conversation in the make-up trailer – about himself: what he was doing, where he was going, the money he was making, his 'bitch of an ex-wife' and his global expansion plans for the Hoff brand.

His only interest in me was how I could help him with his British 'interests'.

'Should I do pantomime?' he asked, rather ironically given that his whole life seems like a pantomime.

'Er, where?' I replied.

'Wimbledon. They want me to play Captain Hook.'

My first ever paper was the *Wimbledon News*, so I know that theatre well.

'Well, it's a big old place and the audiences will be large.'

'I don't know, though,' he said. 'The money's good, but it's panto, you know. It's not real theatre, is it?'

No, I thought, but then you're the Hoff, not Laurence Olivier.

I felt exhausted after twenty minutes in his company. What the hell is it going to be like working with this manic guy for months on end?

At 2p.m., we were called for filming on the first audition show, where an endless procession of 'talented' people would parade before us and perform their act. I met the third judge backstage, a beautiful black pop star called

Brandy, who was a big teenage success but who I only vaguely remembered. She seemed sweet, but very nervous. There is a lot riding on this series for her, too. It must be incredibly hard to be a big star in a celebrity-obsessed country like America and then see your star fade before you're even thirty. I remember talking to Mark Owen from the boyband Take That about the agony of being all washed-up at twenty-four.

'I sat at home for five years, waiting for the phone to ring,' he said sadly. 'Once you've tasted success, it's twice as hard to fail.'

The *America's Got Talent* set was enormous, as was the studio audience of nearly 800 people.

I stood with the Hoff and Brandy, waiting to come on and feeling a bit of a fraud. At least the other two are famous in the US. I'm just a nobody. That made me feel nervous, and not in a nice way. Though as Cowell told me earlier, 'The fact that none of them has ever heard of you, Piers, is probably a distinct advantage in your case!'

We were introduced one by one. The Hoff and Brandy got standing ovations, I got general apathy and bemusement.

Once we started filming, my nerves disappeared and I began to really enjoy myself.

Each act has two minutes to impress us. They can be any age, race, religion or gender, and they can do anything they like. Literally anything goes.

The judges each have loud buzzers and can hit them at any time during the performance. Three buzzes and the acts have to stop immediately.

Some were quite good, others so hopeless they got buzzed off almost as soon as they started.

One of the early acts involved six pirates and a donkey, who all shuffled on stage and pranced about making braying noises.

It was terrible, and all I could think of was one of Cowell's initial sales pitches: 'Piers, we're going to find America's next great superstar, trust me.' On this evidence, we were more likely to find America's next great laughing stock.

Cowell, though, loved every minute of it, and kept hopping up on stage with a massive grin, urging us on. He genuinely seems enthralled with this show.

'I wish I was judging it,' he kept saying. And I could tell he meant it. All the other shows he does involve just singers, this one's completely unpredictable.

The acts kept coming, some rather good but most rather awful. Each of them suffering under the delusion that they are the most talented person in America.

One, a large, cocky bald man called Harry Masters, proudly declared himself 'the greatest singer of all time', then emitted a noise so profoundly awful that half the audience covered their ears with their hands and urged us to hit the buzzers. It was like being in a gladiatorial bear pit.

'That was terrible,' I said.

'What do you know?' he sneered back.

'I know a terrible noise when I hear one,' I replied.

Another group called Blue Velvet wobbled on wearing hideous pink dresses, and as soon as they started singing it was clear we were hearing historically bad voices. We all buzzed them off after less than five seconds, leaving the three members of the band shell-shocked.

'Can't we have another chance?' asked one.

'Absolutely not, no,' I replied.

It was brutal but fair – they were shocking.

We had a break after an hour, and I found Alan Berger outside with a big grin on his face.

'That was great. After fifteen minutes I was already emailing people saying I wanted to renegotiate your deal,' he said.

Cowell came to my trailer, still laughing. 'That was hysterical,' he said. 'I told you it would be fun.'

'But Simon,' I replied. 'Some of them are diabolical.'

'Of course they are, that's half the fun. The audition shows are always the best.'

The show is held together by the host, Regis Philbin. He is a huge star in America – think Parky and Tarrant combined – and the public adore him, as is evident from the standing ovations and chants of 'Regis, Regis' they give him every time he comes on stage.

He is seventy-five now, but looks fifteen years younger and does almost every pre-recorded part in one take. I was seriously impressed.

Towards the end of the day we were all knackered, and it showed. We could barely raise our hands to hit the buzzers, never mind give a quick, witty verdict on a fire-eater.

Cowell appeared again, that permanent smile temporarily gone. 'Come on, guys, I know you're tired, but you've got to raise the tempo a bit, OK?' He sounded slightly irritated and businesslike, and I liked it. He was right, whining about being tired was pathetic. Everybody was tired, the cameramen, the lighting guys, the band, the producers and the acts.

We're the stars of this show, and we have to perform like stars.

We did get things going again, helped by a mad and very bad juggler called Kenny Sheldon, who dropped everything during his two minutes, but it was so funny we let him finish without buzzing him off.

'You're coming back,' shouted the Hoff. He has said that to about 95 per cent of the acts, usually preceding his verdict with the words, 'Man, you were *awesome*.' I think he gets off on the audience applause when he's nice to the contestants. Which is fine for his popularity rating, but not so fine for the credibility of the judging panel.

The public at home are watching the same things we are, and will be baffled and derisive if we praise talentless halfwits to the hilt.

Brandy's not much better. Everyone gives a 'good performance' in her book. Though she did say no to Kenny after I lent over and whispered, 'Brandy, he is the worst juggler in history.'

By the time it got to me, the audience were baying for a bit of blood, so I gave it to them.

'Kenny, juggling is like running the relay. If you drop the baton, it's over.'

He looked like he was going to cry.

'I can do better,' he said.

'OK, go on then,' I replied. 'See if you can juggle for a whole minute without dropping anything. One mistake and you're out. But if you do it, you're through.'

Kenny pursed his lips, took out a load of knives and began juggling them. To everyone's astonishment, not least Kenny, he didn't drop one.

'You're through,' I said. Kenny exploded with orgasmic delight, leaping dementedly around the stage.

However bad he was, Kenny was definitely more talented than a man called Jay Myl, who came on wearing an old sailor's outfit, took a small flute out and stuck it between his nostrils before playing 'Tiptoe Through the Tulips'.

When we buzzed him off, he stood there in disbelief, then laid into all the judges one by one, including the memorable retort: 'When did *you* last have a hit, eh, Brandy?'

The day ended in suitably ridiculous fashion when a giant inflatable break-dancing cow arrived on stage and proceeded to do handstands, before squirting fake milk all over the audience.

The cow didn't make the cut.

As I left the stage, two big guys moved quickly to my side with walkie-talkies.

'OK, we got Piers, he's on the move to the trailer.'

It was like having my own presidential detail, and very, very pleasing. Several of the contestants tried to talk to me but were politely discouraged. They take security *very* seriously over here, and with 250 million firearms out there among the public, I'm rather glad of that fact.

Cowell met me backstage.

'Great job, Piers. Really good, congratulations.'

I've never worked for him before, but Cowell is an inspiring boss. He's smart, amusing, knows his stuff and is ready to dish out praise and criticism when either is due.

Bobby knocked on the door.

'The cart's ready to take you to your car whenever you are, sir.'

'Are David and Brandy still here, thought I'd say goodbye first?'

'No, sir, their limousines left straight after the show.'

Hmmm. I've got to think about how I'm being perceived here. Cowell's last words to me were, 'Remember, Piers, this is a tough town and they will exploit any sign of weakness.'

Driving myself home looks fairly weak compared with hopping into a chauffeur-driven limo straight after filming. Or does it? Perhaps it's a sign of shocking self-confidence. Cowell drives himself around, after all.

I got into my car, a rented Sebring convertible that I've been given for the month, and drove back to the hotel feeling exhausted but exhilarated.

Then I fired off a few emails to several key media gossips back in London, spreading the word that I now had a trailer and bodyguards. I mean, what's the point of having them if nobody back home knows about it?

20 May

Text from Marion: 'Boys most amused by your bodyguards. Spencer planning his book, *The Untold Story*, and signed-photo scam on eBay. Don't you just love him…'

Headed back to the Paramount Studios for another day's filming.

Simon was there already and very focused.

'OK, yesterday was good, but today can be a lot better. We need more chemistry between the judges. The hardest thing when we started *Idol* was getting the chemistry to work between me, Paula and Randy. It's never easy when you don't know each other, but the more you work at it, the better it will be, I promise you.'

We saw sixty more acts in six hours, including a superintendent from the Miami Port Terminal who makes machine-gun noises while playing with a GI Joe doll, a big fat Hungarian bloke called Frank who holds the world record for balancing a motorcyle in his teeth, and an Indian weirdo called the Laughing Yogi, who was memorable for the fact that he never made us laugh once.

Just when I was losing the will to live, a seventy-year-old black woman came on stage, introduced herself as 'the Rapping Granny', and then marched around like Ice-T, snarling and sneering her way through a self-penned rap.

The audience went wild, loving every second, and I found myself, against all expectations, totally enthralled.

'Get on your feet,' said Brandy, forcing me up for a little jig as Granny reached a rousing finale.

'Yo, it's Granny Time!' she cried to tumultuous applause.

'You are what this show's all about,' I said. And she is – bizarre, unique and very entertaining.

But is she *talented*?

That's more difficult to say.

21 May

Got up early to speak to the boys via iChat, an amazing new invention from Apple where you can speak for as long as you like, for free, from computer to computer. And all in normal-time video. For anyone working away from their kids, it's an absolute godsend. My boys love exacting phone terrorism on me, doing things like picking up the handset and groaning, 'I'm tired, bye Dad,' or just emitting stupid noises until I get completely infuriated.

But a video grabs their interest far better and is much more fun to communicate with. They wandered off to eat some more tea, then wandered back to pick up where they left off.

'What car have they given you, Dad?' asked Spencer, who now defines every human being in the world by the vehicle they drive.

'A Chrysler Sebring Convertible,' I said.

I could hear him clicking on his laptop, then groaning.

'Can't you get a Lamborghini?'

'No, Spencer, I can't get a Lamborghini.'

'If the show goes to No 1 will Simon Cowell give you a Lamborghini?'

'I very much doubt it, but I might get a Mini Moke out of him, if I'm lucky.'

Bertie interrupted: 'Dad, I want to say something.'

'Yes, Bertie…'

'You stink.'

All three boys fell on the floor laughing their vile little heads off.

I miss them already, but at least they think I'm finally doing something worthwhile with my life. If I'd gone to America to edit a newspaper they would have been nowhere near as impressed, and nowhere near as tolerant.

I put the phone down, and now I'm wondering what the hell I'm going to do for the rest of the day. It's 9a.m., and I know nobody here at all. Five years of living on my own have taught me how to avoid the pangs of loneliness, but this is different. I'm completely alone here, no family or friends and no work colleagues to call up and have a drink with.

Later, I walked around Beverly Hills, then drove to Santa Monica and had a jog along the beach. I had some lunch, browsed in a bookshop for an hour, bought the Los Angeles Sunday papers, which were dense and worthy, got back to the hotel and had a swim, slept for a bit – the jet lag is still bad – then watched three hours of crap American television. Hardly the most inspiring day of my life, and I've got weeks of it to come.

22 May

I've got nearly two weeks until the next audition rounds are recorded. I've had to stay out here for various production meetings, interviews and stuff, and I've just had my first pang of real loneliness. A fortnight is a long time to be on your own in a place like Los Angeles.

I sat down to write my diary this morning, but ended up just staring at the screen for half an hour. I feel curiously uncreative. Normally words flow easily, but not today. I tried again in the afternoon, but the same blankness enveloped me. Went to the gym and pounded away on the bike for half an hour, but even that didn't get the literary juices going.

I need some human contact, people to have a laugh or get drunk with, something to get me going.

Simon rang at 7p.m. 'Fancy coming to the *American Idol* final tomorrow?'

23 May

I arrived at the Kodak Theatre in Hollywood, where they have hosted the Oscars in recent years. The sheer size of the *Idol* show is extraordinary. It's not just the biggest TV show in the States, it's the biggest TV show in the world. And Cowell is the master of ceremonies, the main attraction, the guy it all revolves around. I watched him work the crowd tonight, and he was a class act. Randy Jackson and Paula Abdul, his co-judges, walked into the 4,000-strong crowd to affectionate applause, stopping along the way to high-five a few fans and sign a couple of autographs.

Then there was silence, followed by a slow build-up of tension and a rumbling roar of anticipation as the show's host, Ryan Seacrest, announced: 'Ladies and gentlemen, please welcome … Mr … Simon … Cowell.'

The place went completely crazy, transforming into a seething cauldron of booing, jeering, screaming and cheering. Half of them loved him, half of them loved to hate him. It was pure theatre, and the pantomime villain had just arrived. To add to the drama, Cowell was flanked by four bodyguards in dark glasses and suits, and he didn't stop for anyone, he just marched to his seat.

Then he looked around the room, caught my eye a few rows back and winked as the audience chanted his name.

It was spine-tinglingly intoxicating.

The show itself was incredible, with endless superstars from Prince to Daniel Powter, Meat Loaf and Toni Braxton, appearing on stage to sing with the ten finalists, all of whom now looked like bona fide stars themselves.

The face-off was between Taylor Hicks, a grey-haired chubby crooner from Alabama, and Katherine McPhee, a beautiful Californian brunette with an equally beautiful voice.

'You have just won *American Idol*,' Cowell told Hicks towards the end of the show, which was a little naughty of him, given that the public hadn't yet had the chance to vote.

But he knew what he was doing. He knew that by giving his verdict now, everyone would vote accordingly. He would therefore be backing the winner. Smart.

24 May

Back to the Kodak Theatre for the live *Idol* results show. Ryan Seacrest announced that 63 million phone votes had been received, more votes than were cast in the last American elections. A staggering, and slightly terrifying, statistic.

Saw Simon backstage, and he told me that nearly 40 million people had watched last night's final – 50 per cent more than the number who watched Charles marrying Diana in Britain.

And the seventy or so thirty-second advertising slots in the two-hour finale had sold for $1.2 million *each*, making it the most lucrative TV show ever – even bigger than the American Super Bowl.

'They call *Idol* the nuclear TV show,' Simon said. 'Because every show that goes up against it gets vaporised.'

He invited me to his dressing room afterwards, but it was complete pandemonium by the time I fought my way through the scrum to get there.

All sorts of unexpected British faces hovered amidst the American stars, including Cilla Black and Lionel Blair.

But the most surprising sight was Simon and his biggest rival, Simon Fuller, chatting like brothers in the corner. Whatever legal problems they have, there's no doubt that these two guys have cracked America like nobody else since The Beatles.

'Let's catch up tomorrow,' Cowell said, as yet more adoring fans barged in to pay homage to the great man. He remained extraordinarily calm amid all the mayhem.

'No probs,' I replied, glad to be released from the frenzy.

There was a big aftershow *Idol* party tonight, to which I'd been invited, but I don't want to be seen strutting around on Simon's coat-tails too much before my show has even aired, so I caught a cab home, ordered a spaghetti bolognese, took a sleeping pill and crashed out.

25 May

Spoke to Celia as soon as I woke up.

'Right, I'm bloody bored and I need a playmate. So get your shapely little backside out here ASAP.'

'I'll come out tomorrow,' she replied.

26 May

Stanley played a guitar solo at his school today, something I would never normally have missed for love nor money.

'How did it go, Stan?' I asked, already knowing the answer.

'I was brilliant, Dad!'

Of course he was. Stanley is like me, he always thinks he's brilliant.

Got a great email from Richard Wallace, my replacement at the *Mirror*. He'd been to a huge pre-World Cup party thrown by the Beckhams.

'Bloody amazing bash. Becks gave me a full-on rapper-style shoulder hug and ordered us to come to Madrid after the World Cup. Ray Winstone and his Mrs were on our table – absolutely top geezers – and we got completely trashed. Met old Rooney and Ronaldo, and my old pal P. Diddy (he arrived with an entourage of eleven!). I tottered out at 3.30a.m. and James Brown was still going strong on stage…'

I don't miss editing the *Mirror* much, but I definitely miss some of the parties.

27 May

Celia arrived, and we decided to go to The Ivy, no relation to the famous London restaurant but just as hot with celebrities and paparazzi.

We were kept waiting a humiliating twenty-six minutes for a table, and were, of course, completely ignored by fellow diners, most waiters and all the photographers as we left.

'I think your campaign to crack America needs a little cranking up,' Celia observed.

'Just wait until we go on air,' I retorted. 'Then they'll be throwing Tom Cruise off his table for us.'

'Of course they will, Piers. I think it's time we put you to bed, isn't it.'

30 May

Celia flew home today. We had hit every hotspot we could think of in three days, but attracted a scale of invisibility only matched by a couple of albino swans in an igloo.

The sheer scale of anonymity I'm enjoying is impressively depressing.

I've not even had the obligatory British tourist calling me a wanker. Absolutely nobody in the entire United States of America has even a modicum of interest in who I am, but I'm determined to change that.

Because if I can pull it off here, then I can kiss goodbye to tedious speeches, crappy TV jobs and all the other nonsense I have to do back in England to pay the bills.

1 June

I'm due to interview Paris Hilton for *GQ* today, which should be most entertaining on many levels. But there's one big stumbling block: her 'people' are insisting I go and listen to her new debut pop album before I can sit down with the great woman.

I tried to wriggle out of it, but they were adamant.

So at 11a.m., I arrived at Warner Records and was met by a smiley-faced PR woman.

'Can I have your mobile phone, please?'

'Why?'

'Security.'

'What do you mean, "security"?'

'I mean this is, like, the hottest record in the world right now, and everyone's trying to get hold of it, so we don't want you secretly recording it with your phone.'

I burst out laughing. 'Trust me, I do not intend to steal Paris Hilton's music on my phone.'

'Well, I'm sorry, sir, but you can't hear it unless I have your phone, and if you don't hear it then you can't do the interview.'

I sighed and handed the phone over. This reminded me of all those incredibly irritating times I'd interviewed American stars for the *Sun* more than a decade ago. The vacuous PRs, their stupid little rules, the sheer scale of annoyance their behaviour can induce.

It was also quite weird sitting on the other side of the fence again. On *America's Got Talent* I am treated like a God and a whole army of people are there to deal with my every whim.

But as an interviewer for *GQ*, I am treated as just another hack.

The contrast is enormous. And I'm not sure I like it!

Minutes later I was buried in the bowels of the building with the PR as she tried to get the stereo to work.

I sensed an opportunity to avoid the impending aural torture.

'Look, don't worry if you can't get it to work, really it's not a problem. I'm sure the album's great...'

She cut me dead: 'No, you *must* listen to it.'

Twenty minutes later it was finally working and the dulcet tones of Paris Hilton filled the room. To be fair, I've heard worse. It was typical bubblegum Eurotrash music, the kind you get in every European nightclub around midnight.

The PR was in a form of mild ecstasy, grinning wildly and gyrating on the floor like she'd just taken a huge acid trip.

'Isn't it, like, FABULOUS,' she cried.

'It's fascinating,' I responded, an ambiguous phrase I always use with PRs because they mistakenly assume it means something flattering.

'Oh I'm so glad you like it, I just LOOOOVVVVE it!'

It was a comical scene – me pretending to make studious notes while actually choosing my all-time greatest Arsenal team; she cavorting with herself on the carpet, having some sort of orgasmic experience.

One of the tracks was a reggae song of dismal quality.

'Doesn't this, like, remind you of Bob Marley?' she squealed.

'Do you think so? How fascinating…'

After four songs I'd had enough. 'Erm, look that's great, I don't need to hear any more.'

'Really? Some of the other stuff is, like, amazing.'

'I'm sure it's fascinating, but I have to get to another appointment. Thanks so much.'

'Oh, no problem. Let me go and get your phone.'

I didn't have the heart to tell her I had another phone with even better recording quality in my pocket.

I got back to the Beverly Wilshire at 1p.m. to find roadblocks all around the place and lots of very excited people running about. It took me twenty minutes to get my car in, past vast swathes of security people.

'Who's this for, the President?' I asked one particularly large and grim-faced policeman. 'No comment, sir.'

Blimey, perhaps it was. Me and Dubya sharing the same hotel, now that could be fun.

I asked another hotel employee if it really was the top man.

'I think it might be his dad,' came the reply.

Further gossip around the pool suggested new names – Bill Clinton, Jimmy Carter, Arnold Schwarzenegger, the Prime Minister of Afghanistan, the Crown Prince of Dubai.

One thing was certain, whoever it was, was very, very important. I saw an FBI SWAT team heading up the stairs, and at 2p.m. everyone was evacuated while sniffer dogs swept the hotel for bombs. Crazy stuff.

At 3p.m. I was due to meet Paris in the hotel bar, but another PR was waiting with some bad news.

'Erm, Paris is, like, worried about the security and wants to meet somewhere else. A restaurant down the road, is that OK?'

We set off, and arrived to find her ensconsed in a booth.

She was petite, and prettier than I'd expected.

I started with a question that I knew would determine how the next hour or so went.

Me outside my trailer on the Paramount movie lot with Bobby the Bodyguard/Mr Fixit, and Jason, one of the show's producers. My wish was their command – well, in my own egotistical mind anyway.

'Remind me, Hoff. Which one of us is supposed to be the talented one again?'

'So you like my new car then boys?' Unfortunately, Spencer's thirteenth birthday present had to go back after five hours, but what fun we had while it lasted.

Water laugh! Stanley and Bertie ignored most of the rides at Universal Studios, preferring to stand under a giant water cannon and get soaking wet.

All friends together in Hollywood. Lisa Kudrow makes the boys' day backstage at the *Tonight with Jay Leno Show*. And their dad looks pretty pleased too.

I think my face tells its own disgusted story. Ellis Watson, topless and wearing a kilt, humiliates me yet again at Muscle Beach.

He never saw us coming … Ellis and I jump Stevie Wonder in a Hollywood restaurant and force him to record a message ordering Celia to marry me.

The word 'crazy' barely does it justice. The Hoff, Simon Cowell, Brandy and me pose with a bunch of exotic stilt-dancers on the set of *America's Got Talent*.

Who's a pretty boy, then? The show's hair stylist Russell and make-up artist Amy launch a double-pronged attack during a commercial break.

'Can you perk it up a bit?' Simon Cowell gives me a pep talk as we enter our eighth hour of judging on the first day of *America's Got Talent* auditions.

XXX – the most formidable weapons in talent show history. Three of these and you're toast.

Bobby Badfingers – the self-proclaimed 'No 1 fingersnapper in the world' – and my favourite contestant on the show.

A dancing cow that spurted milk all over the audience as a finale, thereby winning the 'Most Ridiculous Act' award quite comfortably.

Dave 'the Horn Guy'. I called him the most annoying man I had ever met, and he just grinned back at me with an incredibly irritating smirk.

Hail to the Rapping Granny. She was seventy, had survived breast cancer, but blew the audience away with her sensational stage presence. A truly inspiring woman.

Leonid the Magnificent breaks down, yet again. He was a 6ft 5in Russian transvestite who claimed to be a juggler but looked more like a giant, useless Christmas tree.

Simon Cowell with the show's eventual winner, pint-sized eleven-year-old singer Bianca Ryan. The little girl with the enormous, and amazing, voice.

The Hoff sings 'Jump In My Car' live to the American nation. And millions of people from Colorado to Miami instantly rush to protect their children's ears.

The Hoff does the talking, I do the fixed cheesy grin. Not difficult to smile given that I'd been flown first class to New York for precisely four minutes' work.

'So, Paris, I Googled you this morning and you have over 50 million hits while Nelson Mandela has 10 million hits. Discuss.'

She looked appalled. 'Oh? The last time I looked I had over 90 million hits…'

'I see, perhaps I was only checking the UK version of Google. My apologies. Either way, you appear to be five times as big as Mandela on this planet of ours, what do you think of that statistic?'

She was completely unfazed by the comparison. 'I feel proud of myself actually, that I have accomplished so much at such a young age.'

I asked if she would describe herself as a professional celebrity and she nearly choked on her chicken salad: 'I hate that word.'

I was confused. 'What? "Professional"?'

'No. "Celebrity".'

'Why? You are one, aren't you?'

'It just sounds lame.'

'What are you, then?'

'A brand.'

It was my turn to choke.

'I see. What does that mean exactly?'

'It means I have a fragrance line, my make-up, shoes, hotels. Products I design under my name. And I've made, like, 200 million dollars in the last year, while J-Lo's only made 150 million, so it's doing pretty, like, well. The thing is that there's no one really like me.'

I interrupted. 'There is actually, in Britain. She's called Jordan.'

Paris convulsed on the spot.

'I am *nothing* like her.'

I laughed. 'Well, she was a model, has done a bit of acting, sings a bit, goes to parties, has her own product lines and makes shedloads of cash. You can see the potential comparison…'

'I'm flat-chested,' she responded, 'and she's got huge breasts.'

'So who do you compare yourself to in Britain then? Lady Victoria Hervey?'

'Er … no.'

'Lady Isabella Hervey?'

'Who?'

'Her little sister. A right pair of mingers.'

'What are mingers?'

'Not a good look.'

'So why would you compare me to them, then?'

'Just scrabbling for some sort of British yardstick to judge you by – they're posh, rich and talentless, too.'

'HEY! Stop that.'

'Do you know Abi Titmuss? Blonde, another one with gigantic breasts.'

'No. Never heard of her.'

'Jade Goody?'

'Nope.'

'Posh Spice?'

'Oh yes, of course. I met her and David in LA one night and they were like the most beautiful couple in Britain, and so nice. Victoria is gorgeous, and I always wear her brand of jeans.'

I got to the crux of the debate: 'My only problem, Paris, is that I think you've become the global personification of modern celebrity. Someone with no obvious talent who is incredibly successful.'

'Look,' she snapped. 'I didn't grow up wanting to be a celebrity. I wanted to be a veterinarian and look after animals, but then I realised you had to put them to sleep and give them shots and stuff and I just couldn't do all that.'

I stifled a laugh.

There's a point in most *GQ* interviews where I ask the subject if they think they're good in bed. It always gets a great response, because everyone thinks they are, of course. I mean, I've never heard anyone say, 'I'm a lousy lay.'

But in Paris Hilton's case the question was superfluous because this very morning I watched the infamous internet private sex video she'd recorded with an ex-boyfriend, which he'd then sold all over the world for millions of dollars.

And what was quite clear is that Paris, for all her protestations of being a shy, retiring girl, is rather good in bed.

I put this allegation to her.

'So, I watched your video this morning and the answer is clearly affirmative.'

She blushed but looked delighted.

'I don't know if I am.'

'Yes you do.'

'I don't really do that with men. I've only like done it with two boyfriends.'

She stared straight at me, defying me to be sceptical of this extra-ordinary claim.

'I'm surprised by you, Paris, I had you down as some sort of rampant sex kitten...'

'Well, I'm not. In fact, I'm not going to have sex for a whole year.'

'WHAT? You're going to be celibate for a whole year?'

'Yuh. I'll kiss, but nothing else.'

'But Paris, you're twenty-five and in your absolute prime sexually, why on earth do you want to give it up?'

'I feel good about it. I like the way guys go crazy when they can't have sex with you. If he can't have you, he stays interested; the moment he has you he's gone. Unless he's really in love with you. I have a lot of male friends and I hear the way they talk about girls and I hate it.'

'But come on, Paris, you're supposed to be a partying, sex-mad, posh, rich wild-child wastrel. Not a teetotal, asexual workaholic. This is absurd.'

'I don't like it.'

'What?'

'Sex.'

'Don't be ridiculous. I've seen the video and you definitely like it.'

'I don't. I'm serious. Sex with someone you love is good, but otherwise I hate it.'

There was something attractive about her, definitely. I didn't want there to be, because it's easier to park her on the dumb blonde bench, but the more we talked, the less guarded she became, and the more entertaining the interview got.

'Could you ever go out with an older guy?'

'Maybe.'

'What's your upper age limit?'

'About forty.'

'Can you make it forty-one?'

She got the point and gave me a withering, slightly pitiful look.

'Hmm. I can make it eighty if that helps, Piers.'

Touché.

'What about Tony Blair? Do you fancy him?'

'Who?'

'Tony. Blair. You have heard of him, right?'

'Oh yeah, he's like your President? I don't know what he looks like, though.'

'You must do – greying, balding, dodgy teeth, silly grin, always sucking up to your President...'

'I don't know ... not sure.'

She giggled.

I guess if you're Paris Hilton then knowing what some old politician looks like really doesn't matter.

The scale of her earning power is mind-blowing. She told me she recently got a million dollars to go to Austria and wave at a crowd for half an hour.

'I had to say, "Hi," and tell them why I loved Austria so much...'

'And why do you love Austria?'

'Because they pay me a million dollars to wave at them!' She fell about laughing at the absurdity of this fact.

Paris lives on her own with two monkeys, four dogs and three cats in the Hollywood Hills.

She insists she is sexless and happy, and compares herself readily to Marilyn Monroe and Princess Diana – 'Oh I *loved* her. She was amazing. Her death affected me so much, such a strong and beautiful woman. I just cried for two hours non-stop when I heard she'd been killed. I've been in cars trying to get away from speeding paparazzi before and it's horrible, so I can relate to Diana and the problems she had.'

There's something ridiculous about Paris Hilton, obviously, but there's something smart, too. She knows the game she's playing, and she plays it well. She has more Google hits then anyone apart from George Dubya Bush, and makes tens of millions of dollars while intelligent people dismiss her as stupid.

'What are you doing later?' she asked.

'Oh, I thought I'd head for some crazy bar and dance on tables all night.' She laughed. 'I don't think so somehow...'

'What are *you* doing, then?'

'Going home for an early night with my animals. I've got to be up at 7a.m. for a flight.

'Austria?'

'No, Vegas. They pay me a lot of money to wave at people there, too.'

And with that, Paris Hilton giggled and departed into the Beverly Hills sunset.

She may be the world's No 1 talentless celebrity, but she's no fool.

2 June

Met Rupert's girlfriend, Chloe, and her mum, for a drink in the hotel. She's just landed a job over here working for a UK-based entertainment agency.

It was a fun evening, made memorable by the behaviour of one of the waiters, who served us corked wine from the same bottle twice. When it happened the second time, I asked why he'd brought us wine from the contaminated bottle again and he looked bemused rather than apologetic. 'Well, it was still sitting there, sir, so that's how the mistake occurred. It wasn't my fault.'

Quite extraordinary given that a simple sniff of the wine would confirm it was pungently corked.

When I paid the bill, I included a 10 per cent tip anyway to show goodwill. This is a great hotel and the service is usually excellent, and you don't want a reputation in this town of being a bad tipper because tipping is hugely important here.

We got up to leave, and reached the reception desk before the offending waiter ran over to stop me.

'Excuse me, sir, but was there something wrong with the service?'

'Why do you ask?'

'Oh, because you've only included a 10 per cent tip and it's normal to include a 20 per cent tip if service is good, sir.'

I laughed. 'Look, mate, you served the same corked wine twice and I had to drink it twice. That's not brilliant service now, is it?'

He jutted his jaw out and stood firm.

'But the corked wine isn't my fault, sir.'

Another waitress came to see what the argument was about, heard the story and solemnly agreed with her colleague.

'If it wasn't his fault then the tip should be 20 per cent really, sir.'

I was flabbergasted.

A tip is a gratuity. It's something you give someone out of the kindness of your heart if you like what they've done. It's not a compulsory donation, whatever these two think.

On the other hand, I have to live here for most of this summer, everything else was great and I didn't want a fuss, so I took back the bill and added another 10 per cent to the tip.

'Thank you, sir, I'm glad to have been of service to you.'

5 June

Spencer starts his Common Entrance exams today, which will decide his academic future. He was struggling earlier in the year after missing a lot of school through some weird virus, but recently he's really pulled his socks up and got stuck into his revision. He sounded very nervous on the phone last night, and I feel pretty wretched about being away for his big week.

I drove to the Paramount Studios at 2p.m. The pre-show tedium was enlivened by a quite hilarious meeting with corporate lawyers to discuss the perils of 'non-fraternisation, harassment and prohibited conduct'. The bottom line is that we can't meet, greet, talk to, or most definitely touch a contestant on the show, or their relatives and friends, until four months after the finale.

The Hoff, who is going through a messy divorce, looked downcast. 'You mean I gotta wait till Christmas?' he asked.

'Erm, you have to wait until … to be precise … 9 December 2006,' replied one of the lawyers, trying to hide her dismay at the question.

The Hoff was appalled.

'These rules are ridiculous. Am I allowed to say your pants look hot?'

The lawyer, an undeniably attractive woman, seemed unsure and rather shocked, but she quickly recovered her composure and reassured us that the rules work both ways, and were primarily to prevent contestants trying to harass us.

'Hang on a sec,' I said. 'I've waited forty-one years to be harassed.'

The personal conduct contract went on to stipulate that we could not insult anyone off screen about their marital status, age, disability, medical condition or political beliefs. Nor could we make offensive jokes, or release nude footage of ourselves or anyone else connected with the show. We could not bring firearms, explosives or drugs on to the set, nor take bribes or kick-backs, and we were to be smartly dressed at all times.

I looked at the Hoff, who was wearing an Alf Garnett-style white string vest.

'This *is* smart,' he insisted.

He's a curious beast. Very loud and domineering, but underneath all the 'me, me, me' bombast I suspect there is an insecure, slightly vulnerable guy who just wants to be loved and successful again.

Perhaps the most amusing moment of the day came with my medical check-up. A middle-aged, kindly woman entered my trailer and spent about five minutes checking my ears, eyes and blood pressure. Then she shoved her light device right up each nostril and it didn't take a genius to work out what she was looking for. From what I've heard already about these TV sets, cocaine abuse is almost an occupational hazard for the stars.

I called Spencer from my trailer to see how his exams had gone, and he sounded remarkably relaxed, suggesting they'd gone well.

'What do you actually do out there, Dad?' he asked.

'Well, I judge people.'

'No offence, Dad, but how are you qualified to do that exactly?'

'Well … erm … I was a newspaper editor.'

'Who got sacked.'

'Yes. Thank you for reminding me, Spencer.'

He giggled.

He had a point, though, I'm genuinely not sure that I am qualified to judge a talent show, but then I guess the public at home judge these things in the same way as I do – you either like something or you don't, they're either good or they're not.

The filming today was memorable for a 6 foot 5 inch Russian of dubious sexual orientation called Leonid the Magnificent, who pranced on stage in a pair of white briefs and wings and balanced swords on his nose – until he dropped them anyway. He was hopeless but fantastically charismatic, so after we kicked him off he was tactically invited back to plea for his life, and sobbed his way through a tumultuous appeal to the American nation for clemency.

He got a second chance, not because he has much talent but because he is supremely entertaining TV.

There was also a quite appalling singer who crooned 'I Left My Heart in San Francisco' so badly I thought I'd need eardrops afterwards. I couldn't think of anything else to say but, 'I wish you'd left your voice in San Francisco.'

Just as I was losing the will to live, an eleven-year-old girl called Bianca Ryan crept on stage with mousey hair, a cheap dress and the impression that she'd be happier as a school library monitor. Then she let rip with a voice like Judy Garland, singing Jennifer Holliday's classic 'And I'm Telling You I'm Not Going'. It was a stunning, incredible performance.

'Change your hair, dress and shoes and you can win this competition,' I said. And I meant it, too.

Even Brandy, who is rarely impressed by any of the singers, said she felt goosebumps on her neck.

It was another tiring day. I had a slightly strained conversation with Celia on the phone in my trailer. She's the least high-maintenance girlfriend a man could wish for, but we haven't seen each other for a week, won't do for another week, and the eight-hour time difference makes it hard to have normal conversations. It's usually 5p.m. her time before I wake up, and she goes to bed as I'm off to lunch. It's disorientating. People who say 'absence makes the heart grow fonder' ought to add, 'but it also makes things a lot more difficult than they would be if you stayed on the same continent as each other'.

I am loving this chance-of-a-lifetime gig, but I don't want to sacrifice a possible chance-of-a-lifetime relationship at the altar of shallow Hollywood fame and grubby fortune. If that's what being a celebrity means, then I don't want it. That's something I definitely wouldn't have felt if I was twenty years younger.

We went back in for more filming, and Brandy, who'd been visibly upset all afternoon, confided that she'd split up from her basketball player boyfriend recently and was finding it really hard. I really felt for her. She's a lovely girl and looks distraught in-between takes.

What with the Hoff going through one of the world's worst divorces, me in the process of mine and Regis onto his fifth wife, we're a right bunch of dysfunctional 'celebredee' romantic misfits.

But our mood, especially the Hoff's, was lifted by the arrival of Michelle L'Amour on stage – a very sexy burlesque dancer who proceeded to take most of her clothes off.

Brandy was outraged and hit her buzzer straight away, but the Hoff and I were thoroughly enjoying this unexpected strip show and encouraged Michelle to show us more and more 'L'Amour'.

By the end, the Hoff was physically holding Brandy back while I covered our buzzers for further protection. It was fairly puerile behaviour from men of forty-one and fifty-three, but we were tired and needed some light relief.

'Urgh, you both disgust me,' said Brandy in the break.

'You're just sore because she's prettier than you,' retorted the Hoff.

I finally emerged blinking into the darkness at 10p.m. to find my car battery completely flat. Most people had gone, and I had to wait half an hour for one of the crew to come and help me out with some jump leads.

I stood there wanting to beat the crap out of it, like Basil Fawlty in that memorable scene where he attacks his Mini, but decided against it. I bet De Niro never gets a flat battery at Paramount Studios, though. In fact, I bet De Niro never *drives* to Paramount Studios.

6 June

Woke at 5.30a.m., went for a long walk around Beverly Hills, filled my face with scrambled eggs at the French café, read *Variety*, *Hollywood Reporter*, the *LA Times* and a faxed version of *The Times*, then called Celia and we agreed we were being quite pathetic and had to get a grip immediately. My brother, who has a wife and four young kids, went to Iraq for six months, for goodness' sake.

Phoned Spencer to see how his exams had gone, and he was very upset about a history paper he thought he'd cocked up.

'It was terrible, Dad, just terrible.'

He sounded nervy and tearful, and memories of my own exams came flooding back to me.

'Just keep your cool, and don't worry about the odd tricky paper,' I said. 'These things are a marathon not a sprint.'

He groaned, 'Not another of your stupid sayings, Dad ... please.'

The first programme in my BBC ONE series, *You Can't Fire Me I'm Famous*, went out last night in England. It featured Martine McCutcheon, and did pretty well.

Peter Fincham emailed me: 'I enjoyed that, and I think the audience did, too: 2.7 million – not a bad figure at all for a new series in that slot.'

I'm relieved. If it all goes pear-shaped out here, then I'll need shows like it to keep my British TV career going.

8 June

England played their first World Cup Finals match today against Paraguay, which I watched on my own in my room at 8a.m. Los Angeles time, on ABC with unbelievably annoying American commentators.

Apart from insisting on calling our opponents 'Paragwey', they used bleedingly obvious phrases like: 'It's time to score a goal!' or 'I'll say one thing, Chuck, England need to win!'

Eventually I turned down the volume, it was just easier that way. Michael Owen was injured almost immediately, reminding me of Arsene Wenger's view of his brittle bones and dodgy legs. Not for nothing is Wenger known as the Professor of Football.

Kevin Pietersen texted me tonight: 'Hi, just to let you now that Jess and I got engaged this evening. We are both absolutely thrilled to bits.'

10 June

Final day of auditions, then I can go home for three weeks.

It was another hilarious day of crackpots, oddballs and the odd flash of real talent. I try to be kind to the older or very young contestants.

One seventy-year-old female harpist played a lovely but totally inappropriate mournful song, so I told her, 'The bad news is that you're not right for this competition, but the good news is that I want to book you to play at my funeral.'

But I was less forgiving to another old lady called Sharon, who claimed to have a bird-calling act, and started making a high-pitched whistling noise while peering into the rafters of the studio.

We all waited for a flock of birds to fly down, but none came. She doesn't have any birds.

'Are you sure you're at the right place?' I asked her. 'This is a talent show.'

'Oh yes,' she said defiantly, before twittering away again.

Completely barking.

As was a comic called 'Mark the Knife', whose act involved putting a live scorpion down his trousers.

'OUCH!' screamed the Hoff, who has probably had a lot more dangerous things down his trousers.

Another young girl came out, called Taylor Ware, and started yodelling, something I have never heard done on stage before in my life. I laughed to start with, but then took her more seriously. She's got a fantastic voice, looks like a typical all-American sweetheart, and has a real stage presence. A definite outside chance for the final.

Unlike Buster Balloon, an imbecile of a man who came out, blew up a huge balloon, and tried to dance inside it – only for the balloon to promptly burst.

'Can I do that again?' he said desperately.

'Oh go on then,' I replied, more out of curiosity than anything else.

He came out, blew up the balloon, got inside – and it burst again.

'Can I just have one more go?' he pleaded.

'No.'

'PLEASE.'

'OK, but this is it.'

The balloon burst again.

Towards the end filming we were electrified by a couple called David and Dania, who call themselves Quick Change, and literally change clothes very quickly. It was a stunning, faultless performance, and we were all completely mystified by how they did it.

'I'm using a Hoff phrase,' I said. 'You guys were AWESOME!'

The Hoff gave me a quick glance of disapproval.

In the next break he slid his chair over and said, 'Were you dissing me, then?'

'No, David, I was taking the piss.'

'What does that mean?'

'It means I was complimenting you.'

'Oh, right, OK man. Thanks.'

Then he stood up and went to speak to the audience. He does that a lot and seems to crave the attention. I'm beginning to realise how much he's missed being a big star, and how important this show is to his celebrity rehabilitation.

When filming finished we walked out of the studio to be met with a dozen TV camera crews from all the major showbiz shows, *Hollywood Extra*, *Entertainment Tonight*, *Access Hollywood*.

I flitted from one to another, basking in the attention and loving the growing feeling of being a bona fide celebrity.

There is a much purer, nicer view of the whole fame game here in the States. All the interviewers raved about the show and would never dream of asking anything cynical or personally intrusive.

I've been waiting for my murky scandal-plagued past to catch up with me, but so far nobody seems remotely interested in it.

11 June

Flew home today. The show will go on air while I am back in the UK, and it's going to be fascinating to see how I get treated then.

10

14 June

A long, agonising day spent waiting for Spencer's school not to ring. Apparently, if your child has failed his or her Common Entrance, or not met the required percentage for their chosen school, then the prep school is solemnly informed and the disastrous news instantly imparted back to the offender's parents by phone. So if you get to around 6p.m. without a call, then it's probably good news coming tomorrow when the formal opening of results envelopes takes place.

I spoke to Spencer at 7p.m. 'Looking good, mate.'

'Uh-uh.'

He was now frozen in a monosyllabic world of tense, nervous panicky waiting-for-exam-result hell. It was awful to watch.

15 June

Spencer's D-Day. Marion and I took him up to the school and he was so nervous he could barely speak.

A milling crowd of anxious kids and parents had gathered for coffee in an anteroom a few yards from the headmistress's office, where she was gathered with other senior teachers and a pile of unopened envelopes containing the results for each pupil. The boys and girls were called in alphabetically, so we knew immediately we'd have to wait a while.

I pitied the first child in, but needn't have worried. She was one of the brightest in the year and came back with a beaming grin and a printed sheet full of As. This should have put everyone else at their ease, but instead it only served to double the pressure. Nobody wanted to be the first back with relatively dud results and get that awful outpouring of insincere 'Oh I'm so sorry you're so thick' support.

Spencer was pacing around like a hyperactive caterpillar, slithering from one group of friends to another, inspecting results, craning his neck into the dreaded Head's office, laughing nervously and pretending he had things completely under control.

I tried to take his picture but he was having none of it. 'Dad, go away and stop being so embarrassing.'

Then came the call. 'SPENCER PUGHE-MORGAN.'

I saw his neck twitch almost as much as mine. There must be worse things than watching your oldest son marching into an office to get his Common Entrance results, but right then I couldn't think of any. I was so nervous I could feel sweat patches erupting all over my body. Marion had turned so white, she looked like she was going to expire at any second. She'd worked so hard with Spencer on these exams, and this was the moment of reckoning.

I peered into the Head's office and there was a lot of smiling going on, which had to be good news, then a few handshakes and he was back out.

'Well?'

Marion and I virtually shouted the inevitable question in unison.

'I did OK,' he replied with typical feigned disinterest.

'What does "OK" mean?'

'It means OK.' But then his face cracked into a huge grin.

'Let me see,' I said, and grabbed the sheet of paper.

'A, A, B, B, A, B, A, C.'

Four As, three Bs and a C. Way, way above expectations.

A surge of raw pride ripped through me.

'Spencer, this is brilliant.'

'Dad, stop being so embarrassing.'

'It's fantastic, darling!' cried Marion.

'Mum … shh.'

Spencer's never been one for attention.

He ambled off to his mates, who were all desperate to know how he'd done, and all ecstatic for him when he revealed his impressive sweep.

The results meant he could go to his first-choice school, Charterhouse, which is just as well because there wasn't really a plan B.

He'd pulled it out of the bag when he had to, and when a lot of people doubted he could. I am thrilled for him.

Watched the England/Trinidad and Tobago match with the boys in the afternoon, and spent the match abusing Peter Crouch, our 6 foot 7 inch useless beanpole of a striker.

His sole contribution to English football so far has been that idiotic robot dance he does on the rare occasions he scores.

Stanley rushed to his defence: 'Dad, Crouch is legend, he's amazing.'

'Stanley, he is as much use as a mobile street lamp.'

'No, he's brilliant.'

And with that Stanley launched into his own hilariously over-the-top version of the Crouch robot dance.

It was so funny that I made him do it again for my phone video.

Minutes later, with chilling inevitability, Crouch scored a great goal. Stanley went berserk, shrieking and shouting all over the place before performing another celebratory Robot.

'Told you, Dad, he's LEGEND.'

What could I say? Crouch had made me look a total fool.

16 June

Flew to New York today to appear on their big breakfast programme, *The Today Show*. I was allowed to take Celia after Alan Berger successfully argued that it would be 'potentially relationship-threatening' if I was forced to leave her again so soon after getting back. We settled into Virgin Upper Class, toasted Simon Cowell with champagne and laughed at the sheer absurdity of this ongoing adventure. We'd be staying in one of New York's best hotels for three nights, all expenses paid, and all for a total of just four minutes on air, split between me, the Hoff, Regis and Brandy.

Our joy was shortlived, though.

I'd heard that the queues at JFK customs were bad, but nothing could have prepared me for the snakes of people waiting. It took us over two hours to get to the front of the line, by which time the warm glow of Upper Class and champagne had been displaced by an icy blast of fury, frustration, thirst and starvation.

The atmosphere was intimidating, too, with lots of big, mean armed and hostile policemen staring at us. It all seemed so self-defeating.

America has always been an insular superpower. That infamous statistic stating that just 14 per cent of its population even have passports never ceases to shock and amaze, but it has retreated right back into its shell since 9/11, treating all foreigners as 'aliens', suspecting everyone and everything. It's a sad, if entirely understandable, sight to observe in such a great country.

We finally got to the front and I presented my documents. The customs official grimaced.

'What are you doing in New York?'

'I am appearing on *The Today Show*.'

His shoulders instantly hunched back up.

'You're what?'

'I'm on *The Today Show*.'

'But only celebrities go on *The Today Show*.'

Celia sniggered gleefully.

'Well, I am definitely going on it.'

'But I've never heard of you, Mr Morgan.'

Cue more sniggers from Ms Walden, who was loving every delicious minute of my humiliation.

I toyed with launching into a long-winded explanation of how massively famous I was back in the UK, where I was a household name on the back of share-tipping scandals, offensive 'Achtung! Surrender' front pages and fake photos. But instead I resorted to the verbal equivalent of an instant passport to America: 'I'm a friend of Simon Cowell's.'

The customs man reacted like a large vial of liquid nitrogen had just been injected into his right ear. 'You know SIMON?'

I nodded. 'Yes, and I am doing a new TV show with him here in the States, which is why I'm doing *Today*.'

A huge smile replaced the surly frown. 'That's amazing, man. What's he like, Simon? Is he that mean for real?'

I nodded again. 'Yes, but not as mean as me.' The customs man cackled sycophantically, his menacing demeanour suddenly a distant memory. 'Man, you Brit guys are so funny. Have a nice stay here, sir, and good luck with your show. Tell Simon I love his style.'

Quite extraordinary. I would have had a harder time if I'd said I was a friend of the Queen.

17 June

It was a beautiful sunny day in New York, and we went for an early walk through Central Park, an oasis of calm amid a city of frenzy. We reached the famous lake where so many movie scenes have been filmed, paid our twenty bucks and boarded a small rowing boat.

'You've done this before?' asked Celia nervously as we careered away from the boathouse.

'Yes, of course,' I lied, narrowly missing two boats coming the other way.

We passed a grassy bank, no more than 150 yards wide, where no less than five Japanese couples were posing for wedding photos. It was a riveting scene.

'WATCH IT!'

Celia's warning cry came just too late as our boat entangled itself with two grinning blondes who were just as inept at rowing as me. I desperately grappled with the oars, trying to extricate us from the mess, but to no avail.

'Oh give them to me,' Celia said impatiently, before guiding us gracefully away from the scene of shame.

'You've never rowed before, have you,' she said, more as a statement of fact than a question.

'Yes I have.'

'Have you?'

'No.'

That night we watched *The Way We Were*, and halfway through, by an incredible coincidence, Robert Redford took Barbra Streisand for a row across the same Central Park lake.

'I bet Robert Redford never smashed into anything,' said Celia witheringly.

18 June

Stanley's ninth birthday. I rang him to say how sorry I was to miss his big day.

'Oh that's OK, Dad. Just make sure you buy me a nice present in New York.' That's my boy, always with an eye for turning a negative into a positive.

Bought the Sunday papers and found that the *New York Daily News* has devoted their whole TV guide magazine cover to a photo of me, the Hoff, Brandy and Cowell, flanked by six exotically clad people on stilts.

It summed it all up perfectly.

I phoned Simon to tell him, and the pair of us were soon laughing like drains.

'What I like about you, Piers, is that you get it.'

'Get what?'

'The show, you just get it.'

'Simon, the only thing I get is that it's completely crazy.'

'Precisely!'

19 June

Waiting in the JFK Virgin lounge to fly back London, I started getting texts from people watching my BBC1 interview with Faria Alam in England.

Cowell was one of them: 'Watching your show, very good.'

I thanked him, then suggested he might wish to buy me a gift-wrapped Aston Martin if *America's Got Talent* gets to No 1.

'Hmm,' he replied. 'What's wrong with a mini?'

We finally settled on a Chevy Convertible if the show is No 1 for four consecutive weeks.

20 June

Richard Wallace kindly sent me a posting from the *Guardian* website message boards: 'I had overcome a £500-a-day crack habit until watching Piers Morgan and Faria Alam on BBC ONE last night. I have now realised that life is not worth living any more unless you're blasted off your nut and have well and truly gone back on the pipe. Cheers, Piers!'

21 June

I spent four hours today being interviewed, from London, by thirty-three radio stations across America to promote the launch of the series tonight. It was a bizarre experience, varying from fun to absurd. None of them knew anything about me, other than that I was the 'British dude' on a new talent show.

One DJ in Chicago greeted everything I said with total silence. Literally silence.

'Are you just trying to be like Simon Cowell?' he asked wearily.

'No, I'm much better looking, funnier and more intelligent,' I replied, tongue firmly implanted in cheek.

Silence.

And so on.

The last interview, with a New York station, ended with the immortal words: 'Finally Pierce, can I just ask you: do you think Princess Diana was murdered?'

America's Got Talent finally went on air tonight in America, at 2a.m. UK time. After all the hype and build-up, it will be fascinating to see how it does.

22 June

An agonising day spent waiting for America to wake up. The next phase of my career will depend entirely on how the show rated last night. If the figures are low, my American journey will hit an abrupt, irreparable wall.

I had lunch at The Ivy with Jason Barlow, editor of *Car* magazine. He's just sorted me out a free new Mercedes CLS for six months, so the least I can do is buy him some bang bang chicken.

I went back to the flat and paced about waiting for Cowell to call.

He finally rang at 4.30p.m. from his box at Ascot Races. This was it.

'Piers, the show is No 1, the ratings are huge, it's a hit ... the biggest this summer.'

I've learned not to take everything Mr Cowell says at face value: 'Simon, are you winding me up?'

'No, darling, it's a smash and I'm thrilled. Congratulations!'

He sounded wonderfully merry, in every sense of the word.

I put the phone down and contemplated what this meant. I am now starring in the most popular TV programme in America.

I wish I could say that I took the news calmly, but I punched the air and danced a little jig around the flat. And why not? This is quite possibly the most exciting, and potentially lucrative, thing that has ever happened to me.

An hour later a text arrived from Cowell: 'I feel a little like Dr Frankenstein when the monster came to life.'

23 June

Cowell's been watching the edited version of next week's show and texted me: 'Just watching you tell a guy he was comfortably the worst singer you had ever heard. Absolutely hysterical.' I love his enthusiasm for the show. It's very contagious.

26 June

The Hoff has been named the male entertainment star most likely to appear in 16- to 24-year-olds' emails, according to a new poll by an internet company called Pipex, beating Brad Pitt, Michael Jackson, Tom Cruise and Robbie Williams.

He reacted with customary modesty: 'I'm delighted to be such a hit on the web and to be crowned king of the internet.'

Peter Dubens, chairman of Pipex, which commissioned the survey, said, 'The results of our survey show David Hasselhoff has become a cultural icon.'

Thank God I haven't got to sit in that make-up chair today; he'd be unbearable.

29 June

Breakfast with Russell Brand at Villandry, off Tottenham Court Road. I came prepared to hate him, assuming he would be just as annoying in reality as he is on television presenting *Big Brother's Big Mouth*, but he was disarmingly charming, and much brighter than I thought he'd be, as we romped through his absurd sex, drugs and rock 'n' roll tabloid life.

He is a shocking sexual braggart, though.

'How many women have you slept with?' I asked as a fresh pot of coffee arrived.

He smirked broadly.

'I'm up there with Bill Wyman, mate, that's for sure, though I've slowed down a bit recently.'

Wyman famously claimed to have had sex with 1,000 women.

'How many did you have during your peak?'

'Oh God, five a day.'

He wasn't joking.

'One in the morning, two for lunch and three for tea. A good week would be twenty or so women in various configurations. I've had nights when I've looked down my bed to see a plague of women devouring me.'

'Do you think you're a sexual predator?'

'No, no. I like to think of myself as a conduit of natural forces. After all, it's the most natural thing in the world for people to fuck, isn't it? So all you have to do is remove all the reasons why women don't actually go through with it, like pride and reputation. You just have to unpick the conditions stopping women going to bed with you.'

'Do you care that now you're famous women just want to sleep with you so they can say they shagged Russell Brand?'

He snorted with derision.

'Er, no? Of course not – that seems to work to my advantage, doesn't it?'

30 June

Had a big drinks party at the flat last night. It was a beautiful warm evening, marred only by the relentless abuse I took for allegedly 'disappearing up my Hollywood arse'. At one stage I was cornered on the balcony by the editors of the *Sun*, *Mirror*, *News of the World* and *Observer* and verbally battered from every side. There was only one thing for it – to go on the attack. I strolled over to the TV, stuck the premiere of *America's Got Talent* in the DVD player and played it silently in the background for the rest of the evening. Oddly, it seemed to lose absolutely nothing for having no volume.

Halfway through the evening, Conor raced up to give me some breaking news: 'Hey, your mate the Hoff has nearly killed himself while shaving.'

'You're kidding?'

'Seriously. He's been staying at the Sanderson and apparently slashed his tendons on a chandelier this morning while shaving in the gym.'

'What? Deliberately?'

'Nobody knows, but he was taken to hospital and was pretty badly cut apparently.'

I felt shocked and genuinely concerned. The guy's always struck me as a bit unstable, but not enough to try to kill himself.

I had a number for the Hoff's publicist and called her.

'Is he OK?'

'He's fine now,' she said.

'Well you send him my best and tell him I'm having a party if he wants to come down.'

'I will tell him you called, but I doubt he'll be in the mood for a party. He's only just got out of hospital.'

I begged to differ – the Hoff was *always* in the mood for a party.

3 July

It's my last night in England for six weeks, so I took Celia to the River Café for dinner. We were enjoying a lovely candlelit meal out on the patio when the light was suddenly eclipsed by a gigantic gangly form. It was Peter Crouch, heading for the loo.

When he returned I stopped him. 'Hi, Peter, I've got to show you something.'

He laughed: 'OK, go on then.'

I pulled out my mobile, scrolled through the videos and got to Stan performing the Crouch robot dance.

'That's hilarious,' he said.

I asked if he was going to do his robot again, given the tragic events in Germany.

'No, I think I'm going to retire it,' he said. 'It was only supposed to be a little joke with the lads, but it got completely out of hand. I even saw little Brooklyn Beckham doing it the other day. Crazy.'

In the flesh, Crouch was cheerful, unassuming, polite and even signed my bill 'To Stanley, love your robot, Peter Crouch'. I still think he's a useless footballing beanpole, obviously, but there was something rather charming about him. And to my intense distress, he seems to score a lot of goals.

4 July

Flew back to LA, with Simon Cowell's words ringing in my ear: 'Everything will change when the show goes on air, you'll be mobbed in the street.'

So it was a bit disappointing when the customs guy ignored me, but then he was Mexican and probably didn't watch it.

By the time I got into a taxi an hour later, not one person had flickered an eyelid of recognition in my direction. I even hung around the newspaper stand for a few minutes, willing someone, *anyone*, to stop in their tracks, throw their hands in the air and scream, 'Oh my GOD! It's the star of *America's Got Talent!*'

Instead, my only contact with a member of the public came when I was brushed out of the way by a huge Hawaiian gentleman seeking to buy a bag of peanuts, with the one-word growl, 'Move.'

Far from being mobbed, it feels like I could climb to the top of the Empire State Building in a pair of Union Jack boxer shorts and shout, 'I'M PIERS MORGAN FROM *AMERICA'S GOT TALENT*' and absolutely nobody would take the blindest bit of notice. And pitiful though this may sound, I'm rather disheartened.

I want to be a celebrity out here, because, well, it's exciting, and fun. I've seen the impact Simon Cowell has had, and the amusement he derives from it, and I want a piece of the action.

5 July

I googled the Hoff to see what he's been up to, and there were 400 news alerts about him apparently getting kicked out of the Wimbledon tennis championships yesterday for being drunk and abusive.

Witnesses told the *Sun*, who broke the story, that he was shouting, 'All I want is a drink! Do you know who I am?!'

There will be so much to talk about when we see each other again on Friday for rehearsal.

6 July

Stanley and Bertie had their sports days today; it's the first time I've ever missed them. I rang to see how they'd got on the moment I woke up.

'I won everything,' said Bertie.

'Everything?'

'Everything.'

I spoke to Stanley for confirmation of this astounding fact.

'Well, Bert won nearly everything. He won the sprint, jump and throw, and a few others, I think. And I did really well, too!'

I felt a real tug in my heart.

It's moments like these that get to you the most when you're away. Big days, special days. Days your kids will never forget. Days when their father should be there, cheering them on, not poncing about in bloody Hollywood.

There is no amount of money or success that could ever match the sensation of watching your son win a race on sports day.

A few emails arrived asking if I'd read Kelvin MacKenzie's new weekly column in the *Sun* today. I hadn't, and feared the worst.

It read as follows:

'Two years ago Piers Morgan was unceremoniously fired as the editor of the *Daily Mirror* without even being given the right to pick up his jacket from his office. What has happened to him since? He has written a best-selling book, is much in demand on television and in magazines, and today his TV show in the US, *America's Got Talent*, is a massive hit.

'And what happened to the woman who fired him? Sly Bailey, chief executive of Trinity Mirror, has seen a collapse in circulation, a collapse in revenues and a collapse in share price. As if things couldn't get worse, the noted media analyst Andrew Walsh, from Bridgewell, says of Miss Bailey's company, "The strategy is running on empty." The *Mirror*'s chairman, Sir Victor Blank, has also legged it, and as he reflects on the company's misfortune, I wonder if he says to himself, "Wouldn't this business have been in much better shape if I had fired Sly and promoted Piers?"'

I bought a bagel in a chic Beverly Hills café, sat with the sun streaming onto my tanned face and chuckled. It's so weird how my life has turned out.

7 July

Woke at 6a.m. to find a text from Simon asking me to call. He was at a Little Chef on the M4 when I rang back.

'The figures are great again, congratulations. I'm just treating Terri to a burger.'

Terri grabbed the phone: 'Can you believe he's taken me to a Little Chef for lunch? He knows how to treat a woman, doesn't he?'

I had to laugh. Simon does what Simon wants.

He took the phone back.

'We've got to keep Bernie in.'

He was talking about the world's oldest male stripper, who was up for possible elimination today. We see fifteen acts that have been put through the audition rounds the day before each of the four semi-finals, and kick five of them out.

'He's a bit tacky, Simon. I mean, at the end of the day he's just an old bloke taking his clothes off.'

'Yes, I know, but he's great telly, it's as simple as that.'

I wasn't convinced, and nor was anyone else in the production crew, but it wouldn't be the first time that Simon Cowell's assessment of public taste was more accurate than everyone else's. The man is a populist genius.

Met the Hoff in the make-up trailer at 2p.m., and he was already into a full graphic description of his first London drama – the tendon-slicing incident.

'Man, it was scary. I knew I was going to cut myself, everything there was just so damn dark and trendy. I went to shave in this huge bowl and then I banged my head on this, like, chandelier thing. I pulled my arm up instinctively to feel my head, and cut it on the glass. The next thing I know there's blood spurting everywhere and it was just totally sick.'

He shook his head half in shock at the memory, and half in what appeared to be admiration for his own extraordinary courage.

'God, what happened next?' I asked.

'OK, so then these girls who worked in the gym rushed in and I was standing there naked with blood everywhere and one of them started to faint and I was like, "Don't faint, for God's sake, I need help here."

'They took me off to Thomas's hospital and there was this great plastic surgeon guy – I took some photos to show my plastic surgeon here in Hollywood because it was such great work. Anyway, I was really holding it together and controlling everything until they told me I was going to lose a nerve, and at that moment I just lay back and, you know…'

We waited on tenterhooks for the pay-off line. He threw back his head in anguish.

'And I … I … I cried like a baby.'

It looked like he was welling up again, then and there.

The Hoff is now sporting a big black wrist sling, which he seems quite proud of.

'Sounds like you were a lucky guy, David,' I sympathised.

'Oh man, it was touch and go, you know. If those girls hadn't rushed in when they did, I might have bled to death.'

'And you were completely naked?'

'Absolutely.'

Then he smirked.

'And trust me, those girls were nearly as shocked as I was.'

'I can imagine. So what happened at Wimbledon, then?'

He emitted a long, heavy sigh.

'Oh man, that was such bullshit. It was your paper the *Sun* again; they just make all this shit up, man.'

'It's not *my* paper, David. I just worked there back in the late Eighties.'

'Yeah, well anyway, they said I was drunk and running around trying to annoy the players and stuff. It's all nonsense.

'I was just a bit confused because I'd been taking very strong medication for my tendon injury and it made me feel weird. I had tickets, very good tickets, but they said I was trying to get into the Queen's seats. I was like, "Hey, man, I've got *better* seats than the Queen."'

'You had better seats than the Queen in the Royal Box?'

'Yes, definitely, so why would I need to take her seats? And I hadn't had a drink all day. Not one.

'Anyway, I'm gonna sue their asses off.'

'I wouldn't bother if I were you.'

'Why? Why should I let them print lies about me?'

'I just wouldn't bother suing. It takes two years to reach court, by which time you've long stopped caring, it costs a fortune and your reputation will just get trashed.'

'You think so?'

'I know so. And remember that the *Sun*'s owned by Rupert Murdoch, who owns Fox, who may employ you one day. So why bother suing; just threaten to and get an apology.'

He thought about this for a moment, then surprised me by agreeing.

'Yeah, that makes sense. OK. Thanks.'

The Hoff is a strange and complicated guy. He comes across as arrogant, but that's a classic trait in insecure people, and I think that's the root of his troubles: insecurity. When he's on form, and that seems to depend entirely on whatever 'medication' he is taking at the time, he's great fun, but there are some days when he's miserable, whining and obnoxious.

Later I heard Brandy telling her cousin, 'Just box it up and send it back.'

I asked what it was.

'My engagement ring. He wants to get back with me, but that ain't gonna to happen.'

She was pretending to be all tough about it, but I could see real sadness in her eyes, poor girl.

When we started filtering the fifteen acts, Bernie the Stripper was even more ludicrous than he had been in the first round, lying on the floor wiggling his ageing arse to the world like he was Brad Pitt.

To make it worse, there's no audience for these pre-semi-final elimination rounds, so just a handful of us were there, watching in virtual silence.

It was horrible to behold, and there was no way we could possibly put him through to the semi-final, it would have made a mockery of the whole competition. Bernie, whether Simon liked it or not, was on his bike.

As we wrapped up, the Hoff turned to me and said, 'Hey, did you hear my movie's No 1?'

'Your movie?'

'Yeah, I'm starring in *Click* with Adam Sandler.'

'Really? Well, congratulations.'

'Just think. I'm now in the No 1 TV show and the No 1 movie. All I need next is a No 1 single and I'll be the king of the world!' With that he strutted off to his limo.

As soon as I got back to the hotel I looked up *Click* on the internet to see what kind of role the Hoff has in it.

It would appear from the reviews that his main contribution is to be frozen in time by Sandler, who then farts in his face.

Another triumph for the Hoff brand.

8 July

Saw the Hoff back in the make-up trailer.

'Hey, man, guess what?'

'What?'

'I've been offered a big deal to be the new face of Pipex, some internet company based in England.'

The same internet company who had revealed the survey claiming the Hoff was the world's No 1 internet icon with young people.

'That's great, mate, well done.'

'Yeah, it's quite cool. I'm really big on the internet now. I Googled myself this morning and there are, like, five million hits on me or something.'

'Really? That's amazing. Regis only has eight hundred and fifty thousand.'

The Hoff chortled with delight.

'Really? Ha ha ha.'

I'd heard yesterday that the Hoff refused to start filming on the show back in May when he discovered Regis had a bigger trailer than him. Crisis was averted when they were both given the same, slightly smaller trailers.

Trailer size is hugely important in Hollywood, as it denotes your billing status. I had a lot of fun asking Alan Berger to negotiate me a transfer to the smallest trailer this morning.

'The *smallest*?' he said, incredulous.

'Size isn't everything,' I explained.

'Hey, Piers, in Hollywood, it's the *only* thing,' he snorted.

Back to the make-up trailer.

'So what else have you been doing, David?' I asked.

'Hey, I've got this great new record coming out called "Jump In My Car". I think I'm going to have a big hit with it. The video's incredible.'

The Hoff has only ever enjoyed musical success in Germany, where he became a singing legend by singing "Freedom" as the Berlin Wall came down.

He's sold nine million albums there, but has only ever attracted ridicule for singing in America, and in England for that matter.

'I think this song could be popular here, and with the Brits,' he said. 'Maybe I should sing it on the show? What do you think?'

I stifled a laugh.

'Erm, well, I think that would be very entertaining, David.'

'You do?'

'I do.'

There were some seriously good, as well as off-the-wall acts on the first semi-final today, including a group of young male cloggers called All That who perform like a tap-dancing version of Take That.

They were eclipsed, however, by two brothers called the Millers, or rather one brother, because the young eleven-year-old, L.D. Miller, played rock harmonica like a child prodigy while his twenty-one-year-old big brother Cole sang and played guitar like an adult chump.

The Hoff predictably called them 'awesome', and Brandy, equally predictably, said she 'loved the performance'.

I didn't mince my words: 'Do you want to win this competition, L.D.?'

'Yes.'

'Then you've got to sack your brother.'

Cue complete mayhem. The audience went wild, booing and hissing me; Brandy slapped me on the shoulder; the Hoff shouted, 'No way can you say that, man, that's disgusting!' And L.D. Miller started sobbing on stage, saying, 'There ain't no way you're splitting me up from my family.'

It was great TV.

The Hoff wanted to do the judges' summing-up at the end of the show, because he wanted to say something nice about the cloggers, All That, but he didn't seem to grasp what he had to do, so eventually I was asked to do it instead.

When the show finished, he blew his top.

'I thought I was doing the end bit?'

'They told me to,' I replied firmly.

'No man, it was meant to be me. You just hijacked it.'

I didn't have the energy for this.

'David, I didn't. They told me to do it. You do the next one, it really doesn't matter.'

But it did matter to him. American stars take this kind of thing very seriously. It's all about billing and who appears to be top dog on the show: if I end it, then I am The Man. At least in the Hoff's eyes, anyway.

I got into the Beverly Wilshire lift today, and found a young girl of no more than thirteen with bandages all over her nose. She was with her mother.

'That looks painful,' I said. 'How did she break it?'

The mother looked slightly embarrassed.

'She ... um ... well, she didn't break it.'

The girl looked at me, with vacant eyes, and I suddenly realised that she had obviously just had plastic surgery.

'Oh. I see.'

All three of us then spent the rest of the lift journey looking at the floor in silence.

10 July

The American papers are full of my confrontation with young L.D. Miller.

PIERS MORGAN MAKES LITTLE BOY CRY screamed *USA Today*.

Rebekah sent me some agency copy with a similar headline.

'You must feel very proud,' she said.

Spoke to the boys on iChat over my breakfast, and their tea. Stanley's hair is getting longer and longer. 'Isn't it time you had a trim, Stan?' I suggested.

'I can't, Dad.'

'Why not?'

'Because I'm going to be a Sikh.'

My oatmeal projectile-vomited all over my computer.

'WHAT?'

'If I want to be a Sikh then I have to have the Kesh.'

'What's the Kesh?'

'Long hair. They all have it.'

'I see. Why?'

'So it fits properly in a turban.'

'Right. Do you intend to wear a turban then?'

'Yes, eventually, but my Kesh needs to be a lot longer.'

'And where did you get this idea from, Stan?'

'Rav.'

Who? Ah yes, of course. Marion's new boyfriend, Rav Singh. Think I'm going to have to have a little word with Rav.

11 July

The AGT stylist, Katja, rang this morning: 'Piers, good news, you're going to get some new clothes.'

'Great. Why?'

'Well the show's doing really well, and we've got a lot more shows coming up, so the bosses think you should have some new stuff.'

'Marvellous, what do you suggest?'

'I suggest I meet you at the foot of Rodeo Drive in an hour and we go shopping.'

We met an hour later, and Katja explained how it was going to work.

'You've seen *Pretty Woman*, right? Well, it's going to be like that, only in a gender role reversal. I'm going to take you into lots of smart shops, demand that the assistants perform some major sucking up, and get you lots of new suits and shirts on the company credit card.'

I laughed. 'How much am I allowed to have?'

'Oh, I'm allowed to spend at least ten thousand dollars.'

Katja smiled, I smiled. Shopping is normally a pursuit I would travel continents to avoid, but it's amazing what shopping on somebody else's credit card can do to your enthusiasm levels.

Katja was magnificent, charging into Boss, Armani, Zenga and Versace, and haranguing the staff into pulling out all the stops for this 'major new talent'.

I just stood there silently like a mobile dummy, as endless beautiful suits were draped over me to cries of 'NO!', 'Looking good', 'I'm liking the blue', and 'Now *that's* what I call a man,' from Katja.

We moved to the shirts and I began behaving like Elton John: 'Two of those, three of those, five of those.' It was a delicious experience.

Within an hour and a half we'd blown our budget.

'You're done, young man,' she said, 'leave everything to me and I'll get all the suits measured, tailored and picked up.'

Now I know why Hollywood stars love their stylists so much.

'Do I have to give this stuff back?' I asked.

'I doubt it,' she replied. 'Just ask the producer when he's really busy and I'm sure he'll just wave his hand and say yes.'

I'm beginning to realise that life as a celebrity has a lot of rather nice perks.

12 July

Appeared on an outrageous Los Angeles radio show this morning where the female presenter suddenly asked me, 'So, Piers, have you had sex with Simon Cowell?'

I looked her straight in the eye and said, 'Yes, of course I have. He's my bitch.'

'Was he any good?'

'Not really, he kept judging me in bed…'

It seemed a very odd conversation to be having at 8a.m, especially in somewhere as supposedly puritanical as California. They're an unpredictable bunch, these Americans.

I've hired a personal trainer at the hotel, a 6 foot 6 inch giant called Alex from Austria who, inevitably, wants to be an actor. He puts me through an hour of what I can only describe as gruelling physical torture, but at least he has a sense of humour.

At the end he gives me some weird-looking coconut oil in a brown bottle, which he says will 'burn off your flesh' if I take it three times a day. And some vinegar concentrate that will do the same if I take it twice a day. And then four bottles of fresh organic vegetable juice to replace any tasty meals I may have been tempted to eat. And another huge jar of what looks like green gruel.

'It vill stop you feeling hungry, stop you eating. And BURN all that fat away. Really BURN it.'

'Can I drink alcohol with this stuff?'

Alex looked horrified.

'Vell, if you really have to. But not much, please. If you stick to my regime you will lose a lot of weight very fast.'

Yes, I thought, but I might also die very fast.

I went back to my room and tried them all. They were joined by a common thread – all of them were completely disgusting. They burned my throat, eyes, nose and anything that came within smelling or touching distance.

13 July

Back to the studio for the first live results show. This is where you can make a total twat of yourself in front of 14 million Americans, because there is no editing or re-recording, we just go live at 6p.m.

'Fuck this up and bang goes your career,' said Cowell cheerfully.

Celia's flown out for a fortnight's holiday and was looking forward to meeting the Hoff, but he was still fuming about me cutting him out of the show's finale yesterday, and confronted me before I could introduce her.

'I mean, like, who told *you* you were the king?' he demanded.

I stared him straight in the face and replied: 'I did.'

The Hoff looked bemused and then angry. 'Yeah, well, SAYS WHO?' before stomping off again.

Twenty minutes later he arrived in the make-up trailer as I was fending off Russell's persistent efforts to persuade me to have some highlights.

'David, this is my girlfriend Celia.'

'Hi, I'm surprised he has a girlfriend the way he behaves.'

We sat in our usual chairs, the tension smouldering nicely as Celia stood to one side, trying not to laugh.

After informing us all that his new video for 'Jump In My Car' was 'the, like, second highest watched video on Google', he turned to me and said, 'You were out of order yesterday, man.'

'There was a misunderstanding, David. Forget it.'

'No, man, I didn't misunderstand anything. We agreed I would say something about the cloggers and then you pimped me.'

'No, David, I didn't. But there was obviously a misunderstanding, so why don't we just leave it at that and move on?'

His chest puffed to maximum size as he contemplated my suggestion. 'OK, I accept your apology.'

I laughed. 'Er, I'm not apologising, David.'

'Right, well I accept your misunderstanding.'

'Our misunderstanding, David.'

'Well, whatever. I accept it.'

'Yes, and I accept yours.'

Then he finally laughed too. I can't help liking the guy, however ridiculous he can be sometimes. I think his main problem is that no one has said no to him for about thirty years.

He came and found Celia a little later and was charm personified. Contrary isn't the word.

The live show was memorable for a hilarious middle segment of freaks who never made it even to the audition stage. My favourite was a guy who kicks himself in the head. Literally. First, he gives himself a straight boot to his forehead, then he sticks a balloon there and bursts that, and his finale is sticking an egg to his bonce and then kicking it to smithereens. Totally mad and utterly hilarious.

At the end of the show, the Hoff made a lengthy soliloquoy about almost every act. I high-fived him afterwards, and he looked thrilled by both his own performance and by the fact that I seemed so pleased for him. And to be honest, I was. How could you not love a guy who spent the whole three-minute interval loudly mouthing the words to his speech in front of the audience?

Later, one of the crew told me he'd overheard the Hoff telling a producer: 'What it is with Brandy and Piers? Do they gang up on me because I'm more famous than them?'

14 July

The Hoff had to leave filming early today to record Jay Leno's *Tonight*, the biggest chat show in America. But before leaving Brandy and I to choose the final ten acts to make it through to tomorrow's third semi-final, he made his feelings clear.

'Sugar and Spice go through, you got that? I'm not having you guys ganging up against me again. They are going through.'

He was referring to six young black sisters who did a Jackson Five routine.

Brandy pursed her lips: 'Like hell they are, they're terrible.' I just laughed. They *were* terrible, but they were also quite endearing, a bit like the Hoff. We spent a few minutes taking the piss out of the great man, now that he and his ego had left the building. But we agreed it was easier to put Sugar and Spice through than risk his wrath tomorrow.

Simon rang as I drove home: 'I thought the show was pretty soft last week, Piers. You guys need to make it livelier. Have a row with David and Brandy, kick if off a bit.'

15 July

The Hoff made an arse of himself on Jay Leno last night, even forgetting the name of our show, calling it *American Idol*. By the time I got to the studios today, everyone was talking about his unbelievable clanger. I was sitting in make-up when he careered in.

'Hi, David, I hear Leno went well.' He eyed me suspiciously. 'You did? Who told you that.'

'Oh, everyone's talking about it.' He stared straight ahead, unblinking. 'They are? Well that's nice, it was very emotional actually because my dad was there and Jay was really sweet to him.' He then went off on some lengthy story.

Eventually he paused for breath and I seized the moment: 'I spoke to Simon yesterday, David, and he wants us to spice things up a bit today. He thought last week's show was a bit soft.'

'He did? Well if it ain't broke, don't fix it. The show's No 1 and I'm not changing a damn thing.'

'OK, fine. I'm just warning you that it might get a little more heated in there, so don't take it personally.'

'I just hope you and Brandy stop being such a pair of wankers.'

'I'll try not to be a wanker, David, definitely.'

'Yeah, well I heard what you two were saying about me yesterday. I was still in my trailer waiting to go to Leno and I could hear you talking on the monitor.' Then he stormed off.

Oh. Dear.

When we reconvened on set, you could have cut the atmosphere with a carving knife.

I whispered in Brandy's ear, 'He heard us bitching about him yesterday. The bloody monitor was on in his trailer.'

'He *heard* us?'

'Well, worse than that, actually. He *saw* us as well as heard us.'

'What were we saying?'

'I'm not entirely sure, but I'm pretty certain we weren't saying what a brilliant, lovely man he is.'

Brandy sniggered.

'Well, I don't care. He needs to stop behaving like a diva.'

The second semi-final was amusing, if only for the shameful disbelief we felt at having put some of the acts through from the auditions rounds.

One man called Dave 'the Horn Guy' came out in an orange jumpsuit and began prancing about playing twenty-five horns emblazoned across his body.

'Congratulations, Dave,' I said. 'You're the most annoying man I've ever met in my life.'

He just smiled. He knows it doesn't really matter what I think, he's just performed in front of 14 million people, so business is going to be great for him whatever happens.

One of my favourite acts from the auditions was Bobby Badfingers, the world's only professional finger-snapper. He was great again today.

It's been interesting to judge all these people. I came with an absolute cast-iron belief that only the most genuinely talented performers would get through, but acts like Bobby Badfingers and the Rapping Granny are thrilling the audience far more than some of the acts that have serious talent but lack personality.

If we are searching for a star, then perhaps I need to adapt my strict criteria. I could see Bobby on prime-time television, wowing everyone in a way I could never see some of the excellent but dull singers and dancers we've watched. Being a star isn't just about talent, I can see that now, and it may not even rely on having a great talent.

Look at the Hoff – he's an average actor and a mediocre singer, but he's a household name around the world, mainly because he has a memorable, pulsating, crazy-kinda-guy personality.

The only thing holding him back at the moment is that he takes himself so damn seriously. If he'd lighten up and take the piss out of himself as much as other people take the piss out of him, he could be huge again.

This show is definitely working for him, mainly because he's so keen to come over as a nice, big, cuddly guy.

Sugar and Spice, who he was desperate to see put through yesterday, were awful today, but he just sighed and said, 'Don't worry, girls, you've already won America's hearts.' I could imagine millions of housewives going aah and thinking, The Hoff's not such a bad guy after all.

We've tried to encourage the acts to come back with something new for the semi-finals, but Leonid the Magnificent took this too literally and appeared without all his paraphernalia, dressed in a simple black outfit, no glam make-up and performing a serious juggling act.

'Leonid, I told you last time that the only point of you is that you're the fairy on top of the Christmas tree. But the lights just went out, didn't they?'

He looked angry and his bottom lip started trembling again.

'Oh don't start blubbing, I can't bear it,' I said.

'Blubbing? What's *blubbing*?' shouted the Hoff, and the audience all looked equally bemused. There are so many English phrases that just don't work over here, and you have to be careful or you can quickly become incomprehensible.

16 July

This is getting ridiculous. I'm in the No 1 TV show in America, but Celia and I walked the entire length of Venice Beach without being 'mobbed' by a single human being, apart from a very large, heavily tattooed, shaven-haired gentleman from Essex who stopped me and said, 'You that bloke from the *News of the World*?'

'Yes,' I lied. It was much easier.

'Fucking hot, innit.'

I wasn't expecting Beatlemania, but the lack of recognition is surprising given that the show is top of the ratings and when I'm introduced on stage now, the audiences all go potty, booing and shrieking.

Then, at 10.20p.m. tonight, it happened.

Celia and I got into a cab outside the hotel and the driver stared at me intently in his mirror. This is it, I thought. He *recognises* me. I stared back, looking as important and famous as I possibly could. He continued staring, then broke into a knowing smirk. 'You're an actor, right?'

I nodded – it wasn't strictly true, but hey, this was no time for semantics.

'Yeah, yeah, I know, you're on TV.'

Pause.

Then he burst out laughing: 'I know, I know. You're the Brit judge on *America's Got Talent* right?'

'Right.'

'Yeah, YEAH! I love that show. It's full of idiots, but I love it.'

I felt irrationally smug. This was one very small moment for that cab driver, but one giant leap for my American fame-hunting campaign.

17 July

Felt completely knackered after a week of press and recordings, so booked Celia and I into a famous old beach hotel in Santa Monica called Shutters.

'Ah, Mr Morgan,' said the reception man with a huge grin. 'Good news, sir, we've upgraded you ... to the Presidential Suite.' I tried to hide my shock.

'Erm, right, well that's very kind of you, thanks.'

Now *this* is more like it...

20 July

Simon Cowell's girlfriend Terri Seymour interviewed me in my hotel suite for *The Xtra Factor*, a big TV show over here. I sent Simon Cowell a text: 'Terri grilled me in my bedroom.'

He replied, 'Terri told me. I think she has a little crush on you...'

I said this was hardly surprising: 'After all, nobody cared about Dr Frankenstein once his monster was on the loose, did they?'

He replied, 'There is a horrible element of truth in that. Off to the Earls Court motorshow now.'

This reminded me. 'Ah yes, talking of motors, I do believe we are No 1 for the fourth week, so you owe me a Chevy convertible.'

'That has occurred to me – did we specify new?'

'Yes.'

21 July

Had to attend a big press conference today, part of NBC's bi-annual report to the media about their plans for the next couple of seasons. Before it started, we were told that the show was definitely being recommissioned for the winter season. This was not entirely surprising given how well it's been doing in the ratings, but it was still a thrill to have it confirmed.

A second series is what everyone craves out here – it validates you and separates you from all the losers who crash and burn after one series, which applies to the vast majority of shows launched in the States.

The Hoff dominated the press conference, answering almost every question, and taking up to five minutes with each rambling, incoherent statement.

I just sat there bored out of my brains, raising an eyebrow at some of his more ridiculous comments and waiting in vain for someone to ask me something, anything.

Brandy was so fed up she started pulling faces behind his back, and he eventually caught her doing it.

'Hey, why are you doing that? It's not respectful.'

It wasn't 'respectful' to take over a whole press conference in such a shameless way, but that argument would have been lost on the Hoff. It was perfectly normal behaviour for him to make it all about himself.

I left him and Brandy bickering, and went back to my hotel.

Took Celia to The Ivy for dinner, and a drunken, rather crazed woman came up to me, started eulogising about the show and then began ostentatiously massaging my back.

After five minutes of this, I suggested that perhaps she should return to her table.

'Yes, of course, I'm so sorry. I just love you and wanted to touch you.'

This has definitely never happened to me at the London Ivy ... but I could get used to it.

22 July

The Hoff and Brandy said nothing to each other during the recording, simmering like a pair of volcanos. Eventually the Hoff had a little dig I didn't hear properly and it all kicked off.

'Just leave it, David, OK?' said Brandy, with a steely glint in her eye.

'No, Brandy, I won't "just leave it". Your behaviour yesterday was fucking disgusting, pulling all those stupid faces behind my back and stuff.'

'I didn't,' she said icily.

'You did, and I'm sick of you doing stuff like that, so stop it.'

His tone was aggressive and increasingly loud. Audience members near to the judges' seats looked amazed, unsure if this was real or part of the show, but it was real all right.

'You were totally out of order, so don't pretend otherwise,' he shouted.

Brandy looked shocked. 'David, this is not the right place to be having this discussion. If you have something to say, then say it after the show.'

He sprang out of his chair. 'NO! If I want to say something I'll fucking well say it whenever I feel like it.'

It was an unedifying spectacle, to put it mildly.

Brandy ignored him and the recording started again.

Later, in an effort to lighten the mood, I told the Hoff about my Presidential Suite upgrade at Shutters. He was appalled: 'I've been going there for years and they've never put *me* in the Presidential Suite.' He carried on shaking his head in disbelief for some time afterwards.

'You know,' he eventually mused, 'I was thrown out of the Dorchester in London once. I insisted on walking out of the front door, though, with my head held high.'

Donald Trump was a surprise guest on the show today, in his capacity as star of the hit US show The Apprentice. He was plastered in more make-up then even Dale Winton would consider decent on a man, but he was friendly enough and congratulated me on the success of the show. I mentioned that I knew Alan Sugar, star of the British version of The Apprentice. 'Oh, really? I know Alan, he's a nice guy. Send him my regards.'

The Hoff later mused, 'Donald shared my lowest ever moment in the business. I had this huge pay-per-view TV gig lined up that was going to be my big singing break in America. Donald had put a lot of the money up and everything was perfect right up until an hour or so before the concert was due to start. Then O.J. fucking Simpson went on the run, every TV network switched to live coverage of his escape and 93 million Americans ended up watching O.J. in a van while only 30,000 watched David Hasselhoff singing. It was a total disaster!'

He laughed out loud, and in that moment I felt myself warming to him again. When he laughs at himself he can be very funny; it's when he takes himself seriously that it all gets rather irritating.

Had a chat with Bobby by my trailer during a break.

'I have a funny story for you,' he said.

'What is it?'

'Gary Oldman turned up at the studios the other day while I was waiting by the entrance in the golf buggy for you.

'He saw me and said, "Hey, you for Gary Oldman?" And I said, "No, I'm here for Piers Morgan." He was so shocked, man, it was incredible. He kept shaking his head.'

The third semi-final was surprising.

Bianca Ryan, the eleven-year-old singer I thought was a shoe-in for the finale, disappointed, shrieking way too much, whereas the Rapping Granny blew the audience away again with a thunderous new rap song. I still can't assess with any certainty how much talent she has, but I do know for a fact that she is consistently the most popular act in this competition.

The funniest moment today came when Stiltworld, a group of dancers who perform on stilts, started their act, only for one of them to fall over and lie helplessly thrashing on the ground waiting to be rescued.

I felt for the poor girl, but it was hilarious to watch.

23 July

I rang Alan Sugar to pass on Donald Trump's regards. He snorted, 'I've never met the man. We had a row on the phone a while back about something I'd said about him, but that was it.'

24 July

The boys flew in today and I don't think I've ever been so excited to see them. Stan and Bertie ran towards me and flung their arms round me excitedly. Spencer, in a bright pink shirt and shades, strolled nonchalantly behind, but I could tell he was quietly thrilled too.

As we walked to the car an airport porter stopped me and shrieked, 'Hey! *America's Got Talent*!'

I nodded.

'Man, I love that show. You are *so* mean!'

The boys found it highly amusing.

'So are you really famous here, Dad?' asked Stanley.

I didn't have the heart to say that this was only the fifth time I'd been recognised.

'Erm, well, a tiny bit, yes.'

'Cool,' said Stanley. He loves all the fame-game nonsense just as much as Spencer hates it.

'Can I get a magazine?' Spencer asked as we drove to the hotel. He studied the rack for five minutes before buying a Lamborghini specialist magazine with a brand-new peach-coloured L640 Murcielago on the cover.

'See, Dad, *that* is like, just the coolest car ever. Much better than your crappy little thing.'

'Is that so...' I replied, chuckling to myself.

25 July

An email arrived from the production team today, informing me of the following: 'Just giving you a formal heads-up that we will be switching your dressing room with Brandy's dressing room, so our female judge is further away from the contestant holding area.'

Hmm. Let me think about this for a second. They are moving the nicest judge away from the contestants and moving Mr Nasty next to them?

I don't think that's the real reason.

Could it possibly be that Brandy wishes to be in a trailer far enough from

Mr Hasselhoff that she can say what she really thinks of him without him hearing?

26 July

It was Spencer's thirteenth birthday today and I decided to make it a day to remember. We all had breakfast downstairs before I announced that just Spencer and I would be going shopping.

His eyes lit up. 'Great, am I getting a trolley dash in Abercrombie & Fitch?'

'No, it's better than that.'

'It can't be, that's the ultimate present,' he replied.

I raised a conspiratorial eyebrow and led them all to the drive-through car park.

'Right, there's the taxi, in you get.'

There was indeed an LA cab waiting, but not for Spencer.

'No, not that taxi ... *that* taxi.'

His eyes swivelled in the other direction and alighted on a brand-new peach-coloured Lamborghini Murcielago L640.

He blushed slightly, cleared his throat, and looked at me with slightly crazed, desperate eyes. 'Is that ... is that ... are we ... erm ...'

'Yes, son, happy birthday. For the next four hours we're driving in the world's like, just coolest car ever.'

I don't think I have ever seen a happier expression than the one that enveloped Spencer's face. It hadn't been cheap tracking down the only one of these cars available to rent in Hollywood, but in that moment the reward was priceless.

We got in through doors that slide up, and I strapped him in.

'Dad, can you actually drive one of these?'

'Of course I can. I've had, oh, at least ten minutes' practice in one this morning before breakfast.'

I started up the engine, which emitted a King Kong like roar that reverberated through Beverly Hills, and we sped off down Wilshire Boulevard, turning head after head as we did so. It was fabulous to drive, and surprisingly easy. We raced down to the sea, joined the Pacific Coast Highway and surged on up to Malibu. It was exhilarating, even breathtaking at times. Flying down the freeway with the soft rock music up and our shades on, father and son shared one of those moments you know you'll never forget. We stopped by a particularly dramatic stretch of Malibu coast, where huge white-crested waves crashed onto black rocks. It was the perfect backdrop for souvenir photos.

'Thanks, Dad,' said Spencer. 'This has been my best birthday ever.'

'It's not over yet,' I replied, as we headed back up Sunset Boulevard, through the Hollywood Hills. 'This birthday's only just begun.'

We arrived back at the hotel bang on time to find a very excited Stanley and Bertie waiting as they'd been instructed to.

'Dad, there's an absolutely ginormous stretch Hummer over there, *look*!'

I laughed. 'God, yes, it's huge isn't it. Right, let's get in that taxi and go to the next surprise.'

The boys started clambering into another normal LA taxi before I stopped them.

'No, no, no – not that taxi, *that* taxi.'

I pointed to the Hummer, which was embarrassingly long and could seat fourteen comfortably in the back.

The boys squealed with joy and raced inside to find an assortment of their favourite drinks and sweets.

'Where are we going, Dad?' asked Stanley, almost too excited to speak.

'It's a secret.'

Forty minutes later we pulled up at the Los Angeles Dodgers baseball stadium, one of the most famous in America.

'Oh COOL!' they cried in unison.

I arranged the pick-up with the driver, sorted the boys out with some caps, giant foam hands and hotdogs, and we sat in our VIP dugout seats just twenty yards from the batter.

It was swelteringly hot, over 110 degrees, but still great fun. Baseball is basically a simpler version of cricket. All American sports have to be fast, the average fan's attention span just won't tolerate anything slow or boring. They find the whole idea of watching a five-day test match that might still end in a dull, meaningless draw completely ridiculous.

At 2.30p.m. we went to meet the Hummer again. I had a very precise timetable because I'd arranged one last surprise: a party by the hotel pool in one of the VIP cabins, complete with balloons and cake – the only problem being that the pool was shutting for a private function at 4p.m. That still gave us about an hour to party if we got back quickly, and it would round off a perfect day for Spencer, and the other boys for that matter.

The Hummer was nowhere to be seen, though. I called the driver.

'Where are you?'

'I've been getting some gas.'

'But I said be here by 2.30p.m., why didn't you get gas earlier?'

'I did, but I couldn't get back into the stadium.'

'Well why didn't you call me?'

'Because I thought I'd get back in.'

'Right, well where are you now?'

'I'm back in and will be there in a minute.'

'OK, please hurry because I've got a party waiting for us.'

'OK, got it.'

Fifteen minutes later there was still no sign of him.

I rang again. 'Where are you?'

'I can't find you.'

'What do you mean? We're where you dropped us.'

'Yes, but they are not letting cars in.'

'But you said you were already in.'

'I tried to come in but they wouldn't let me.'

'Well where are you now?'

'I'm trying to come in.'

'Oh for fuck's sake, stop lying and get on with it.'

Fifteen more minutes elapsed. It was now 3p.m. and we were running out of time to get back to the pool for the party.

I rang again: 'Where. Are. You?'

'I'm trying to find you.'

'Are you inside yet?'

'Yes.'

'Are you?'

'Well I'm trying to get in, yes.'

'Stop lying to me. Tell me exactly where you are and I'll walk to you.'

He told me where he was and we started walking. The heat from the sun and my increasing fury was almost unbearable.

We got to where he said he was.

I rang again.

'Where are you?'

'I'm just coming round now.'

'But you said you were here.'

'I will be in a minute.'

Finally, at 3.15p.m., I saw the Hummer approaching. I wanted to deflate his tyres, steal his keys and leave him trapped inside with the air-conditioning on high for a week.

'You've ruined everything,' I said a little melodramatically, but by now the boys were exhausted, thirsty and they knew that the last surprise wasn't going to happen because of the delay.

'It wasn't my fault.'

I stared at the driver's face. He just looked stupid, there is no other way to describe him.

'Just drive, all right?'

Five minutes later he stopped at a gas station.

'What the hell are you doing?'

'Getting some gas.'

'But that's what made you late, isn't it?'

'Yes, but I only put five dollars worth in.'

'Why?'

'I thought that was all I'd need.'

A sudden thought hit me.

'Is this some TV wind-up show?'

'No, sir, this is not a TV show.'

He shuffled off to refill his tank with gas. I wanted to fill him with gas, too, and blow him into the ether.

We finally got back to the hotel at 4.20p.m. Waldo, the bright, genial manager who supervises guest arrivals and departures, and who had fixed the cake and balloons for the pool, looked quizzical.

'What happened, Mr Morgan?'

'*He* happened,' I said, pointing at the driver with loathing in my voice.

We went up to the room and had the cake and balloons transferred from the pool. The boys didn't seem to mind, but I did. One dumb driver had taken the gloss off an otherwise perfect day.

Simon rang as I simmered on my balcony.

'Piers, it's Simon. I need some help with something.'

'Of course, whatever you want.'

'I want to know what tomorrow's *Mirror* front-page headline says.'

'*Right*. Why?'

'Because they've got photos of me with a young lady.'

'I see. What kind of photos?'

'Well, she's leaving my house at 2a.m.'

'*Right*. And what are you doing?'

'Apparently I'm peering round the door.'

I laughed. 'All completely innocent, obviously?'

'Obviously, Piers. There were other people there, including Paul McKenna. It's not what it seems.'

I hung up and tried to raise any of the *Mirror* guys who might give me a steer on what they were up to. But it was 1a.m. in the UK by now, and they'd all be asleep.

Eventually I got hold of someone on another paper who'd just found a *Mirror* with the headline SEX FACTOR.

The young lady was called Jasmine Lennard, she's twenty-one, and according to the report she's a bisexual model. She was wearing a fur coat in the photo, just to complete the amusement.

I phoned Simon back, but he'd already heard the good news.

'What with you and Hasselhoff hitting all the headlines in London, I'm starting to think I'm in the wrong city,' I said.

He laughed: 'Yes, just when you thought all the craziness was in LA.'

Talking of craziness, news broke later that the Hoff might miss the live results show tomorrow.

'Why?' I asked one of the production team.

'Oh, because of some incident at Heathrow.'

I checked the internet and discovered that the *Sun* had run an exclusive saying the Hoff had been kicked off a British Airways flight from Heathrow to LA yesterday because he was blind drunk. But his publicist was now reassuring everyone that this was not the case.

'Due to a new medication prescribed on Tuesday by his doctor in London for an infection to his injured hand, Mr Hasselhoff became ill at Heathrow airport and requested to be put on a later flight.'

That damn medication keeps causing him problems.

27 July

I took the boys to the live results show tonight, and they loved it, especially being ferried to and from my trailer in their own golf buggy and having their own bodyguards.

I introduced them to the Hoff, who couldn't have been nicer.

'Hey, boys, you gonna help me boo your dad when he's mean?'

'YES!' they cried back.

And they did.

When filming started and I received my first crescendo of booing, I looked over and saw the boys joining in, giving me the thumbs-down and the Hoff the thumbs-up.

The cheeky devils.

'Dad, they all really hate you, don't they?' said Stanley during one of the breaks, with a massive grin.

'No, Stanley, they just pretend to.'

He wasn't convinced.

The Hoff talked me through his latest drama at Heathrow as we had our make-up retouched.

'I was stitched up, man. The photographers were all waiting for me, so someone at BA must have stitched me up.'

'Was the story true?' I asked.

'No way, man. I wasn't drunk. I don't drink. It was the medication for my arm; it made me feel all weird.'

'David, have you considered changing your medication? It seems to be getting you into a lot of trouble.'

'Yeah, you're right,' he said. 'It does.'

And we went back to our respective eyebrow-plucking.

As I drove the boys back, Stanley announced, 'I like the Hoff, he's cool.'

The others concurred. I didn't know whether to laugh or cry.

28 July

Woke up to a flurry of emails and texts from concerned 'wellwishers' asking if I was OK.

'OK about what?' I demanded of one them.

'OK about the Hoff claiming you're gay in the *Daily Telegraph* today.'

WHAT?

I found the offending article on the *Telegraph* website. It was an interview he'd done with the lovely Jan Moir.

The pertinent part read: 'Piers! Piers is piercing. Piers is rude. All of America hates him because he made a little boy cry on the show, ha. But now that he's a star, I've taught him that he's fair game because of all the crap he used to write about us. Welcome to our world, Piersy, pal. I'm going to tell everyone that he's gay and see how he likes it.'

The cheeky bastard.

Though he's got a point, of course. I have rather crossed the fence. Going from tabloid editor to celebrity is about as poacher-turned-gamekeeper as you can possibly get.

I got to the studio at 3p.m. and found him in the make-up trailer.

'Why are telling everyone in Britain that I'm gay, David?'

He started convulsing with laughter.

'Oh man, have they run that? That's *hilarious*. How do you like it? Not nice is it?'

'I think it's funny,' I replied.

'Yeah, so do I,' he roared.

'Quite brave, though.'

'Brave? Why?'

'Well, because now I'm going to have to retaliate.'

He laughed again. 'Do your worst, man, you tabloid guys always do anyway. But I'm gonna have a lot of fun telling everyone you're gay.'

He was still laughing an hour later. And he was right, of course. There is absolutely nothing I can possibly say or do that could tarnish the Hoff now. He is fast becoming an untouchable celebrity icon, whose every scandalous incident merely serves to enhance the brand.

It's not the kind of celebrity I would like to be, but it works for him because he *needs* to be famous and *needs* to be loved. And right now, he is probably as famous and loved as he's ever been in his life, even if it's mostly for reasons entirely unconnected to his acting or singing skills.

There was high drama at rehearsal when I heard this almighty bang and a flurry of people raced over to where the band play.

Regis had taken a tumble, which is never good news when you're seventy-five. It must have been quite a drop because there was no sign of him.

Ken Warwick, the show's executive producer, was talking to the Hoff with his back to the stage and didn't realise what had happened, so I interrupted: 'Ken, there's something you should know...'

'Yeah, yeah. OK, mate, in a minute.'

'No, Ken, this could be quite serious.'

He wasn't really listening. 'OK, mate, just a sec.'

'Ken. Regis is down.'

He carried on talking, then suddenly stopped, turned round to see the increasing melee around where Regis had been standing and shouted, 'Fucking hell, where *is* he?'

Ken raced over to find Regis slowly picking himself up somewhere between the drum kit and the keyboards.

He'd cut his leg, but thought he'd be OK. It's at moments like that, that a producer can suffer severe emotional trauma. If Regis had broken his leg, our show would have been in *big* trouble. Because he is the star, no question, even if sometimes he seems very tired, particularly on the live show nights when he has to fly in from New York, where he hosts a daily morning TV show, and go straight to work.

He admitted to me today, 'It's exhausting. I can't pretend otherwise. But there is no other way of doing it, and I love the show.'

Regis is a tough, shrewd guy, and very entertaining. Even when he's tired he's great.

29 July

A Riverdance-style group of Irish-American dancers called Celtic Spring performed on the show today and were very talented and entertaining, apart from the mum, dad and little brother, who just got in the way of the five older kids.

It was like *The Waltons* meets the *Little House on the Prairie*, and they all had these slightly mad eyes and big gleaming Osmond-style teeth.

I told them the truth: 'I think you should lose your mum, dad and little brother if you want to progress in this competition.'

The little boy, aged four, burst into tears, as did two of his sisters. The audience loudly booed and jeered me, and the oldest boy grabbed the microphone and effectively told me to stick my views where the sun don't shine.

'I bet the public vote them through,' I said to Brandy in the next break. 'All it takes is a few tears.'

She agreed. 'You're right, though, they should be just the five older kids.'

It's a tricky thing, this judging lark. A lot of it needs to be tactical. If I make anyone cry, they get voted through by the public as a sympathy vote, but if I rave about an act, they tend to get voted through, too. So perhaps the smarter thing to do in order to guarantee my favourite acts get through to the final is to talk up the acts I don't want put through, but not too much.

Michelle L'Amour, the burlesque stripper, was up next, performing a tribute to the Hoff – complete with Knight Rider car – and prompting the boys to exchange embarrassed, shocked looks, first with themselves and then with me.

I did the thing any father would have done, pretended to be outraged and voted her off.

The Hoff was devastated and went over to tell her personally.

He came back grinning. 'We're going to have a drink at the end-of-series party.'

'But she's not in the final, David,' I said.

'No, I know. But she can still come to the party.'

30 July

Kelley, the NBC press officer in charge of *America's Got Talent*, rang today and asked what I was doing on Tuesday.

'Nothing much, why?'

'There might be something rather special we'd like you to do.'

'What is it?'

'I can't say yet because it may not happen.'

I waited on tenterhooks all day until Kelley called again at 7p.m.

'OK, I think you're going to like this … how would you like to appear on Jay Leno's show?'

YEEESSSSSSSSS!

That was my silent reaction anyway. It's important for perception to stay cool, though.

'Erm, well now, Kelley, let me just consult my diary … yes, I seem to be available.'

I put the phone down and punched the air.

'What is it, Dad?' the boys chorused.

'I'm going on the *Tonight* show with Jay Leno!'

They all looked completely bemused.

'Who the hell is Jay Leno?' said Spencer.

'He's the most famous chat-show star in America.'

'If he's so famous how come I've never heard of him?' he replied with undeniable logic.

The other two had already gone back to watching *The Simpsons*.

Kelley rang back again.

'I forgot to say that the other guest is Lisa Kudrow.'

'Who?'

'She played Phoebe in *Friends*.'

I relayed this information to the boys.

'Oh my GOD,' said Stanley. 'Phoebe from *Friends* – that's amazing!'

Even Spencer was impressed.

'That's quite cool, Dad. Can we get her autograph?'

31 July

A stunning brand-new Jaguar XK convertible arrived today, courtesy of Jason Barlow at *Car* magazine. It's the sexiest car I've ever driven, and even the Korean guys who do the valet parking at the hotel were impressed.

I'm relieved, too. You can't continue driving a rented Chrysler Sebring convertible if you want to be taken seriously as a celebrity in this town.

1 August

Arrived at the Jay Leno studios to find I'd been allocated my own dressing room with my name on the door. Not just a handwritten scrawl like you get with the BBC, but a properly printed laminate plate.

I went in to make-up and Jay came to say hello. He was incredibly friendly, no airs and graces or bigshot stuff. The NBC people had all told me what a down-to-earth bloke he was, but he really is.

He arrived in my dressing room twenty minutes later with giant cookies for the boys – another nice touch – and then posed for pictures with all of us.

'Is it true you've got eighty cars?' said Spencer.

'Yes, I keep them all in an aircraft hanger near this studio.'

'Cool! Have you got a Lamborghini?'

'Yep, and some Ferraris, Bugattis, Bentleys, a McLaren F1 ... oh, and eighty motorbikes as well.'

Spencer was stunned. Jay Leno had suddenly become his favourite celebrity in the whole world.

As showtime approached, I began to feel unusually nervous. This was a big moment, potentially one of the biggest of my career. A good performance on Leno really matters out here. Everyone watches it, and your profile goes through the roof. Conversely, a bad interview can cause irreparable damage to one's 'brand', and it was this sobering thought that was pre-occupying me now. I paced the small dressing room, twitching after drinking too much Red Bull, and going over potential anecdotes again and again. They'd given me a rough guide to Jay's line of questioning, and thanks to all the speeches I've done back home I had a few 'banker' stories I was sure would work.

'When in doubt, talk about Diana,' was the advice one agent gave me yesterday.

I walked out to generous applause from the studio audience – and a few jokey boos, which made me feel better. At least it meant they'd seen the show.

I sat between Jay and Lisa Kudrow, took a deep breath, and off we went.

I started a bit fast, rattling out answers and behaving like an overexcited puppy, but Jay was great, making me instantly relaxed and laughing cheerily at my jokes. We talked about the Hoff – 'He says I'm gay, which I must say came as news to my three sons and girlfriend.' – and then moved swiftly on to Diana, triggering three or four 'my friend the Princess' stories. The audience seemed to enjoy it, and by the time the interview finished eight minutes later I'd really enjoyed myself, too.

Lisa lent over as Jay wrapped up the show and said, 'God, so many amazing stories,' which was nice of her.

'Thanks, my boys are so excited about me doing this with you. They just loved *Friends*. Is there any chance they could have a photo with you later?'

'Of course, bring them to my dressing room.'

Minutes later I took the boys in. They were shy and tongue-tied, but she was very sweet. I pulled a chair out and asked her to sit in the middle, then we all stood around her like some sort of formal school picture with the headteacher.

What struck me most was that Lisa Kudrow treated me as an equal, a TV 'star' like herself, and not as an ex-tabloid editor.

I am increasingly living two completely separate lives. In Britain I'm still very much seen as the ex-editor, a figure of scandalous contention and occasional revulsion. But in America, they don't care about all that. They just see me as the new mean Brit on the block making them laugh on *America's Got Talent*. It really has been a chance to reinvent myself, and I'm finding the whole experience quite liberating.

In fact, I can see an almost perfect world developing, where I assume a smaller and smaller profile back home, enabling me to lead a contented, normal, fairly anonymous life in the UK, while enjoying a celebrity profile in the States, together with all the benefits that status brings in a country where they love you for it.

2 August

Took the boys to Universal Studios, which was unbelievably busy and very, very hot. We had VIP tickets, which meant we didn't have to queue for any of the big Hollywood-themed rides, but the boys were more interested in standing under a giant water cannon that blasted them with gallons of cold water every three minutes.

By the side of the cannon was a shop, selling cheap, nasty little towels for twenty dollars each, and it was doing a roaring trade.

Not stupid these theme park owners, are they?

3 August

The boys went home this morning, and I found a handwritten note from Spencer on my computer – an unprecedented act. 'Thanks for a great holiday, Dad, and for the best birthday ever. Love, Spencer.'

It had been fantastic fun having them here, and even more so to see how much they enjoyed the show and all the razzamatazz that goes with it.

The boys used to love coming to see me at the *Mirror*, sitting in my editor's chair and inhaling the excitement of a newspaper office. It's felt really satisfying seeing them embrace my new career move with the same enthusiasm.

The truth is that I'm loving this American adventure. It's fun, exciting and challenging. I don't know how long it's going to last, but I do know that I'm going to enjoy every single delicious second of it.

11

3 August

The Hoff, after much pestering of the producers, finally got his wish earlier this week and was told he could sing on the show.

This was incredibly annoying for me and Brandy because it meant we'd have to come in six hours earlier just so they could film our reactions to his pre-recorded performance for the later live show.

I got to the studios just before midday to find a lot of tense faces. It turned out the Hoff had pulled out late yesterday after one of his daughters told him the reason he had two million hits on the internet for his song 'Jump In My Car' was because it had been voted the worst music video of all time.

She'd also told him she would die of embarrassment if he even thought about singing it on the show.

So the Hoff phoned in and said he was going to the beach instead, throwing the production into complete turmoil.

Frantic phone calls followed, and eventually he had been persuaded to return and do the song as planned. But he was nervous, very nervous.

We sat in the make-up trailer and he asked me, 'Is this a good idea, man? Are people just going to laugh at me?'

'Only if you take it too seriously,' I said.

'But I can sing, man. I'm huge in Germany.'

And indeed he is. But in the States he's a musical laughing stock, and this performance could either repair that situation or, much more likely, endorse every American's worst fears.

He was twitchy, jabbering and totally lacking in his usual crushing self-confidence. I felt for the guy.

I went back to my trailer and received a visit from one of the producers.

'There are some issues we need to clear up with you concerning David's performance.'

'Right, OK, what are they?'

'Well you can't pull any funny faces during the recording for one.'

'Don't be ridiculous.'

'I'm not being ridiculous. If you do, he will walk off stage.'

'But that's absurd, am I supposed to just sit there expressionless for three minutes?'

'Yes.'

'I can't do it. It would make *me* look ridiculous. I trash all these other acts, but have to stare at Hasselhoff as if he's bloody Frank Sinatra?'

'It would be helpful if you did, yes.'

I could tell the whole production team had spent twenty-four hours in purgatory trying to make this happen. They knew it would be great telly, whether people at home laughed at him or not, but logistically it was too late to do anything else now, so they needed me on board to ensure there were no last-minute hitches.

'OK, I'll do it. Anything for an easy life.'

'There's one other thing…'

'Don't tell me, I can't give a verdict when he finishes either?'

'Erm … no.'

I laughed. 'This is nonsense. Everyone at home's going to be waiting for me and Brandy to let him have it.'

'Exactly, which is precisely why he doesn't want you to.'

'Do you think you could sit there without saying a word or even raising an eyebrow as David Hasselhoff prances about on stage singing "Jump In My Car"?'

Silence.

'Come on, be honest.'

More silence.

'Your silence says everything.'

A raised eyebrow.

'Well I'll do it because I don't want to give you guys any more trouble, but can I just record the fact that this is a total farce?'

'You can, yes. And thanks.'

I sat there in my trailer, shaking my head for several minutes. This could well turn out to be one of those TV clips people watch for decades to come – the moment Hasselhoff died on his backside on air and Morgan watched without even a titter.

We were called to the stage, and Brandy and I took our seats as the Hoff prepared to perform.

One of the dozen or so Knight Rider cars was on stage to add some 'colour' to his act, as were numerous scantily clad pretty young girls.

The Hoff did a rehearsal and then we went for the first record. As instructed, I sat motionless and expressionless throughout as he bounded around singing such scintillating lyrics as, 'Jump in my car, I wanna take you home … mmm, it's too far to walk, jump in my car!'

It was ludicrous.

At the end of the first run-through, the Hoff came down and spoke to me and Brandy at the judges' desk.

'Hey, guys, that was great, wasn't it!'

'No, not really,' I replied.

'Why, man? I thought it worked really well?'

'David, it's just stupid to have me and Brandy sitting here saying and doing nothing. It looks obvious to everyone that we've been ordered to, and it makes it obvious that you must be taking all this terribly seriously.'

I thought he'd go mad, but instead he looked thoughtful for a moment, then he said, 'Do you think so?'

'Yes, mate, I know so. I've told you before how important it is for you not to take yourself too seriously. The Hoff is a great, growing brand that is based around you sending yourself up a bit, and the only thing that can fuck it up for you is if you start taking yourself seriously.'

'What would you suggest, then?'

'I suggest you do it again, and this time Brandy and I will take the mickey, pull faces, laugh a lot and at the end we'll rip you to pieces with our judges' comments.'

He stared at me, taking in the full enormity of what I'd said.

Then, to my surprise, he rocked his head back with laughter and said, 'You're right man. You're absolutely right. Let's do it again.'

The producers came over.

'It's all OK,' I said. 'I've persuaded David that it's a very good idea to let us take the piss.'

We did a second take, with me and Brandy hamming it up to full effect – giggling, looking horrified, pulling quizzical faces at the cameras and hugging each other in disbelief.

And the Hoff joined in, laughing along with us.

At the end, I was asked for my verdict and said, 'The only phrase that springs to mind is "Kit, get him outta here."'

He burst out laughing, and I found myself adding, 'No, seriously, to borrow a phrase from you, David, "YOU WERE AWESOME, MAN!"'

The studio audience loved it, and so did he.

And I came away from the whole incident thinking that my relationship with this big, crazy guy had entered a new phase. I'd gone from untrustworthy ex-tabloid scumbag to someone he might actually be able to pick up a few tips from.

'Hey, man, thanks,' he said as we retired to our trailers.

'No problem, mate. It was fun, and the audience at home will think it's great because you're so obviously laughing at yourself as well as performing really well. It's a win-win.'

He bounded down the road to his trailer with a spring in his step and a smile on his face. For the first time since we'd been working together he looked genuinely happy.

After the live show finished, I was followed out of the studio by one of the contestants who had failed to get through to the final. He was a singer called George Kelly who I'd thought had real potential. He had a desperate look in his eye.

'Piers, can you speak to Simon for me? Can you do anything to get me into the final? I will do anything? Please help me.'

A bodyguard quickly came forward to remove him, but he carried on pleading until I was out of earshot. He was a desperate man, and I guess it's hardly surprising given the winner of *America's Got Talent* gets $1 million.

5 August

Ellis Watson has come out for a long weekend, which promises, on past performances, to be more testing than ten days with my three sons. He has brought his video camera with him and says he wants to make a movie of me in Hollywood.

His first 'interview' came this afternoon as we lounged by the pool.

'Fuck me, it's Jerry Springer!' he exclaimed, pointing to a man under an umbrella near the bar. It was, indeed, the reality-TV legend, the man who hilariously calls his show the worst TV show in history. I'd met him once, but he'd never remember.

Ellis waited until he got up to go, then pounced, stuffing his video in a startled Jerry's face and pumping him with questions about me.

Then he summonsed me over.

'Piers, Jerry wants to meet you.' Which seemed very, very unlikely, given the look of apathetic thunder on his crinkled face.

'Hi, Jerry, how are you?'

'I'm fine, congratulations on the success of your show.'

'Thanks very much, it's been a lot of fun.'

Ellis interrupted: 'How big a star do you think Piers is right now, Jerry?'

'Oh. Piers is huge, just huge,' he replied. 'Anyway, I have to go, but good luck with everything.'

The whole encounter was cringe-makingly embarrassing from start to finish, but Ellis was thrilled.

An hour later we were waiting for my car to be brought round when John Malkovich emerged from the hotel with his family. I stood there next to him for several minutes while Ellis prowled nearby with his video, wondering what to do.

Then he came over, asked me to hold the camera while it was still filming, walked in front of the Malkovich, and broke wind.

Everyone stared ahead, pretending we hadn't just heard what we knew we'd heard.

Ellis calmly came back, stood next to me and whispered, 'Did you get that?'

'Yes. What on earth did you do that for?'

'Because it's funny,' he said, spluttering with laughter.

John Malkovich's car arrived and he and his family departed without once looking in our direction, showing supreme dignity in the face of quite outrageous provocation.

My car pulled up and we set off, me in shocked silence, Ellis still cackling at his comic genius.

As we pulled away down Wilshire Boulevard, a large truck came alongside us and the driver started giving me strange looks. Ellis spotted this and turned the camera on again.

We reached some traffic lights and the man shouted, 'Hey, you're the actor, right?'

I smiled and Ellis shouted back: 'What's his name?'

The man looked puzzled: 'God, he's an actor, on TV I think. He's famous.'

Ellis zoomed in. 'Yes, but what's his name?'

The man turned to his wife. 'Hey, honey, look at that guy – who is he?'

She peered at me. 'Oh my God, he's from that TV show!'

Ellis was unimpressed: 'What TV show?'

We moved on before they could answer, but soon arrived at a second set of lights.

'Hey, man, we know him – we just can't remember his name.'

Ellis carried on filming as I drove off again. The truck followed us, the man, his wife and their two kids now craning out of the windows, trying to solve the mystery.

As we approached another set of lights, the kids suddenly started squealing, '*America's Got Talent! America's Got Talent!*'

The man whooped with joy. 'Yes! You're that mean Brit judge. We love that show. Can I take your photo on my phone?'

'Sure.' I beamed like a gurning imbecile.

Ellis still wasn't satisfied.

'Yes, but what's his name?'

The man looked straight down his video lens and shouted, 'I don't know man, but he's better than Simon.'

'That's a wrap!' I shouted.

We turned off Wilshire and both fell about laughing.

For the rest of the day, everywhere I turned Ellis was filming me with that bloody video – in my trailer, in make-up, in wardrobe, backstage, onstage, in the loo. He was like the worst kind of nagging paparazzi.

When we filmed the show, which was a special 'Wildcard' show to allow two losing semi-finalists back in for the final – I became slowly aware of a constant torrent of abuse coming from my right every time I spoke.

It was Ellis, shouting 'wanker' in response to everything I said.

The Hoff heard him, laughed his head off and joined in – 'He *is* a wanker, you're so right', and so on.

The highlight of the show came when Quick Change returned for their latest performance. I'd asked them in the semi-final if they did anything else in their act, given that we're looking for something that can last ninety minutes, and they had assured me they did, but today they just did the same old thing, changing the same clothes in the same way for two minutes. It was a new audience, so they whooped and cheered as everyone does the first time they see it, but I've now seen it four times, including the rehearsal for the semi-finals, and I'm bored with it.

It was time for a confrontation.

'You're either deaf, dumb or arrogant,' I told David. 'Which is it?'

He exploded with rage, grabbed the microphone and shouted, 'Don't you call me *dumb*!' while Dania fled the stage in tears.

I let him rant away for thirty seconds, sounding dumber and more arrogant every second, before saying, 'Are you familiar with the phrase "Give a man enough rope and he'll hang himself."'

He looked like he wanted to come over and hit me.

I bet they go through, though, everyone who cries gets the public phone vote. Why should they be any different?

We left the studios and headed for Asia de Cuba, the Hollywood restaurant that also boasts the famous Sky Bar, with stunning views of the city. We were joined by Chloe, a lovely PR woman from the Four Seasons called Sarah Cairns, and Caroline Graham – a great old friend of mine from my *Sun* days, who is now the American correspondent for the *Mail on Sunday*.

There was a private party going on in the bar when we got there, but Ellis decided it would be fine for us to gatecrash.

'Sorry, sir, but if you're not on the list you can't come in,' said an officious security man.

'I beg your pardon,' replied an indignant Ellis. 'Have you any idea who I'm with?'

The security man eyed me up and down without a flicker of recognition. 'No, sir.'

'I am with Piers Morgan, the superstar judge on *America's Got Talent*, the No 1 show in your country.'

The security guard yawned and turned away.

At that point Kiefer Sutherland arrived and was let straight in.

'Oh, I get it, it's one rule for Kiefer and another rule for us, is it?' exclaimed an indignant Ellis.

The guard stared at him with total disdain.

'No, sir, it's *his* party.'

Just when the day couldn't get any more surreal, I nipped to the loo and on the way came across a long table of people celebrating what appeared to be some sort of family event, judging by the wide range of ages. At the foot of the table was a head that even in the dim light sent a bolt of electricity through my drunken body: there's only one bloke I know with a laugh, and a ponytail, like that: Stevie Wonder. It was, indeed, the great man. Who, apart from being one of the world's great superstars, is also Celia's favourite singer. I ran over to Ellis. 'Mate, get the video back out, we're going for the big one.' Seconds later we were standing two feet from Mr Wonder, both of us gently swaying from the effects of champagne, Montrachet and mojitos, pleading with his very tall yet curiously unthreatening bodyguard to let us meet his charge, describing it as a matter of 'extreme urgency'. Five minutes elapsed, then the bodyguard lent down, whispered to his boss, and Stevie promptly stood up to say hello. *Carpe diem* and all that...

'Good evening, Mr Wonder, my girlfriend is your biggest fan and I need your help with something.'

He smiled. 'Whatever I can do, my friend, what is it?'

'Well, I'm hoping to persuade her to marry me one day, but if you were to, erm, encourage her, then that would be massively helpful.'

He laughed loudly.

'OK, well what did you have in mind?'

'Right, well we have a video camera here, my name is Piers, her name is Celia and the rest is down to you.'

Ellis fired up the video and pointed it straight at Stevie Wonder, who was giving every indication of having tucked into a few mojitos himself. The master cleared his throat: 'OK, Celia, Piers says that he wants to marry you. And you know what, if he makes you feel happy, and you make him feel happy, I say this to you: time is too long, and life is too short to waste it. Hand me your business.'

I didn't quite understand what he meant, but what I knew for sure was that I had Stevie Wonder virtually ordering Celia Walden to marry Piers Morgan – on tape. Which might be very handy.

Ellis and I had a still photo done with Stevie for further proof, then thanked the great man and made our exit.

At that point, several of his female relatives stopped me with excited looks in their eyes. 'Hey, you're that guy off the TV, right? *America's Got Talent*? We love that show.'

I admitted my crime. 'Can you get us tickets? We'd love to come.'

It was my turn to laugh. 'Sure, no problem, and bring Uncle Stevie if you like.'

6 August

Ellis's last day in Hollywood. It has felt like a year. 'Let's go rollerblading in Santa Monica,' he cried at 6a.m. I nodded, there was no point arguing with him any more: it would be as futile as telling John McEnroe there was no chalkdust. Two hours later we were indeed rollerblading along the beach in Santa Monica. Me in conventional shorts and T-shirt, Ellis in a tartan kilt – despite the fact that it was 90 degrees in the shade. Neither of us had any idea what we were doing, and the whole spectacle bordered on the ridiculous as we careered into walls and lamp posts to the intense amusement of passers-by and a group of stoned tramps on the sidewalk. After ten minutes, I heard a huge bang and an even bigger yelp. Ellis was lying in a mangled heap on the ground, blood pouring from a leg wound. 'Right, that's it,' I said wearily. 'I'm stopping this nonsense before you kill me.'

'What about cycling?' he begged.

'Fine.'

'Tandem?'

'Ellis, fuck off.'

We cycled in virtual silence for an hour, by which time I was almost ready to resume civilities – at which point he drove straight into a wrought-iron fence.

'What a laugh, poppet,' he cackled.

8 August

Simon rang this afternoon. 'Hi, Piers, I've got the results of NBC's research into the show.'

This was an important moment, he'd told me before that the networks place a lot of importance on viewer research. They poll a lot of people and make decisions based on what they say. It was no good to me being in the No 1 show if the public all hated me. All that would happen then is that I would get ditched for the next series and they'd bring in someone else.

'It's all disappointing,' said Simon, his voice laden with gravity.

'Oh dear.'

'Yes, disappointingly good.'

He'd done me again.

He began reading out some of the findings.

'Majority find you fair, brutal but honest, and funny. A few think you're too cruel, but most think you're the most credible judge. There's only one thing that should worry you.'

'What's that?'

'Two-thirds of them think you're not as good-looking as Simon Cowell.'

'What? You can't be serious.'

'I'm completely serious. It doesn't surprise me...'

'I can't believe that.'

Simon laughed. 'No, well, that's because I made that bit up. Look, this is all very good, Piers. It's similar to the research I get on *Idol*, and NBC will be really pleased.'

'So how should I be turning this to my advantage, then?'

He laughed again.

'I'd hang up on me right away and give Alan Berger a call as fast as you can!'

I hung up immediately and called Alan Berger to tell him the good news. 'That's great,' he said. 'Just great. Leave it to me.'

9 August

BREAKING NEWS! I've been exposed by the *National Enquirer*. Under the headline REVEALED: DARK PAST OF *AMERICA'S GOT TALENT* STAR the world's most scurrilous tabloid rag devotes a whole page to my sinister background, focusing on share scandals and my getting fired over the Iraq photos. There's a huge mean-looking photo with it – caption: MORON OF THE YEAR: Piers's past seems to be catching up with him – adding to the impression that I'm a thoroughly repellent piece of work.

I laughed out loud when I saw it at the newsstand, not a reaction I would imagine is typical of *Enquirer* victims, but as far as I'm concerned, the only words that matter are 'The show's star judge Piers Morgan'. The Hoff will be furious.

10 August

I spent ten minutes waiting for my car at the hotel and experienced another hilarious vignette of Hollywood life: Sidney Poitier shuffling around looking lost, Jerry Springer (again) looking purposeful and then a weird commotion as a vast stretch limousine swept up to the main entrance. I could tell by the staff reaction that somebody very important, even by Hollywood standards, was about to emerge from the car. The door was opened by a large bodyguard, and out popped an absolutely tiny creature dressed in pink and turquoise. Christina Aguilera, no less, currently the hottest pop star in America. One of the reception guys walked forward, hand outstretched to greet her with the words, 'Welcome to the Regent Beverly Wilshire, Ms Aguilera' – and at that moment I discovered everything I'd feared about the jumped-up little diva is absolutely justified. She just ignored him, I mean completely blanked the guy. Bustling past him, head down, grim-faced. There was no crowd, just me, him and a couple of other reception people. We all just stood there, gobsmacked. It had been a despicable piece of prima-donna behaviour, and yet thoroughly entertaining too. I just wish I'd run after her and said, 'Hey, Christina, lost your manners, luv?'

One thing's for sure, however big I may or may not become over here, I will never, ever behave like that.

I learned working in the ruthless British media that if you kick people on the way up, they will kick you twice as hard on the way down.

Everyone who works with Simon says the same thing: 'He treats everyone the same way, he is as courteous to the make-up staff and drivers as he is to the network executives.'

And it won't be your peer group who will cause the biggest reputational problems; it will be the secretaries, cab drivers, sandwich sellers and hotel managers who bury you.

A little bit of respect goes a very long way.

When I got to the studio, the first person I saw was the Hoff.

'Hey, man, I see the *Enquirer* got ya!' He could barely contain his glee. 'You suing them, man?'

'Suing them?' I said. 'I'm absolutely thrilled.'

He looked totally bemused, then saw Ken Warwick and got distracted.

'Hey, man, I gotta thank you for persuading me to play the other day – women are just going crazy for me, man. CRAZY! They all say I looked incredible. I mean girls are just walking up to me in the street and saying, "David, you're amazing."'

Ken smiled. 'That's great, David, I'm so pleased for you.' Then he winked at me.

Ken came into my trailer a few minutes later and broke the good news.

'Congratulations, Quick Change won by a mile...'

I didn't know whether to laugh, or beat the air-conditioner vent into submission.

Ken continued, chuckling, 'Do you think we can have a little chat next time about who you intend to make cry, so we can get the act we want through the public vote?'

'Yes, I have worked that out for myself, but I think they cry deliberately now, just to win the million.'

I got back to the hotel tonight, turned on the news and discovered that a massive terrorist plot to blow up ten transatlantic flights has been foiled. Apparently the intention was to set off simultaneous blasts using explosives smuggled into passenger cabins inside hand luggage.

It's obviously brilliant news that they stopped it, but Celia's supposed to be flying out tomorrow for the final, and the disruption to flight schedules is already horrific. She's also due to fly on British Airways to America, which was the main target route of the bombers.

I rang her.

'Am I worth dying for?'

Pause.

'No, but the Hoff is. See you tomorrow.'

11 August

Celia rang from Heathrow.

'We're in a makeshift marquee out the back of Terminal One, it's pouring with rain, flights are being cancelled all over the place and nobody knows what the hell is going on.'

'Other than that, you're having a good day, though?'

She forced a laugh. It was difficult enough enduring the twenty-two-hour round trip to LA for a long weekend. But the delays were going to add hours more to the total. And in addition to that there was general tension in the air about a possible further terrorist attack. This truly was dedication beyond the call of duty.

'You don't have to come if it's too tricky,' I said.

'You don't mean that, do you?' she replied.

'No, of course I don't.'

'Then I'll be there, I'll just be a little bit late.'

I checked the departures board on the BA website throughout the day – her plane was finally due to arrive five hours late at 8.30p.m.

I drove down to LAX and found complete chaos at the airport.

In a ridiculous overkill reaction to the threat, all passengers on BA flights from London were being kept in the baggage hall for up to four hours after landing so their luggage could be treble-checked. Word filtered through that they had no drinks or food, it was hot and dusty and babies were, understandably, making a hell of a racket. Poor Celia. I felt suddenly very guilty about making her come all this way.

The tannoy announced her flight would not be coming through customs for at least three hours, so I sat in a plastic chair drinking disgusting coffee and reading the American tabloids.

A woman came and sat next to me after half an hour, middle-aged but very well-preserved.

'Who are you waiting for?' I asked eventually to kill some time.

'Oh, my boyfriend and my grandson,' she replied in a posh English accent. 'And you?'

'My girlfriend. Keeping them out the back like this is ridiculous, isn't it?'

'Totally absurd. Typical American over-reaction.'

We chatted for another twenty minutes about all sorts of random stuff. She was amusing company, bright and opinionated.

'So what do you do?' she eventually asked.

'Oh, I'm doing a TV show out here.'

'Really, which one?'

'*America's Got Talent.*'

She eyed me with sudden curiosity. 'Are you Piers Morgan?'

I laughed. 'Well, yes, but I don't admit it obviously.'

We discussed the show for a few minutes, and she seemed surprisingly knowledgeable about the American TV business.

'What do you do?' I asked.

'I'm in the same line of work, actually.'

It was my turn to eye her curiously.

'Really? Should I know you?'

'I don't know. I'm Stephanie Beacham.'

I burst out laughing. She certainly was in the 'same line of work'. Only in her case that work included being one of the world's biggest TV stars in *Dynasty*, a movie actress whose first break came doing love scenes with Marlon Brando, and a perennially successful TV personality in Britain, starring in shows like *Tenko* and, currently, the ITV drama *Bad Girls*.

'I'm so sorry for not recognising you,' I said. 'How embarrassing.'

She just laughed.

'Oh don't be ridiculous, why the hell should you when I look this rough sitting in an airport?' She didn't look rough at all.

We spent the next two hours talking about Brando – 'such a kind man, one of my best friends out here' – Charlton Heston – 'It's so sad, he's got Alzheimer's now and rang me a while ago to say he wanted to tell me he loved me before he wasn't able to any more' – and Michael Winner, who directed that original Brando movie, *The Nightcomers*.

'He was a brilliant director,' she said. 'Really underrated.'

The time flew by, and I enjoyed every minute, until Celia finally came through and we said our goodbyes.

Things like this happen in Hollywood. You never know who you're going to be sitting to next...

12 August

Rupert's over for a week, so he came to see the finale with Chloe and Celia today. The Hoff took about three minutes to do his favourite joke. 'Hey, Rupert, did you know your brother's gay?' Rupert nodded and laughed, displaying shocking disloyalty.

During one of the audience warm-ups, a ten-year-old girl murdered some Britney Spears song, so I jokily pressed my buzzer to try and stop her wailing any longer. The audience roared with laughter, but she didn't. For the rest of the day, every time I looked at her, she stuck her tongue out, and when she wasn't doing it, her mother was. The pair of them kept it up for over three hours. Quite extraordinary.

I'd hoped that the eventual winner of the show would be a non-singer, to reaffirm the point of principle that we were not just an *American Idol* clone, but the stand-out performance tonight was by Bianca Ryan, the eleven-year-old girl from Philadelphia with the incredible voice. She was the only act where you felt goosebumps, and everyone knew it. I'll be amazed if she doesn't win.

We tried to crash the Sky Bar, Hollywood's coolest venue, after dinner tonight, but were foiled by two amusingly effete goons on the door.

'Can we come in?' I asked.

'Are your names on the list, sir?'

'Yes, I think so,' I lied. There's usually a Morgan on a guest list somewhere.

He studied his list for several minutes, pulling endless histrionic faces, shook his head solemnly and finally puffed his cheeks and whistled.

'I'm sorry, sir, there is no Morgan on the list.'

'Well can we come in anyway?'

'No, sir, we are completely full and you can only come in if you're on the list.'

My brother intervened. 'But he's the star of *America's Got Talent*.'

The goons peered at me suspiciously with no sign of recognition bar a tiny flicker of derision for the name of the show.

'That's just great, sir, but I'm afraid the list is full.'

I played my trump card: 'If I told you I was a close personal friend of David Hasselhoff's, would that make any difference?'

They exchanged horrible smug little smiles.

'No, sir.'

I wasn't quite beaten yet.

'Can I book us in for another night?'

'Of course, sir.'

'Great, 5 October 2011, please.'

They nodded.

'OK, sir.'

'Thanks, chaps.'

'No problem, sir, enjoy your evening.'

13 August

Met Rupert and Chloe at The Ivy for lunch. We got a great table, and the waiters fussed over us with considerably more enthusiasm than they had the last time I was here. As we came out afterwards I was stopped by a group of English people who had been watching the show. As we spoke, I caught the eye of an attractive blonde woman in the middle of the party and thought she looked familiar, then I realised who she was, Sara Dallin from Bananarama.

'Last time I saw you was the Rock in Rio festival in 1991,' she said. 'I was out there with George Michael.'

What a laugh that had been, two weeks on the Copacabana beach doing what the hell I liked because every other British hack had their trips cancelled when the first Gulf War started.

Suddenly a black range rover screamed to a stop on the opposite side of the road and two big guys pulled out absolutely enormous cameras and began papping us. I assumed they were after Sara, who's been making a comeback in the States, but as I stepped back, I saw the lenses were following me.

'They're after you.' She laughed.

I was getting papped outside The Ivy in Hollywood, in front of someone who had sold 40 million albums. Splendid!

Sara found the whole thing hilarious.

'Oh the irony,' she laughed. 'Piers Morgan getting hunted down by paparazzi.'

'I know,' I said. 'The trouble is that I *want* to be hunted down by paparazzi.'

It was only after they'd sped off again that Celia realised she was clutching an Agent Provocateur bag.

I could see the *National Enquirer* headline now: KINKY SECRET OF *AMERICA'S GOT TALENT* STAR'S GIRL. Well, hopefully anyway.

We drove from The Ivy to the Chateau Marmont, a castle-shaped hotel that rises above Sunset Strip and which has become infamous for being the place where comedian John Belushi died in 1982 after injecting a 'speedball' cocktail of heroin and cocaine.

Everyone's stayed here – Errol Flynn, Clark Gable, John and Yoko Lennon, Greta Garbo. James Dean met Natalie Wood at the Chateau, Paul Newman wooed his wife in the restaurant, Jim Morrison dangled from one of the drainpipes and Robert De Niro has apparently lived in the penthouse on and off for years.

Sandra Bullock summed it up in a recent *LA Times* interview saying, 'No wonder people come here for affairs, it's got that air of history, where you know a lot of people did things they weren't supposed to do.'

Our car was valet parked for us as we headed for reception, where a camp young man with thespian delusions awaited us.

'Please remember that no photography is allowed in the Chateau,' he announced, like some sort of SS guard.

'What, none at all?' said Celia with understandable surprise. Photography is, after all, permitted in every other hotel on the planet.

'None. At. All. Madam. If you want photographs of the Chateau you must call our publicity department in New York.'

This had to be the most pretentious thing I'd yet heard in Los Angeles, which is quite an accolade.

'What happens if I whack off a couple of sneaky photos in my bedroom when you're not looking,' I said.

He stared at me for several seconds, his eyebrow furrowing in an imperious manner.

'Then we'll assassinate you, sir.'

It was quite a funny line, only he wasn't smiling.

We went to the room, which was dimly lit and rather musty-smelling. The bathroom was sparse and had no soaps or anything in it, which seemed odd for a supposed five-star hotel. Celia took a couple of photos, just on a point of principle, and I took out a bathrobe, only to find several rather unsightly stains on it. Everything seemed a bit, well, grubby. I'm all for rock 'n' roll, but I prefer it to be at the Rolling Stones high end of the market than the down-and-dirty Pete Doherty and Kate Moss end. However, it was 3.30p.m., the sun was shining and the Chateau has a famous pool that was awaiting us, so we ignored the lingering odour of stale cigarettes and headed off. It was busy, in fact there were no spare sunbeds, so I walked up to the only attendant in sight and asked for a couple.

He smirked. 'Erm, well we don't have any right now, I'm afraid.'

'Well can you go and get some?' I asked.

'Not really, these are all we have.'

'But there are only about thirty people here, surely you have other beds for when it gets busy?'

'No.'

We both stood there, saying nothing.

'What about a towel?'

'Over there.' He pointed to a basket by the pool, but when I walked over I found numerous dirty towels lying around it, but no clean ones inside.

I went back. 'There are none left.'

He shrugged his shoulders.

'Can you get some more?'

'I doubt it. It's getting late now.'

This was like something out of *Fawlty Towers*.

'OK, well, can we get a drink then?'

He was standing by a mobile bar.

'I'm sorry, but we're just shutting up.'

'Shutting it? Why? It's only 3.30p.m. and it's busy.'

'Yes, but we've run out of most things.'

'You've run out? Can't you get some more? You're a five-star hotel, aren't you?'

'We could but we're not going to, sir. I'm sorry.'

He didn't give a flying monkeys, but I did. We were paying $450 to stay here, and I was damned if we were going to be treated like a couple of annoying barnacles stuck to the bottom of a boat: 'We are paying good money to stay here and I don't think it's unreasonable to expect a bed, towel and drink by the pool.'

He seemed bemused by my remarks and just shook his head.

'Look, mate, what exactly do you propose to do about this?'

He shrugged again. 'I can try and get a towel, and we can get you a drink from the main hotel if you really want one.'

'Fine. I'd like a bottle of dry white wine, please.'

Celia and I sat by the pool on burning hot tiles. This was not turning out to be the wonderfully smart, decadent experience we'd hoped it would be.

I spotted a familiar face sitting under a parasol in the corner. It was Annie Lennox. She looked in great shape, but was as white as a sheet. Quite extraordinarily white, in fact, as if she'd never once set foot in direct sunshine.

Another guest came over. 'We're leaving in a minute if you'd like our sunlounger.'

It was a nice gesture and we accepted. They left soon after and I waited for the waiter to clean up their mess. He didn't. He just stood there, ignoring us.

We sat on the bed, surrounded by dirty glasses, cigarette butts and dirty towels. It was deeply unpleasant.

The other guests around the pool all seemed the same – loud, tattooed, obnoxious English people all trying to be cool. I hated it all.

The waiter returned with the wine. It was red.

'What's this?'

'It's your wine, sir.'

'I ordered white, not red.'

He sighed theatrically. 'OK. Well if you want me to change it, I guess I'll go back and change it.'

'What about the towels?'

'They've run out. We're trying to find some.'

I looked at Celia, who screwed up her face in that way that suggested enough was enough.

'Shall we just leave?' she said.

I nodded and turned back to the waiter.

'I tell you what, forget the towels, forget the wine, forget it all. This is the worst service I've ever experienced.'

He looked down at the floor.

'Seriously, it's just terrible. I never usually complain, but this has been stratospherically awful. And we're not just leaving the pool, we're checking out of the hotel after less than an hour. It's over. And I doubt you even care.'

'To be honest, I don't blame you,' he said.

It was a pathetic end to a pathetic hour.

Celia and I went back to get our bags, stopping at reception on the way. Our smart alec friend was there.

'Can I help?'

'Yes, we're leaving.'

He raised an eyebrow.

'You're *leaving*? Why?'

'Because we've just had the worst service of all time and we're fed up. Your hotel is dirty, your staff are dreadful, nobody seems to care and we're going home to the Beverly Wilshire. But before we do, I'd like a quick word with your manager.'

'OK, I'll try and find him.'

Smart alec tried three numbers, but to no avail.

'He doesn't seem to be around.'

'You surprise me.'

'I can get him to call you.'

'Just tell him I'm at the Beverly Wilshire and I don't expect to pay a dime for this nonsense, but if he does want to charge me he can call me and explain why.'

I drove like a maniac and got us back to the Beverly Wilshire in fifteen minutes. We went straight to the pool and found Vivienne, the beautiful and amusing Latino waitress from New York who has been looking after me for six weeks.

'You guys look like you need a nice jug of sangria.'

We sighed with relief. We were home.

17 August

The last day, the last show and I'm ready to go. I've been here for six weeks on this second stretch, and I suddenly feel an absolutely burning need to go home.

I wasn't due to fly out until tomorrow afternoon, but I made a call to the production team and asked if they could get me on the last flight, a BA jumbo, at 9.20p.m.

They said they'd sort it out and to bring my bags with me.

Ratings for the final the previous night were brilliant, the highest since the premiere, so everyone was bouncing off the walls by the time I got to the studio to film the live results show, where the winner's revealed.

Normally, I'd be given a steer on who had won – the phone votes are all calculated by first thing in the morning – but to preserve a bit of excitement we were kept in the dark this time.

The travel co-ordinator, Everett, came to my trailer and said he'd fixed it for me to catch the BA flight.

'But it's going to be pretty tight, so here's what we're going to do. There will be a limousine waiting outside the studio doors for you the moment filming ends. It will take you to a heliport ten minutes away where a helicopter will fly you to LAX. The journey takes seven minutes, and a BA special services lady will be waiting for you when you land to check you in. If everything goes according to plan, you'll catch the plane.'

This is all sounded rather thrilling. A limo, a chopper, a 'special services' aide, then the sumptuous luxury of a BA first class cabin. What a perfect end to an extraordinary trip.

Halfway through the show, Bobby came up: 'Piers, good news, the flight's delayed by two hours so you'll definitely be able to catch it. Oh, and you won't need the helicopter now so we cancelled that.'

I was distraught.

'Bobby, the chopper was going to be my James Bond exit.'

He smiled. 'If I could fix it for the plane to leave on time...'

'I know, I know, you would!'

God I'll miss Bobby, and his fellow production assistant (and girlfriend) Cher. They have bust a gut for all of us.

Bianca Ryan won the show, and the $1 million, and burst into tears. She will be a big star one day, I'm sure of that.

I said my goodbyes, hugged Brandy and the Hoff and got in the limo. What a laugh it had been.

Two hours later, I walked through to the gate and went to board the plane.

A BA security woman saw me and said sternly, 'You, over here!'

I was mortified. What the hell had I done?

She glared at me menacingly as other passengers began to point and mutter.

'Have I done something wrong?'

'Yes, you have.'

I was racking my brains but couldn't think of anything that might be even remotely problematic, other than my signed copy of the Hoff's new video, which I guess might be construed in some quarters as an offensive weapon.

She stuck her face close to mine.

'Stop making those poor kids cry on TV...'

I got to my seat, lay back and fell fast asleep.

EPILOGUE

19 August

I'm back. Jet-lagged, as usual, but thrilled to be home. I went straight round to pick up the boys and take them to see Arsenal's first Premiership match at the new 60,000 seater Emirates Stadium. It's a stunning space-age creation, but seems at first sight to be lacking the intimacy of Highbury.

As we walked up the steps to our block, a bloke clocked me and said, 'There's that wanker Piers Morgan,' rather loudly.

I pretended not to hear, but Stanley ran up to me with a cheeky grin and said, 'Dad, Dad, that man just called you a wanker.'

'Did he? How nice.'

We walked on.

'Dad, why does he think you're a wanker?'

'Well, Stanley, not everyone thinks your father is a lovely guy, unfortunately. It's one of the problems of having once been a tabloid editor.'

He dwelt on this for a few moments.

'But, Dad, they all think you're a wanker in America, too, and they didn't know you were a tabloid editor there, did they?'

'No, Stanley, they didn't. But they're only joking in America, because of the judging I do. They don't really hate me.'

30 August

Spencer's first day at Charterhouse. He's going to be a weekly boarder, which effectively means he's leaving home. We arrived an hour early, having beaten the non-existent traffic. We unloaded his various enormous trunks and went up to his small but cosy little room. He looked as white as a sheet and said he was feeling ill, but I could tell it was just nerves. It must be such a weird psychological thing to go from being the big boy at school to a minnow again.

Later we listened to the headmaster give an amusing and rather thoughtful speech about what the boys, and parents for that matter, could expect. I looked round the room and spotted Gary Lineker and his estranged wife Michelle. One of their four sons must be coming here, too. Excellent ... I'd always fancied Lineker and Morgan as a strike pairing.

Marion, as she had confidently predicted for weeks, was in floods of tears when the time came to say goodbye.

Spencer, equally predictably, told her to 'stop being retarded'.

I realised a kiss from his father would mortify him, so offered a jokey stiff formal handshake instead. Spencer was so relieved he gripped my hand and gave it a hearty shake back. We laughed. It was nearly as absurd as that ridiculous photo where the Queen shook Prince Charles's hand on the train platform when he was five and she hadn't seen him for weeks.

Drove home and spoke to Marion tonight to find she was *still* crying. For thirteen years she has tended to Spencer's every need and whim, put up with his moods, laughed at his jokes and made his beloved cups of tea. Now his bedroom is empty, and will be for weeks on end.

Her emotions had been further wrenched, she said, by the events earlier this morning when Stanley and Bertie queued up to say goodbye to their big brother.

Stan formally presented him with his favourite CD by the Arctic Monkeys and a £5 note from his savings.

Spencer returned the CD saying, 'I know it's your favourite, Stan, you can keep it.'

He kept the money though, obviously.

Then Bertie's sad little face looked up at the big brother he worships and said, 'Spence, how many days until you come home?'

2 September

Spencer has now declined to respond to any of my five texts and two phone messages. I texted him again, suggesting that it might be nice if he could at least confirm he was still alive.

'Sory, my fone was of,' came the disingenuous reply, spelled in that deliberately illiterate way early teens use in their text messages and which seemed designed to annoy me further.

'Well are you free to speak now?' I asked.

'Wil txt when u can cal,' came the response.

An hour later a further message arrived. 'Cal.'

We had a ten-minute chat, mainly comprising of 'fine', 'yup', 'yeah, whatever', and 'no, Dad, don't be retarded'.

But I could tell from his voice that he was happy and obviously settling in well.

'Keep in touch, son,' I said at the end.

'Yes, OK, Dad. Now can I *please* go?'

4 September

Spoke to Spencer in the afternoon.

'Everything OK?'

'Erm, well, I've got to sleep on Harry's floor tonight.'

'Why?'

'Erm, well, I sort of lost my alarm clock down the back of my wardrobe.'

'Right, why does that mean you have to sleep on Harry's floor, though?'

'Erm, well, the thing is that I accidentally set the alarm for 4a.m., and it went off behind the wardrobe and I couldn't reach it to turn it off, so it woke everyone up. Everyone's been trying to get it, but nobody can reach it, so until the battery runs out I'm going to have to sleep in Harry's room.'

There are many things you can legislate for as a parent, but I must admit that this particular scenario had not entered my thought process.

Spent the evening at Rachel Johnson's launch for her new book, *Notting Hell*, which was held in the appropriate surroundings of her Notting Hill square and attended by the very cream of Notting Hill society.

I bumped into her brother Boris when I got there, who ordered me to fetch him a bottle of wine. 'I'm absolutely gasping, old man,' he explained.

When I came back and started pouring it for him, three photographers appeared from nowhere and started snapping away. 'Two naughty boys together,' observed a bystander.

A few minutes later I caught the other 'naughty boy' chatting to Celia with the usual lustful glint in his eyes. This is not a visage designed to engender anything but immediate suspicion and fury, so I marched straight over and made my feelings clear.

'Down, boy.'

Boris feigned bemusement.

'Whatever do you mean, old boy?'

'I mean, down boy, Boris. It's what you say to dogs on heat when they get a little overexcited with the family poodle.'

'No, no, no, no … you've got it all wrong. Celia and I are just chums.'

'Yes, I know that, but your reputation unfortunately makes this kind of pre-emptive strike necessary. I like you, Boris, I just don't want to have to kill you with my bare hands.'

By then he had already moved on to a gaggle of gagging Notting Hill fillies by the marquee, all agog with excitement at the prospect of meeting their heart-throb.

I moved on to the bar, where an attractive middle-aged woman stopped me. 'I loved your book,' she said.

'Thank you. I appreciate that very much.'

'I'm Felicity Osborne, George's mother.'

We swapped Shadow Chancellor stories for half an hour, and she was highly entertaining company.

Then she suddenly panicked.

'Don't put any of this in your next book, will you?'

'Relax, you have my word.'

5 September

The annual *GQ* awards, and what a hilarious night it turned out to be. Celia and I were bombarded with flashbulbs as we arrived.

Tragically, they were all for Eva Herzigova, who was prancing around semi-naked on the red carpet behind us like Marilyn Monroe on speed.

I passed Graham Norton, who shook my hand and said, 'Congratulations on *America's Got Talent*.'

He had a definite new-found look of respect in his eyes. It's easy to forget that so few Brits actually succeed in America, at anything. I've got massively lucky.

I reached my table and discovered that Naomi Campbell was sitting three feet away. Another of Dylan's little jokes, clearly. I hadn't seen Naomi since we'd clashed in the High Court over her drug problems. But her PR, Alan Edwards, is an old mate and suggested it might be a good time to kiss and make up. My appetite for long-running feuds is fading these days. What seemed such fun in my adrenalin-fuelled days as an editor now seems like a waste of energy.

Alan came back with good news: Naomi was ready to greet me.

I walked to her table and she proffered her hand in a regal manner. I took it and kissed it.

'Naomi, how lovely to see you again.'

She smiled. 'Nice to see you, too, Piers.'

We were like sharks circling off the Bay of Biscay – one drop of blood and it could turn nasty.

A friend of hers had a video camera pointed straight at me, so I turned and we conducted a live interview.

'Are you going to say sorry at last?' the guy asked.

'Well I certainly think the court case was very regrettable,' I replied. A useful way of making them think I was apologising when of course I wasn't.

I turned back to Naomi. 'It should never have gone as far as it did. We were genuinely trying to do the story in a positive way and it backfired. And I'm sorry that you got trashed so badly in court because it was all a bit ridiculous.'

Naomi stared at me intently, trying to work out if I was being sincere or not.

'Well at least one good thing came out of it,' she said 'I'm still sober.' And she reached for her glass of water.

I laughed: 'Two good things actually, I'm still getting drunk.' And I reached for my wine glass.

'I saw your interview with Rachel,' she said, referring to the BBC ONE show I'd made with Rachel Hunter for *You Can't Fire Me, I'm Famous*. 'It was fun.'

'Well, let's do one together then,' I replied. 'Now *that* would be fun, wouldn't it?'

'It might be...'

'Oh go on, Naomi, life's too short. I still fancy you, if that helps.'

She giggled. 'Well maybe we'll do something together...'

I returned to my table chuckling, and found David Furnish, Elton's other half, chatting to Rebekah.

'Nice suit,' I observed. Furnish is always immaculately attired.

'Thanks,' he said. 'You don't look so bad yourself.' Which was a complete lie because I'd turned up in full black tie only to find that it was not a black tie do.

'We should do a feature together for *GQ*,' he said.

'What kind of feature?'

'A makeover.'

I felt my blood run cold.

'What kind of makeover?'

'I'd like to take you clothes shopping and write about it for *GQ*.'

'What's in it for me?'

'Free clothes.'

'Fair enough.'

'And I'll make you look great.'

Rebekah scoffed. 'Now this I've got to see ... you getting a David Furnish makeover.'

But he seemed very serious, and it could be quite fun.

'I'd be up for it,' I said. 'I've always fancied being kidnapped by you and Elton and taken on one of your endless shopping sprees.'

'I'll sort it with Dylan,' he said.

The awards themselves have an almost religious rite of passage: the presenter, in this case the comedian Jimmy Carr, is met with almost complete derisory silence, ensuring he falls flat on his arse. Each presenter of an award is noisily mocked and the winners politely booed. The acceptance speeches tend to be nasty, tasteless, humourless and long-winded. All in all it's usually a thoroughly enjoyable couple of hours, and tonight was no exception.

Carr was, appropriately, a car crash. But went down fighting by telling more and more puerile jokes about things like AIDS and gay masturbation, which were met with open-mouthed faux horror.

As Justin Timberlake prepared to receive his award, Celia sidled up to his two enormous bodyguards for a laugh, said she was a massive fan and wondered if she could meet Justin afterwards. The goons whispered to themselves, gave her a long, lingering full-length physical assessment and said, 'You are the perfect kind of girl. Give us your phone number and we'll call you from the hotel.'

Given that Justin's currently engaged to Cameron Diaz, it seems unlikely that he would be playing any part himself in the rendezvous, and much more likely that his bodyguards intended crooning 'Cry Me A River' to Celia over ten hot dogs and a bottle of Cristal.

She returned to the table giggling, and I saw the goons exchange sudden worried glances as I showed Celia my phone camera snaps of the momentous encounter. Suffice to say, the call never came...

The funniest moment of the night came when Rod Stewart berated Russell Brand for claiming he'd slept with his daughter, Kimberly.

Rod directly challenged him from the stage: 'You didn't, did you, Russell?'

Brand, caught like a randy rabbit in the headlights, stood up and admitted he hadn't.

'Well stop claiming you have, then,' said the protective father to raucous cheers.

I found Rod by the bar after the awards and congratulated him on his stoic paternal defence.

'I fucking enjoyed putting that twat in his place,' he laughed. 'I don't mind a shagger, obviously, but you shouldn't claim you've shagged a bird when you haven't. And he has definitely not had anything to do with Kimberly, so I thought we'd just clear that up for everyone. He didn't know where to fucking look, did he?'

Rod looked absurdly fit and youthful. He is one of the genuinely nicest guys in the tawdry word of showbusiness – always polite, charming, fun and with a heart of gold. I remember his brother Don telling me once how when their mother was dying, Rod used to sit at the end of her bed for hours singing songs to her with tears rolling down his cheeks.

At midnight the hard-core players were gathering to head to the Groucho and get even more monumentally drunk than they already were.

We headed home instead and jumped straight into a cab waiting outside, then got pursued down the road by a dozen photographers, firing away into the back of the cab. One of them hilariously shouted, 'It's the girlfriend!' at the top of his voice.

I've been papped before, but never chased by the pack down a street.

There's only one reason they're doing it, and that's because they now view me as a celebrity they can make money out of. And that's fine by me, to be honest. I am the perfect kind of celebrity because I actively enjoy being harassed, photographed and generally used and abused by the media. This might be because I have a brother who spends most of his time dodging bullets and bombs rather than lenses.

11 September

The following story appeared in the news this morning:

'David Hasslehoff has some unique plans for his body after he is dead. He said, "I was actually thinking of being buried under my Hollywood star, looking up so people could look down and watch me decompose."'

Everyone else will think he's joking, but I know he's being deadly serious.

13 September

The Hoff has published his autobiography and flown to Britain for a week-long promotional tour. There's just no escaping the bloody man…

He excelled himself today by claiming during one book-signing that Princess Diana wanted to have sex with him. It was something he'd hinted at one morning in the make-up trailer, with a knowing smirk and eyebrow raise. 'We had a kind of thing going,' he'd told me, but refused to elaborate.

The whole notion seemed ludicrous to me, but today he insisted, 'She was smitten with me since I'm so tall, and I was smitten with her since she was so tall.' He said the pair would have slept together 'if circumstances had been different'.

I walked through Soho this afternoon, and a youngish man stopped in his tracks when he saw me and exclaimed, 'Hey, can you stop printing all that shit in your paper, mate?'

I turned towards him slowly and replied: 'Mate, I haven't printed any shit in any paper for two and a half years.'

'Really? What happened to you?'

'I got sacked.'

'What, for printing all that shit? Good.'

Then we both walked off, and I wondered what must it be like if you're really famous in Britain today? You must spend literally every hour of your life fending off a member of the public who wants a chat, a photo, an autograph, a whine, or just to use you as a platform for abuse.

The more well known I've become, the more sympathetic I am to the celebrity cause. Not, I hasten to add, to those who systematically sell their private life to the media – they're fair game – but to those celebrities – and there are still some out there – who don't sell their privacy to the highest bidder or play the media game. The loss of anonymity for them is restrictive, invasive, unpleasant and usually unfair.

In the evening I took Celia to a testimonial dinner for Liam Botham, Ian's son, who had to quit sport last year because of a neck injury.

'Can I meet Shane Warne?' she asked. And I scratched my head for several seconds, contemplating the right answer to this perplexing question.

Kevin Pietersen's one of Shane's best mates but still hasn't let him meet his fiancée Jessica, and most people would say that was very wise.

It's not that Shane is a letch, it's more that he radiates a quite phenomenal animal magnetism to the opposite sex. He's the sporting equivalent of Bill Clinton, with a success rate to match.

'You can come and say hello,' I said, 'but I will be there at all times. Think Hannibal Lecter and Agent Starling – it's just too risky to let you near him without security.'

As Celia went to powder her nose, I went to find Shane.

I saw his right index finger first, pointed at me in the position more commonly known as 'the Bird'.

Such cultured people, these Australians.

'Mr Warne, how lovely to see you again.'

'Hey, mate, how the fuck are you?'

He looked slightly grotesque thanks to a heavily stitched, bloodstained eyebrow where a ball had whacked him through his helmet grill yesterday while playing for Hampshire.

'Fine, mate. Hope there's no permanent injury to that eye of yours.'

'Nah, don't think so…'

'Oh, what a shame.'

'Fuck off, you pommie bastard. Tell you what though, mate, it's bloody painful.'

'Oh good.'

This is no time for sentiment with the Aussies. The Ashes are two months away and an injured Shane Warne would help us enormously.

'So what are you up to, mate?' he asked.

'I'm starring in a smash-hit TV show in America with David Hasselhoff,' I said.

'You're not?'

'I am.'

'Fuck me sideways. Good on yer, mate.'

'Never mind me though, Warney, how are you?'

He sat back and laughed: 'Well, it's not been the easiest of times since we did that *GQ* interview, mate, that's for sure. Christ!'

That had to be the understatement of the century.

'Yes, well, if you'd just kept your trousers up, like I told you to…'

'I know, I know, mate. I just can't help myself.'

He cackled again, like Sid James on acid.

'The trouble is that all the mates I used to go out with are behaving themselves now. When I was married and shouldn't have been doing it, loads of blokes wanted to come along. Now I'm single, I can't find anyone to join me. Bloody typical!'

I asked him how his long-suffering wife Simone was treating him since they split up.

'Oh, mate, it's been pretty rough and I don't blame her, given everything that happened. The last few weeks it's been better, though. I got a bit pissed the other day when I heard she'd been out for dinner with some fella.'

I laughed. 'How disgraceful of her … you sleep with half of Britain and Simone goes on one date.'

'I know, mate, rank hypocrisy. But I still love her and I didn't like it. Maybe we should try for a reconciliation.'

'But, Shane, how would that work given your love of misbehaviour?'

'Er, well, that's the trouble, isn't it? I've got to stop behaving like a big kid, but the problem is I quite like behaving like a big kid.'

He laughed again, loudly. There's something utterly hilarious about Shane Warne. You might disapprove of his morals, but he doesn't try and hide anything, and he is incredibly funny to talk to.

I came to the big question:

'Now look, my girlfriend Celia wants to meet you, but obviously I am very concerned about this, so just keep your hands to yourself.'

'I'll try, mate, which one is she?'

Celia appeared on cue at the other side of the table.

'That one.'

'Christ, mate, she's a beaut. Can't make any promises, I'm afraid.'

'Thirty seconds, Warne, that's all you get.'

He cackled. 'More than enough time, mate, trust me.'

I believed him, too.

When it came to the actual meeting, Shane was utterly charming. He's the ultimate lovable rogue, and both women and men adore his company.

After thirty seconds I pulled Celia away. 'Sorry, Shane, can't take any chances.'

'Understood, mate, don't blame you. I was just starting to crack it.'

Celia's enthralled eyes confirmed this was, indeed, probably the case.

A full minute and I might have lost her.

We bumped into Freddie on the way back to our table. He looked absurdly lean and fit.

'You coming out to the Ashes, then?'

'I'd love to, mate, but I'll probably be back in Hollywood then.'

'You flash ponce.'

His wife Rachel was next to him, wearing a rather fetching leopard-skin number.

'Cost me fifty-seven pounds,' she said proudly. Freddie will never be a flash ponce with Rachel around.

As we drove in a taxi down the Embankment at around 12.30a.m., a chauffeur-driven Mercedes pulled up alongside us and a grinning Chris Tarrant poked his head out of the window.

He's been in the papers all week after he was caught 'snogging' a woman in a Surrey pub and incurring the wrath of his wife.

I lent out of the cab and shouted, 'You should have kept your trousers up!'

'Thanks for your support, Morgan, as ever.'

Another surreal celebrity encounter.

15 September

A whole morning of TV interviews to promote a poll we commissioned a while ago for *First News*. It was fun nipping around the various BBC and ITV studios, particularly by the time I got to a live chat with Phillip Schofield on *This Morning*.

'I can't believe I'm saying this, but you're now a ... well   you're now a massive star in America, aren't you?' he said, utter incredulity in his voice.

I hesitated. 'Well, that's very kind of you, but, erm, well I wouldn't, er ... well ... yes.'

The irony of sitting on the *This Morning* sofa, scene of my three days of presenting humiliation two years earlier, wasn't lost on me, Phil or most of the show's superb production crew.

They even played me a special video message from the Hoff, who'd been on the day before – he is haunting my every move, just when I thought I could get some peace in my own country.

I was whisked straight to the Sky News studio at Millbank afterwards for a live interview with Kay Burley, which descended into farce when I used the word 'bullshit' to illustrate what modern kids are fed up with hearing.

Kay froze.

'You can't say that word on live television.'

'Er, can't you?'

It hadn't even occurred to me that 'bullshit' was an after-the-watershed word.

'No, you can't. Not at lunchtime.'

'I see. Well, do you want me to issue another apology to the nation, then?'

'Yes, please.'

'Righto. I am very sorry to anyone who was offended.'

Kay wrapped up the interview by asking if there was any message I'd like to convey to children in light of the survey.

'Yes, don't swear.'

Only I could get into a swearing row on TV while promoting a children's newspaper survey.

I picked Stanley and Bertie up this evening, both of whom had suffered what could be politely termed as 'behavioural lapses' this week.

They ran to the front door excitedly, then stood there with sheepish faces and said, 'Sorry, Dad,' before presenting me formally with two presents: a lighter shaped like a golf club from Stan and a little metal motor car made from bottle tops from Bertie.

People without kids often ask me what the best thing about being a father is, and it's always hard to specify an exact aspect, but it's the little moments like this that move you the most.

I took them back to the flat for a movie and Chinese takeaway – they both love sweet and sour pork and noodles – before they crashed out on my sofa. It was a sublimely pleasant evening.

18 September

Question Time called. 'Hi, Piers, how do you fancy coming on in Labour Party Conference week?'

I laughed. 'Now *that* would be fun.'

'Yes, we thought so, too.'

'Who else is on?'

'Jack Straw…'

I laughed again. The man who probably hates me more than any other Labour politician, mainly because I exposed his son for selling drugs to a *Mirror* journalist, but also because we'd done a front page around the time of the Iraq War asking, WHAT IS THE POINT OF JACK STRAW? One of those rhetorical newspaper questions for which there is only one answer: nothing.

Straw had dinner with an editor friend of mine soon after I was sacked, and apparently he spent ten minutes chortling about it and saying how thrilled he was that I'd finally got my comeuppance.

'I'm cancelling all other engagements. See you in Manchester.'

19 September

Celia took me to the Rodin exhibition at the Royal Academy, all part of her campaign to 'culturally enrich' me. She was a few minutes late, and as I waited, a short, plump young American woman came up to me.

'Excuse me, have we met before?'

'I don't think so, no.'

She looked puzzled.

'I'm sure we have. Weren't you here for my interview two weeks ago?'

'I wasn't, no.'

Usually when this sort of thing happens I put the person out of their misery, tell them who I am, they look slightly appalled – if they've even actually heard of me – and we both get on with our day. But sometimes I just can't be bothered, and today was one of those days.

'But you seem so familiar. Are you an art dealer?'

'No, I'm not.'

She was blushing now.

'This is so embarrassing, I'm sorry.'

'No problem, have a nice day.'

An hour later an English woman came up to me as we sat down for lunch at Cecconi's and exclaimed, 'Hi, how are you?'

'I'm fine thanks, how are you?'

'Great, just great. So good to see you again. Are you going to the Rodin?'

'Just been actually, it's very good.'

'So I've heard, so what else have you been up to?'

'Oh, this and that, you know.'

'Are you putting on any more exhibitions?'

'Unlikely, no. I've never put on an exhibition in my life.'

I could see a strange look envelop her face as the penny dropped that I wasn't who she thought I was.

'You're not who I think you are, are you?'

'I don't think so, no. I'm Piers Morgan.'

'Oh my God, how embarrassing, I thought you were an art dealer friend of mine.'

I've never been mistaken for an art dealer in my life, and now it's happened twice in one hour. Still, better than being mistaken for a bloody gardener I suppose.

I'd read a story in one of the papers this morning about Michael Winner fighting to save his local cinema in Kensington. What stood out was a reference low down the page to one of the reasons for his distress: he gets unlimited free pick 'n' mix sweets whenever he goes. No wonder he's so upset.

'You should ring him up and ask what his favourite pick 'n' mix sweets are?' I suggested to Celia, and we both laughed at the potentially huge amusement value we'd get from making that call.

Shortly afterwards I went to the loo at Cecconi's and met … Michael Winner. A quite extraordinary coincidence.

'Hello, darling,' he said, slobbering me with a big wet kiss.

'Michael, just the man. Follow me.'

I dragged him outside and round the corner to where Celia was sitting.

'Michael, this is Celia, and we were literally just talking about you. She has something she wants to ask you.'

'Righto, off you go, dear.'

Celia was trying to keep a straight face.

'Well, the thing is that I've heard you got free pick 'n' mix at the Kensington Odeon, and I just wondered what your favourites were?'

Winner guffawed.

'Absolutely true, dear. They caught me nicking them one evening, and someone complained to the manager, so I resolved the crisis by sending a cheque for £500 to the Variety Club in their name. The manager offered me a load of free tickets to thank me, but I said I'd rather have free sweets whenever I wanted them, so he agreed. Best bit of business I've done in years.'

'So what are your favourites?'

Winner considered this momentous question for a few seconds, giving it very serious thought.

'I love the little fried eggs, they're lovely.'

Celia had her scoop.

Ironically, Winner looked like he'd stopped eating sweets altogether.

'You're wasting away,' I said.

'I've lost three and a half stone, and it's all because of you,' he confirmed.

'Me?'

'Yes, every Christmas your photographers used to catch me on the beach at the Sandy Lane hotel in Barbados, and one year you ran a bloody great picture of me with a headline saying something rude like WHAT'S PINK, ENORMOUS, ABSOLUTELY DISGUSTING AND HANGS OUT OF MICHAEL WINNER'S SWIMMING TRUNKS?'

'And the answer would be Michael Winner.'

He does look incredibly slim.

'How have you done it?' I asked.

'I stopped eating so much. It's not rocket science, darling. I just have vegetable juice for dinner now.'

'Well, you should look slightly less revolting on the beach anyway.'

'So long as Simon Cowell doesn't sit next to me, I'll be fine.'

'Why, because he's in such good shape?'

'No, because he attracts all these yobbos and insists on talking to them for hours on end. I'm going to get the management to ensure we are placed at different ends of the beach. It's intolerable.'

Cowell, coincidentally, rang to update me on the next series of *AGT* an hour later.

'It's going to be *so* much better,' he said.

'Fancy a drink tonight to discuss it in more detail?' I replied.

'I'd love to, darling, but I'm having dinner with Philip Green.'

20 September

Dinner with Andy at The Ivy, and a bizarre encounter with Brian Paddick, the controversial gay Met Police commander. I had dealt with him a few times on the *Mirror*, and always rather admired his courage. But nothing quite prepared me, or Andy, for him coming over, sitting next to us and pouring his heart out about the shooting of the innocent Brazilian Jean Charles de Menendez in the wake of the 7/7 bombings.

Paddick made it absolutely clear that he thought senior police officials knew within half an hour of the shooting that a terrible mistake had been made, and he said he believed there had been a deliberate cover-up afterwards.

Furthermore, he had told investigators there were big discrepancies in other people's accounts, and said he found it 'inconceivable' that Met Police chief Ian Blair didn't know what was going on, although Sir Ian has strenuously denied this.

The implications of what Paddick was telling us were obvious.

It was a startling outburst from one of the country's top cops, and Andy and I were both left slightly dumbstruck.

'Did he say what I think he said?' Andy asked.

'I think he did, yes.'

As we digested this sensational piece of news, a sexy blonde plonked herself down where Paddick had been sitting.

It was Sara Dallin from Bananarama again – just a few weeks after we'd met at the other Ivy in Hollywood.

I hadn't seen her in fifteen years, then twice in a month. Bizarre.

We had a very friendly chat, and then Brian Paddick suddenly returned and addressed her: 'I'm sorry to interrupt, but I just wanted to say I'm one of your biggest fans ever, and it's great to meet you.'

Sara was very gracious, as Paddick continued with his eulogy.

'I've been a fan since the start, you girls were brilliant and you still look amazing…' And so on.

I was beginning to wonder if someone had spiked his wine.

Sara went back to her table, and minutes later Barbara Windsor tottered over and let rip one of her wonderful trademark cackles.

'How are you, darlin'? Congratulations on America – that's amazing!'

It's funny how impressed other TV people are by what I'm doing in the States. It's obviously considered to be the Holy Grail of television, unlike the newspaper industry, where Britain is seen as the best in the world and America's viewed as pretty dull and mediocre.

I went to the loo and bumped into a visibly shocked Neil Morrissey.

'Have you heard the news?' he said.

'What news?'

'Richard Hammond's had a massive car crash at 300mph trying to break the land speed record. He's in a coma and it's very serious.'

As well as being one of *Top Gear*'s presenters, Hammond is also a *Mirror* columnist.

'God, how awful.'

'Terrible. I'm a good friend of him and his wife, it's just dreadful.'

I offered my sympathies and went back to my table.

Celia arrived, and the three of us headed off to Matthew Freud's house for a party in honour of Bono and Georgio Armani.

We were all pretty merry to put it mildly, which may explain Andy's bizarre insistence on playing Johnny Cash music incredibly loudly in his car. His chauffeur, Rudi, just raised his eyes to heaven when I asked how long he'd had to suffer the noise.

We arrived at the party and I bumped into George Osborne.

'What the hell did my mother tell you?' he demanded.

'Oh, I'm sorry George. She swore me to secrecy.'

'You bastard. It's my mother. If you put anything she told you into print, I'll...'

'George, relax, I won't.'

He laughed, probably out of relief.

'How's it all going?' I asked.

'Pretty well, I think. Just waiting for Blair to go, and then the real battle can start.'

'Do you think you can win the next election?'

'Absolutely. It's all about momentum, and with Labour tearing itself apart at the moment, the momentum's all ours.'

We discussed Gordon Brown.

'He's looking old,' said Osborne. 'David will look fresh and dynamic by comparison.'

'I'm not so sure. He'll hit the ground running, trust me.'

'Well, we will be lying in wait, don't worry about that.'

I'd never met Bono before, and was absolutely convinced that he'd be insincere, self-absorbed and worthy to the point of tedium.

How wrong can you be? I found him in the downstairs garden and introduced myself.

'The last time I saw you, Bono, was at the Greenbelt Christian rock festival, where you were third on the bill after Cliff Richard and Charlene.'

He rocked back with laughter.

'Oh my God, that was Eighty-two. I remember it well. We were just breaking it, then.'

'Well you were good, but Charlene was brilliant.'

'Charlene ... yes ... she had that one big hit...'

'I've been to paradise but I've never been to me.'

Bono roared again.

'That was it! I've been to fucking paradise but I've never been to me. A classic!'

We started singing it, as a duet, right there on the lawn.

'So what are you doing now?' came the inevitable question.

'I'm judging a talent show in America with David Hasselhoff.'

'You're joking ... that's hilarious!'

'I know, you should come on and have a go. You might get past the auditions if you take the shades off and don't make any speeches about world poverty.'

At which point, Rebekah arrived and tried to lure him away.

'Watch her, Bono, she'll be trying to nail you down for more worthy campaigns in the *Sun*.'

'Piers, do piss off,' Rebekah smiled sweetly as she steered Bono to a nearby table. 'I wish to talk to Bono without you shouting in his ear.'

'Look, I just want to ask him if I can borrow some of his bodyguards when I'm back in Hollywood, and see if he has any tips on dealing with being mobbed by fans.'

Rebekah feigned instant nausea. 'Urgh. You disgust me.'

'Seriously, Bono mate, can you lend me some security, it's getting crazy for me out there.'

'Sure, man, no problem. I quite understand.'

Rebekah made more vomit sounds.

'The fans and paparazzi are getting a bit heavy, you know what it's like…'

He laughed. I was warming to him very quickly. He wasn't a twat at all.

Rebekah motioned to him: 'Come and sit over here with me, Bono, I want to get to know you.'

I wasn't going to let her get away with that.

'Rebekah, has it crossed your tiny mind that Bono might be relaxing and enjoying himself here, and that the last thing he probably wants is some crazed fan boring him to tears.'

He chuckled again; he was enjoying this.

'Piers, go away.' Rebekah was determined to see me off, but I was equally determined to stay.

'What do you want to talk to Bono about anyway?'

'I want to talk to him about Bono.'

I looked at him.

'Be honest, Bono, how bored are you of talking about Bono?'

'Fucking bored.'

'Exactly. Rebekah, with the greatest of respect, Bono doesn't want to talk about Bono, because that's all people ever want to do – talk about Bono.'

'Well, what do you suggest we talk about then, smartarse?'

'Something more interesting.'

'What? Like you, I suppose?'

'Yes, why not. I mean, come on, Bono, have you ever in your entire life spent an evening at a party talking about me.'

He chuckled. 'No, I can honestly say I haven't. You're right.'

'See, Rebekah. He wants to talk about me. Sorry.'

'I didn't say that, Piers,' he said.

'No, Bono, but you implied it. Would you rather sit there having Rebekah blow endless smoke up your arse, or hear me tell you how I cracked America.'

Rebekah was incensed. 'Actually, I want to talk to Bono about Africa.'

I burst out laughing. 'Africa? *Africa*? The editor of the *Sun* has one of the world's most charismatic rock stars sitting next to her and she wants to talk about *Africa*. Give the guy a break, for fuck's sake.'

Bono was almost in hysterics now.

'Are you two always like this?'

'Pretty much, yes,' said Rebekah. 'Piers can be very irritating around celebrities.'

'Rebekah, I *am* a celebrity. But let's ask him. Bono, do you really want to talk about Africa again tonight with the editor of the *Sun*?'

He smiled. 'I never get bored talking about Africa.'

'Why don't we talk about tax instead?' I suggested.

Bono has recently been criticised for paying hardly any tax on his income.

'Oh very good,' he said.

'Seriously, when you guest-edited the *Independent* you should have done a bloody great photo of yourself on page one with the headline, OVER-PAID AND UNDERTAXED.'

He laughed again. He seems a totally natural, charming guy. I was completely wrong about him.

'Right, well I'll leave you two to it, then,' I said. 'I'm sorry, but it's midnight and I'm off to find 50 Cent. I bet he doesn't want to talk about Africa.'

I walked upstairs and saw George Osborne again.

'George, haven't seen 50 Cent, have you?'

'Yes, he just went that way.'

'Thanks. If he comes back, tell him One Dollar wants to have a word with him.'

22 September

After a quite magnificently long lunch at Petrus with Gerard Greaves, editor of the *Mail on Sunday*'s new *Live* magazine, I've agreed to join his organ as a weekly columnist. It will be in diary form, similar to *The Insider*. 'Just write about your ridiculous life,' said Gerard, laughing into our fourth glass of port.

25 September

I received an emailed invite to a film premiere today from a PR woman I'd met once at a screening. At the end of the email she said, 'Thank you for the myspace add!' I didn't know what on earth she was talking about, so I tapped my name and myspace into Google.

There was my entry, in full glory: my photo, my correct age, star sign, marital status, bibliography and a mini introduction entitled 'About me' that read as follows:

'Some of you may now know me as one of the judges on NBC's *America's Got Talent*, but my career has primarily been in the publishing industry. I became editor of the *News of the World* at 28 – the youngest national newspaper editor for more than 50 years. Two years later, I was headhunted to edit the *Daily Mirror*.

'Since then my career has had its share of controversy which I'm sure you've managed to read about if you've Googled me enough. But all in all, it's been a great ride.

'One of my favourite projects took hold just a few months ago when I launched *First News*, a weekly paper aimed at 9–12-year-olds, where I am now editorial director.'

It then listed 118 'friends', including Simon Cowell, Donald Trump, a delightful young lady called 'Fabs', and a variety of bearded hippies, weirdos and wannabes.

I flicked down the page and found forty-two comments from people about my entry, including various women asking me to 'drop by sometime', strange-looking men asking, 'Do you remember me?' (I didn't), and on, and on. The only common denominator being that I had apparently 'added' all these people to my entry.

I have no idea what any of this means, but I do know one thing for sure: I have never created an entry on myspace, and wouldn't know where to start. The internet is a celebrity curse. Rumours spin out of control in seconds, and regulation, censorship or even legal remedy is virtually impossible.

There is also, as I have just discovered, absolutely nothing to stop people pretending to be a celebrity. The implications of which are fairly serious.

26 September

Simon was grilled about me on a US radio show today: 'Now, you're known as a tough judge, but Piers, he made little children cry. Do you think he was too tough on the little ones?

Simon replied, 'I think any judge on these shows is liable to make little people cry. Young singers on these shows, I think they cry in any competition they go into. It certainly wasn't intentional. When you enter these shows as a judge, you have got to be realistic and honest, and that's what I think he was trying to be. It certainly wasn't intentional.'

Who would have thought it? Simon Cowell defending me to the American nation about upsetting people.

28 September

Question Time in Manchester. I've been looking forward to this ever since they asked me. Jack Straw and I have unfinished business.

I boarded the train at Euston to find that co-panellists Ken Clarke and Baroness Jenny Tongue were sitting with me.

Within fifteen minutes they were both fast asleep. Ken, comfortably portly and glowing with ruddy health, woke as we pulled into Manchester.

'Good sleep?' I asked.

'Marvellous, thank you.'

'I must say you look very well, have you been away?'

'Oh yes, I try and have as many holidays as I possibly can now.'

He chortled happily. I've always thought Ken Clarke would have made a splendid Prime Minister. He seems so blissfully happy in his own skin and doesn't care what people think of him. There's also something incredibly comforting about those brown Hush Puppies he always wears.

We reached the studio and were taken to the makeshift green room, where the usual array of alcoholic temptations lay in wait. I resisted. This is definitely not the kind of TV programme you want to try and wing while fuelled with Chablis.

'You looking forward to the Tory conference, Ken?'

He looked a bit sheepish.

'Actually, no, because I'm not going.'

'Not going? But you always go?'

'Yes, haven't missed one in decades. But I've ... well ... I've had a better offer.'

'What is it?'

'I'm flying to Shanghai tomorrow on a business trip.'

He was trying not to laugh.

'What kind of business?'

'Oh, sod it, there's no point hiding it. I'm going to the Grand Prix!'

Everyone, including him, fell about laughing.

Then the door swung open and there was Jack Straw.

'Hi, Piers,' he said, offering me a handshake and beaming grin. It was a masterclass in how to greet someone you secretly want to kill.

'Hi, Jack. How are you?'

'Fine, fine. Apart from having to miss the bloody Blackburn game tonight.'

For the next five minutes he had an animated discussion with the show's production team about where he should sit on the panel. He's completely deaf in his right ear, and wanted to be sure that he would be sitting where he could best hear things.

It's funny to think that if he ends up as Gordon Brown's deputy, as he desperately wants to be, then we could end up with a leadership duo with one good ear and one good eye.

The seating plan sorted – he would sit to Dimbleby's right and my left, which would be quite helpful if he wanted to pretend he couldn't hear me – we all had a rather entertaining chat about politics, life and the universe.

Cherie's 'He's a liar' outburst at Brown during his Labour Party conference speech this week had them all enthralled.

'I think spouses should stay in the background,' said Ken firmly.

'Yes, quite agree,' said Straw.

'So do I,' I concurred.

Straw turned to me.

'Yes, unless you're putting mine all over your front page, of course, you bastard!'

I smiled. There was no point getting into all that again.

The subject moved on to the government's obsession with our diet.

'It's bloody nonsense,' growled Ken, lying back in his chair with his large pot belly proudly on display. 'When I was young we lived on chips and sweets and it never did us any harm at all. Labour want to stop us smoking, drinking and eating. They are the ultimate nanny state.'

'Perhaps you should launch the pro-obesity party, Ken,' I suggested.

'Not a bad idea,' he laughed. 'I just want to spend the rest of my life eating good food, drinking fine wine, smoking great cigars and enjoying myself. What the hell is wrong with that?'

Straw suddenly popped up on TV, saying something about John Prescott's farewell speech to conference, which we couldn't hear because the sound was turned down.

'Were you saying what a great guy Prezza is?' I asked.

Straw raised his eyebrows to the ceiling. 'Yes, something like that. Duty calls, etc.'

Next on the news was John Reid, who'd made a typically combative speech.

'He's good, isn't he?' I said.

'Yes, he is,' replied Straw with just the whiff of a conspiratorial look on his face.

'Think he will stand as leader against Gordon?'

He paused. 'I hope so, yes.'

Extraordinary people, politicians. Straw's been publicly backing Brown, but clearly wants to hedge his bets with Reid. They all go where they smell power.

Bizarrely we got into a discussion about trains, prompting Ken to recall the famous time Geoffrey Howe lost his trousers on a sleeper train to London.

'I was on that train!' cried Straw. 'It was hilarious. Geoffrey was supposed to lock his door but forgot, and then some thief came along and thought it was easier to steal his trousers than try and pull out the wallet.

'Geoffrey didn't care about the wallet, all he cared about was the fact that he now had no trousers. He was wandering around asking any of us if we had a spare pair. I don't know what he did in the end.'

Mention of Howe revived memories of his finest hour, when he tore Margaret Thatcher to pieces in his resignation speech to the Commons after she'd fired him.

Ken recalled, 'I was sitting on the Front Bench, just a few seats from Margaret, and you could almost feel the knives plunging into her back. She just sat bolt upright, with a startled look on her face.'

'Did you think Thatcher would go so soon after?' I asked.

'Good God, no. I had no idea at all, just never saw it coming. I thought it was a blip and she'd come through it all as usual. It was quite amazing to discover how wrong I was.'

The show's editor arrived: 'OK, we're ready for you.'

Everyone began clearing throats and straightening ties. The fifth panelist was Lance Price, a former Blair spin doctor. This was his first *Question Time*, though he'd briefed countless ministers on their appearances.

'Nervous?' I asked.

'A bit, yes,' he admitted. I felt for him, the first time you do this show it's scary.

We were introduced to the audience, and then I went first and got a mixture of cheers and boos – just the way I like it.

Ken got the biggest cheer, Straw the most boos.

The show started in a pedestrian fashion, but kicked off when a young woman in the audience launched into an extraordinary attack on most of the panel, branding Straw a 'total disgrace'.

Finally she targeted me: 'And as for you, Piers Morgan, you should be absolutely ashamed of yourself.'

What?

I turned to look at my accuser, who was working herself into a mad fury. Her face was pinched and angry.

'What have I done?' I asked, genuinely bemused.

'You've been an absolute disgrace for the last two years.'

I laughed. It hasn't been my finest career period, granted, but I hadn't, to my knowledge, done anything to this ranting woman.

'You are single-handedly responsible for dumbing down this country,' she shouted, really getting into her stride. 'You should be ashamed of yourself.'

The audience were loving it, and so was I. Hecklers are always good because you can come back with a joke and everyone thinks you've handled it really well.

I waited for the right moment, then responded, 'I think you're labouring under the massive misapprehension that I'm still editing the *Mirror*,' I said. 'But unfortunately I was cruelly removed from that job more than two years ago ... however, if you'd like me to take responsibility for the government, then I happily will. I apologise unreservedly for Iraq, Afghanistan...'

The audience roared with laughter. Even the mad woman smiled. Her intervention lifted the atmosphere a few notches, though, and we had some spicy exchanges about Blair and Brown before finally getting to the question I'd been waiting, and praying, for.

Iraq.

Straw hadn't been on *Question Time* since the war, in fact, none of the Cabinet big-hitters had. This was the chance to finally pin him to the floor. He was, after all, Foreign Secretary at the time.

I've done *Question Time* at least ten times and have only had the odd moment of true electricity running through me. A clash with William Hague on the night the war started was one, and this was another. I went toe to toe with Straw, lambasting him for the biggest cock-up in modern military history, haranguing him for not resigning, scoffing at his pathetic attempts to justify what had happened and generally abusing him.

The audience, as always when Iraq comes up, were united in their fury against him, too, and with Ken Clarke – who'd opposed the war from the start – joining in the fray, it rapidly descended into a gladiatorial bearpit, with Straw as the helpless young slave being torn to pieces in front of the baying crowd.

He began to physically shrink back into his seat, panic in his eyes.

He'd only come on the show to try and show his credentials for the deputy leadership, now his worst nightmare had come true and he was getting well and truly buried.

Desperate to win back the audience somehow, he admitted Iraq was now in a 'dire' state, and even conceded that it had been when he was Foreign

Secretary and insisting everything was fine. He said 'mistakes had been made', mainly by the Americans. But this only prompted more jeers and whistles. By the end, he sat there in silence, realising it had all gone horribly wrong.

Dimbleby made his usual joke – 'Now, we just have to check we got all that on film' followed a minute later by 'I'm really sorry but … it seems to have worked' – and we filed out.

Straw was gone in a flash.

Ken was chortling. 'That was great fun.'

And Dimbleby looked happy. He loves it when it gets fiery, though he'd never admit it.

Afterwards we had dinner elsewhere in the college, and I found myself sitting next to Alison Jackson, the brilliant photographer who does 'double take' images of famous people's doubles doing stupid things.

She'd been gripped by the drama earlier.

'God, it was amazing. Just extraordinary. Do you get nervous when it kicks off like that?'

'Nervous? No … I love it like that.'

And it's true, I do.

Conor texted me: 'Did you pull the heckler? Definite sexual tension going on there.'

Other texts started streaming in, either about the heckler or Straw, but all agreed it had been a great show to watch.

Mum rang, sounding emotionally exhausted.

'That was so nerve-wracking.'

It must be awful being my mother sometimes. Having to sit there, utterly powerless, waiting to see if I do well or make a complete tit of myself.

I got back to my hotel at midnight, feeling wide awake. I know why so many entertainers get into so much trouble – they come off stage, adrenalin pumping, and the last thing they want to do is go to bed. I watched the news for a bit, had a glass of wine, replied to a few texts, then suddenly felt desperately tired and crashed out.

29 September

The Hoff was on *GMTV* this morning, and gave every appearance of being drunk as a skunk, manhandling the presenter Jenni Falconer and trying to persuade her to go on a date with him.

Afterwards apparently, 250 viewers rang up to ask what was wrong with him.

But his publicist reassured us, yet again, 'David was just very tired. His schedule has been non-stop. He took a sleeping pill at 7p.m. last night and another at 4a.m. and was up at six. It's no surprise that he is absolutely exhausted.'

That infernal medication. I do wish he'd try something else.

I was sitting on the train back to Euston, chuckling over the internet reports, when Conor emailed.

'The Hoff is sitting in your old chair.'

'What chair?'

'Your old editor chair. He's come in to edit the 3a.m. Girls column for the day and just barged into conference.'

Hilarious.

'How is he behaving?'

'He's a bit odd, isn't he?'

'Yes, you could say that. He's entertaining, though.'

'Oh, very. He still thinks you're the editor here, so he keeps asking where you are. And when we told him you were fired two years ago, he looked all serious and said, "Oh yeah, I remember, he stole some oil or something, didn't he?"'

The Hoff has just released a new single in the UK, called 'Jump In My Car' – the one he sang on *America's Got Talent* – and there's a huge internet campaign going on to get him to No 1.

If he does, I think I'll jump in my car – then drive off a cliff.

4 October

Went to Claridges for the launch of Gordon Ramsay's autobiography.

There aren't many things at which I can beat Gordon Ramsay, other than sperm count, judging by recent comments from his wife, Tana.

He's fitter, richer, better looking, tougher, funnier and infinitely more capable where it really matters: in the kitchen.

But we're both currently starring in American TV shows, and not only is mine – *America's Got Talent* – thrashing his *Hell's Kitchen* in the ratings, I've also beaten him in a recent US internet poll to find the Biggest British Asshole in America.

My charming citation read: 'Morgan is a humorless ponce who loves to make women and children cry.'

Simon Cowell, of course, was first, and Anne Robinson second.

Then there's me at No 3, leaving poor old Gordon, a ferociously competitive soul, trailing in fourth, only just ahead of Jo 'Supernanny' Frost.

He wasn't happy when I broke the news to him tonight.

'That's ridiculous,' he said. 'I'm a much bigger asshole than you'll ever be.'

6 October

Dinner at The Ivy tonight. David Walliams, the *Little Britain* 'Ladyeez Man', arrived halfway through the evening and sat at the table next to me with two attractive young women.

Walliams is the perfect A-list celebrity – incredibly talented, cool, charming and always surrounded by beautiful females.

We exchanged jibes.

'What's it like discovering you're a better swimmer than comedian so late in life?' I asked him.

'Oh it's hilarious,' he replied, with not a semblance of humour.

'Who are your friends?'

'I'm Tamara,' said one, with just a hint that perhaps I should know who she is. 'Tamara Mellon.'

Ah yes, the multi-millionairess Jimmy Choo founder and socialite.

I turned to the other, a small Australian brunette.

'Don't tell me you're famous as well?'

The others sniggered.

'You are, aren't you, how embarrassing. Who are you?'

'I'm Natalie.'

Still a blank. But she'd said it as though her first name ought to be enough to identify her, like Kylie or Naomi.

'Natalie?'

'Natalie.'

More sniggers.

I stared at her face, but nothing registered at all.

Eventually she put me out of my misery.

'I'm Natalie Imbruglia.'

These pop beauties look so different with their clothes on.

7 October

A Russian journalist was shot dead in Moscow yesterday by a hitman.

I didn't give it much thought until I saw the victim's photo in the papers this morning and realised it was Anna Politkovskaya, the courageous anti-Putin reporter I met in Sweden last year.

It was profoundly shocking and, when I thought of her two young children, incredibly upsetting too.

10 October

Drove Stanley and Spencer to school.

'Hey, Stanley, what do you tell your mates I do for a living now?'

Pause.

'I tell them you're the second most hated man in America, Dad. After Simon Cowell.'

'And what do they think of that?'

'They think it's much cooler than being editor of the *Daily Mirror*.'

I turned on the radio to hear the new Top 40, and find out what happened to the Hoff's single.

'I hope he's at number one,' said Stanley, at which point all three boys began singing 'Jump In My Car', mainly, I suspect, to annoy me.

'And we're down to the top three now,' said the DJ. 'Has the Hoff done it?'

Cue a pre-recorded interview with the Hoff urging Britain to buy his record.

'And at number three ... is ... you'll find out after this short commercial break.'

I pulled the car into a layby and we waited anxiously for the news.

'Come on, Hoff!' shouted Bertie.

'Please God, no,' I whispered, head in hands.

'And at number three ... he hasn't made it to the top. It's the Hoff with "Jump In My Car".'

'YES!' I shrieked.

'NO!' the boys shouted back.

I have never been so pleased to see someone fail at something in my entire life. He would have been literally unbearable.

11 October

Bumped into Sandra Howard at a drinks party at the Mandarin Hotel tonight to launch the *Business* magazine.

She was still recovering from doing *Question Time* last week, where at times she'd appeared almost paralysed with fear.

'It was utterly nerve-wracking,' she said.

'I thought you were very brave,' I replied. 'And the audience were definitely warming to you by the end.'

Michael Howard interrupted, 'What do you mean "by the end?" They loved her from start to finish.'

I admired his blind loyalty – it reminded me of my mother after I train-wrecked on *Have I Got News For You*: 'Well, I thought you were *very* funny, darling.'

'What I mean is that it took the audience a while to believe that some-one so nice could actually be Mrs Michael Howard,' I said.

Took Celia to The Ivy for dinner afterwards, and there, sitting at a corner table on the opposite side of the room were Marion and Rav.

After ten minutes of slightly awkward waving and giggling on both sides, Marion sent over a note saying, 'Well, dear, it had to happen eventually.'

I sent it back, adding: 'Yes, don't fancy yours much.'

Before we left, though, I took Celia over and introduced her to Marion.

It seemed somehow entirely appropriate that this should all have happened in the very epicentre of luvvie Britain.

12 October

Tom Parker Bowles had his new cookbook launch tonight at Kensington Place, and when I saw the red carpet lined with twitchy policemen it could only mean one thing: mummy was there, too.

I spied Camilla talking to ultra-cool portrait painter Jonny Yeo, and seized the moment.

'Is he trying to get you to pose nude?' I asked. 'He does that with every woman. Be careful.'

Camilla smirked.

'You are a very naughty boy, Piers. No, he's not. Now, how's my rhino?'

Ah, yes, Camilla's rhino.

She's only ever sold one of her paintings, a rather good watercolour of a rhinocerous in the African bush, at a charity auction. And to her horror, the *Daily Mirror* bought it. We couldn't decide what to do with it, so it hung for several years behind my editor's chair, and now resides on my loo wall at home as a getting-sacked momento.

'It's … erm … in safe hands,' I said, not wanting to be too specific about its current location, for obvious reasons.

'Charles and I used to see it behind your head when you did interviews; we were horrified!'

Camilla's a charming woman. Funny, smart, far more glamorous in the flesh than you might think, and with a mischievous streak.

'What did you think of *Tatler* voting you the sixth most powerful blonde in Britain last week?'

'Was I? How ridiculous.'

'Yes, particularly as young Chelsy came second.'

She roared with laughter.

'So what's Tom's best dish?' I asked.

'Oh, he does wonderful roast potatoes. In fact his whole Sunday roast is marvellous.'

'I'm available if you ever need a guest to make up the numbers.'

'How kind of you, but I don't think we'll ever be that desperate,' she laughed.

At the Press Ball later, a splendid festering pit of cynical hacks and Christopher Biggins, I was grabbed by Tara Palmer-Tomkinson.

'How's your love life?' I asked.

'Wonderful. I'm snogging eight boys at the moment.'

'I see. Who are they?'

She began rattling off names, but stopped after five.

'Um, I can't remember who the others are, but I've definitely snogged them.'

13 October

Sarah Botham rang: 'Hi, Dad hasn't forgotten your promise, so see you on Tuesday for the final leg of the walk...'

'But Sarah, my back's got a twinge and I...'

'Not listening, sorry. And nor will Dad be, especially after two hundred and fifty miles so far.'

She hung up, and I was doomed.

16 October

Sharon Osbourne invited me on to her heavily criticised ITV chat show today. I realised things may not have been going brilliantly well with the run when a researcher came to see me in my dressing room and said, 'Hi, feel free to swear, we could do with the £250 you get for sending it in to one of those TV blooper shows.'

An hour later I was sitting in the green room waiting to go on when I heard Sharon come out to record the opening of the show.

It was the perfect opportunity to see if she really is as bad with the autocue as everyone says she is.

'... And later on we've got America's new Nazi, Piers Morgan.'

I spat out my tea.

'Oh fuck I just called him a Nazi, didn't I?' she said, to much hilarity in the audience.

'I meant to call him Mister Nasty.'

They re-recorded her intro, but the researcher was jubilant – that cock-up would fetch at least £500, and we hadn't even got to the interview yet.

Sharon was fascinated by *AGT*.

'It's the biggest show in America,' she told the audience. 'Ozzy and I watch it every time it's on. It's hilarious!'

Off camera, she was just as ecstatic. 'God, what a show! I love it. Are you having fun out there?'

'God, yes,' I replied. 'It's fantastic fun.'

'Well, just enjoy it. Too many people forget to enjoy it,' she said.

'Are you enjoying this show?' I asked.

'It's OK,' she said, 'but so tiring. I don't think I'll do another series.'

17 October

The day of reckoning: Ian Botham's walk.

I woke at 8a.m., stiff and creaking from a little practice walk yesterday.

It's only five miles today, through the streets of central London, but at the speed he walks – a punishing 4.5 miles per hour – it will feel like a sprint to me.

My general spirit wasn't improved by the sight that awaited me – Beefy, Ernie Els, Daley Thompson and Barry McGuigan, four of the fittest men you will ever meet, and just a handful of other walkers, including Sarah and Kath Botham.

We set off, and after half a mile I was 20 yards behind and struggling.

'Come on, Morgan, keep up, it's embarrassing,' cried Beefy, steaming ahead.

'When do we get a break?' I asked to general derision.

The lead car had a tannoy whose owner compounded my ordeal by blaring out every ten minutes or so, 'And here's Ian Botham, followed by Daley Thompson ... and finally, bringing up the rear, is Piers Morgan.'

By the time we finished in Oxford Street, I was absolutely knackered, as were some of the others.

'I did twenty miles with him on Sunday, and didn't run the next morning for the first time in twenty years because my blisters were so bad,' moaned Daley.

'I need to go and lie down,' groaned Ernie.

'That was hard,' admitted Barry.

Botham looked like he could do another 50 miles.

'Do you like doing this, Beefy?' I gasped, as the oxygen canister kicked in.

'Well, it tears my feet to pieces and creaks my ageing bones,' he said, 'but we've raised more than eight million pounds in eleven walks now, and during that time survival rates for leukaemia have risen from twenty to eighty per cent.

'I think that puts a few blisters into perspective, don't you?'

It does. And it also puts the whole celebrity circus into perspective, too.

Many celebrities do charity work just to look good, putting in little effort and reaping more reflected kudos than they deserve.

Ian Botham does it the hard way, and has has been doing it the hard way for over a decade. And that makes him, in my eyes, a worthy 'celebrity', someone who had a fabulous talent for cricket, but an even more fabulous talent for taking on leukaemia.

18 October

The papers are full of Paul McCartney's bitter split from Heather Mills, and in particular leaked divorce claims from Heather about what a nasty piece of work Macca is.

I read her statement with mounting incredulity, and anger. Paul might be a vain old rocker, but he's essentially a decent man, and he doesn't deserve this appalling character assassination.

I also feel partly responsible. It was me, after all, who introduced them in the first place at the *Mirror*'s Pride of Britain Awards. I've always defended Heather in public before, but this is indefensible.

At the very moment I was thinking this, my phone rang – it was the *Daily Mail* inviting me to write a piece to that very effect.

'I'd love to,' I said, and started venting my spleen onto an iMac.

19 October

The *Mail* ran my article over a whole page with the headline: I'M SORRY MACCA FOR EVER INTRODUCING YOU TO THIS MONSTER.

I never called her a monster in the piece, of course; it was just one of those general summation headlines the *Mail* love so much.

My phone rang just after midday.

'Piers, it's Heather. WHAT THE FUCK ARE YOU DOING TO ME?'

Before I could even reply, she started shouting at me in that high-pitched, slightly demonic way that I would imagine is very familiar to her husband.

'Why have you written all this shit? *Why?*'

'Because you're behaving appallingly, that's why,' I replied, as she finally drew breath. 'Those divorce papers were absolutely shocking; you should never have said all that stuff about Paul.'

'I've done *nothing* wrong,' she shrieked. 'Every single word in those divorce papers is true. I'm not going to lie when I go to court.'

She sounded completely bonkers.

'Heather, whoever is advising you to do all this is making a massive mistake. Just think about…'

I was going to say 'your daughter Beatrice', but she cut me dead.

'It's *not* a mistake. It's the truth. I can't believe you've turned on me like this, too. Paul always said I should never trust a tabloid journalist because you're all *scumbags,* but I trusted you.'

'Yes, well I guess we've both seen the light then, Heather.'

She carried on shouting, before suddenly stopping mid-rant.

'I know what it is,' she sneered, after a second's pause.

'What?'

'I know why you've done this.'

'Really? Why have I done this, then?'

Another pause, and a huge theatrical sigh.

'Because you're a Paul fan, that's why.'

'I'm a Paul fan?'

'Yes, you're a Paul fan.'

I contemplated this allegation for a second or two, letting my mind saunter back to my teenage fifty-six-album Beatles collection, including that rare Japanese import of *Abbey Road.*

'Yes, I guess I am a Paul fan,' I replied. 'In fact, I've always been a Paul fan.'

Another pause.

'I knew it.'

And the phone went dead.

20 October

Clare Short has quit the Labour whip on 'principle'. The same Clare Short who said she'd quit the government if there was no second UN resolution sanctioning the invasion of Iraq, then changed her mind when there wasn't.

Principle? That's one thing our Clare's been rather 'short' of.

21 October

I opened the *Daily Mirror* and a four-page leaflet fluttered to the floor.

I picked it up.

'*The Hoff's Guide To Life*.'

What? I read on...

'A modern manual for the chest-hair challenge.'

There was a huge, heavily airbrushed photo of the great man giving me the thumbs-up on the cover.

I turned the page to find a whole series of 'life tips' from the Hoff.

'FAMILY – Stay on good terms with your family. After all, one day you may need them to run your fan club.

'DIPLOMACY – Not only am I witty and charming, I can also speak a little Puerto Rican, which is important if you have as much international appeal as I do.

'LOVE – Of course, if you look like me you never have any trouble attracting the laydeez. But for you less famous people, I have advice: 1) Leather trousers are both stylish and breathe well in nightclub environments. 2) Girls whose names end in 'I' like Candi, Bambi and Cindi, are usually very friendly. 3) If all else fails, undo another button and show a little more chest hair.

'FASHION – When shopping remember three key words: tight, leather, black. This is true for everything from underpants to a suit for your wedding. And don't be afraid of spandex; it's your friend.'

I turned another page to find it was all a spoof advert for Pipex, his internet sponsors. Two and a half million *Mirror* readers would be reading this now, and laughing. Not *at* him, but *with* him.

The Hoff may not be No 1 in the pop charts, but from the moment he stopped taking himself so seriously he has become, indisputably, the No 1 popular celebrity cult icon in the world.

And he's got there on medium talent, but maximum personality.

24 October

I've never quite got the Kate Moss thing.

How this stroppy, pinch-faced little coke-snorter from Croydon ever made it to become the world's No 1 supermodel is quite beyond me, but even that fact is not as incomprehensible as her obsession with that filthy, talentless, junkie Pete Doherty. Each to their own, though, and it's undeniable that they are currently the hottest showbiz couple out there.

So when I found I was at the same party as them tonight, I was intrigued.

It was a stunningly glamorous masked ball in an extraordinary gothic villa in Twickenham, attended by the most beautiful crowd imaginable, and I spent a happy hour flitting around various themed rooms, finding that brilliantly mad culinary scientist Heston Blumenthal in one, making sizzling moss-flavoured sorbets and egg-and-bacon ice cream, and Scarlett Johansson and Gisele in another, just sizzling.

Then a jittery PR woman from the sponsors Moët et Chandon marched up and demanded: 'Could you move?'

'Why?'

'Because Kate and Pete want to come through, but they're terrified of you.'

'Kate and Pete who?'

'You *know* who.'

Of course, silly me. But why so 'terrified'?

Perhaps they think I'm still editing the *Mirror*, which famously exposed Kate's drug problem last year.

'Where are they?' I asked a photographer.

'They're in the karaoke room out the back.'

Curious to see this iconic duo in their natural habitat, I headed down there, sporting my *Phantom of the Opera*-style face mask, and found Kate, Pete and their ten-strong entourage sprawled across some leather sofas.

Kate was curled up into a little ball, writhing and shaking and guzzling greedily from a bottle of champagne. She looked tiny, pimply, wide-eyed, and with a nose like Danniella Westbrook's.

Pete was not much bigger, wearing black eye goggles and a coat in the hot dark room, and swaying from side to side as the entourage guffawed at every word he slurred.

This was supposed to be the personification of crazy, fun-loving, rock 'n' roll, A-list cool, but instead I observed a joyless, pathetic scene of self-absorbed artificiality.

Then, with wonderful irony, 'Itchycoo Park' by the Small Faces – chorus: 'It's all too beautiful' – started playing on the karaoke machine. Pete grabbed the microphone and started singing. Well, when I say singing, I mean he began emitting a tuneless, whining noise more akin to a live lobster being brought to the boil.

I assumed it was a wind-up and laughed, but it wasn't.

Kate flashed me an angry stare: there was a non-worshipper in the room.

Pete was shambling around like a hyena on acid, which probably wasn't far from the truth. He looked dirty, sweaty and puffy-cheeked, and he was murdering the song, literally killing it with every agonising groan he made. Yet Kate and the entourage cooed and drooled as if they were having a collective orgasm.

Then Pete bumped into a wall and I laughed louder, provoking another ferocious stare from Kate, which made me laugh even louder. And if you laugh that loudly while wearing a mask then eventually you need air.

I dropped the mask.

Kate saw my face and gasped in horror.

'Oh fucking hell, what the fuck is he doing in 'ere?' she snarled in a rough south London twang.

The entourage turned and hosed me down with menacing 'evils'.

'Just fucking get 'im out of 'ere,' Kate shrieked, before nearly falling off the sofa.

A security man hastily ran to her side, and then to mine.

'I'm sorry, Mr Morgan, but you must leave the party.'

'Er, why?'

'Because there have been complaints about you.'

'But I haven't said or done anything, this is not a private room, and it's not their party, is it?'

'No, sir, but you're still going to have to leave.'

I glanced back at Kate, who scrunched her face into a tight, merciless ball of blind, triumphant fury.

Pete didn't know what was happening – I doubt he ever knows what's happening – and so I left the masked ball, frogmarched out by security, to the cheers and jeers of the entourage.

But I'm glad I've finally met Kate Moss, because at least now, when people ask me what she's *really* like, I can answer with some authority: 'Well, just as I thought, she's a drunken, foul-mouthed, ill-mannered, paranoid Croydon girl with a cocaine-desecrated hooter and spots.

'And Pete's a filthy, talentless junkie who can't sing.'

As for me, well I learned once again that there is no greater truism than, 'If you lie down with dogs, you get fleas.'

25 October
The *Daily Mail* reported today that Kate Moss left the masked ball an hour after me, shouting, 'Where the fuck is Piers Morgan?'

It's too late now, darlin'.

26 October
Had dinner with Simon Cowell at his favourite London restaurant, Cipriani, where he spent two hours fending off a string of beautiful young female admirers.

'Let's go to Stringfellows,' he said, at midnight, so we did – and I spent a further two hours watching Simon sit on a large red throne fending off another string of young, rather more scantily dressed female admirers.

'Is it the money or the fame they're after?' I asked.

'Neither,' he replied with an even smugger grin than usual. 'They just want me to be rude to them.'

I wouldn't have minded so much if I hadn't been persistently harassed by a mad-eyed tattooed Polish lap dancer who insisted on reciting great chunks of quite terrible poetry to me.

'If you won't let me dance for you, then let me inspire you with my words,' she said, before shrieking with manic laughter, slapping my thigh, and launching into another appalling ten-minute monologue.

27 October
I watched Kate Winslet sobbing uncontrollably on *Parkinson* tonight, as she revealed how husband Sam Mendes sobbed equally uncontrollably as he told her how utterly brilliant her new film is. I tried to remember how nice Kate was before fame ripped into her soul and turned her into this ghastly creature. She has become a complete caricature of a celebrity – someone who genuinely believes she is something very special indeed, and wants everyone, sob, to know it, sob.

29 October
Feuds are wonderful things. I've had quite a few in my life and always thoroughly enjoyed them.

As the noted anthropologist Michael Bobick observed, 'People in small towns have feuds because they don't have cablevision and there's nothing else to do.'

But I've got cablevision now, and anyway, there should always be a moment when you finally down cudgels, kiss and make up.

So when the editor of *Kent on Sunday* newspaper called me on Friday asking what I thought of Ian Hislop – a local resident – slating me yet again in an interview 'celebrating' his twenty years as *Private Eye* editor, I felt curiously benign.

'Right,' I said, 'here's a scoop for you. The war is over. I am officially calling an end to hostilities, at least from my end. I'm sure it won't stop him carrying on his "Piers Moron" stuff, but you can't buy *Private Eye* in Hollywood, so I don't have to worry any more.'

The paper published this historic declaration today, with a quote from Hislop saying, 'Is it an armistice, or an unconditional surrender?'

Call it what you like, Ian, but it's sincere. I just don't wish to seal things with a public handshake, because the last time we shook hands I remember vowing never to clutch your clammy, limp-wristed little paw again if I could possibly help it. (Leave it, Piers, LEAVE it.)

A friend rang after seeing the paper and laughed: 'God, what next? Jeremy Clarkson?'

31 October

It was midnight, and I'd been partying hard at the National TV Awards – always one of the more entertaining celebrity bunfights of the year – when Simon Cowell sidled up to me and whispered, 'We're all going on to Baglioni's.'

What he meant was that *he* was going on to Baglioni's – a lively Italian restaurant in Kensington – and as a result, so would anyone who mattered.

I left it half an hour, then caught a cab down there.

It was quite dark inside, and there were lots of noisy tables. I craned my neck for any sign of Cowell, but instead alighted on another friend, Ross Kemp, sitting in the corner with a small group including Patrick Kielty, and *The X Factor*'s Louis Walsh. I walked over, reached the table, saw Ross's wife – *Sun* editor Rebekah Wade – went to say hello, and then froze.

There, sitting next to her in the dim recesses of Baglioni's, was Jeremy Clarkson.

Now the last time I'd seen Jeremy was at the British Press Awards in 2004, when he punched me three times in the head (the *Mirror* had incurred his wrath by running a couple of suggestive photos of him and a lady who wasn't Mrs Clarkson).

I didn't hit him back because there were 1,000 journalists in the room, I was surprisingly sober and I thought I'd get sacked if I did. Ironically, I was sacked three weeks later anyway.

But I digress.

The table fell silent. Jeremy stared at me and mouthed the words, 'Oh, fuck.' I stared at Jeremy and mouthed something rather similar. Ross stared at both of us and put his head in his hands.

Then an extraordinary thing happened: Jeremy stuck his hand out. And then an even more extraordinary thing happened: I shook it.

'Want a drink?' he asked

'OK, thanks,' I replied.

It was all very British, very civilised.

We sat next to each other for the next two hours, sharing a magnificent bottle of red wine and swapping tales of agony from the infamous fight, as the entire *Top Gear* production team looked on in utter astonishment.

'I've still got a scar on my forehead where your ring nicked me,' I bleated.

'I don't wear a bloody ring,' he snorted. 'It was pure knuckle. And my injuries were far worse.'

At which point he showed me the little finger on his right, punching, hand. It was crocked and gnarled.

'I broke it on your head,' he said, 'and it's never reset properly.'

As the atmosphere continued to thaw faster than a globally warmed Antarctic ice cap, he reflected, 'You know, other people always tell me that we're quite similar. In different circumstances we might have been friends.'

'Let's not be too hasty here, Jeremy,' I replied. 'One step at a time.'

As for Simon Cowell, he swept in with Sinitta at 1a.m., took one look at the scene before him, burst out laughing and exclaimed, 'Fuck me! I feel like Kofi Annan.'

We sat at a side table chatting about the extraordinary year we'd shared together.

'What's it like being a celebrity, then?' Cowell asked, chuckling.

'It's just great,' I replied. And most of the time, to be honest, it is – although my journey from tabloid editor to celebrity has given me a fascinating insight into fame, the fastest-growing career option in the country.

Fame invades your privacy, of course it does, and it can invade your personality, too, making you more arrogant and less self-aware.

It's not easy being exposed in the media, or criticised. Britain has the most liberated press in the world, but that makes it the most dangerous and aggressive, too, and being on the receiving end can be a brutal experience.

But the benefits of the media to anyone choosing to play the fame game – and you make a clear choice about this path – are obvious: you get well paid, you get tables in fully booked restaurants, you get limos and make-up artists, you get fêted and admired everywhere you go, you even get more physically attractive to the opposite sex (that *must* be true or how would John Prescott ever be able to have an affair?).

But where I have slightly changed my mind on fame is in this business of who deserves it.

As an editor I despised the explosion of celebrities from reality TV shows, mechanical pop-music factories and kiss-and-tell bimbos. I hated the fact that someone could become a star just by eating filthy bugs in a jungle, or having sex in the *Big Brother* house. And to a large extent, I was right. It *is* bloody ridiculous that we salute so many talentless people.

And yet … and yet … is it actually a talent to have a personality that people love? Who am I to look down my nose at Jordan, Bobby Badfingers or the Rapping Granny? If you can entertain through sheer force of character, then that, surely, is a genuine talent.

Perhaps spending so much time with the Hoff has cemented my view. In him I see a man who has become, indisputably, the world's top cult iconic celebrity. And he's done it, essentially – and after some prompting – by taking the piss out of himself.

I realised the power of self-deprecation when I changed my after-dinner speeches to include constant self-parody and found it worked much better than arrogantly assuming everyone is fascinated by my life.

We are living in a celebrity-obsessed country now, but it's also a country that likes its celebrities to be real people, warts and all. They want honesty, soul-searching, confession and incident, and they're beginning to reject the cosseted, saccharine stars like Tom Cruise in favour of heroes who tell it like it is.

It's one of the reasons why Tony Blair's bubble burst – nobody believed him any more – and one of the reasons why Freddie Flintoff has replaced David Beckham in the nation's affections.

After some initial teething problems, I have grown to rather like being a celebrity. It brings me lots of perks, a lot of fun, and the occasional humilation. And there is, as I know, an alternative liftestyle out there called real work, in the real world.

Yes, it would be lovely to think that only supremely talented people became stars, but did Frank Sinatra really bring more joy to the world than the Hoff?

9 November

Tatler magazine threw a party tonight for their annual 'Little Black Book' of Britain's most eligible young men and women.

'Come with me,' said Celia. 'It will be fun.'

'OK,' I replied.

We arrived at 8p.m. and Celia fluttered straight inside.

I, however, was stopped by a burly bouncer on the door.

'Where's your ticket?'

'Erm, I don't have one. I think my friend must have it…'

'No ticket, no entrance,' he growled.

'Oh for goodness' sake, I'm on the guest list.'

The goon summonsed two young PR women with clipboards.

'Is he on the guest list?'

They studied me intently like medical students peering at their first real slab of membrane.

'Name?'

'Morgan.'

'Morgan who?'

'Piers Morgan.'

Not an eyebrow flickered in anything even approaching recognition, and both girls spent several long, tedious minutes studying page after page looking for my name, as the bouncer gripped the red-carpet curtain tightly in his hand.

'I can't find a Morgan,' said one.

'No, nor can I,' said the other.

At which point, sensing blood, several sniggering paparazzi swooped and took photos of me standing there.

It began to rain.

CAST OF CHARACTERS

A.A. Gill — absurdly smug and annoying TV critic

Abi Titmuss — reality TV person and sex tape star

Ainsley Harriott — TV chef

Alan Berger — top Hollywood agent

Alan Clark — legendary Tory MP (deceased)

Alan Edwards — top showbusiness PR

Alan Rusbridger — editor of the *Guardian*

Alan Sugar (Sir) — permanently angry tycoon

Alicia Monckton — Rod Liddle's young lover

Alison Jackson — brilliant fake photo artist

Alison Sharman — ITV executive

Alistair Darling — very serious Labour cabinet minister

Amanda Platell — journalist and broadcaster

Andrew Gilligan — journalist sacked by BBC over Iraq dossier report

Andrew Neil — broadcaster, media star and bon viveur

Andy Coulson — editor of the *News of the World*

Angus Deayton — fading sarcastic TV personality

Anil Bhoyrul — former City Slickers columnist on *Daily Mirror*

Ann Widdecombe — fearsome Tory MP

Anna Politkovskaya — outspoken Russian journalist (deceased)

Anne Robinson — *Weakest Link* TV star

Anton Mosimann — top chef

Antony Worrall Thompson – TV chef

Arsene Wenger – Arsenal manager and superior life force

Aunt Lorna – my Irish aunt, sister of my natural father (deceased)

Barbara Windsor – bubbly *EastEnders* star

Baroness Jenny Tongue – Liberal Democrat MP

Barry McGuigan – former boxing champion

Benazir Bhutto – former prime minster of Pakistan

Bertie Pughe-Morgan – my youngest son

Bianca Ryan – eleven-year-old singer who won *America's Got Talent*

Bill Anslow – former *News of the World* production editor

Bob 'The Cat' Bevan – legendary after-dinner speaker

Bono – singer in Irish band

Boris Johnson – TV star, and part-time MP

Brandy – American singer, and my co-judge on *America's Got Talent*

Brian Paddick – controversial gay Met Police chief

Bruce Waddell – editor of the *Scottish Sun*

Camilla Parker Bowles – Prince Charles's wife

Carol Vorderman – counts numbers on daytime TV

Caroline Jones – my sons' occasional nanny

Celia Walden – *Daily Telegraph* journalist who has the misfortune to be
  my girlfriend

Charles Clarke – jug-eared, rotund Labour MP

Charlie Brooker – TV critic for the *Guardian*

Charlotte Tomlinson – my sister

Chris Cairns – New Zealand cricket star

Chris Evans – TV and radio star

Chris Grieve – *Daily Mirror* photographer

Chris Hughes – *Daily Mirror* reporter

Chris Tarrant – TV star, host of *Who Wants to be a Millionaire*

Claudia Schiffer – German-born supermodel

Conor Hanna – *Daily Mirror* deputy editor

Courtney Love – rock star wife of the now deceased Kurt Cobain

Craig Plestis – NBC executive

Dale Winton – TV star

Daley Thompson – former Olympic decathlon champion

Danniella Westbrook – former *EastEnders* actress

David Aaronovitch – fat, miserable *Guardian* columnist

David Blunkett – former Home Secretary, now serial whinger

David Cameron – leader of the Conservative Party

David Dimbleby – host of BBC's *Question Time*

David Folb – founder of the Lashings all-star cricket team

David Hasselhoff – TV legend and my co-judge on *America's Got Talent*

David O'Keefe – producer of my Channel 4 show *Morgan and Platell*

David Trimble – former leader of the Ulster Unionist Party

David Walliams – the tall, straight half of *Little Britain*

Davina McCall – TV presenter, host of the ghastly *Big Brother*

Dennis Skinner – fiery Labour MP

Dermot Murnaghan – BBC presenter

Des Kelly – my treacherous former deputy editor of the *Daily Mirror*

Diarmuid Gavin – TV gardener

Dickie (Richard) Wallace – editor of the *Daily Mirror*

Dorothy Byrne – head of news and current affairs at Channel 4

Duchess of York – Fergie to her mates

Dylan Jones – editor of *GQ* and style guru

Eamonn Holmes – TV presenter

Eamonn Matthews – executive producer of *Morgan and Platell*

Ed Balls – Labour MP and senior courtier to Gordon Brown

Ed Victor – top literary agent

Eddo Brandes – rotund Zimbabwe cricketer

Ellis Watson – media legend (in his own mind)

Elton John – singer and pianist

Erin O'Connor – model

Ernie Els – top South African golfer

Eugenie Furniss – my brilliant literary agent

Faria Alam – former FA secretary who had affair with Sven Goran Eriksson

Fern Britton – Presenter of ITV's *This Morning*

Fiona Phillips – Presenter of *GMTV*

Frank Bough – former breakfast TV presenter brought down by drugs and prostitute scandal

Freddie Flintoff – England cricket star and Herculean drinker

Gary Farrow – top showbusiness PR

Gary Lineker – TV sports presenter

Gavyn Davies – former chairman of the BBC

Geoff (Buff) Hoon – plodding Labour cabinet minister

Geoff 'Dusty' Miller – former England cricketer, and top after-dinner speaker

George Galloway – firebrand anti-war MP

George Graham – former Arsenal manager

George Kelly – contestant on *America's Got Talent*

George Michael – singer

George Osborne – Tory Shadow Chancellor

Gerald Ronson – businessman

Glenn McGrath – Australian cricketer

Gordon Brown – Chancellor

Gordon Ramsay – top chef and TV star

Graham Norton – TV star

Grande – my grandmother, Margot Barber

Greg Dyke – former Director-General of the BBC

Grover Norquist – leading American republican

Guy Adams – diary editor of the *Independent*

Harriet Harman – Labour MP

Helen Fielding – author of *Bridget Jones's Diary*

Hilary Benn – Labour cabinet minister, son of Tony Benn

Ian Blair (Sir) – boss of the Metropolitan Police

Ian Botham (Beefy) – England cricket legend

Ian Hislop – professional cynic and part-time editor of *Private Eye*

Ian Wooldridge – *Daily Mail* sportswriter

Ian Wright – former Arsenal and England football star, now TV presenter

Jack Straw – Labour cabinet minister

Jade Goody – reality TV star

James Hipwell – former City Slickers columnist for *Daily Mirror*

James Naughtie – co-presenter of Radio 4's *Today* programme

James Nesbitt – TV star

Jamie Oliver – TV chef

Jamie Theakston – TV star

Jan Moir – food eater for *Daily Telegraph*

Janet Street-Porter – journalist and broadcaster

Jason Barlow – editor of *Car* magazine

Jay Leno – American TV chat-show star

Jean-Christophe Novelli – French chef

Jenny Willott – Liberal Democrat MP

Jens Lehmann – Arsenal goalkeeper

Jeremy Pughe-Morgan – my brother, an army officer

Jeremy Clarkson – TV pugilist

Joe Pasquale – TV comedian with very annoying voice

John Humphrys – co-presenter of Radio 4's *Today* programme

John Mortimer – lawyer and author, famous for Rumpole character

John Prescott – political laughing stock

John Reid – Labour cabinet minister

John Walsh – literary editor for the *Independent*

John Webber – top TV agent

Jonathan Isaby – ebullient deputy editor of *Daily Telegraph*'s Spy column

Jonny Yeo – portrait painter to the stars

Judith Keppel – woman who won £1 million on *Who Wants to Be a Millionaire*

Karen Smith – BBC TV executive

Kate Moss – spotty little girl from Croydon

Kate Winslet – very-pleased-with-herself actress

Kath Botham – Ian's wife

Katja Cahill – stylist on *America's Got Talent*

Kay Burley – Sky News presenter

Kelvin MacKenzie – media legend, former editor of the *Sun*

Ken Clarke – former Tory home secretary

Ken Warwick – executive producer of *America's Got Talent*

Kerrie Hutton – my former PA at the *Daily Mirror*

Kevin Lygo – Channel 4 boss

Kevin Pietersen – England cricket star

Lance Price – former Labour spin doctor

Larry Lawrence – *Daily Mirror* librarian

Liz Murdoch – TV mogul, daughter of Rupert and wife of Matthew Freud

Lord Jeffrey Archer – writer, jailbird and charity auctioneer

Lord Levy – Labour fund-raiser

Marco Pierre White – top chef, now successful businessman

Marcus Trescothick – England cricketer

Margaret Hodge – Labour MP

Mark Owen – Take That pop star

Martine McCutcheon – TV star, former *EastEnders* actress

Mary Riddell – journalist

Matthew Freud – PR guru

Matthew Hoggard – Engand cricketer

Max Boyce – Welsh singer and comedian

Melvyn Bragg – TV presenter and Arsenal fan

Meredith Ahr – NBC executive

Michael Ancram – Tory MP

Michael Cohen – sports agent

Michael Gambon (Sir) – great British actor

Michael Heseltine – former Tory deputy prime minister

Michael Howard – former leader of the Conservative Party

Michael Parkinson – TV and radio star

Michael Portillo – former Tory minister and broadcaster

Michael Vaughan – England cricket captain

Michael Winner – movie director and food critic

Michelle L'Amour – burlesque dancer on *America's Got Talent*

Mike Graham – former editor of the *Scottish Mirror*

Mitchell Everard – restaurant manager

Mohamed Al Fayed – Harrods tycoon

Naomi Campbell – supermodel with anger management issues

Natalie Imbruglia – famous singer (apparently)

Naynesh Desai – lawyer to stars including Ian Botham

Neil Morrissey – TV star

Nicholas Witchell – BBC royal reporter

Nicky Cox – editor of *First News*

Nigella Lawson – TV chef

Paris Hilton – professional talentless celebrity

Patricia Hewitt – Labour cabinet minister

Paul Beck – tycoon and cricket fan

Paul Burrell – former royal butler

Paul Dacre – editor in chief of the *Daily Mail*

Paul Danan – reality TV 'star'

Paul O'Grady – TV star

Paul Routledge – political commentator for the *Daily Mirror*

Paul Scott – author

Paula Abdul – singer and star of *American Idol*

Penny Junor – royal pundit

Pete Doherty – singer (allegedly)

Peter Fincham – BBC ONE boss

Peter Mandelson – Labour MP

Philip Green (Sir) – business tycoon

Phillip Schofield – co-presenter of ITV's *This Morning*

Rachel Flintoff – Freddie Flintoff's wife

Rachel Royce – ex-wife of Rod Liddle

Rachel Stevens – pop star

Randy Jackson – judge on *American Idol*

Rav Singh – *News of the World* showbusiness columnist

Ray Snoddy – media commentator

Rebecca Loos – my second cousin, also known for having fling with David Beckham

Rebekah Wade – editor of the *Sun*

Richard Compton-Miller – journalist

Richard Dreyfuss – movie star and left-wing political activist

Richard Madeley – TV presenter

Richard Stilgoe – former TV presenter

Richard Wallace – editor of the *Daily Mirror*

Richie Richardson – former West Indies cricket captain

Rob McGibbon – journalist and author

Robbie Williams – singer and egotist

Robert Clark (Sir) – former chairman of the Mirror Group (deceased)

Robert Kilroy-Silk – former TV presenter

Rod Liddle – Britain's ugliest man. Also writes

Roger Alton – editor of the *Observer*

Roly Keating – BBC TWO controller

Ross Kemp – TV star

Rupert Pughe-Morgan – my little brother, a nightclub manager

Russell Brand – TV star

Sam Carter – the second-best batsman for Newick CC

Sandra Howard – wife of former Tory leader Michael

Sarah Botham – Ian's daughter

Sarah Brown – Gordon Brown's wife

Sara Dallin – Bananarama pop star

Sarah Jane Thomson – media mogul, boss of Thomson Intermedia

Shane Warne – Australian cricket star

Sharon Osbourne – TV star and wife of rock star Ozzy

Shaun Wallace – first black winner of *Mastermind*

Simon Cowell – TV superstar and my current boss

Simon Hattenstone – feature writer for the *Guardian*

Simon Jones – England cricketer

Simon Kelner – editor of the *Independent*

Simone Warne – wife of cricket star Shane

Sly Bailey – current chief executive of Trinity Mirror

Sophie Raworth – BBC TV newsreader

Spencer Pughe-Morgan – my oldest son

Stanley Pughe-Morgan – my middle son

Steve Coogan – TV comedian

Sue Nye – Gordon Brown's right-hand woman

Tamara Mellon – fashion designer

Tana Ramsay – wife of chef Gordon

Tara Palmer-Tomkinson – professional socialite

Terri Seymour – girlfriend of Simon Cowell

Tom Parker Bowles – Camilla's son, and top food writer

Tracey Chapman – my PA

Tracey Emin – artist

Tracey Temple – John Prescott's mistress

Ulrika Jonsson – former TV weathergirl

Veronica Wadley – editor of the *Evening Standard*

Victor Blank (Sir) – former chairman of Trinity Mirror

Victor Lewis-Smith – TV critic

Vincent O'Meara – my natural father

Vinnie Jones – former footballer, now movie star

Virginia Bottomley – tedious former Tory politician

Vivienne – singer and pool attendant at the Beverly Wilshire hotel

Wendy Spence – my personal trainer

Will Hutton – journalist and broadcaster

William Hague – former Conservative leader